MIKE FOUNTAIN

BRITAIN AND THE JEWS OF EUROPE
1939–1945

W9-BGT-103

Property of Holocaust Resource and
Information Project. UWM, Curtin Hall,
Phone 922 4701

The Institute of Jewish Affairs gratefully acknowledges the assistance of the Memorial Foundation for Jewish Culture which made the preparation and publication of this volume possible.

*In memory of
my grandparents*

BRITAIN AND THE
JEWS OF EUROPE
1939–1945

BERNARD WASSERSTEIN

INSTITUTE OF JEWISH AFFAIRS, LONDON

OXFORD UNIVERSITY PRESS

Oxford   New York

1988

Oxford University Press, Walton Street, Oxford OX2 6DP

Oxford New York Toronto
Delhi Bombay Calcutta Madras Karachi
Petaling Jaya Singapore Hong Kong Tokyo
Nairobi Dar es Salaam Cape Town
Melbourne Auckland

and associated companies in
Berlin Ibadan

Oxford is a trade mark of Oxford University Press

© Institute of Jewish Affairs 1979

First published by Oxford University Press and the Institute
of Jewish Affairs 1979. This edition first issued as an Oxford
University Press paperback 1988

All rights reserved. No part of this publication may be reproduced,
stored in a retrieval system, or transmitted, in any form or by any means,
electronic, mechanical, photocopying, recording, or otherwise, without
the prior permission of Oxford University Press

This book is sold subject to the condition that it shall not, by way
of trade or otherwise, be lent, re-sold, hired out or otherwise circulated
without the publisher's prior consent in any form of binding or cover
other than that in which it is published and without a similar condition
including this condition being imposed on the subsequent purchaser

British Library Cataloguing in Publication Data
Wasserstein, Bernard, 1948–
Britain and the Jews of Europe 1939–1945.
—(Oxford paperbacks).
1. Europe. Jews. Policies of British
government, 1939–1945.
I. Title   II. Institute of Jewish Affairs.
940.53'15'03924
ISBN 0–19–282185–7

Library of Congress Cataloging in Publication Data
Wasserstein, Bernard.
Britain and the Jews of Europe 1939–1945/Bernard Wasserstein.
p.   cm. Bibliography: p.
Includes index.
1. Holocaust, Jewish (1939–1945)   2. Refugees, Jewish—Government
policy—Great Britain.   3. Great Britain—Emigration and
immigration.   4. Palestine—Emigration and immigration.   I. Title.
D804.3.W37 1988
940.53'15'03924—dc19
ISBN 0–19–282185–7

Printed in Great Britain by
Richard Clay Ltd.
Bungay, Suffolk

Preface

THE PURPOSE of this book is to describe and explain the policy of the British Government towards the Jews of Europe during the Second World War. The story has many faces: the question of immigration to Palestine; the attitude towards Jewish refugees entering Britain and the British Empire; the reaction of the British Government to the news of the German 'final solution' to the Jewish problem in Europe; the effect on the Jewish problem of Britain's relations with her allies (most notably the United States) and with neutral states; the extent to which the British Government was prepared to give help to Jewish resistance efforts in occupied Europe; the Government's response to schemes for rescuing Jews from Nazi territory. These are some of the main themes. The question of Jewish immigration to Palestine is of crucial importance to the discussion, because it was there that the British Government was most directly and continuously involved in the problem. The internal history of Palestine in this period lies beyond the scope of this study, and no attempt has been made to deal with it except where this is necessary to an understanding of the central theme.

The sombre nature of the subject and the depth of feeling which it evokes alike dictate precision in the use of evidence. Fairness requires that the evidence be presented in as complete a form as possible. The most faithful way of communicating to the reader the considerations in the minds of policy-makers is through their own contemporary words. I have therefore not hesitated to quote, often extensively, from the sources. These are all documentary, and include diplomatic notes, minutes of meetings, private letters and diaries, some published but most stored in archives. The documentation is extremely rich and I am greatly indebted to the generous assistance of archivists and librarians in Britain, Israel, and the U.S.A. All the official papers concerning this subject in Israel and the U.S.A. are freely open to inspection by historians. Most of the relevant official papers in Britain are now similarly available in the

Public Record Office. But the British Government continues to bar access, beyond the normal thirty-year period, to a small number of files, among which are some dealing with Jewish illegal immigration to Palestine and the wartime internment of aliens in Britain as well as other matters relevant to the subject of this book. The Foreign Office refused a request for permission to examine for the purposes of this study certain of these withheld files. However, in response to a similar request, the Home Office agreed to make available to me a number of such files. I have been greatly helped in my efforts to make sense of the documents by interviews with some of those who were involved in the events here described, and I am very grateful to them. However, the conclusions of this book are based entirely on documentary evidence.

The essence of this story is a clash of priorities. For the Jews of Europe the essential goal was survival, for which victory over the common enemy was an indispensable, but not a sufficient, condition. For the British Government the first priority and chief preoccupation was, of necessity, victory in the war. 'Everything for the war, whether controversial or not, and nothing controversial that is not *bona fide* needed for the war'[1]—Churchill's dictum in October 1943 neatly encapsulates the principle on which British wartime policy-making was founded. The problems discussed in this book were, for the Jews of Europe, a matter of life and death; they were of only secondary importance in the eyes of the British Government. The clash in priorities was the natural result of discrepant interests. Yet the question arises, and it is the fundamental question which echoes through this book: was Britain's wartime policy towards the Jewish problem the *only* possible one compatible with the overriding end of victory?

Paperback edition

For this new edition a few minor corrections have been made to the original text.

BERNARD WASSERSTEIN

Brandeis University,
1987

[1] Quoted in Paul Addison, *The Road to 1945: British Politics and the Second World War*, London 1975, p. 253.

Acknowledgements

THIS WORK was written at the invitation of the Institute of Jewish Affairs, London, and I wish to express my particular gratitude to the Institute and all its staff for their co-operation at all stages of the project. Much of the initial research work was done by Dr A. J. Sherman (at that time of St Antony's College, Oxford), and his advice has been most helpful to me in the course of my continuation of the project. The Memorial Foundation for Jewish Culture (whose original endowment derives from reparations payments made by the Government of the Federal Republic of Germany to the Conference on Jewish Material Claims against Germany) made substantial grants towards the expenses of the project.

In addition to the above I benefited from the generous assistance of the following individuals and institutions: Professor Chimen Abramsky; Professor Benjamin Akzin; Professor Yehuda Bauer; Sir Isaiah Berlin; the Board of Deputies of British Jews; the Bodleian Library, Oxford; the British Library; Mr David Brown; Cambridge University Library; Dr William Carr; Central Zionist Archives, Jerusalem; Royal Institute of International Affairs; Mr Derek Chambers; Professor Lucy Dawidowicz; Dr Elizabeth Eppler; Professor Leon Feldman; Dr Joel Fishman; the Foreign Office; Dr John P. Fox; Dr Józef Garliński; Mr Martin Gilbert; Professor S. J. Gould; Dr Lukasz Hirszowicz; Mrs Pat Holland; Dr Colin Holmes; the Home Office; House of Lords Record Office; Israel State Archives; Jewish National and Hebrew University Library; Dr Lionel Kochan; Dr Israel Kollat; Mr I. J. Linton; Mr V. D. Lipman; Lloyd's Register; Dr R. M. Littlewood; Mr S. Lorant; Dr N. Lucas; Dr Aubrey Newman; St Antony's College, Oxford; Nuffield College, Oxford; Rabbi Dr Maurice L. Perlzweig; Polish Underground Movement Study Trust (London); Public Record Office, Kew; Mr Chaim Raphael; Dr Gerhart M. Riegner; the late Dr Jacob Robinson; Dr S. J. Roth; Professor Leonard B. Schapiro; Sheffield Central Library;

Sheffield University Library; Dr Lewis Spitz; Professor Aryeh Tartakower; United States National Archives, Washington D.C.; Professor and Mrs A. Wasserstein; Miss Celia Wasserstein; Mr David Wasserstein; Yad Chaim Weizmann, Rehovot; Yad Vashem Archives, Jerusalem; Mr Ron Zweig.

My great indebtedness to all the above for their help renders it all the more incumbent on me to stress that responsibility for the whole contents of this book is that of the author alone.

Contents

Abbreviations

BD	Archives of the Board of Deputies of British Jews, London
BL	British Library Additional Manuscripts
CZA	Central Zionist Archives, Jerusalem
FRUS	*Foreign Relations of the United States*
HC	House of Commons Debates, 5th Series (*Hansard*)
HL	House of Lords Debates (*Hansard*)
ISA	Israel State Archives
PRO	Public Record Office, Kew
USNA	United States National Archives, Washington D.C.
VAT	*Actes et Documents du Saint Siège Relatifs à la Seconde Guerre Mondiale*
WA	Weizmann Archives, Rehovot
WJCL	World Jewish Congress Archives, London
WJCNY	World Jewish Congress Archives, New York
YV	Yad Vashem Archives, Jerusalem

Britain and the Jewish Problem

THE JEWISH problem in the modern world was not a matter of primary British concern; yet it was one in which British Governments in the first half of the twentieth century found themselves inextricably involved. There were several reasons for this involvement. The most important was the assumption by Britain at the end of the First World War of responsibility for the government of Palestine under a League of Nations mandate, and the obligation under the mandate to facilitate the establishment in Palestine of a national home for the Jewish people. But there were also other reasons for British involvement, for the Jewish question in this period was a secondary but recurrent theme both in British domestic politics and in Britain's relations with other powers. Within Britain the arrival before 1914 of large numbers of Jewish refugees from Russia, and the further influx in the 1930s from the Third Reich produced significant, though not lasting, social and political tensions. In foreign affairs, the Jewish question, while never of central importance, was an element in British relations with several central and east European states between the wars, notably Poland, Roumania, and (after 1933) Germany; and British relations with Russia and the United States of America were to some extent affected by assumptions (not always correct) about the nature and influence of Jewish opinion in those countries.

The entanglement of several of these strands may be seen in the origins of British involvement with Zionism. The first expressions of interest by the British Government in some form of territorial solution to the Jewish problem were made in 1902 and 1903 when there was serious consideration of proposals for British sponsorship of Jewish settlement around El Arish in the Sinai peninsula, or in part of east Africa. These schemes were put forward at a time when the 'aliens question' was a major subject of political controversy in Britain, and one object,

particularly in the mind of Joseph Chamberlain, the chief
proponent of the east African offer, appears to have been to
divert the flow of Jewish refugees away from Britain.[1] These
plans came to nothing. But during the First World War the
Government again took up the possibility of promoting large-
scale Jewish settlement, this time to Palestine. Among the
reasons for this renewal of interest was a rather exaggerated
belief in the effect which would be produced on Jewish opinion
in Russia and the U.S.A. by British support for Zionism, at a
time when the attitude of both powers was considered of vital
importance in deciding the outcome of the war. In November
1917 the British Government issued the Balfour Declaration in
which it undertook to facilitate the establishment in Palestine of
'a national home for the Jewish people', with the proviso 'that
nothing shall be done which may prejudice the civil or religious
rights of existing non-Jewish communities in Palestine, or the
rights and political status enjoyed by Jews in any other country'.

Subsequent British Governments found cause to regret that
this pronouncement had ever been issued, for Britain derived
little benefit and less credit from three decades of rule over
Palestine. In December 1917 General Allenby entered
Jerusalem, and by the end of the war the entire country had
been occupied by his army, which included three Jewish battalions. British administration of Palestine was regularized in
1922 when the League of Nations confirmed the terms of the
mandate accorded to Britain: the text of the Balfour Declaration was incorporated in the mandate. Between 1918 and 1939
the Jewish population of Palestine grew from 56,000 to 475,000,
and the Jewish proportion of the population from under ten per
cent to thirty-one per cent.[2] Fuelled by a capital inflow of over
£100,000,000 between the wars, a resilient Jewish economy
grew up, dominated by the *Histadrut*, the Jewish trade union.
Quasi-governmental institutions of the Jewish community
were formed with official recognition, the most important being
the Jewish Agency for Palestine, which, while it included non-
Zionist elements, was dominated by the World Zionist Organisation. Under the political supervision of the Jewish Agency

[1] Leonard Stein, *The Balfour Declaration*, London 1961, p. 33.
[2] D. Gurevich *et al.* eds., *Statistical Handbook of Jewish Palestine*, Jerusalem 1947, pp. 34
and 47.

and of the *Va'ad Leumi* (the National Council of the Jews of Palestine) there developed an underground Jewish army, the *Haganah*. The numerical, economic, institutional, and military growth of the Jewish National Home was rapid and impressive, but it was vitiated by the opposition of the Arab majority of the population.

Arab hostility to Zionism, manifest as early as the 1890s, became a serious political force in the wake of the Balfour Declaration. After 1918 there developed a nationalist movement which, although riven by personal and clan rivalries, by suspicions between Muslims and Christians, and by social and economic differences among townsmen, bedouin, and fellahin (peasants), commanded widespread support among Arabs. The dominant motif in the ideology of this movement was total opposition to Zionism, to the Balfour Declaration, and to the Jewish National Home. In so far as the mandate incorporated a British obligation to support the national home, the nationalist movement also declared total opposition to the mandate. Arab hostility to Zionism was demonstrated in a series of riots in 1920, 1921, and 1929, in which large numbers of Jews were attacked and many killed. These riots, and the military and political cost of repressing them, raised for British Governments the questions of whether the Balfour Declaration policy should be continued, and whether a British presence in Palestine should be maintained. During the 1920s these two questions were regarded as being connected, since it was felt that the British presence in Palestine derived much of its justification from the Balfour Declaration. The continuation of the policy was therefore seen as a necessary corollary of British rule. Serious consideration was given to the possibility of withdrawal from Palestine, but the fear was expressed that to withdraw would be to invite another power—France, Italy, or a renascent Turkey—to move into the vacuum created. No such potentially hostile presence could be tolerated in the vicinity of the Suez Canal, the jugular vein of the Empire, and an essential interest of the highest priority which no British Government could afford to imperil. Britain therefore remained in Palestine, and the Balfour Declaration policy was maintained, although some concessions were made on marginal issues in deference to Arab opinion.

So long as the post-war settlement in Europe remained stable, British dominance over much of the Middle East secure, and Jewish immigration moderate, it continued to be possible for the British to rule Palestine in relative isolation from political currents elsewhere in the Middle East or in Europe. But these conditions were challenged by the convulsive changes in European politics in the mid-1930s, which drew Palestine inexorably into the whirlpool of world diplomacy and induced the British Government to change course both in its international policy, and, as a by-product, in its attitude to the government of Palestine. The essential reason for these changes was the conduct of the German Government, under Nazi control from 1933, in domestic and international politics, and the example which its behaviour set for other European states to follow.

Anti-Semitism was a European, not a specifically German phenomenon, but it was the policy of the German Government after 1933 that turned it into a European political problem of the first importance. As a popular force anti-Semitism probably struck deepest roots in the heartland of Jewish settlement in Poland, Roumania, and the western regions of Russia. However, from the 1880s onwards, a massive westward emigration of Jews from the Russian Empire, Roumania, and Austrian Galicia into the cities of central Europe, especially Vienna, Berlin, and Budapest, helped to stimulate the growth of anti-Semitism in a new form. Political anti-Semitism became in central Europe a vital ideological element in the mobilization of the masses, particularly (although not exclusively) by anti-liberal and anti-socialist parties. Several explanations have been offered for the endemic grip of anti-Semitism on the popular mentality: it may be understood as a relic of the ancient hatred of the different; as a mutation of Christian beliefs in a post-Christian society; as part of the débris of romantic nationalism; as a product of the social and intellectual upheaval resulting from rapid and uneven industrialization; as a collective psychopathy in which the Jew is identified with the devil; or as a modern version of the witch craze. In countries such as Poland, Roumania, and Hungary between the wars two further reasons stand out: first, the important role of Jews in the development of commerce and industry, their heavy concentration in certain professions such as law, medicine, and journalism, and their importance in the arts, all of which aroused nationalist resentment; secondly, the tendency in these countries to identify Jews with the communist threat. Such fears helped to produce widespread killings and massacres of Jews in Poland and the Ukraine between 1917 and 1921. (It is a significant pointer to the British reaction during the Second World War to what were often regarded as atrocity stories that the British Foreign Office, on the basis of reports from Polish Government sources, was convinced that Jewish descriptions of the pogroms of 1917 to 1921 were greatly exaggerated.)[3] In Germany and Austria similar fears and resentments, although with much less grounding in the social and economic relations actually existing between Jews and non-Jews, were prominent in the rhetoric of anti-Semitism. In eastern Europe the nominal equality accorded to Jews under the post-war constitutions and the apparent protection afforded them by special minority treaties appended to the general peace settlements failed to get rid of anti-Semitism. But it was only after the revolutionary change in government policy towards Jews in Germany after 1933 that political anti-Semitism acquired an irresistible momentum as a force in European politics.

Following the Nazi capture of power in January 1933 the half million Jews of Germany were subjected to a series of legal enactments whose cumulative effect was to exclude Jews from the civic and economic life of the country. In 1933 laws were passed barring the employment of Jews in the civil service, universities, and schools, and in the legal profession. Jewish

[3] Estimates of the number of victims vary: C. Abramsky, in 'The Biro-Bidzhan Project', in Lionel Kochan ed., *The Jews in Soviet Russia since 1917*, p. 64, considers reliable an estimate of 200,000 Jews massacred in the Ukraine alone. S. Ettinger, in *A History of the Jewish People*, ed. H. H. Ben-Sasson, London 1976, p. 954, estimates 75,000 deaths in the Ukraine and 'several thousand' in Poland. Norman Davies, in 'Great Britain and the Polish Jews, 1918–20', *Journal of Contemporary History*, April 1973, vol. 8 no. 2, seeks to justify the scepticism of the Foreign Office regarding the ferocity of the pogroms in Poland. He argues: 'That fewer than 1,000 Jewish civilians died when the Polish Army during the same period suffered over 250,000 casualties is a fair indication of the scale of the disaster.' Davies, however, admits that in the Ukraine, as distinct from Poland, 100,000 Jews died. The occupation of Ukrainian territory by the Poles in the Russo-Polish war renders the distinction somewhat academic. For a contemporary account by Israel Cohen, who visited Poland as special commissioner to investigate reports of the outrages, see Israel Cohen, 'Diary of a Mission to Poland, December 1918 to January 1919' and 'The Lemberg Pogrom December 1918' in Israel Cohen, *Travels in Jewry*, London 1952, pp. 48–92. Cohen's report, on his return from Poland, substantiated the earlier Jewish accounts of serious and widespread violence.

immigrants who had been naturalized since 1918 were denaturalized. This legislation was extended in 1935 with the enactment of the more far-reaching Nuremberg laws, which attempted to lay down close definitions of various categories of 'non-Aryans', and prohibited intermarriage between Jews and 'Aryan' Germans. The anti-Jewish campaign gathered momentum in 1938. After the *Anschluss* in March the Nuremberg laws were extended to Austria. Decrees issued in April greatly accelerated the 'Aryanization' of Jewish property throughout the Reich. In the late spring the atmosphere of violent anti-Semitism was heightened and Jewish shops in the Kurfürstendamm in Berlin were daubed with swastikas and anti-Semitic caricatures. In November there took place the *Kristallnacht* pogrom in which ninety-one people were killed, large numbers of synagogues destroyed, and at least twenty thousand Jews arrested and sent to concentration camps where many perished. During the next few months most remaining Jewish property was confiscated, Jewish organizations were forced to disband, and Jewish newspapers closed. The intended, and the actual, effect of all these measures was to drive masses of Jews out of Germany.

From 1933 onwards emigration was a central element in the German Government's Jewish policy. By the end of 1938 an estimated 150,000 Jews had emigrated.[4] The attitude of the German Government towards Zionism and the Jewish National Home was ambivalent, but its enthusiasm for Jewish emigration led it in September 1933 to conclude a special arrangement with the Jewish Agency for Palestine: the *ha'avara* (Hebr. 'transfer') agreement enabled Jewish emigrants to Palestine to retain part of their assets by providing payment in marks for German exporters to Palestine and obtaining in return Palestinian currency from the importers in Palestine. This procedure (which the German Government favoured as a means of increasing German exports) facilitated the emigration of some forty thousand Jews from Germany to Palestine between 1933 and 1938 and made an important contribution to the inflow of capital to Palestine. As time went on the proportion of assets which it was possible for the Jewish emigrant

---

[4] Karl A. Schleunes, *The Twisted Road to Auschwitz: Nazi Policy Towards German Jews 1933–1939*, London 1972, p. 199.

to transfer abroad decreased. A *Reichsfluchtsteuer*, or emigration tax, first introduced in 1931 in order to curb the flight of capital, was greatly increased in 1934. By 1938 it was almost impossible for Jewish emigrants to transfer any of their remaining assets abroad. Yet, while despoiling Jews of their property, the German Government remained anxious to encourage Jewish emigration, and indeed expressed dissatisfaction with what was regarded as the slow progress made in the ejection of Jews. From the autumn of 1938 it resorted to more direct methods of stimulating emigration. In August 1938 a Central Office for Jewish Emigration was established in Vienna under Gestapo auspices. Henceforth the German authorities increasingly resorted to physical extrusion as a way of getting rid of Jews. In October 1938 more than fifteen thousand Jews of Polish nationality, many of them long resident in Germany, were rounded up and taken to the Polish frontier where they were expelled from German territory. In the last year of the peace similar scenes became commonplace on the eastern borders of the Reich.

By 1939 Jewish emigration from the Reich had become a major European problem. A total of 226,000 Jews are estimated to have left Germany between the Nazi seizure of power and the beginning of the war. A further 134,000 to 144,000 emigrated from Austria and the 'Protectorate of Bohemia and Moravia'. A total of some 360,000 to 370,000 Jews therefore left the borders of the expanded Reich between 1933 and 1939: this represented more than one third of the approximately 913,000 Jews who lived in this area in 1933. Of the emigrants, about 57,000 went to the U.S.A., 53,000 to Palestine, and about 50,000 to Britain. France absorbed 40,000, Belgium 25,000, and Switzerland 10,000.[5] Other countries which admitted significant numbers before the war included Argentina, Brazil, Australia, and Canada. However, as the exodus threatened to become a flood, most countries began to impose restrictions on

[5] Figures for the U.S.A. from A. Tartakower and K. R. Grossmann, *The Jewish Refugee*, New York 1944, p. 348; for Palestine from Gurevich, *Statistical Handbook*, p. 108; for other countries from A. J. Sherman, *Island Refuge: Britain and Refugees from the Third Reich 1933–1939*, London 1973, pp. 264–5. The figures given for France, Belgium, and Switzerland include both Jews and non-Jews; however, in these countries as elsewhere the majority of refugees from the Reich were Jewish. The total number of refugees from the Reich admitted to Britain between 1933 and 1939 was 56,000, of whom ninety per cent are estimated to have been Jewish.

the entry of refugees. Moreover, the governments of east European states, aping the Germans, intensified discrimination against their own Jewish citizens, and, particularly in Poland, Roumania, and Hungary, increased the pressure for the emigration of what they regarded as their surplus Jewish populations. These countries showed no inclination to welcome Jewish refugees extruded from the Reich. When the thousands of Polish Jews from Germany were driven over the German-Polish frontier in October 1938 the Poles refused to admit them: many remained for several months in a makeshift camp at the village of Zbąszyn in the no-man's-land between the two countries. Hungary refused to admit a similar group of sixty Jews expelled from the Austrian Burgenland, who were obliged to take refuge on a verminous barge on the Danube. Thousands of refugees, expelled from their countries of residence, found themselves without any country ready to receive them. In desperation many fled to the International Settlement in Shanghai, the only city in the world where refugees could enter without visas; in 1939 every third European in Shanghai was said to be a refugee, the majority of them paupers; by 1941 there were 20,000 Jewish refugees in Shanghai.[6]

In July 1938, on the initiative of President Roosevelt, an international conference met at Evian to seek a co-ordinated international solution to the refugee problem. The rudiments of an international organization to deal with the problem already existed in the League of Nations 'High Commission for Refugees (Jewish and other) coming from Germany', which had been set up in 1933. But the body lacked funds, authority, or support from governments, and the first High Commissioner, James G. McDonald, an American, resigned in December 1935 in protest against his inability, with restricted powers, to make any effective contribution to solving the refugee problem. The Evian Conference established an Inter-Governmental Committee on Refugees, with a mandate to seek, by negotiation with the German and other governments, 'to improve the present conditions of exodus and to replace them by conditions of orderly emigration'.[7] From January 1939 the Director of the I.G.C.R. and the High Commissioner for

---

[6] Tartakower and Grossmann, *The Jewish Refugee*, p. 322.
[7] Quoted in Sherman, *Island Refuge*, p. 119.

Refugees were combined in one person, Sir Herbert Emerson, a former Governor of the Punjab with a reputation as an efficient administrator. The I.G.C.R. evolved several schemes for the financing of Jewish emigration from Germany to various destinations, but by the outbreak of the war there was little to show for its efforts apart from numerous lengthy memoranda. At the insistence of President Roosevelt it was maintained in a shadowy limbo existence after the outbreak of the war. However, in the history of international action on behalf of refugees it proved a weak reed unable to stem or direct the engulfing tide of refugees. A child of the Evian Conference, the I.G.C.R. inherited many of its defects from its parent. The birth of the committee was, indeed, the only notable product of the conference, which, organized primarily in order to find places of refuge for fugitives from the Reich, in fact proved to be the occasion for a dismal series of speeches by the delegate of country after country, each of whom demonstrated the inability of his nation, notwithstanding the deepest sympathy and generosity towards refugees, to absorb further significant numbers of immigrants. The proceedings at Evian turned out to have been a dress rehearsal for the similar Anglo-American conference on refugees at Bermuda in April 1943.[8]

In comparison with other countries Britain's pre-war record towards Jewish refugees was relatively generous. Few other countries in this period, with the exception of Palestine, admitted a larger number of Jewish refugees in proportion to population. There was a considerable degree of public sympathy in Britain for the persecuted Jews fleeing the Reich. It has been argued that 'Nazi treatment of the Jews' before the outbreak of the war 'did more than anything else to turn English moral feeling against Germany'.[9] The immigration of refugees to Britain was greatly facilitated by an undertaking given in 1933 by representative leaders of the Anglo-Jewish community who promised the Government that 'all expense, whether in respect of temporary or permanent accommodation or maintenance will be borne by the Jewish community without ultimate charge to the State'.[10] This undertaking was honoured by the

[8] See chap. 5.

[9] A. J. P. Taylor, *English History 1914–1945*, Oxford 1965, p. 420.

[10] Quoted in Sherman, *Island Refuge*, p. 30.

Jewish community until after the outbreak of the war, although the numbers of refugees who arrived in Britain far exceeded the expectation when the undertaking was given. Generous assistance was also given to Jewish refugees by non-Jewish bodies and individuals. The Academic Assistance Council (later the Society for the Protection of Science and Learning) helped to find positions in British universities for many refugee scholars. Many private citizens offered refuge to Czech or German Jews in their homes: for example, Harold Macmillan M.P. sheltered forty Czech refugees in his house in Sussex. The former Prime Minister, Lord Baldwin, launched an appeal fund for aid to refugees. Although the Government made no contribution to the maintenance of German Jewish immigrants, a grant of £4,000,000 for aid to Czech refugees (non-Jewish as well as Jewish) was made by the Government, perhaps as a gesture of contrition, after the Munich Conference. In December 1938 a Movement for the Care of Children from Germany was formed, which arranged for the immigration of nearly ten thousand children (ninety per cent of whom were Jewish) by September 1939: most were lodged with foster parents, many of whom were non-Jews. In January 1939 the 'Kitchener Camp for Poor Persons' was opened at Richborough in Kent, where over three thousand Jewish refugees were temporarily housed pending their re-emigration to other countries.

But, in spite of this relatively hospitable reception accorded to fifty thousand Jewish refugees between 1933 and 1939, there was a definite undercurrent of antagonism towards the arrivals. There was some opposition to immigration on the ground that it aggravated unemployment. The British Medical Association opposed the admission of more than a small number of refugee doctors, and Lord Dawson of Penn, President of the Royal College of Physicians, told the Home Secretary in 1933 that 'the number that could usefully be absorbed or teach us anything could be counted on the fingers of one hand'.[11] The *Daily Mail* warned against the 'misguided sentimentalism' of those who called for the admission of larger numbers of refugees: 'Once it was known that Britain offered sanctuary to all who cared to come, the floodgates would be opened, and we should be inundated by thousands seeking a home.' Expressing a similar view,

[11] Quoted ibid., p. 48.

the *Daily Express* felt it 'would be unwise to overload the basket'. Six trades unionists wrote to the *Daily Herald* to complain of that paper's support for refugees, and averred that 'charity begins at home.' And *The Observer* argued that a mass influx might lead to outbreaks of anti-Semitism.[12] In a discussion in the Cabinet in July 1938 on the results of the Evian Conference, the Home Secretary stated that 'while he was anxious to do his best, there was a good deal of feeling growing up in this country—a feeling which was reflected in Parliament—against the admission of Jews to British territory'.[13] The Cabinet was also informed in 1938 of an M.I.5 report 'suggesting that the Germans were anxious to inundate this country with Jews, with a view to creating a Jewish problem in the United Kingdom'. Jewish representatives themselves, (who, together with church, trades union, and other representatives served on the Co-Ordinating Committee for Refugees which had been established to advise the Home Office) were said to have told the Home Secretary that they were 'averse from allowing very large numbers of Jews to enter the country or from allowing the entry of Jews whom they had not themselves approved, since they were afraid of an anti-Jew agitation'.[14] During the war similar public attitudes towards refugees, both more and less welcoming, persisted; but, as will be seen, it was by the latter that, after September 1939, the Government allowed itself to be swayed in the determination of its refugee policy on the 'home front'.

It was not, however, in Britain, but in Palestine that the British Government was confronted by the most acute problems as a consequence of the exodus of refugees from central and eastern Europe. Jewish immigration to Palestine, which had been relatively stagnant between 1927 and 1932, suddenly increased in 1933 to over 30,000, more than the combined total of the previous six years. In 1934 it rose further, to 42,000, and in 1935 to 62,000. These were the highest immigration figures in the history of Palestine under the British mandate. In these three years the Jewish population of Palestine grew from 192,000 to 355,000, an increase of more than eighty per cent. The Jewish proportion of the total population as a result rose

[12] Quoted ibid., pp. 94, 124 and 126.
[13] Quoted ibid., p. 121.
[14] Quoted ibid., pp. 88 and 175–6.

from 17.9 per cent to 27.2 per cent. In addition to the 53,000 immigrants from the greater Reich between 1933 and 1939, even larger numbers arrived from elsewhere. The largest number came from Poland, some 74,000, but significant numbers also arrived from Roumania, Greece, Lithuania, and Latvia. The total number of Jewish immigrants to Palestine between 1933 and 1939 was 215,232.[15] This large influx, which more than doubled the size of the *Yishuv* (the Jewish community of Palestine), led to a dramatic change in the politics of the country.

In April 1936 there broke out a widespread Arab general strike which developed into a full-scale rebellion. An Arab Higher Committee, composed of representatives of all the main Arab nationalist parties, and headed by the Mufti of Jerusalem, Haj Amin al-Husseini, called for an end to Jewish immigration, a ban on the sale of land to Jews, and the establishment of democratic government in which the Arabs, as the majority element in the population, would have the predominant voice. The strike continued until October when it was called off by the Higher Committee in response to an appeal to the Palestinian Arabs by King Ibn Saud of Saudi Arabia, King Ghazi of Iraq, and the Emir Abdullah of Transjordan, who called on the Palestinians to 'rely on the good intentions of our friend, Great Britain, who has declared that she will do justice'.[16] The appeal of the Arab kings had been previously concerted with the British Government, and marked a significant stage in the internationalization of the Palestine problem.

Meanwhile a Royal Commission, under Lord Peel, had been appointed by the British Government 'to ascertain the underlying causes of the disturbances' and to decide whether 'upon a proper construction of the terms of the Mandate, either the Arabs or the Jews have any legitimate grievances'.[17] The Commission's report, one of the most penetrating analyses of the nature of the struggle for Palestine, was published in July 1937. It decided that the mandate was unworkable, and that the existing form of government tended to exacerbate the

---

[15] Gurevich, *Statistical Handbook*, *passim*. These figures relate to the country of last residence, not to the citizenship, of immigrants.

[16] Quoted in *Palestine Royal Commission Report*, Cmd. 5479, London 1937, p. 101.

[17] Ibid., p. ix.

Arab-Jewish conflict. 'The disease', declared the commission, 'is so deep-rooted that, in our firm conviction, the only hope of a cure lies in a surgical operation.'[18] The commission therefore recommended the partition of Palestine into sovereign Arab and Jewish states. The Jewish state was to comprise Galilee, the valley of Esdraelon, and the coastal plain to a point a little south of Jaffa. The larger Arab state was to comprise the remainder of the country except for a small residual British mandatory enclave stretching from Jerusalem and Bethlehem to Jaffa (which would form part of the Arab state). During the 'period of transition' to partition, it was recommended by the commission that 'steps should be taken to prohibit the purchase of land by Jews within the Arab Area . . . or by Arabs within the Jewish Area'.[19] During the same period there should be a territorial restriction on Jewish immigration: no Jewish immigration to the Arab area should be permitted, and the volume of Jewish immigration should be determined by the economic absorptive capacity of Palestine less the Arab area. If, however, the mandatory government were maintained in its existing form without partition, the commission recommended that the criterion of economic absorptive capacity by which the permitted level of Jewish immigration had hitherto been assessed by the government should be replaced by a 'political high level'. The commission added: 'This high level should be fixed for the next five years at 12,000 per annum, and in no circumstances during that period should more than that number be allowed into the country in any one year.'[20]

The Royal Commission's report provoked a bitter controversy within the Zionist movement. The dominant figure in the movement, Dr Chaim Weizmann, was cautiously in favour of the partition proposal, although not of the borders proposed by the Peel Commission. His first reaction to the idea of partition, when giving evidence to the commission, had been: 'Of course it is cutting the child in two.' After the session Weizmann declared that 'the long toil of his life was at last crowned

[18] Ibid., p. 368.
[19] Ibid., p. 393.
[20] Ibid., p. 306.

with success. The Jewish state was at hand.'[21] Weizmann was supported in his approval of the principle of partition by the most powerful of the Palestinian Labour Zionists, David Ben Gurion. Among those who opposed partition were Menahem Ussishkin, chairman of the Jewish National Fund, Vladimir Jabotinsky, head of the break-away militant New Zionist Organisation, Berl Katznelson, of the Labour Zionists, Rabbi Stephen Wise, one of the leading American Zionists, the *Jewish Chronicle* of London, and Viscount Samuel, who had served as first High Commissioner of Palestine under the mandate from 1920 to 1925, and who made an influential speech in the House of Lords in July 1937 attacking the idea of partition. The issue came to a head at the twentieth Zionist Congress at Zurich in August 1937. Weizmann delivered a two-hour speech in which he defined the dilemma facing the Zionists in terms of a Talmudic saying: 'If the jug falls upon the stone, woe to the jug. If the stone falls upon the jug, woe to the jug.' He bitterly attacked the proposed restrictions on Jewish immigration:

I say to the mandatory power: you shall not play fast and loose with the Jewish people. Say to us frankly that the National Home is closed, and we shall know where we stand. But this trifling with a nation bleeding from a thousand wounds must not be done by the British whose Empire is built on moral principles—that mighty Empire must not commit this sin against the people of the Book. Tell us the truth. This at least we have deserved.'[22]

At the same time Weizmann urged that the principle of partition should be considered in the light of two criteria:

Firstly, does it offer a basis for a genuine growth of Jewish life . . . Secondly, does the proposal contribute to the solution of the Jewish problem, a problem pregnant with danger to ourselves and to the world.'[23]

One of the listeners described the speech as 'an inspired utter-

[21] Quoted in N. A. Rose. *The Gentile Zionists: A Study in Anglo-Zionist Diplomacy 1929–1939*, London 1973, p. 128.

[22] Quoted ibid., p. 141.

[23] Quoted in J. L. Meltzer, 'Towards the Precipice' in M. Weisgal and J. Carmichael, eds., *Chaim Weizmann: A Biography by Several Hands*, New York 1963, p. 242.

ance'.[24] The Congress voted by 299 to 160 to reject the Peel Commission scheme, but it empowered the Zionist Executive 'to enter into negotiations with a view to ascertaining the precise terms of His Majesty's Government for the proposed establishment of a Jewish state'.[25]

The reaction of the Palestinian Arabs to the Royal Commission's proposals was less equivocal. The publication of the commission's report proved to be the signal for a renewal of the Arab rebellion. The Arab Higher Committee appealed to Arab rulers to rescue the Palestinian Arabs 'from imperialism, Judaisation, and dismemberment'.[26] At a conference of Arab nationalists at Bludan in Syria, in early September 1937, delegates from Syria, Palestine, Egypt, Iraq, Lebanon, and Transjordan took a collective oath 'to continue the struggle for Palestine until she had been liberated and Arab sovereignty over the land had been attained'.[27] On 26 September the acting District Commissioner for Galilee, Lewis Andrews, was murdered with his escort by Arab insurgents outside the Anglican church in Nazareth. The Arab revolt now entered its most serious stage. Although it took the form of internecine Arab warfare and attacks on Jews as much as of direct attack on the mandatory government, the British eventually found it necessary to resort to vigorous repression in an effort to curb the rising. In October 1937 the Arab Higher Committee was outlawed, and warrants were issued for the arrest of its members, several of whom were deported. The Mufti of Jerusalem evaded arrest and fled to Lebanon disguised as a bedouin. Martial law was finally declared throughout the country, and over one hundred Arabs were hanged after trial by military courts between 1937 and 1939. In spite of military action by the British, however, the revolt continued in 1938. In the summer of 1938 the Arab rebels were in control of most of the hill country, and paraded openly in the streets of Nablus. In October 1938 the Arab flag was raised in the Old City of Jerusalem, and the entire area within the walls was occupied by rebels. It was five days before British

[24] N. A. Rose, ed., *Baffy: The Diaries of Blanche Dugdale 1936–1947*, London 1973, p. 57 (entry dated 4 Aug. 1937).

[25] Quoted in Meltzer, op. cit., p. 243.

[26] Quoted in Y. Porath, *The Palestinian Arab National Movement vol. 2 From Riots to Rebellion 1929–1939*, London 1977, p. 230.

[27] Quoted ibid., p. 232.

soldiers, using local Arabs as human shields, were able to re-occupy the area.[28] The revolt which persisted into 1939 represented a major challenge to British authority, and diverted British military resources on a massive scale. At the height of the revolt more than two British division strengths were committed to the repression of the rebels. It has been estimated that forty per cent of the total British field force was tied down in Palestine—the equivalent of what British strategic planners reluctantly considered committing to France in the event of a European war.[29] As a result Palestine became a major element in British strategic calculations. As the European scene darkened in the autumn of 1938 British policy in Palestine began a drastic change of direction.

Although the Government had at first accepted the Royal Commission's report, its enthusiasm for partition gradually waned. In September 1937, the Foreign Secretary, Anthony Eden, told the Council of the League of Nations: 'partition is the only solution'. But in December the Government announced that it was 'in no sense committed' to the Peel Commission's partition plan.[30] A new commission under Sir John Woodhead was appointed to redraw the frontiers of the proposed Arab and Jewish states. The commission's conclusion in the autumn of 1938 was that partition was impracticable and would not afford a solution to the Palestine problem. These findings were reached with the aid of hints from the Government that such a decision would not be unwelcome. When the report was published in November 1938 the Government published a White Paper in which it announced its abandonment of partition because of the 'political, administrative and financial difficulties involved'.[31] A round-table conference was to be called by the Government at which Arabs and Jews would seek a new solution. If no accord were reached at the conference the Government would impose its own solution. The conference opened in February 1939 at St James's Palace in London. It was attended by representatives of the Jews (both Zionist and non-Zionist) and of the Arabs (among whom were delegates

[28] Ibid., p. 240.
[29] Rose, *Gentile Zionists*, pp. 111–12.
[30] Quoted in J. C. Hurewitz, *The Struggle for Palestine*, New York 1950, pp. 90–1.
[31] *Palestine: Statement by His Majesty's Government in the United Kingdom* (Cmd. 5893), London 1938.

from Egypt, Saudi Arabia, the Yemen, Iraq, and Transjordan, as well as Palestinian Arabs drawn from the members and supporters of the Arab Higher Committee; on British insistence, however, the exiled Mufti of Jerusalem was excluded from the Arab delegation). The Arab delegation refused to confer formally with the Jews (although there were unproductive private meetings), and the Government was obliged to hold separate sessions with the two delegations. By the middle of March no agreement had been reached, and the Government declared the conference closed. The way was now open for the Government to impose its own policy.

The direction of the Government's thinking had been clearly revealed in the conference discussions. In a candid speech to the Jewish delegates on 14 February, the Colonial Secretary, Malcolm MacDonald, laid bare the strategic preoccupations which governed official planning. He emphasized that in the event of war 'the security of British forces in the Middle East and lines of communication with India and the Far East' depended on the maintenance of friendly relations with governments in the region. He stressed the importance of the Suez Canal, of the British naval base at Alexandria, and of British oil interests in Iraq. All the Government's dispositions in the Middle East, MacDonald declared, were based on the assumption that it would enjoy in any war the active support of its allies and the benevolent neutrality of other states. A 'continuation of the estrangement in Palestine' would not only threaten the entire British position in the Middle East; it might also produce 'a good deal of unrest among the Moslems of India'. The Government, he continued, had received 'strong and unanimous warnings' from its military advisers and from British representatives in the Middle East and in India as to the dangerous effects which might be predicted in the event 'of the pursuance of certain policies in Palestine'. If war broke out the Middle East might be the British Empire's 'Achilles' Heel'. The defeat of the British Empire, he reminded his audience, would be a disaster as much for the Jews as for Britain.[32]

The Government's policy was set forth in a White Paper, published in May 1939. The White Paper, which was to remain

[32] Extract from minutes in Yehuda Bauer, *From Diplomacy to Resistance: A History of Jewish Palestine 1939–1945*, New York 1973, pp. 361–3.

the formal basis of British policy in Palestine throughout the war, represented a total reversal of the Balfour Declaration policy which, notwithstanding some concessions to Arab views on inessential matters, had been the anchor of British administration of Palestine for the previous two decades. The White Paper was divided into three sections, the first dealing with the Government's constitutional proposals, and the others with land and immigration policies. In the first section the Government declared (for the first time in such a policy statement) 'unequivocally that it is not part of their policy that Palestine should become a Jewish State'. Partition was dismissed; while it was admitted that it would have afforded 'clarity', the establishment of separate Arab and Jewish states had been 'found to be impracticable'. The objective of the Government was now pronounced to be 'a State in which the two peoples in Palestine, Arabs and Jews, share authority in government in such a way that the essential interests of each are secured'. A single independent Palestinian state was to be established within ten years in treaty relations with Britain. During the intervening period Palestine was to remain under the mandatory regime. Palestinians, both Arabs and Jews, were to be invited to serve as heads of government departments 'approximately in proportion to their respective populations'. No proposals were made for the establishment of an elective legislature, but it was stated that the Government 'would regard this as an appropriate constitutional development, and, should public opinion in Palestine hereafter show itself in favour of such a development, they will be prepared, provided that local conditions permit, to establish the necessary machinery'. Neither the legislative assembly nor the appointment of Palestinian heads of departments was realized by the Government during the war. The administration of the country between 1939 and 1945 therefore remained frozen as a bureaucracy responsible only to the Colonial Office (and indirectly to the Westminster Parliament) and without any elective character.

The Government made greater (although not wholly effective) efforts to implement the land provisions of the White Paper. The policy statement declared that 'owing to the natural growth of the Arab population and the steady sale in recent years of Arab land to Jews, there is now in certain areas no room for further transfers of Arab land, whilst in some other areas such transfers of land must be restricted if Arab cultivators are to maintain their existing standard of life and a considerable landless Arab population is not soon to be created.' The High Commissioner was therefore to be given powers 'to prohibit and regulate transfers of land'. The Land Transfer Regulations, foreshadowed in the White Paper, were promulgated in February 1940. They divided Palestine into three zones. In the first zone (comprising 63.4 per cent of the country) the sale of Arab-owned land to Jews was prohibited. In the second zone (31.6 per cent of the country) Jews might acquire land only from owners who were not Palestinian Arabs. In the third zone (five per cent of the country) land transfers were to remain uncontrolled. The land regulations were administered with some rigour, but it was still possible by various means for Jews to acquire title to land. The total area in Jewish possession increased between 1939 and 1945 from 1,533,400 to 1,778,300 metric dunams.[33] The proportion of Jewish-held land owned by the Jewish National Fund increased sharply in this period, and some fifty new settlements were established. Although the land provisions of the White Paper aroused great resentment among Zionists they did not, therefore, completely preclude the possibility of further Zionist land settlement. But if the land regulations were a stinging irritant for the *Yishuv*, the immigration provisions of the White Paper were a matter of burning outrage to them.

The White Paper stated that the Government had decided in principle 'to permit further expansion of the Jewish National Home by immigration only if the Arabs are prepared to acquiesce in it'. The Government, however, felt that 'abruptly to stop further immigration would be unjust to the Jewish National Home'. Moreover, the statement continued, 'His Majesty's Government are conscious of the present unhappy plight of large numbers of Jews who seek a refuge from certain European countries, and they believe that Palestine can and should make a further contribution to the solution of this pressing world problem.' Jewish immigration would therefore be permitted to continue for a further five years 'at a rate which, if economic capacity permits, will bring the Jewish population

[33] Gurevich, *Statistical Handbook*, p. 140. One metric dunam = 0.247 acre.

up to approximately one-third of the total population of the country.' It was calculated that this would allow for the admission of 75,000 new immigrants. These would be admitted in accordance with economic absorptive capacity, and on the following basis:

For each of the next five years a quota of 10,000 Jewish immigrants will be allowed on the understanding that a shortage in any one year may be added to the quotas for subsequent years, within the five-year period, if economic absorptive capacity permits.

In addition, as a contribution towards the solution of the Jewish refugee problem, 25,000 refugees will be admitted as soon as the High Commissioner is satisfied that adequate provision for their maintenance is ensured, special consideration being given to refugee children and dependants.

No further immigration would be permitted at the end of the five-year period 'unless the Arabs of Palestine are prepared to acquiesce in it'. The section on immigration concluded:

His Majesty's Government are satisfied that, when the immigration over five years which is now contemplated has taken place, they will not be justified in facilitating, nor will they be under any obligation to facilitate, the further development of the Jewish National Home by immigration regardless of the wishes of the Arab population.[34]

The White Paper came as a shattering blow to the Zionists. The immigration restrictions, in particular, were seen as 'a breach of faith and a surrender to Arab terrorism'. A public statement by the Jewish Agency for Palestine underlined the Zionist feeling of betrayal:

It is in the darkest hour of Jewish history that the British Government proposes to deprive the Jews of their last hope and to close the road back to their Homeland. It is a cruel blow, doubly cruel because it comes from the government of a great nation which has extended a helping hand to the Jews, and whose position must rest on foundations of moral authority and international good faith. This blow will not subdue the Jewish people. The historic bond between the people and the land of Israel cannot be broken. The Jews will never accept the closing to them of the gates of Palestine nor let their national home be converted into a ghetto.[35]

[34] *Palestine: Statement of Policy*, Cmd. 6019, London 1939.
[35] Text of Jewish Agency statement in Walter Laqueur, *The Israel-Arab Reader: A Documentary History of the Middle East Conflict*, London 1969, pp. 76–7.

An interview between Malcolm MacDonald and Chaim Weizmann on 13 May at MacDonald's country house (held at the Colonial Secretary's insistence) showed how far removed the Anglo-Zionist relationship now was from the spirit of 1917:

Dr Weizmann [said] that there was really nothing he had to tell Mr MacDonald, except that everything he had done, and the way in which he had done it, had aroused their uncompromising hostility . . .

Mr MacDonald said that the Jews had made many mistakes in the past, to which Dr Weizmann replied: 'Oh, yes, certainly we have made mistakes; our chief mistake is that we exist at all . . .'

The conversation reached its crisis when *Dr Weizmann*, in analysing the Government's new policy, said that at least in Hitler one found the virtue of an absolutely frank brutality, whereas Mr MacDonald was covering up his betrayal of the Jews under a semblance of legality. He added that Mr MacDonald was handing over the Jews to their assassins. *Mr MacDonald* showed great indignation and said that it was of no use to talk to him like that. He said he knew that the Jews had been calling him a hypocrite and a coward. *Dr Weizmann* replied: I have never called you a coward.

After this staggering insult, the Colonial Secretary attempted a rather feeble defence, but Weizmann swept MacDonald's words aside with a further vehement tirade:

Mr MacDonald said it was all very well to stand by and criticise. *Dr Weizmann* replied that he surely did not belong to those who just stood by and criticised. He had worked; he had worked his hardest to try and explain the British to sixteen millions of Jews. He went on to say that he pitied the Prime Minister, who was the innocent victim of specious advisers. He then said that the Government would have to use troops against the Jews, and the troops would have to shoot. Their masters would certainly be delighted. *Mr MacDonald* asked: 'Who are our masters?' And *Dr Weizmann* replied: The Mufti and his friends. He said that the troops would have to shoot at the Jews when the latter went to take possession of lands acquired contrary to the new laws, and added that he thought *Mr MacDonald*, as a young man, was taking upon himself a very great responsibility.

MacDonald, who must by this stage have been regretting that he had pressed Weizmann to come to tea, said that it needed courage to face the problem and make a decision; it would be much easier to postpone the decision. Weizmann commented, with sarcasm, that no doubt much courage was required when warships and troops were available. MacDonald returned to the strategic priorities which had dictated the Government's change of policy, but Weizmann said 'that all this talk about the strategic necessities was just bunk'.[36] Seldom can a Colonial Secretary have been subjected to such slighting admonitions. Weizmann described the occasion as 'the worst afternoon of his life' and said 'that he had never spoken so rudely and so straight to any man and that it left a bitter taste in his mouth'.[37]

The Zionists used every means at their disposal to mobilize opposition to the Government's policy. In the past, when British Governments had momentarily wavered in their commitment to the Jewish National Home, the Zionists had often succeeded in stiffening the Government's pro-Zionist resolve by skilful deployment of support in Parliament, the press, and abroad. But on this occasion these tactics failed to influence the Government. In a debate in the House of Commons on 22 and 23 May MacDonald defended the White Paper, repudiating the charge that it involved a breach of faith by the British Government, and reminding the House: 'We have some interests of our own in Palestine. We have, for instance, certain vital strategic requirements'. The White Paper was subjected to withering criticism from the Government's two most eloquent critics, both former Colonial Secretaries, and both now on the Conservative back benches. Leopold Amery speaking on the first day of the debate announced that he would defy the Government's three-line whip and vote against the motion calling for approval of the White Paper: 'I could never hold my head up again to either Jew or Arab if I voted to-morrow for what, in good faith, I repeatedly told both Jews and Arabs was inconceivable, namely, that any British Government would ever go back upon the pledge given, not only to Jews, but [to] the whole civilised world when it assumed the Mandate.' Amery's words were echoed on the following day by another speaker who, after lunching with Weizmann, told the House of Commons:

As one intimately and personally and responsibly concerned in the earlier stages of our Palestine policy, I could not stand by and see solemn engagements into which Britain has entered before the world

[36] Note on conversation, CZA S25/7563.
[37] Quoted in Rose, *Gentile Zionists*, p. 203.

set aside for reasons of administrative convenience or—and it will be a vain hope—for the sake of a quiet life. Like my Right Honourable Friend, I should feel personally embarrassed in the most acute manner if I lent myself by silence or inaction to what I must regard as an act of repudiation.[38]

Winston Churchill's words made a powerful impression, but the Government's motion was nevertheless carried, albeit by a smaller than usual majority.

Outside Parliament the Zionists achieved some success in arousing support for their views, but again with little perceptible effect on the Government's determination to adhere to the White Paper policy. A survey conducted by the British Institute of Public Opinion in March 1939 (that is, before the publication of the White Paper) on the question whether the Government should continue to allow Jews to settle in Palestine revealed a marked pro-Zionist tendency among the respondents: sixty per cent said that they favoured the continuation of Jewish immigration to Palestine; twenty-six per cent expressed no opinion; only fourteen per cent gave negative replies.[39] But this was long before the period when public opinion polls assumed a dominant position in the calculations of British politicians. The White Paper was, in any case, of little concern to the general public, who, in so far as they were interested in foreign affairs at all, saw much more pressing dangers in Europe, where Hitler, having occupied Prague in mid-March, was now turning his attention towards Poland. More important to the Zionists than public opinion was the press. The *Manchester Guardian* condemned the White Paper as 'disastrous'. But this was only to be expected of the organ of Manchester liberalism, which (with contributors such as Harry Sacher and Lewis Namier) was in any case traditionally identified with Zionism. Its views on the subject were as a result habitually discounted in official quarters. Criticism of the White Paper by *The Times* might consequently be of greater value to the Zionists. Its editor, Geoffrey Dawson, told Weizmann that he thought the White Paper 'folly'. But he failed to

[38] HC vol. 347, cols. 1937–54, 2015–16, and 2168 (22–23 May 1939).
[39] See S. Levenberg, 'Zionism in British Politics' in Paul Goodman, ed., *The Jewish National Home 1917–1942*, London 1943.

express himself with equal pungency in print. Other Conservative and independent newspapers tended to support the White Paper: the *Daily Telegraph* thought it 'fair'; *The Observer* considered it 'logical'; the *Daily Sketch* pronounced it 'sound'; and the *Daily Express*, in self-congratulatory vein, acclaimed it as a 'supremely wise act of statesmanship . . . which has been urged by this newspaper unceasingly for close on a quarter of a century'. As for the left, the *Daily Worker* seized the strangely inopportune moment to denounce the Jewish Agency as 'open supporters of British imperialism'. Finally, the *New Statesman*, with characteristic muddleheadedness, suggested that a greater number of immigrants might be allowed into Palestine, while at the same time dismissing 'the appeal to mercy, so to speak'.[40] The Zionists could not expect to make much headway in Whitehall by relying on the effect of public or press opinion.

There remained the international arena. In a cable to the former French Prime Minister, Léon Blum, in April, Weizmann had appealed for French pressure on the British Government to delay publication of the White Paper and to reconsider its policy.[41] The socialist leader was a convinced Zionist, but he was now out of office and in no position to induce the French Government to make such a *démarche*. Nor would much notice have been taken of such a French approach at this time. The position was, however, different in the U.S.A., for the British Government was acutely conscious of the capacity of American Jews to influence the United States Government and American public opinion, and feared that, as Malcolm MacDonald told the Cabinet at the end of April, the Jews in the United States 'would do their best to make the publication of the White Paper the occasion to stir up agitation'.[42] At the behest of Weizmann, Zionist pressure on President Roosevelt was concerted by Supreme Court Justice Louis D. Brandeis. The President notified the British of his interest in the matter, but without any impact on British intentions.[43] Upon publication of the White Paper, Roosevelt expressed 'a good deal of

[40] See Rose, *Gentile Zionists*, pp. 206–12; and Andrew Sharf, *The British Press and Jews under Nazi Rule*, London 1964, pp. 184–6.

[41] Weizmann to Blum, 18 Apr. 1939, WA.

[42] Cabinet minutes, 26 Apr. 1939, PRO CAB 23/99/66.

[43] Weizmann to Brandeis, 19 Apr. 1939, WA; Moshe Sharett (Shertok), *Yoman Medini* (Political Diary) *vol. 4: 1939*, Tel Aviv 1974, p. 278 (entry dated 11 May 1939).

dismay', and the American Ambassador in London, Joseph Kennedy, was instructed to warn the Foreign Office that there was widespread disappointment in the U.S.A. with the White Paper, and in particular with its immigration provisions.[44] But Kennedy, who had a tendency to act with a haughty disregard for the directions of the State Department, had already vitiated any effect which such representations might have had, by privately assuring MacDonald that while American Jews might cause a certain public commotion over the White Paper, the policy of the Administration would not be affected.[45] Having failed to exert pressure through the Americans, the Zionists turned to one final hope: the Permanent Mandates Commission of the League of Nations. The commission included at least two strongly pro-Zionist members, and the Zionists hoped that the White Paper might be declared by the commission to be contrary to the terms of the mandate by virtue of which Britain ruled Palestine. The commission met in June and unanimously declared that 'the policy set out in the White Paper was not in accordance with the interpretation which, in agreement with the mandatory Power and the Council, the Commission had placed upon the Palestine mandate.' Four of the seven members of the commission further stated that 'they did not feel able to state that the policy of the White Paper was in conformity with the mandate, any contrary conclusion appearing to them to be ruled out by the very terms of the mandate and by the fundamental intentions of its authors'. Three members dissented, arguing that the White Paper policy might be justified by existing circumstances; among the dissenters was the British delegate, Lord Hankey, who had been Cabinet Secretary at the time of the Balfour Declaration.[46] But the commission was merely an advisory body responsible to the Council of the League of Nations which was due to consider the commission's report at a meeting in September 1939. The outbreak of the war prevented the meeting from taking place, and dealt a death-

[44] Cordell Hull, *The Memoirs of Cordell Hull*, 2 vols. London 1948, p. 1530.

[45] Sharett, *Yoman*, p. 278 (entry dated 11 May 1939, reporting a conversation between MacDonald and Tom Williams M.P.); see also Sharett, *Yoman*, p. 288 (entry dated 16 May 1939, reporting a conversation between Kennedy and Weizmann); and Cabinet minutes, 26 Apr. 1939, PRO CAB 23/99/66.

[46] Hurewitz, *Struggle for Palestine*, pp. 105–6; Rose, *Gentile Zionists*, p. 211; Stephen Roskill, *Hankey: Man of Secrets vol. III 1931–1963*, London 1974, pp. 405–9.

blow to the League. In consequence, the British Government felt free to interpret the mandate according to its own lights.

Having failed to persuade the Government to change its policy the Zionists resorted to direct attack: they undermined it by illegal action. As early as 1934 there had been attempts to avoid the Palestine Government's immigration controls by the landing of illegal immigrants on the shore of Palestine. During 1937–8 the Government had decided to take immediate action on the Peel Commission's proposal of a 'political high level' of Jewish immigration of not more than 12,000 per annum. Jewish immigration shrank from 29,727 in 1936 to 10,536 in 1937 and 12,868 in 1938.[47] A severe economic depression in 1937–8, as a result of which Jewish unemployment rose to 9,000 in July 1938, suggested that even had the principle of economic absorptive capacity been applied without any political considerations, officially permitted immigration in this period would have decreased. Unemployment continued to rise after 1938, reaching a peak in July 1941 when 26,406 Jews were out of work. Thereafter the wartime economic boom led to a speedy recovery to almost full employment.[48] But the Zionists refused to accept the legitimacy of the 'political high level', and contested the Government's conservative assessments of economic absorptive capacity. In the face of the dire peril confronting Jews in Europe, they were prepared to contemplate some temporary economic difficulties in Palestine. From late 1938 onwards illegal immigration was organized on an increasing scale: in 1939, out of a total of 27,561 Jewish immigrants to Palestine, 11,156 were illegal arrivals.[49] The promotion of illegal immigration, which (contrary to Weizmann's wish) was publicly espoused by some speakers at the twenty-first Zionist Congress at Geneva in August 1939, brought the Jewish Agency and the Government of Palestine into direct confrontation. The result was what amounted, after September 1939, almost to a war within the war, with the most terrible consequences.

Faced with the challenge of Jewish illegal immigration, the

[47] Gurevich, *Statistical Handbook*, p. 102.

[48] 1938 figure from Hurewitz, *Struggle for Palestine*, p. 84; figures for 1939–45 from Gurevich, *Statistical Handbook*, p. 309.

[49] Gurevich, *Statistical Handbook*, p. 102.

Government resorted to several counter-measures. Coastal patrol vessels sought to intercept the ships carrying illegal immigrants and prevent them from landing their passengers. But the ships would often unload the refugees outside Palestinian territorial waters, leaving them to row ashore in small boats or rafts. Illegal immigrants were placed in internment camps upon arrival, and from mid-1939 their number was subtracted from the official quotas permitted under the White Paper. The Government applied pressure on European states from which illegal immigrant vessels plied, and on those from which the immigrants originated. In March 1939 the British Ambassador in Berlin was instructed to join his American colleague in protesting against the 'large, irregular movement from Germany of Jewish refugees' which was said to be 'a cause of great embarrassment to His Majesty's Government'.[50] Brazil, China, Liberia, Panama, and other countries under whose flags of convenience illegal immigrant ships sailed, or with the dubious protection of whose passports or visas many refugees travelled, became the object of a strenuous British diplomatic effort in 1939 designed to halt the exodus.[51] The attempt to confine Jewish refugees to the countries in which they lived earned approval in exalted quarters. In February 1939 King George VI's private secretary wrote to the Foreign Secretary: 'The King had heard . . . that a number of Jewish refugees from different countries were surreptitiously getting into Palestine, and he is glad to think that steps have been taken to prevent these people leaving their country of origin.'[52] But, in spite of its counter-measures the Government found it impossible to stem the flow of refugees.

The British Government recognized that, as Sir Alexander Cadogan, Permanent Under-Secretary at the Foreign Office, put it in February 1939: 'If we have to limit drastically, or stop altogether, Jewish immigration into Palestine, we shall be on stronger grounds if we can find a refuge elsewhere.'[53] Both the British and the American Governments devoted considerable resources to the investigation of settlement opportunities for

[50] Quoted in Martin Gilbert, *Britain, Palestine and the Jews 1891–1939* (Sacks Lecture 1976), Oxford 1977, p. 19.
[51] Sherman, *Island Refuge*, p. 239.
[52] Quoted ibid., p. 205.
[53] Quoted ibid., p. 191.

Jewish refugees in obscure recesses of South America, Africa, and Australasia. The possibilities of such an outlet in the British colonial empire were exhaustively explored. The results were not encouraging. The Governor of Kenya declared that 'a Jewish enclave of this kind would be an undesirable feature', although he was prepared to permit 'the carefully regulated influx of Jews of the right type—i.e. nordic from Germany or Austria . . . in small groups'.[54] The number allowed to enter the colony turned out to be a maximum of twenty-five families a year.[55] The proposed settlement of Jewish refugees in Northern Rhodesia encountered strong opposition from white settlers there.[56] Similarly negative responses were received from most other colonies. There was some official enthusiasm in 1939 for the proposed settlement of large numbers of Jewish refugees in British Guiana. An initial small-scale settlement was approved by the Government, but before the pioneer group could sail in September 1939, war broke out, and the scheme was abandoned. The total number of refugees from the Reich who found refuge in the British colonial empire between 1933 and 1939 was officially estimated as 'in the neighbourhood of 3,000'.[57] During the war a no less restrictive policy regarding colonial immigration was to be pursued by the British Government. The empire therefore made only a marginal contribution to alleviating the Jewish refugee problem. Nor had the British Government succeeded, by September 1939, in discovering any alternative solution.

The White Paper was to remain the formal basis of British policy in Palestine, and by extension of Britain's general approach to the Jewish problem, throughout the war. There were some faint hopes among Zionists in the course of the war that the White Paper, which had been criticized as an example of Britain's policy of 'appeasement', might now be jettisoned. But the White Paper, although enacted and supported by the appeasers, is more plausibly to be understood as a measure designed to help fight a war than to help preserve the peace.[58] It was, it is true, intended to 'appease' the Arab population of

[54] Quoted ibid., p. 106.
[55] Ibid., p. 174.
[56] Ibid., p. 188.
[57] Ibid., p. 255.
[58] See Bauer, *From Diplomacy to Resistance*, p. 41.

Palestine, and thereby to help prevent outbreaks of anti-British feeling in the Middle East at a time when Britain could ill afford to keep large numbers of troops there for internal security duties. In this, the White Paper may have had some success. There was a brief anti-British *coup d'état* in Iraq in April 1941, but this was swiftly and decisively repressed. Rumblings of discontent in Egypt were successfully contained. The Palestinian Arab revolt had been crushed by the spring of 1939. The White Paper, although by no means acceptable to many Arab nationalists, secured grudging acquiescence from some. The Arab nationalists in Palestine were in any case by now in some disarray, their most prominent leader, the Mufti, having fled. After taking part in the *coup* in Iraq in 1941, the Mufti made his way to Berlin, where he sought to concert Arab support for the Axis powers against Britain. But, although he retained much personal loyalty among Palestinian Arabs, his words, broadcast on Berlin radio, had little effect in the Middle East. Palestinian Arab nationalism, cowed for the moment by defeat in the revolt of 1936–9, and the exile of its leaders, remained quiescent throughout the war. The Palestine conflict did not (apart from the Iraqi *coup*) have major reverberations on the British position in the Arab world during the war. This was the primary purpose of the White Paper, and it was fulfilled. The extent to which the fulfilment of this aim was dependent upon the maintenance of the White Paper was, however, questioned.

The Zionists and their supporters (most notably Churchill) argued that the White Paper was not the only possible path to the achievement of this object. Conceding that in time of war it would be essential to reduce the number of British troops tied down on internal security duties in Palestine, they suggested the deployment of alternative military resources—those of the Jews themselves. In the early stages of the Arab revolt, the underground *Haganah* had pursued a policy of *havlagah* (Hebr. 'self-restraint'), refraining from retaliation against Arab attacks. As the revolt continued, this gradually gave way to a more activist policy. In 1937 a militant fringe of the *Haganah* re-grouped as the *Irgun Tsevai Leumi* (National Military Organisation); repudiating *havlagah*, the *Irgun* resorted to retaliatory terrorism, most menacingly in Haifa in July 1938, when land mines planted by the *Irgun* in the Arab fruit market killed seventy-four people, and wounded 129.[59] The *Haganah*, although it did not resort to such indiscriminate attacks, moved away from *havlagah* towards a policy of direct attack on Arab guerrilla bands operating in the hill country of the north and the interior of Palestine. The most effective expression of this new policy was the organization in 1938 of 'Special Night Squads', composed mainly of Jews with some British officers and N.C.O.s. The Special Night Squads were not *Haganah* formations (although most of the recruits were drawn from the *Haganah*), but were authorized by the British commander in Palestine, General Wavell. Their leader, and chief originator, was a young British officer, Orde Wingate, who was a passionate pro-Zionist, and an inspiring influence on the fledgeling Jewish army. The Special Night Squads did not long survive Wingate's departure from Palestine after a stay of only a few months, and the Government never adopted the proposals made by Wingate and others for official recognition and mobilization of the *Haganah*. Throughout the war the British authorities, fearing an adverse Arab reaction to the arming of Jews, displayed great reluctance to recruit Palestinian Jews to the British armed forces. There was, as will be seen, particularly strong official hostility to the idea of a separate Jewish force. The British army and British intelligence in the Near East made occasional use of *Haganah* personnel for special missions during the war, but no official recognition was given to the underground force, and there were periodic arrests and arms searches by the Palestine Government in an attempt to suppress it. Nevertheless, the *Haganah*'s strength and capability developed greatly during the war, especially with the formation in 1941 of its full-time spearhead, the *Palmach*.

The foremost exponent among British statesmen of the argument that British security in the Near East should be preserved not by reliance on the White Paper but by British sponsorship of a Jewish army in Palestine was Winston Churchill. Unlike his predecessor as Prime Minister, Neville Chamberlain (who had not inherited his father's interest in the Jewish problem), Churchill had a long history of involvement in the Jewish refugee problem and Zionism. As a young M.P. he had denounced the pogroms in Russia. In 1905, as Liberal

[59] Hurewitz, *Struggle for Palestine*, p. 92.

parliamentary candidate for North-West Manchester, a constituency with a heavy concentration of Jewish voters, Churchill
had campaigned strongly against the Aliens Act, which Balfour's Conservative Government had devised in order to limit
Russo-Jewish immigration to Britain. In December 1905
Churchill's election agent wrote to Weizmann (at that time
resident in Manchester) asking him to use his influence among
the Jews in Churchill's favour.[60] As Colonial Secretary in
1921–2 Churchill had visited Palestine and displayed
enthusiasm for the Jewish National Home.[61] In private evidence to the Peel Commission in 1937 he had spoken strongly in
favour of Zionism, and he had advocated continued immigration leading to a Jewish majority in Palestine and the eventual
establishment of 'a great Jewish State there, numbered by
millions'.[62] He expressed opposition to the Peel Commission's
partition proposals, arguing that the project was 'a mirage',
that the Government were 'a lot of lily-livered rabbits' who
would 'chip off a piece here and there' from the Jewish state and
that the Zionists should 'persevere, persevere, persevere'.[63] In
November 1938 he told the House of Commons that all the
Government had done in Palestine in 'three whole years of
classic incapacity is to palter, and maunder, and gibber'.[64] As
we have seen he denounced the White Paper in May 1939, and
he remained opposed to it throughout the war. In an interview
with Weizmann in December 1939 the Zionist leader said to
him: 'You stood at the cradle of this enterprise; I hope you will
see it through.' When asked what he meant Weizmann
explained that he envisaged 'a state of some three or four
million Jews in Palestine'. Churchill responded, 'Yes, I quite
agree with that.'[65] As First Lord of the Admiralty in Chamberlain's War Cabinet, from September 1939 to May 1940, Churchill repeatedly took up the Palestine question in the Cabinet,
stressing the deleterious effect of the White Paper on American
opinion.

As Prime Minister after May 1940 Churchill maintained a

[60] Stein, *Balfour Declaration*, p. 150.
[61] See Martin Gilbert, *Winston S. Churchill*, vol. IV, London 1975, chaps. 29–36.
[62] Quoted in Martin Gilbert, *Winston S. Churchill*, vol. V, London 1976, p. 847.
[63] Rose, *Gentile Zionists*, pp. 132–3.
[64] HC vol. 341, col. 2031 (24 Nov. 1938).
[65] Note on meeting on 17 Dec. 1939 in WA.

similar stance. To General Wavell, British Commander-in-Chief in the Middle East, he insisted: 'The essence of the situation [in Palestine] depends on arming the Jewish colonists sufficiently to enable them to undertake their own defence.' He lambasted the Colonial Secretary, Lord Lloyd, for opposing this policy, pronouncing it 'little less than a scandal that at a time when we are fighting for our lives' large British forces should be 'immobilised in support of a policy which commends itself only to a section of the Conservative Party'.[66] On several occasions in the course of the war he intervened in order to secure more compassionate treatment of Jewish refugees than was advocated by the Colonial Office. In a note to the Cabinet Secretary in October 1941 Churchill wrote: 'If Britain and the United States emerge victorious from the war, the creation of a great Jewish state in Palestine inhabited by millions of Jews will be one of the leading features of the Peace Conference discussions. The Liberal and Labour Parties will never agree to the pro-Arab solutions which are the commonplace of British Service circles; nor, so long as I remain in British public life, will I.'[67] He returned to this theme on several occasions during the war. He told Roosevelt in August 1942: 'I am strongly wedded to the Zionist policy of which I was one of the authors.'[68] He suggested that the dismissal of 'anti-Semite officers and others in high places . . . would have a very salutary effect'.[69] He remained unswervingly opposed to the White Paper—'this low-grade gasp of a defeatist hour' as he termed it in January 1944.[70] His friends found him immovable on the subject. Sir Edward Spears wrote in 1943:

On the previous evening the Prime Minister had laid down his Zionist policy in the most emphatic terms. He said he had formed an opinion which nothing would change. He intended to see to it that there was a Jewish state. He told me not to argue with him as this would merely

[66] Churchill to Wavell, 12 Aug. 1940, in Winston S. Churchill, *The Second World War* vol. II *Their Finest Hour*, eighth ed. London 1966, p. 377; Churchill to Lord Lloyd, 28 June 1940, ibid. pp. 154–5.

[67] Churchill to Sir Edward Bridges, 1 Oct. 1941, PRO PREM 4/52/5/1366.

[68] Churchill to Roosevelt, 9 Aug. 1942, in F. L. Loewenheim *et al*., eds., *Roosevelt and Churchill: Their Secret Wartime Correspondence*, London 1975, p. 234.

[69] Churchill to Colonial Secretary, 5 July 1942, PRO PREM 4/51/9/Part 2/938.

[70] Churchill to Deputy Prime Minister and Foreign Secretary, 12 Jan. 1944, PRO PREM 4/52/5/Part 2/1028.

make him angry and would change nothing. If I was impelled for conscientious reasons to take an opposite point of view he would regret it but would have to blast me with all the means at his disposal. There is simply no arguing with him on this subject.[71]

No British statesman had a more consistent and more emphatic record of sympathy for Jewish refugees and support for Zionism as a solution to the Jewish problem than Winston Churchill.

Yet, notwithstanding the unprecedented authority which Churchill aggregated to himself during the war as Prime Minister and Minister of Defence, the White Paper remained the official basis of his government's Palestine policy throughout the war. One reason was that Churchill stood almost alone among senior ministers in his attitude to the Jewish question. Of his Cabinet, only Leo Amery, Secretary of State for India, and the Liberal leader, Sir Archibald Sinclair, Secretary of State for Air, shared Churchill's pronounced view on the subject. The balance of ministerial opinion tended strongly in a contrary direction. In the Labour Party there was widespread sympathy for the plight of Jewish refugees and support for Zionism, but this was not reflected in the actions of Labour ministers in the wartime coalition, whose failure to press the matter in government induced Harold Laski, the socialist theoretician and member of the Labour National Executive (and son of one of Churchill's most active Jewish supporters in Manchester in 1905), to write to the Prime Minister in 1943: 'What hurts me so deeply is the realisation that among my own colleagues in your Government Dr Goebbels has induced a spirit of caution [on the Jewish refugee problem] when you have so amply shown that audacity is the road to victory.'[72] Among ministers departmentally concerned with the problem the Prime Minister's views found little favour. Lord Moyne, Colonial Secretary in 1941–2 and later Deputy Minister Resident in the Middle East, wrote to the High Commissioner for Palestine in April 1942 of the 'extreme Zionism of the Prime Minister' which he said was 'bound to . . . clash [with] the unchangeable

---

[71] Note by Spears, 27 June 1943, Spears Papers, Middle East Centre, St Antony's College, Oxford, Box II, file 7.

[72] Laski to Churchill, 1 July 1943, PRO PREM 4/51/8/476.

facts of the Palestine situation'.[73] The other wartime Colonial Secretaries felt similarly: Malcolm MacDonald and Lord Lloyd were among the most unwavering supporters of the White Paper; only Viscount Cranborne, who occupied the office for nine months in 1942, questioned the wisdom of the policy. Lord Halifax, Foreign Secretary from March 1938 until December 1940, put the issue in the form of a moral dilemma:

In the world today there was a contest between the profoundest philosophies of human life ... [and] if this diagnosis be correct, they would see how necessary it was for them to reconcile administrative necessity and fundamental and eternal spiritual claims and rights.[74]

Halifax's successor, Anthony Eden, while sharing his support for the White Paper, did not join him on this elevated ground. He regarded the White Paper as a diplomatic imperative if Britain were to retain her position in the Middle East. Eden was not a Zionist; nor did he have a notable predilection for Jews. His private secretary, Oliver Harvey, recorded: 'Unfortunately A.E. is immovable on the subject of Palestine. He loves Arabs and hates Jews.'[75] Eden himself, in a private note commenting on a pro-Zionist memorandum by Harvey, admitted in September 1941: 'If we must have preferences, let me murmur in your ear that I prefer Arabs to Jews.'[76]

The preponderant weight of ministerial opinion dissented from the Prime Minister's view of the Jewish question; moreover, the strong support for the White Paper among politicians reflected the received opinion among senior civil servants in both Whitehall and Jerusalem. The 'departmental view' in the Colonial Office, for long disillusioned and frustrated with the consequences of the Balfour Declaration policy in Palestine, was overwhelmingly in favour of the White Paper. It was at the behest of the Colonial Office that from 1939 onwards the Government resorted to every practicable administrative, diplomatic, and legal device to counter illegal immigration to Palestine. The fear that the White Paper policy

[73] Moyne to Sir Harold MacMichael, 25 April 1942, MacMichael Papers, Middle East Centre, St Antony's College, Oxford.

[74] Quoted in Rose, *Gentile Zionists*, p. 115.

[75] Diary of Oliver Harvey, entry dated 25 Apr. 1943, BL 56399.

[76] Eden to Harvey, 7 Sept. 1941, BL 56402.

might tend to alienate American public opinion from Britain at a time when American support was desperately required greatly influenced Churchill. But these apprehensions were not shared in the Colonial Office, where Sir John Shuckburgh, the Deputy Under-Secretary (who, as head of the Middle East Department of the Colonial Office under Churchill in 1921–2, had helped to fashion his pro-Zionist Palestine policy), wrote in 1940:

The importance in present circumstances of retaining the goodwill of the United States needs no demonstration; but it is very doubtful whether the influence of the American Jews over the United States Government or over general opinion in America is really as potent as the Zionists and their supporters would have us believe . . . There is evidence to show that Jewish stock in the United States is on the decline. Generally speaking, I doubt whether we need be unduly alarmed over the American bugbear. In any case we ought not to allow it to deflect us from the policy which we have deliberately adopted on the Palestine question.[77]

The Colonial Office view faithfully mirrored that of the men on the spot: the British officials in the Government of Palestine (Palestinian Arabs and Jews held only subordinate positions) had, since the inception of the mandate, been, with rare exceptions, dubious about the value to Britain of the Jewish National Home; to them the White Paper appeared as a welcome relief from some of their burdens. Sir Harold MacMichael, High Commissioner (i.e. head of the Palestine Government) from 1938 to 1944, was a staunch advocate of the White Paper policy (although at the end of his term of office he veered towards partition as a solution *faute de mieux*) and rigidly restrictive in the implementation of its immigration provisions.

The same view held the field in the Foreign Office, albeit with certain modulations. The Eastern Department, which was responsible for the foreign relations of Palestine and for Britain's relations with several Middle Eastern states, hewed closely to the Colonial Office line. Reports from British representatives in the Middle East throughout the war unanimously endorsed this position. Elsewhere there were occasional reservations. The Refugee Section of the General Department (later a fully-fledged Refugee Department) evinced passing irritation

[77] Minute by Shuckburgh, 7 Feb. 1940, PRO CO 733/426/75872/14.

at the perplexities of tackling refugee problems within the constraints imposed by the White Paper policy in Palestine (and by the Home Office's refusal in wartime to admit to Britain refugees from enemy or enemy-occupied territory). The American Department and the British Embassy in Washington were alive to the potential danger that the enforcement of the White Paper might alienate influential sections of American public opinion. As British Ambassador in Washington from January 1941, Lord Halifax, while holding to his earlier favourable opinion of the White Paper, now tended to view it in a less metaphysical context as a sore point in British public relations in the U.S.A. In April 1941 he noted:

As you can imagine, I greatly dislike having to listen to and answer the criticisms of our policy in Palestine which we receive from the Jewish organizations in this country. But tiresome as it is, I am afraid that we shall have to go on doing it. . . . The Jewish community here is extremely influential, in and out of the administration, and particularly in the Press . . . Very large numbers of important people in this country are watching our Palestine policy with a critical eye.[78]

But, at the same time, it was known to British diplomats that Zionism did not command the support of all (nor perhaps even a majority among) American Jews, and that some of the most influential members of the American Jewish community were lukewarm or hostile towards the movement; it was only after about 1942 that American Jewry turned massively and decisively to support for the Zionist cause. Moreover, British diplomats found, in discussion with Middle East experts from the State Department, that there was much understanding for Britain's Palestine policy among American officials. As for Roosevelt's attitude, his Secretary of State, Cordell Hull, wrote: 'In general, the President at times talked both ways to Zionists and Arabs, besieged as he was by each camp. Rabbis Wise and Silver believed that the President had made pledges to them. The State Department made no pledges.'[79] In the event of American criticism of British policy in Palestine, it remained, of course, open to the British to remind their critics that the United States Congress (in this accurately reflecting American public opinion) was consis-

[78] Halifax to R. A. Butler, 4 Apr. 1941, PRO CO 733/444/75872/102/28.
[79] Hull, *Memoirs*, p. 1536.

tently hostile to any easing of American immigration laws to permit a larger number of refugees (many of whom were barred under the quota restrictions based on national origins) to enter the U.S.A.

The essence of the official attitude to the Jewish problem in the Second World War was summed up in a Foreign Office minute in 1941: 'When it comes to the point, the Jews will never hamper us to put the Germans on the throne.'[80] World Jewry, which to British official eyes in 1917 had presented an aspect of mysterious and pervasive international power, now appeared a negligible political quantity. In the last resort only the lunatic fringe of Palestinian or American Jews would wish to see Hitler 'on the throne' as the price of getting rid of the White Paper. In so far as Jewry had any political value, it could in any case be taken for granted by Britain in the war effort against Hitler. Jewish organizations therefore had no basis for bargaining with the British Government. In any case, the Government showed little inclination to treat for Jewish support. The Jewish Agency with which, because of its recognized position under the mandate, the Government was obliged to deal, was viewed with increasing suspicion and hostility in official circles, mainly because of its involvement in the organization of illegal immigration to Palestine. Weizmann, for a generation the key figure in the Anglo-Zionist relationship, continued to be regarded with a grudging (sometimes a rather apprehensive) respect by British statesmen and officials; but his health and his standing within the Zionist movement deteriorated in the course of the war. The younger Zionist leaders, David Ben Gurion and Moshe Shertok, lacked Weizmann's 'mesmeric charm'.[81]

Other Jewish organizations carried less weight. The right-wing New Zionist Organisation was regarded with contempt in official quarters. The British section of the World Jewish Congress was frequently accorded a hearing, but the aspirations of the Congress to represent 'the permanent address of the Jewish people' (as its co-founder, Nahum Goldmann, described it in

[80] Minute (signature not identified) 14 June 1941, PRO FO 371/26172 (A 4441/44/45).
[81] The apt phrase of Robert Boothby in Lord Boothby, *Recollections of a Rebel*, London 1978, p. 208.

1932)[82] were not taken seriously by the Government and were vigorously contested by other Jewish organizations. More attention was paid by the Government to representations made by the Board of Deputies of British Jews, since the early nineteenth century the recognized representative body of Anglo-Jewry. However, in late 1939 a member of the Zionist Executive, Professor Selig Brodetsky, was elected President of the Board, and by 1943 it had a clear majority of Zionist deputies. As a result its stock with the Government tended to decline. One consequence of the Zionist capture of control over the Board of Deputies was the dissolution of the Joint Foreign Committee through which since 1878 the Board had made common representations to the Government with the Anglo-Jewish Association. The latter body, small in numbers and unrepresentative in nature, but including many of the notables of Anglo-Jewry, remained distinctly cool towards Zionism; but the era of the notables had passed, and after the severance of the link with the Board the Association's influence decreased. Of other Jewish organizations three were of political weight. The Chief Rabbinate was occupied by the combative J. H. Hertz, who, although tarred with the Zionist brush, was perforce treated with respect by the Government. The Jewish Refugees Committee, founded in 1933 by Otto M. Schiff, continued during the war to help in the integration of Jewish refugees in Britain. The Central British Fund for Jewish Relief and Rehabilitation, also formed in 1933, raised substantial sums for the relief of Jewish refugees at home and abroad. The latter two organizations eschewed political agitation and often worked in close cooperation with government departments.

However, the Jewish organizations and their non-Jewish sympathizers proved powerless to effect any significant departure from the guiding principles of British policy towards Jewish refugees during the war: no retreat from the immigration provisions of the Palestine White Paper; no admission of refugees from Nazi Europe to Britain; and no entry for significant numbers to the colonial empire. These principles enjoyed the wholehearted endorsement of Whitehall opinion, a dangerous creature when roused, and one in the neighbourhood of

[82] Quoted in *Unity in Dispersion: A History of the World Jewish Congress*, New York 1948, p. 33.

which even the most pugnacious Prime Minister was obliged to tread warily. Upon the outbreak of the war these principles froze into axioms of official decision-making, and so it continued until the end of the war. The first fruit was a concerted British effort to seal the escape routes used by Jewish refugees from Nazi Europe.

2

Sealing the Escape Routes

On 2 September 1939, the day after the outbreak of the war in Europe, two Jews were killed when a British coastal patrol vessel opened fire on an illegal immigrant ship, the *Tiger Hill*, as it landed 1,400 Jewish refugees from Poland, Roumania, Bulgaria, and Czechoslovakia on Tel Aviv beach.[1] These were probably the first hostile shots fired by British forces after the German attack on Poland. They marked the opening of a new and bitter phase in the British struggle against Jewish illegal immigration to Palestine.

The German invasion of Poland led to a catastrophic change in the position of the Jews in Europe. The rapidity of the German advance prevented the majority of Jews in the areas occupied by the Nazis from escaping before the arrival of German forces. A few thousand Polish Jews were able to flee to Hungary, Roumania, Slovakia, and Lithuania. Between 200,000 and 300,000 were estimated to have fled eastwards to the Soviet-occupied areas of eastern Poland.[2] However, none of these countries evinced hospitality towards their uninvited guests: in several cases borders were closed, and in some instances refugees were ejected. In the frontier districts of German- and Soviet-occupied Poland the occupation forces engaged at times in co-operation at others in conflict over Jewish refugees. In December 1939 General Keitel complained of 'repeated wrangles' on the boundary, where German attempts to extrude large numbers of Polish Jews into Soviet territory 'did not proceed as smoothly as had apparently been expected'. In a typical incident, according to Keitel, a thousand Jews had been expelled by the Germans 'at a quiet

[1] Ben-Zion Dinur, ed. *Sefer Toldot Hahaganah*, vol. III, part 1, Tel Aviv 1972, pp. 87–8; joint Foreign and Colonial Office memorandum on 'Jewish Illegal Immigration to Palestine', 17 Jan. 1940, PRO FO 371/25238/274 ff. (W 766/38/48).
[2] Tartakower and Grossmann, *The Jewish Refugee*, pp. 43–4.

place in the woods . . . Fifteen kilometres away, they came back, with the Russian commander trying to force the German one to readmit the group.'[3] In other instances, however, 'close cooperation between the German Gestapo and the Soviet OGPU' [NKVD] was reported. Sometimes, it was stated, 'the Russians had shown mercy by putting the fugitives into prison rather than sending them back'.[4] There were similar scenes on a smaller scale on the border between the German zone and Lithuania.[5] Within a few weeks of the German invasion the boundaries of Poland were effectively sealed to Jewish refugees, less by the Germans (who in general appeared eager to expel Jews wherever possible) than by the neighbouring states which were unwilling to receive Jewish refugees. In mid-November it was estimated that 1,875,000 Polish Jews found themselves in the Russian-occupied zone, 1,250,000 in the German zone, and 125,000 in Lithuanian-occupied Vilna.[6]

The position of the Jews in German-dominated areas of Europe grew steadily worse as the war proceeded. In Poland, in the wake of the German invasion, widespread pogroms and massacres were committed by German military and police forces, in particular by special units known as *Einsatzgruppen*. In November 1939 all Jews in the 'General Government' were ordered to wear the distinctive yellow Star of David. Jewish property was confiscated. Synagogues were destroyed. Men were seized for forced labour. Jews in villages and small towns were compelled to leave their homes and forced to move into urban areas. From the spring of 1940 onwards ghettos were created in the major Polish cities into which most Polish Jews (and many from other countries) were concentrated in conditions of terrible overcrowding. Jewish rations were reduced to levels below those of all other categories of the population. Hundreds of thousands died of starvation, disease, or lack of heat and inadequate hygiene. Many Jews were driven to

---

[3] Memorandum by State Secretary Weizsäcker, reporting telephone conversation with Keitel, 5 Dec. 1939, in *Documents on German Foreign Policy 1918–1945, Series D (1937–1945)* vol. VIII, London 1954, p. 489.

[4] 'Jews in Eastern Poland', report to Joint Foreign Committee of Board of Deputies of British Jews and Anglo-Jewish Association, 21 March 1940, BD C11/2/34.

[5] *Jewish Chronicle*, 1 Dec. 1939; Tartakower and Grossmann, *The Jewish Refugee*, p. 44.

[6] *Jewish Chronicle*, 17 Nov. 1939; similar figures (from Polish and Jewish sources) in Kirk (Berlin) to State Dept., Washington, 7 Aug. 1940, *FRUS 1941* vol. I, p. 221.

suicide. Arbitrary arrests and killings continued. Atrocities and persecution were worst in Poland, but in the Greater Reich and Czechoslovakia, where Jews had already been deprived of most of their property, excluded from the professions, and subjected to various forms of humiliation, conditions deteriorated further in the course of 1940 and early 1941. In Roumania, Hungary, and Bulgaria, as governments fell increasingly under German influence, the Jewish situation became increasingly insecure. In the Soviet zone of Poland Jewish religious and political organizations were crushed and their leaders gaoled, sent to labour camps, or murdered. From early 1940 the Soviet authorities began the mass deportation to the east of suspect elements from Soviet-occupied Poland, and later from Bessarabia, the Bukovina and the Baltic states; Jews numbered about twenty per cent of an estimated 350,000 deportees; large numbers perished of cold, hunger, or harsh labour conditions. Everywhere in Europe the pressure for Jewish emigration to safe havens became overwhelming.

During the early part of the war German policy was not opposed to Jewish emigration. On the contrary, the Germans favoured, encouraged, and even promoted Jewish movement out of the Reich as well as from certain occupied areas. Between 1939 and mid-1941 expulsion, in addition to expropriation, persecution, and sporadic murder, was one of the central goals of Germany's Jewish policy.[7] The main agency concerned with the implementation of German policy towards the Jews was the Reich Central Bureau for Jewish Emigration, headed from October 1939 onwards by Adolf Eichmann. As head of similar offices in Vienna and Prague since the *Anschluss* of 1938, Eichmann had considerable experience of supervising the policy of extrusion, under which large groups of Jews were rounded up, transported to frontiers, and dumped in neighbouring countries or (in cases where the neighbouring authorities proved recalcitrant) in no-man's-land. Under war conditions the Germans found this procedure more difficult but not impossible. In addition to driving masses of Jews across the Russian and Lithuanian frontiers, the German authorities made efforts to stimulate emigration from the Reich and from Czecho-

---

[7] Raul Hilberg, *The Destruction of the European Jews*, Chicago 1961, p. 3 ff; H. Krausnick and M. Broszat, *Anatomy of the SS State*, London 1970, pp. 60–76.

slovakia by all possible means, overt and covert. The German authorities made it clear to enemy governments, during the early stages of the war, that they wished Jewish emigration to continue, provided only that the emigrants were despoiled of their property before departure. In the absence of any welcoming gesture from the Allies, Eichmann's office took advantage of the Zionists' desire to organize illegal immigration to Palestine from central Europe. According to Ehud Avriel, a Zionist agent, Jewish Agency representatives who applied to Eichmann's office for exit permits for Jewish emigrants 'were treated like preferred customers'.[8] In 1940 German officials considered also the possibility of deporting all the Jews of Europe to Madagascar.[9] Although Hitler seems to have been attracted by this idea (an old anti-Semitic project which had been suggested in the *Völkischer Beobachter* in the 1920s), nothing came of it.

Immediately after the outbreak of the war, Helmut Wohlthat, an official of Goering's Economics Ministry, and a central figure in German efforts to foster Jewish emigration during the last year of the peace, sent an official message to the British Government through the United States Embassy, stating that the German Government wished to adhere to their policy of getting as many Jews out of Germany as possible.[10] At the same time the Germans informed the Jewish Agency that Jewish emigrants would still be permitted to leave for Palestine by way of neutral countries.[11] The Germans sent a similar message through the Netherlands to Sir Herbert Emerson of the Inter-Governmental Committee, in which they stated that pressure for Jewish emigration would be intensified, and urged that the work of the I.G.C. in promoting emigration should be continued in spite of the outbreak of the war.[12] In a letter to the Foreign Office on 27 September, Jan Masaryk wrote that he too had learnt that 'Gestapo authorities represented by Mr Eichmann are prepared even now to abide by the undertaking' to

[8] Ehud Avriel, *Open the Gates*, London 1975, p. 91.

[9] Krausnick and Broszat, *Anatomy of the SS State*, pp. 72–5.

[10] Memorandum to Foreign Office from U.S. Embassy, London, 3 Oct. 1939, PRO FO 371/24085/280 (W14428/520/48).

[11] L. Herrmann (Jewish Agency) to Sir Henry Bunbury (Czech Refugee Trust Fund), 12 Sept. 1939, PRO FO 371/24095/338 ff. (W13874/1369/48).

[12] J. Kennedy (U.S. Embassy, London) to State Dept., Washington, 29 Sept. 1939, *FRUS 1939* vol. II, pp. 149–50.

permit Jews to leave.[13] In January 1940 the British Embassy in
Rome reported that Nino Pizzinato, agent in Berlin of the
Italian Tourist Agency, C.I.T., had told a member of the
embassy staff that nothing was put in the way of Jewish emigration from Germany, and, indeed, that 'Jewish emigration [was]
about the only form of travelling left for his company to cater
for'.[14] In the same month the High Commissioner for Palestine
complained to the Colonial Office that, according to information received, bookings were being accepted by offices in Germany of the Hamburg-Amerika line on behalf of a foreign
travel company which was organizing travel from Europe to
Palestine.[15] A report prepared for the Foreign Office in February 1940 by Professor Arnold Toynbee of the Royal Institute for
International Affairs stated that the Jewish offices in Prague
had been ordered to arrange for the migration to foreign countries of 120 Jews daily.[16] In September 1940 Eichmann suggested that German transit visas should not be granted to
Hungarian Jews seeking to emigrate via German territory; he
feared that such emigration might limit the possibilities for
emigration by Jews from Germany.[17] That the Germans still
hoped to induce other countries to accept an influx of Jews from
the Reich was demonstrated in late 1940 when special sealed
trains carrying Jewish refugees travelled from Germany to
Lisbon and Spanish ports.[18] In May 1941, in an official German decree, Goering ordered that Jewish emigration from the
Reich and from the Protectorate of Bohemia and Moravia was
to be 'stepped up in spite of the war, in so far as this was
humanly possible'. In order to facilitate the emigration of Jews
from those areas, no Jewish emigration was to be permitted

[13] Copy in Livia Rothkirchen, 'The Czechoslovak Government-in-Exile: Jewish and
Palestinian Aspects in the Light of the Documents', *Yad Vashem Studies*, vol. IX,
Jerusalem 1973, pp. 174–6.

[14] Sir N. Charles (Rome) to Foreign Office, 25 Jan. 1940, PRO FO 371/24387/400
(C 1484/6/18).

[15] High Commissioner, Jerusalem, to Colonial Office, 20 Jan. 1940, PRO FO
371/25239/233 (W 2743/38/48).

[16] 'Notes on the Jews in Poland' by A. J. Toynbee, Feb. 1940, PRO FO
371/24471/127 (C 2393/116/55).

[17] Eichmann to Rademacher (German Foreign Ministry), 4 Sept. 1940, in R.
Braham, *The Destruction of Hungarian Jewry: A Documentary Account*, 2 vols., New York
1963, p. 5.

[18] David S. Wyman, *Paper Walls: America and The Refugee Crisis 1938–1941*, Amherst,
Mass. 1968, p. 172.

from France and Belgium.[19] However, it was only in August 1941 that emigration of Jews from German-occupied lands was prohibited (at first the restriction applied only to Jews between the ages of eighteen and forty-five, later to all others).[20] It was not until 23 October that Himmler issued an order banning all further Jewish emigration from the Reich.[21]

During the first two years of the war, therefore, the German Government was not the primary obstacle to Jewish emigration from Nazi-controlled areas of Europe. Not all Jews, of course, were permitted or able to emigrate. Those incarcerated in concentration camps, prisons, or ghettos had little opportunity of escape. Much often depended on the whim of a bureaucrat and the venality or soft-heartedness of a police or customs official. Jews who left Germany were forced to surrender their property and were often subjected to brutal treatment before departure. Some tens of thousands of Jews managed to escape: in 1940 36,945 Jews entered the U.S.A., and 8,398 were admitted to Palestine; a few thousand more reached Argentina, Canada, and other countries.[22] But these numbers constituted only a small fraction of the vast multitudes desperately seeking an escape route from Nazi-dominated Europe. That the great majority of Jews failed to emigrate was primarily due to the extreme reluctance of all countries to admit them. The only two countries, indeed, to which any significant numbers of Jews could still emigrate after the outbreak of the war were the U.S.A. and Palestine. But even in these cases the door was now almost closed. Fifty-two per cent of all immigrants to the U.S.A. in 1939 and 1940 were Jewish; the Jewish proportion of the total was the highest in American history; but in absolute terms the numbers admitted (43,450 in 1939 and 36,945 in 1940) fell far short of the peak years of Jewish immigration between 1899 and 1914 when about 1,300,000 Jews had arrived (out of a total immigration to the U.S.A. in those years of 13,700,000). The main obstacle to larger Jewish immigration was the quota system imposed under American law, which laid down the numbers of immigrants of each national origin to be

[19] Krausnick and Broszat, *Anatomy of the SS State*, p. 84.
[20] Mark Wischnitzer, *To Dwell in Safety*, Philadephia 1948, p. 235.
[21] Krausnick and Broszat, op. cit., p. 85.
[22] Gurevich, *Statistical Handbook*, p. 116.

admitted in any year. The law prevented many applicants from qualifying for admission, and long queues developed for visas several years in advance. In spite of the intense pressure for visas, there was formidable public and congressional opposition to any change in the immigration laws. The interpretation of the law by the State Department was, in general, stringent and restrictive, particularly towards refugees 'likely to become a public charge'. After July 1940 hardly any visas were issued to applicants from Germany.[23]

Throughout the war the British and United States Governments continued the futile search among the waste places of the earth for suitable havens for Jewish refugees. In the course of 1940 there was extensive discussion in the Foreign Office about the possibility of reviving the scheme for a 'second Jewish National Home' in the interior of British Guiana; the provision of such a refuge was seen, as one Foreign Office official put it, as 'desirable . . . to salve the conscience of H.M.G. in relation to European Jewry'.[24] But the Colonial Office insisted that Britain was 'under no *special* obligation to assist the settlement of Jewish refugees within the United Kingdom or the Colonial Empire'. It was pointed out that the scheme 'would be open to objection on the ground that the British subjects in the West Indian area were in greater need of and had a far stronger claim to such assistance'. And the fear was expressed that 'any reference to the establishment of a Jewish National Home, however vague, would give rise to strong opposition in British Guiana . . . [and] to difficulties comparable with those experienced in Palestine'.[25] The project was abandoned. Exotic proposals for Jewish refugee settlement in a number of improbable places, among them North-West Australia, Eritrea, Ethiopia, and the Mindanao area of the southern Philippines, flourished briefly in the official files, and were speedily consigned to the oblivion of the archives. The United States Government was particularly attracted to the notion of large-scale Jewish settlement in Angola; the Government of Portugal (which ruled Angola) betrayed no interest in the idea. A suggestion that Jews might

[23] Wyman, *Paper Walls, passim.*

[24] Minute by R. T. E. Latham, 26 Dec. 1940, PRO FO 371/24568/47 (E 1063/1063/31).

[25] Colonial Office memorandum, June 1940, PRO FO 371/24568/160 ff. (W 1063/1063/31).

settle in Alaska was similarly discarded. For a time much faith was placed in the prospects for Jewish refugee settlement in the Dominican Republic, whose government manifested considerable enthusiasm for Jewish immigration. With the active support of the Inter-Governmental Committee and of the U.S. State Department, an agreement was signed in January 1940 between the Dominican Government and the Dominican Republic Settlement Association, an American-financed company: the agreement provided for the immigration of up to 100,000 refugees who were to be settled under the auspices of DORSA. By June 1942 a total of 472 settlers had been established (at a cost of $3,000 a head). Plans for expansion of the settlement were abandoned after the disappointing beginning.[26] Repeated efforts by the British Government to induce Dominions and colonial governments to accept some Jewish refugees met with frustratingly negative replies. In a typical comment, in January 1941, on a Foreign Office query about the possibility of Jewish emigration to the colonies, a Colonial Office official wrote:

Apart from the obvious difficulties in the way of their getting to any Colony, the hard fact remains that they are not wanted by any Colonial Government for a number of very good reasons, the most important of which perhaps are that they are certain sooner or later to become a charge on public funds . . . The introduction of a body of people, however small, which is entirely alien in every sense of the word, would be greatly resented by the working classes in the Colony and might well lead to serious trouble . . . I am thinking particularly of the West Indies.[27]

Such replies evoked a feeling akin to despair in the Foreign Office, where one official minuted: 'This was to be expected. I don't know what is wrong with the colonial Empire, but its absorptive capacity seems to be nil.'[28]

As the door of the U.S.A. closed, as the British Empire was discovered to be filled to capacity, as the far-fetched settlement programmes for obscure regions collapsed, as all sovereign states closed their borders to all but a trickle of refugees, and as

[26] Dana G. Munro *et al.*, *Refugee Settlement in the Dominican Republic*, Washington 1942.
[27] K. E. Robinson to P. J. Dixon (Foreign Office), 13 Jan. 1941, PRO FO 371/30000 (R 425/122/37).
[28] Minute by E. M. Rose [?], 20 Jan. 1941, ibid.

the vice tightened round European Jewry, thousands of Jewish refugees, fearing for their lives, struggled to reach any safe destination. In the course of 1940 and early 1941 over two thousand Jews travelled over the Trans-Siberian railway to Kobe in Japan, whence they made their way to Shanghai, swelling further the Jewish refugee population there. The *Yeshiva* of Mir arrived in Shanghai *en bloc*, having been issued with visas to Curaçao in the Dutch West Indies, by a sympathetic Dutch Consul in Kaunas, Lithuania; they were able to make the journey after receiving Japanese transit visas from the Japanese consul. But immigration restrictions to Shanghai, first imposed by the Japanese occupiers in August 1939, were after 1941 stringently enforced.[29] Except for Jews in Lithuania, able somehow to obtain Soviet transit visas, Shanghai was, after the outbreak of the war, no longer a practicable destination. There appeared to be only one alternative: Palestine. During the autumn and winter of 1939–40 boats heavily laden with Jewish refugees continued to set out for Palestine from ports on the Black Sea and the Aegean. The Jewish Agency's Immigration Department, with its network of Palestine Offices (which, in some cases, were permitted to operate in Nazi Europe), was officially charged with the administration of legal immigration to Palestine in co-operation with the Government of Palestine; but its officials simultaneously organized part of the illegal (or as the Agency preferred to term it, 'uncertificated') influx. Larger numbers of illegal immigrants were organized by the Revisionist Zionists and by shady figures from the Roumanian and Greek underworld who perceived an opportunity to combine humanitarianism with an easy penny.

The reaction of the British Government was to implement the immigration provisions of the White Paper policy. Apart from the general political objectives which lay behind the policy, war conditions introduced new reasons which were held to justify the policy. These were set forth in a memorandum on Jewish illegal immigration to Palestine, prepared jointly by the

[29] David Kranzler, 'The Jewish Refugee Community of Shanghai, 1938–1945', *The Wiener Library Bulletin*, 1972/3, vol. XXVI, nos. 3/4, new series nos. 28/9, pp. 28–37; Yehuda Bauer, 'Rescue Operations Through Vilna', *Yad Vashem Studies*, vol. IX, Jerusalem 1973, pp. 215–23.

Foreign and Colonial Offices, and distributed in January 1940. The memorandum began by characterizing the motives for illegal immigration as 'largely political'. It continued with the surprising statement: 'Illegal immigration is not primarily a refugee movement.' While admitting that there were 'of course, genuine refugees among the immigrants', the memorandum insisted: 'The problem is . . . an organised invasion of Palestine for political motives, which exploits the facts of the refugee problem and unscrupulously uses the humanitarian appeal of the latter to justify itself.' Particular concern was expressed regarding the role of the Germans: 'The Gestapo are known to assist the Jews in organising and despatching these parties. It is clearly to the interest of the German Government to promote this traffic, since it serves the double purpose of ridding them of Jews and causing embarrassment to His Majesty's Government.'[30] An anxiety repeatedly expressed in official discussion of illegal immigrants was 'the possibility of there being agents of the German Government amongst them and the consequent danger to the internal security of Palestine'.[31] No such agents were, in fact, ever discovered; this in spite of the fact that British intelligence authorities in the Middle East succeeded in penetrating Axis espionage networks in the area to an extent and by methods similar to those of the celebrated 'Doublecross System' in the United Kingdom. At one stage the Foreign Office expressed considerable irritation at the habit of the Colonial Office and of the High Commissioner for Palestine of invoking the threat of enemy agents, without being able, when invited to do so, to produce any evidence that pro-Nazi operatives had ever been introduced into the Middle East in the guise of illegal Jewish immigrants.[32]

Irritation over such matters led to occasional friction between the Foreign and Colonial Offices regarding Palestine during the first two years of the war. In the Colonial Office there developed an attitude towards the illegal immigrants, and Jews in general, which bordered on paranoia. In April 1941 J. S. Bennett, one of the Office's Middle East experts, in a

[30] Memorandum dated 17 Jan. 1940, PRO FO 371/25238/274 ff. (W 766/38/48).

[31] Memorandum by J. E. M. Carvell, 5 Feb. 1940, PRO FO 371/25239/150 ff. (W 2500/38/48).

[32] T. M. Snow (Foreign Office) to H. F. Downie (Colonial Office), 14 Jan. 1941, PRO CO 733/445/Part II/76021.

minute deploring a statement by the American Zionist, Rabbi Stephen Wise, commented:

The Jews have done nothing but add to our difficulties by propaganda and deeds since the war began . . . The morally censorious attitude of the United States in general to other people's affairs has long attracted attention, but when it is coupled with unscrupulous Zionist 'sob-stuff' and misrepresentation, it is very hard to bear.[33]

Sir John Shuckburgh, the Deputy Under-Secretary at the Colonial Office, writing in 1940 of the Jews of Palestine, remarked:

I am convinced that in their hearts they hate us and have always hated us; they hate all Gentiles. . . . So little do they care for Great Britain as compared with Zionism that they cannot even keep their hands off illegal immigration, which they must realise is a very serious embarrassment to us at a time when we are fighting for our very existence.

The Colonial Office official principally concerned with Palestine, H. F. Downie, went further. Commenting in March 1941 on an article by the American Labour Zionist, Hayyim Greenberg, Downie declared: 'This sort of thing makes one regret that the Jews are not on the other side in this war.'[34] Such views, although widely prevalent in the Colonial Office (and among senior officials of the Government of Palestine) were not shared to quite the same degree in the Foreign Office, where there was greater respect for the importance of Jewish opinion in the United States, and some resentment at being obliged to undertake distasteful diplomatic initiatives at the behest of the Colonial Office in order to bolster the White Paper policy. One Foreign Office official, in a comment in April 1941 on a paper from H. F. Downie, wrote:

One has, in matter emanating from the Middle Eastern Department of the Colonial Office, to take into account Mr Downie's inward and spiritual conviction that illegal immigration is only the outward and visible sign of a world-wide scheme to overthrow the British Empire. It is only if one realises that he regards the Jews as no less our enemies than the Germans that certain features of this draft become explicable

---

[33] Minute by J. S. Bennett, 18 Apr. 1941, PRO CO 733/444/75872/102/3.
[34] Minute by Shuckburgh dated 27 Apr. 1940, PRO CO 733/426/75872/16; minute by Downie, 15 Mar. 1941, PRO CO 733/445/Part II/76021/308.

... It is for this reason that the argument about enemy agents has such a fatal attraction for the Middle East Department, like the candle-flame for the moth—though they get burnt every time they come near it . . . If one has a personal conviction that the Jews are our enemies just as the Germans are, but in a more insidious way, it becomes essential to find reasons for believing that our two sets of enemies are linked together by secret and evil bonds, and it becomes our duty to say that they are so linked, irrespective of the evidence we can produce . . . The Foreign Office should, I submit, be careful not to tar itself with the brush of Mr Downie's curious and unprofitable beliefs.[35]

However, such friction between the two departments did not lead to any alteration of the White Paper policy, in the implementation of which the Foreign Office was generally prepared to collaborate.

The rigour with which the Government was determined to enforce the White Paper policy became apparent immediately after the outbreak of the war. No attempt was made to introduce the constitutional provisions of the White Paper, but in early 1940 the Government decided, over fierce Zionist protests, and in spite of vociferous opposition in the Cabinet from Churchill, that the restrictions on Jewish land purchase in Palestine, foreshadowed in the White Paper, should be implemented.[36] But it was the Government's restrictive interpretation of the immigration provisions of the White Paper which aroused the deepest Zionist indignation. The White Paper had laid down that a total of 75,000 Jewish immigrants were to be admitted in the course of five years: the policy was applied with retroactive effect from April 1939. However, so strict was the application of the policy that, in spite of the great outward pressure from Europe in 1939 and 1940, the numbers admitted fell far short even of the figure set by the White Paper. In July 1939 the Government had announced that because of the large number of illegal immigrants who were arriving in Palestine no quota at all would be issued for legal immigration in the six months October 1939 to March 1940. Upon the outbreak of the war the principle was enunciated that no

[35] Minute by R. T. E. Latham, 27 Apr. 1941, PRO FO 371/27132 (E 1240/204/31).
[36] Churchill to Cabinet, 25 Dec. 1939, PRO CAB 67/3/365; Cabinet minutes, 16 Jan. 1940, PRO CAB 65/5; Cabinet minutes, 12 Feb. 1940, ibid.

refugees from Germany or from German-occupied territory were henceforth to be admitted to Palestine. 'So far as we and France are concerned,' minuted a Foreign Office official, 'the position of the Jews in Germany is now of no practical importance.'[37] As a result of insistent Zionist pressure, the Colonial Office conceded that persons in enemy territory who already held Palestine immigration certificates would be allowed to proceed.[38] With the co-operation of the neutral Italian Government, and the full acquiescence of the Germans, 2,900 certificate-holders (including 1,019 from Prague, 717 from Berlin, and 448 from Vienna) were transported to Palestine via Trieste by an Italian shipping line.[39] But this was the only significant exception to the rule. For the six months April to September 1940, a quota of 9,060 certificates was authorized; but under half that number were actually admitted to Palestine. From October 1940 until June 1941 legal immigration was again suspended. In fifteen of the first thirty-nine months of the war no legal immigration schedules were issued. The result of these measures was that by the end of 1942 (when three-quarters of the five-year period laid down by the White Paper had already passed) barely half of the 75,000 immigrants theoretically permitted under the White Paper had been admitted to Palestine: since April 1939 a total of 38,930 had arrived; of these a majority, 19,925, were illegal immigrants.[40]

In order to counter the 'invasion', as it was termed, of illegal immigrants, the Government considered every possible diplomatic, legal, and military means at its disposal. In an effort to block the escape routes from central Europe which were used by illegal immigrants, energetic diplomatic action was undertaken by the Foreign Office to try to persuade the governments of south-east European states to co-operate. The Bulgarian Government was warned in December 1939 that 'in the event of any further instances of Bulgarian ships being involved in the illegal immigration traffic with Palestine, His Majesty's Government will expect [the] Bulgarian Government to take [the]

[37] A. W. G. Randall minute, 5 Sept. 1939, PRO FO 371/24078 (W 13132/45/48).
[38] M. MacDonald to C. Weizmann, 3 Oct. 1939, PRO FO 371/24095/54 (W 14438/1369/48).
[39] H. Barlas, *Hatzalah Bimei Shoah*, Tel Aviv 1975, pp. 20–3.
[40] Hurewitz, *Struggle for Palestine*, pp. 109 and 138–9.

immigrants back'.[41] Under pressure from the British Embassy in Bucharest, the Roumanian Government promised that Roumanian vessels would be prevented from carrying Jewish refugees down the Danube.[42] In February 1940 the Yugoslav Government, as a result of similar representations by the British Government, promised 'to exercise a strict control over the passports of all Jews who are embarking on vessels under the Yugoslav flag . . . taking a particular care that the passports are labelled with the necessary letter "J" and that in every respect they are provided with all the necessary visas and other formalities allowing the bearer to proceed to and disembark in Palestine'. The Yugoslav Foreign Ministry added that the measures were being taken 'with the sole object of responding to the urgent requests made by the British Government . . . although such a measure will inevitably deprive our shipping companies of a very substantial sale of transport tickets'. The Foreign Office instructed the British Ambassador in Belgrade to convey 'an expression of the appreciation of H.M. Government' to the Yugoslavs.[43] The Panamanian Government was induced to take preliminary steps towards the cancellation of the Panamanian registration held by many of the ships engaged in the illegal traffic.[44] The Liberian Government was asked to prevent the circulation of bogus Liberian entry visas.[45] Summarizing the diplomatic action taken, a Foreign Office memorandum stated:

The Foreign Office has asked countries of transit to refuse transit visas; . . . it has asked the nations where the owners of such [illegal immigrant] ships reside to take action against them; it has asked the nations whose ports are used by such ships to put administrative difficulties in the way of their sailing; and it has explored the possibilities of evading the legal provisions concerning freedom of transit

[41] Foreign Office to Rendel (Sofia), 6 Dec. 1939, PRO FO 371/24096/347 (W 17689/1369/48).

[42] Sir R. Hoare (Bucharest) to Sir R. Campbell (Belgrade), 30 Jan. 1940, PRO FO 371/25238/405 (W 1384/38148).

[43] 'Translation of Note Verbale from the Yugoslav Ministry of Foreign Affairs', 19 Feb. 1940, PRO FO 371/25240/86 (W 3207/38/48); Foreign Office to Belgrade (draft), 29 Feb. 1940, PRO FO 371/25240/87 (W 3207/38/48).

[44] Panamanian Ministry of External Affairs to British Envoy Extraordinary, 13 Dec. 1939, PRO FO 371/25238/215 (W 318/38/48).

[45] Foreign Office to Monrovia, 11 Apr. 1940, PRO FO 371/25241/143 (W 5819/38/48).

on the Danube and through the Straits in order to enable the riparian governments at our request to hinder the traffic. Representations have been made to twelve European and Mediterranean governments and to several American governments. In Roumania, Turkey, Greece, Bulgaria and Yugoslavia these representations have been carried to a point which has made the question of illegal immigration a factor constantly present in our relations with those countries.[46]

Yet this far-reaching British diplomatic effort to stanch the flow of refugees out of Europe had only a limited effect: it raised the prices paid for tickets to shipping agents and in bribes to officials of Balkan and other states, but it did not stop the illegal movement. The Governments in London and Jerusalem therefore considered other measures. The Admiralty was persuaded to divert ships of the Contraband Control Service in the eastern Mediterranean to intercept ships carrying illegal immigrants to Palestine. This action was taken in spite of legal advice given to the Foreign Office that the action was in contravention of international law, since interference with ships on the high seas for the purpose of preventing illegal immigration did not form part of the maritime rights of belligerent powers.[47] On 30 December 1939 an Admiralty order was dispatched, at the request of the Colonial Office, to the Commander-in-Chief of British naval forces in the Mediterranean, instructing him to intercept an illegal immigrant vessel and conduct it to Haifa 'giving as reason for this diversion [the] necessity of examining cargo for enemy exports or if no cargo for enemy agents'. As a 'test case' it was proposed, in the first instance, that the s.s. *Rudnitchar*, a Bulgarian river steamer, which was reported to have left Varna on 26 December with a large number of illegal immigrants on board, should be thus detained.[48] The Admiralty order had, however, been dispatched without the prior concurrence of the First Lord, Churchill. When he learnt of it he sent a stiff personal letter to the Colonial Secretary, Malcolm MacDonald, stating that while the order issued would be carried out 'in this case', he would not allow it to become 'a general

[46] Memorandum by J. E. M. Carvell, 5 Feb. 1940, PRO FO 371/25239/150 (W 2500/38/48).

[47] Foreign Office to Admiralty, 21 Nov. 1939, PRO FO 371/24094/219 (W 16266/1369/48).

[48] Admiralty to C.-in-C., Mediterranean, 30 Dec. 1939, PRO FO 371/24097/151 (W 19367/1369/48).

practice'. Churchill also inquired: 'I should be glad to know how you propose to treat these wretched people when they have been rounded up. Where are they to be sent, and what will be their fate?'[49] MacDonald replied that the intention was to seek to confiscate the ship, imprison the captain and officers, and, if possible, send the passengers back to Bulgaria; if, however, it proved impossible to deport them, they would be interned in Palestine for a while and then released for settlement there.[50] The 'test case' proved to be something of a fiasco for the Government of Palestine, since the *Rudnitchar* evaded capture by the navy, and succeeding in unloading its passengers into small landing craft near Haifa. The authorities captured 505 illegal immigrants, whom the High Commissioner proposed to deport to Bulgaria.[51] But, on examination, deportation was judged impracticable, because only two of the captured passengers were Bulgarian, and because the Foreign Office was so pessimistic about the likelihood of Bulgarian compliance that it was reluctant even to inquire in Sofia whether the deportees would be admitted into Bulgaria.[52] They therefore remained in Palestine.

In spite of this débâcle it was decided to attempt another 'test case'. On 17 January 1940 a Greek vessel, the s.s. *Hilda*, was intercepted by the Contraband Control Service. On board were 728 illegal immigrants of whom 675 held German or Czecho-slovak passports and were included in a collective entry visa for Paraguay supposedly issued by the Paraguayan consul in Prague (some doubt was cast on the authenticity of the visa when the government in Asunción denied that it had any recognized consul in Prague).[53] The ship was escorted to Haifa and detained there with all the passengers on board; on 28 January, after medical reports of ill health and insanitary conditions on the ship, the passengers were permitted to disembark and were placed in a detention camp at Athlit, near Haifa.[54] In

[49] Churchill to MacDonald, 4 Jan. 1940, PRO CO 733/429/76021/10/58.

[50] MacDonald to Churchill, 6 Jan. 1940, PRO CO 733/429/76021/10/56.

[51] High Commissioner for Palestine to Colonial Office, 9 Jan. 1940, PRO CO 733/429/76021/9/99.

[52] H. F. Downie minute, 1 Feb. 1940, PRO CO 733/429/76021/9.

[53] Beard (Asunción) to Foreign Office, 1 Feb. 1940, PRO FO 371/25239/54 (W 1943/38/48).

[54] High Commissioner, Jerusalem, to Colonial Office, London, 18 Jan. 1940, PRO

order to deter future illegal immigration, the Colonial Office prepared an account of the arrest of the ship and the internment of the passengers for transmission by the BBC in broadcasts to the Balkans. Presumably in anticipation of criticism, the Colonial Secretary gave instructions that the item was to be withheld from the British and foreign press, and was not to be broadcast on the BBC's English-language news bulletins.[55] The case of the *Hilda*, however, proved to be a further humiliating set-back for the Government, for, even as the ship was being taken into harbour, it was discovered that there was no legal power for such an arrest in international waters. The Attorney-General advised the High Commissioner that it was 'quite hopeless to expect to get conviction' of the master of the vessel in the Palestine courts.[56] There followed consideration in London and Jerusalem of the practicability of enacting 'retrospective legislation making the aiding and abetting of illegal immigration outside the territory of Palestine and its territorial waters an offence'.[57] The retrospective and extra-territorial aspects of the proposed legislation aroused a distinct sense of unease among the legal experts, and a lengthy wrangle ensued without any immediate decision.

Meanwhile yet another illegal immigrant vessel, the s.s. *Sakarya*, flying the Turkish flag, was sighted nearing the shores of Palestine. The High Commissioner suggested that the Contraband Control Service should intercept the ship, and, rather than bring it into port as in the previous instance, escort it to the limit of Palestinian territorial waters without permitting a landing.[58] However, the Admiralty did not favour this procedure, arguing that it would be necessary to take the boat well beyond the territorial waters limit in order to ensure that the passengers did not later attempt to land in smaller craft: it was now not considered that the navy had legal powers to take such action beyond territorial waters.

FO 371/25238/339 (W 1145/38/48); sim., 24 Jan. 1940, PRO FO 371/25238/316 (W 1210/38/48); sim., 26 Jan. 1940, PRO FO 371/25239/21 (W 1544/38/48).

[55] J. E. M. Carvell minute, 3 Feb. 1940, PRO FO 371/25239/59 (W 1988/38/48).

[56] High Commissioner to Colonial Office, 18 Jan. 1940, PRO FO 371/25238/336 (W 1157/38/48).

[57] Minute by R. T. E. Latham, 24 Jan. 1940, PRO FO 371/25238/379 (W 1371/38/48).

[58] High Commissioner to Colonial Secretary, 3 Feb. 1940, PRO FO 371/25239/88 (W 2105/38/48).

The Colonial Office pointed out a further objection 'on political grounds':

There is a possibility that Jewish passengers might resist forcible removal from Palestinian waters, and might for example attempt to jump overboard and swim to land. In that event our action would be open to serious misrepresentation.[59]

On 13 February the *Sakarya* was escorted into Haifa. She was found to be carrying no fewer than 2,176 refugees, of whom 801 were women and children. German passports or other travel documents were held by 1,383 of the passengers; the remainder included 180 holders of Hungarian passports. Some passports contained visas for Bolivia, Liberia, or China, but 1,094 of the travel documents contained no visas at all. The passengers were interned in the Athlit camp, while, as in the case of the *Hilda*, the captain of the *Sakarya* and his vessel were detained under emergency defence regulations.[60] In order to make way for the *Sakarya* arrivals, all the passengers from the *Rudnitchar* and the women and children from the *Hilda* were released from internment.[61]

With the landing of the passengers from the *Rudnitchar*, the *Hilda*, and the *Sakarya*, it was apparent that the Government's attempts to halt the flow of immigrants were failing, and that further deterrent measures would have to be considered if the policy was to be maintained. The Admiralty made it clear that following the questionable results obtained in the 'test cases', the naval authorities would not be issued with standing instructions to intercept further ships; if naval patrols happened to intercept such ships in the course of their normal duties they would be sent to Haifa; but beyond this the Admiralty refused to go.[62] Meanwhile, the Colonial Office had asked for Foreign Office help in another deterrent measure: it had been learnt that a party of at least a thousand Jewish refugees, fleeing down the Danube had found themselves blocked by ice on the river and forced to remain at the river port of Kladovo in Yugoslavia; they were reported to be in dire straits and with no money or

[59] Colonial Office to High Commissioner, 5 Feb. 1940, PRO FO 371/25239/114 (W 2280/38/48).
[60] High Commissioner to Colonial Office, 17 Feb. 1940, PRO CO 733/425/75852/96.
[61] High Commissioner to Colonial Office, PRO FO 371/25239/140 (W 2451/38/48).
[62] Admiralty to Colonial Office, 14 Mar. 1940, PRO CO 733/429/76021/10.

food, and had appealed to the American Jewish Joint Distribution Committee for aid. The Colonial Office suggested that some means might be found to prevent such assistance reaching the party because 'assistance of this kind amounts to not only conniving at, but also actively helping, the passage of illegal immigrants towards Palestine'.[63] The suggestion was rejected by the Foreign Office where R. T. E. Latham, noting that intelligence reports indicated that several of the refugees had died and a large number were ill, minuted:

This time the C.O. is really carrying too far its policy of calling upon other Departments to do its dirty work . . . American public opinion would protest against our inhumanity: 'You won't help these people yourselves; and now you won't let us help them.' In the spirit though not in the letter, American public opinion would be right. Such action on our part would savour of real malice against the refugees, more worthy of our enemies than of us.[64]

The Colonial Office proposal was not implemented—but the Kladovo group did not escape from Europe. They were interned by the Yugoslav authorities in a camp near Belgrade. Immediately after the German occupation of Yugoslavia in April 1941 they were murdered.

A more drastic deterrent was next considered by the Government of Palestine and the Colonial Office: deportation of illegal immigrants to their country of origin. J. S. Bennett of the Colonial Office suggested on 20 February that, as a beginning, the 180 Hungarian passport-holders from the *Sakarya* should be deported to Hungary 'if only for the publicity value which this would have, both as a deterrent to future illegal immigrants and as a sign to the Arabs that the law is being enforced vigorously'.[65] The High Commissioner favoured the suggestion, declaring 'We must be prepared to face up to the consequences and enforce our declared policy', but he pointed out that deportations would 'create very serious feeling amongst the Jews, probably disorder' which might necessitate the maintenance in Palestine of British troops required for service elsewhere; he therefore suggested that the Colonial Secretary

[63] H. F. Downie to J. E. M. Carvell, 19 Jan. 1940, PRO FO 371/25238/322 (W 1087/38/48).
[64] Minute by Latham, 22 Jan. 1940, PRO FO 371/25238/319 (W 1087/38/48).
[65] Minute by Bennett, 20 Feb. 1940, PRO CO 733/429/76021/11.

might 'not think the game is worth the candle for the sake of deporting these 175 Hungarians'.[66] The Colonial Office reluctantly decided not to turn to mass deportation as a deterrent.[67] In the event only a few individuals were deported, including three of the Hungarians from the *Sakarya*.[68] At the instance of the High Commissioner prolonged efforts were made in 1940 to persuade the Hungarian Government to accede to the return to Hungary of two Jews who had left the country for Palestine as tourists in 1934 but had remained there for six years.[69] However, little could be done in face of the Hungarian Government's stated view 'that the number of Jews in the country is excessive and they have made it clear that far from being prepared to facilitate the repatriation of Jews who have left Hungary, it is their aim that as many as possible should be encouraged to emigrate'.[70] As similar sentiments were voiced by the governments of all European countries from which illegal refugees originated, deportation to the country of origin, it became apparent, would not provide the necessary buttress for the government's policy.

As a partial solution the High Commissioner secured Colonial Office approval for the promulgation of new emergency regulations under which ships carrying illegal immigrants to Palestine would be liable to forfeiture; penalties of £1,000 fine and imprisonment for three years were laid down for the 'owner, agent or master' of such vessels; and illegal immigrants themselves were made liable to a fine of £100 and imprisonment for six months.[71] The regulations encountered some criticism in the Foreign Office, one of whose legal advisers termed them 'rather a pathetic commentary on the Palestine authorities and particularly on the judicial authorities'.[72] Under the new

[66] High Commissioner to Colonial Office, 23 Mar. 1940, PRO CO 733/429/76021/11.
[67] Minute by H. F. Downie, 4 Apr. 1940, PRO CO 733/429/76021/11.
[68] High Commissioner to Colonial Secretary, 7 June 1940, PRO FO 371/25241/239 (W 7473/38/48); sim., 16 Aug. 1940 PRO CO 733/429/76021/11.
[69] High Commissioner to Colonial Office, 23 May 1940, PRO FO 371/25240/35 (W 2908/38/48).
[70] J. S. Somers Cocks (Budapest) to High Commissioner, Jerusalem, 14 Feb. 1940, PRO FO 371/25240/28 (W 2908/38/48).
[71] High Commissioner to Colonial Office, 29 Feb. 1940 PRO FO 371/25240/114 (W 3232/38/48); Colonial Office to High Commissioner, 15 Mar. 1940, PRO FO 371/25240/207 (W 4257/38/48).
[72] P. Dean minute, 11 Mar. 1940, PRO FO 371/25240/200–1 (W 4257/38/48).

regulations 1,725 of the passengers from the *Sakarya* and the 512 men from the *Hilda* were held in internment camps for six months.[73] But the regulations failed to achieve their object of halting the refugee traffic; to many Jews in Europe in 1940 a six-month spell in a Palestinian detention camp seemed preferable to what might await them in Europe. Nor were the organizers of the exodus deterred by a warning, issued by British representatives in the Balkans, that 'Palestine coast defences, being now on the *qui vive* to repel possible Italian raiders, would be unable to distinguish illegal immigrants attempting clandestine landings from enemies'.[74] In July the s.s. *Libertado*, flying the Uruguayan flag, was captured off the Palestinian coast and escorted to Haifa. The 343 passengers (who included 80 Hungarians and 60 Bulgarians, as well as several other nationalities) were interned, and a strong British protest was lodged with the Bulgarian Government, from whose territory the expedition had been organized.[75]

The conflict over illegal immigration now moved to a climax, culminating in a tragedy which was to haunt the Zionist memory for a generation—the explosion of the *Patria*. In September 1940 British intelligence reports indicated that a new wave of several thousand refugees was gathering in south-east Europe and appeared about to move towards Palestine. Among these refugees were some of those who had spent the entire winter of 1939–40 marooned on icebound boats or river barges on the frozen Danube. In spite of the attempt of the Colonial Office to prevent aid reaching the stranded Jews, they had received some food, clothing, and money from Jewish organizations and from a relief committee of British women in Bucharest (who had not sought the advice of the Colonial Office); but many of the refugees had died, victims of cold or hunger, and a large number were ill.[76] On 3 September 1940 more than 3,000 further refugees from Prague, Vienna, and Danzig, who had been permitted to leave by the German authorities, set sail down the Danube in four river steamers 'under the Swastika

[73] High Commissioner to Colonial Office, 27 June 1940, PRO CO 733/425/75852/51.

[74] Foreign Office to British Consul, Burgas, 22 June 1940; Foreign Office to Bucharest, Sofia, Athens etc., 25 June 1940, PRO FO 371/25241/292 and 299 (W 7899/38/48).

[75] Foreign Office to Rendel (Sofia), 3 Aug. 1940, PRO CO 733/429/76021/9.

[76] *Jewish Chronicle*, 2, 9, and 23 Feb. 1940; Jewish Agency memorandum, 'The Refugee Ships in Haifa Bay', 26 Nov. 1940, PRO FO 371/25242/410 (W 12506/38/48).

flag'. The convoy of refugees had reached the Roumanian port of Tulcea (near the mouth of the Danube) on 11 September. There they boarded three Greek cargo boats, which were renamed the *Atlantic, Pacific*, and *Milos*, and in these they continued the voyage to Palestine under the Panamanian flag. The *Milos* was reported to be carrying 709 passengers, the *Pacific* 1,015, and the *Atlantic* 1,875.[77]

Conditions on all three boats were appalling. The overcrowding on the *Atlantic* was such that many passengers had sitting room only and were unable to stretch their limbs for the whole duration of the voyage.[78] A statement by a group of passengers described the ordeal of the *Atlantic*:

The 'Lebensraum' was restricted to a space of 45 cm. per person. In this way children, babies, women, old people, cripples, were pressed together . . . The boat was supplied with a little fuel and food which may be stretched to last us a fortnight with utmost thrift. The crew were apparently 'pirates'. In front of the lavatories, the number of which was by no means sufficient, there were long queues of people waiting. These conditions became almost unbearable when due to the bad food and the spoiled water, the majority of the passengers suffered from diarrhoea . . . When the wind blew up people got sea-sick. So we sailed and lived almost for three months.[79]

At Istanbul the local Jewish community provided the boat with some provisions, but these soon ran out. By the time the *Atlantic* reached Crete on 16 October there was no fuel, water, or food left; typhoid broke out. On 28 October while the ship was still immobilized at Heraklion, Italy attacked Greece. The Greek captain and crew, frightened to continue the voyage, tried to escape in the only usable lifeboat. The harbour police, however, brought them back to the ship which, supplied with some inferior-quality coal, was ordered to move on. Soon after leaving Heraklion the captain and crew threw most of the coal overboard and, docking at another Cretan port, refused to

---

[77] Foreign Office to Cairo, 2 Nov. 1940, PRO FO 371/25242/38 (W 11006/38/48); High Commissioner, Jerusalem, to Colonial Office, 15 Oct. 1940, PRO FO 371/25242/45 (W 11091/38/48); Aaron Zwergbaum, 'Exile in Mauritius', *Yad Vashem Studies*, vol. IV, Jerusalem 1960, pp. 191–257.

[78] Zwergbaum, loc. cit., p. 195.

[79] Deposition by Dr. Erwin Enoch, Dr. Robert Hirsch, and Engineer Erwin Kovac, 19 June 1942, BD C 14/26/2.

carry on. The passengers, with a few sympathetic crew members, took over the ship and continued through the Dodecanese. After three days the boat again ran out of fuel. The passengers began demolishing the superstructure of the vessel to provide wood to keep the boat moving. On the fifth day out of Crete they saw land; most of the ship's instruments did not work, and they thought they were near the coast of Anatolia. The passengers' account continued: 'After some hours of desperate waiting, a motor boat approached us . . . At last we were able to discern a British flag in the motor boat; we cried, we laughed, we were saved at last.' On 12 November the *Atlantic* was towed into Limassol by tugs. The Governor of Cyprus reported that an inspection of the vessel had revealed 'indescribably shocking' conditions:

Gross overcrowding; standing room on deck only; below lack of ventilating light; no ablution or laundry facilities at all; no proper cooking facilities for such numbers . . . Director of Medical Services considers that every day's delay in taking passengers off increases risk already high of epidemic death toll which would probably be very heavy as passengers are suffering from exposure and hardship and are emaciated.[80]

While the *Atlantic* had been moving slowly from Tulcea to Limassol the *Pacific* and *Milos* had made much faster progress, and at the beginning of November they reached Palestinian waters, confronting the Government of Palestine with a renewed challenge to the White Paper policy. Alarmed by reports of the movements of all three ships, the High Commissioner on 21 September cabled to the Colonial Office expressing his anxiety about the danger to public security represented by 'an influx of young toughs who may or may not be Jews and are sure to include enemy agents'. He urged that the possibility be considered of diverting the illegal immigrants to Australia.[81] The Colonial Office replied on 15 October that it was impracticable to send the refugees to Australia, but that the possibility of sending them to Mauritius or some other colony would be investigated. Meanwhile, any illegal immigrants who arrived

[80] Governor of Cyprus to Colonial Office, 18 Nov. 1940, PRO FO 371/25242/117 (W 12017/38/48).

[81] High Commissioner, Jerusalem, to Colonial Office, 21 Sept. 1940, PRO FO 371/25242/204 (W 11091/38/48).

should be interned and kept in safe custody or held on board the ships in which they arrived.[82] In anticipation of the arrival of the three boats, the High Commissioner promulgated new emergency regulations giving himself power to intern illegal immigrants for an indefinite period.[83] Meanwhile the Colonial Office investigated the possibility of deporting the refugees to a British colony. A telegram to the Governor of Mauritius on 15 October inquired:

Could you as a matter of urgency provide accommodation for a considerable number of Jews who are endeavouring to enter Palestine illegally? They would have to be kept under restraint and this involves the construction of a camp surrounded by barbed wire and the provision of guards.[84]

The Governor agreed to accept a total of 4,000 refugees on condition that they brought their own bedding, crockery, and cutlery with them, and provided that they were accompanied by 'a necessary proportion of guards, doctors, and interpreters'. He also specified that 'they should all be inoculated against typhoid, vaccinated, and their persons and clothing cleaned of all vermin before embarkation or on the voyage'. In a later telegram the Governor added that an adequate supply of chamber-pots should also arrive with the refugees. To accommodate them, the main prison hall and courtyard would be divided into makeshift cells. The Governor expressed some surprise at the ration scale suggested for the immigrants which, he stated, 'indicates higher class of immigrants than anticipated'. He warned that European guards were not available in Mauritius and that it was impossible to say how many would be required 'without details as to type and culture of immigrants, whether quarrelsome, degree of discipline required, extent to which leaders among immigrants will co-operate with guards to maintain internal order'.[85]

[82] Colonial Office to High Commissioner, Jerusalem, 15 Oct. 1940, PRO FO 371/25242/208 (W 11091/38/48).

[83] High Commissioner to Colonial Office, 17 and 18 Oct. 1940, PRO FO 371/25242/105–7 (W 11823/38/48).

[84] Colonial Office to Governor of Mauritius, 15 Oct. 1940, PRO FO 371/25242/219 (W 11091/38/48).

[85] Governor of Mauritius to Colonial Office, 17 Oct. 1940, PRO FO 371/25242/212 (W 11091/38/48); sim., 11 Nov. 1940, PRO FO 371/25242/272 (W 12017/38/48).

While these arrangements were being made the *Milos* and *Pacific* were intercepted off Palestine by coastal patrol vessels and brought into Haifa harbour. The passengers were not permitted to land; instead they were held on board the two ships while preparations were made for their transport to Mauritius aboard the *Messagerie Maritime* liner, the *Patria*. There were energetic Jewish protests in Palestine and in the U.S.A. against the Government's reported intention to deport the refugees, and on 20 November a general strike was observed by the Jews in Palestine. In defence of its position the Government of Palestine issued an official communiqué:

There can be no doubt that these persons must be classed as illegal immigrants, that is to say persons seeking to enter Palestine against what is well known to be the law of the country. H.M.G. are not lacking in sympathy for refugees from territories under German control. But they are responsible for the administration of Palestine and are bound to see to it that the laws of the country are not openly flouted. Moreover they can only regard the revival of illegal Jewish immigration at this present juncture as likely to affect the local situation most adversely and prove a serious menace to British interests in the Middle East. They have accordingly decided that the passengers of the s.s. *Pacific* and s.s. *Milos* shall not be permitted to land in Palestine but shall be deported to a British Colony as soon as arrangements for safe transport and building accommodation can be made, and shall be detained there for the duration of the war. Their ultimate disposal will be a matter for consideration at the end of the war but it is not proposed that they shall remain in the Colony to which they are sent or that they should go to Palestine. Similar action will be taken in the case of any further parties who may succeed in reaching Palestine with a view to illegal entry.[86]

Four days later the *Atlantic* arrived in Haifa under British escort (the Governor of Cyprus having refused to allow the passengers to land on the island 'as political reaction to their land[ing] here will be most undesirable'[87]). By this time the passengers from the two previous ships had already been transferred to the *Patria*, and it was decided to delay the liner's departure for

[86] Text in PRO FO 371/25242/285 (W 12017/38/48).
[87] Governor of Cyprus to Colonial Office, 18 Nov. 1940, PRO FO 371/25242/117 (W 12017/38/48).

Mauritius in order to transfer also the passengers from the *Atlantic*; the process of transfer from the *Atlantic* to the *Patria* began immediately on the afternoon of 24 November, but had to be suspended at nightfall.

These proceedings in the eastern Mediterranean had not failed to arouse dissension in London both among the Zionists and within the British Government. Weizmann took a surprisingly acquiescent attitude to the Government's actions, apparently concerned by the reports of Gestapo involvement in the illegal immigration traffic, and worried that large-scale immigration might imperil the restricted legal immigration schedules under the White Paper. After discussing the matter with the Colonial Secretary, Lord Lloyd, Weizmann, in a 'painful scene' in the Zionist Executive (as it was described by Mrs Blanche Dugdale, Balfour's niece, who was present), argued that 'they must not have anything to do with this business just for the sake of getting an additional 3,000 people into Palestine—who might later turn out to be a millstone round their neck'. Berl Locker, a Palestinian Labour Zionist, strongly disagreed, reminding the Executive that 'among these refugees were many of their own people—*halutzim*,[88] Zionists, and persons having near relatives in Palestine'. But Weizmann said that the refugees would probably be safer in Mauritius and suggested that 'Mr Locker was perhaps taking too sentimental a view of the matter'.[89] Weizmann offered the Government his co-operation in calming Jewish feeling in Palestine and the U.S.A. by the dispatch of reassuring messages to Zionist leaders. However, so locked into conflict with the Zionists was the Government by this stage that this (and other such Zionist overtures around this time) met with a distinctly ungracious response. The High Commissioner told the Colonial Office that he did 'not much like [the] appearance of making use of Weizmann as favour and so increasing obligations which will of course be cited later'.[90] In the event Weizmann's messages were dispatched through official channels, but it was explained to him that the Colonial Secretary did not regard

[88] Hebr., 'pioneers'.

[89] Rose ed., *Dugdale Diaries*, p. 178 (entry dated 15 Nov. 1940); minutes of meeting of Zionist Executive, London, 15 Nov. 1940, CZA Z4/302/24.

[90] High Commissioner to Colonial Office, 18 Nov. 1940, PRO FO 371/25242/289 (W 12017/38/48).

himself as under any obligation to the Zionist leader for his assistance.[91]

A more respectful attitude was taken towards the views expressed by another prominent supporter of Zionism, Winston Churchill. On 13 November Lloyd sent the Prime Minister a memorandum outlining the proposal for deportation of illegal immigrants to Mauritius, and asking for Churchill's support 'as the Jews are making a grievance about the non-admission of these illegal immigrants into Palestine'. Churchill replied: 'Provided these refugees are not sent back to the torments from which they have escaped and are decently treated in Mauritius, I agree.'[92] However, a few days later the Prime Minister's Private Secretary, J. M. Martin, drew his attention to the fact that the arrangements apparently being made for the illegal immigrants in Mauritius included the construction of 'a concentration camp with barbed wire and guards'.[93] When Churchill saw this he sent Lloyd one of his celebrated 'Action this day' minutes:

I had never contemplated the Jewish refugees being interned in Mauritius in a camp surrounded by barbed wire and guards. It is very unlikely that these refugees would include enemy agents, and I should expect that the Jewish authorities themselves, as Weizmann can assure you, would be most efficient and vigilant purgers in this respect.

Churchill suggested that the proposed action 'should be confined to future illegal immigrants, and that those in the country, after careful vetting, be allowed to stay'.[94] This minute was written on 20 November, the day of the Jewish general strike in Palestine and of the Government of Palestine's public announcement of the deportation policy. As soon as Lloyd received the Prime Minister's minute he sent a 'most immediate' telegram to the High Commissioner instructing him to defer the announcement, but it arrived too late. Lloyd replied to the Prime Minister asking him to agree that since the deportation policy had been announced it should be carried out. He

[91] Colonial Office to High Commissioner, 20 Nov. 1940, PRO FO 371/25242/290 (W 12017/38/48).

[92] Lloyd to Churchill, 13 Nov. 1940; Churchill to Lloyd, 14 Nov. 1940, PRO CO 733/429/76021/Part I/63 and 53.

[93] Martin to Churchill, 17 Nov. PRO PREM 4/51/1/88.

[94] Churchill to Lloyd, 20 Nov. 1940, PRO PREM 4/51/1/87.

argued that the illegal immigrants 'generally include a proportion of militant young Jews who are likely to cause trouble', and dissented from the Prime Minister's view that the Germans were unlikely to try to smuggle in agents among the refugees:

Is it indeed likely that the Nazis would neglect so good an opportunity of getting their agents into the Middle East? I put it to you that there can be only one answer to this question, and that in the circumstances it is absolutely necessary to keep refugees under strict guard . . . The position is that the intention of the Government to remove these refugees from Haifa to a British Colony has now been officially announced in Palestine. Its revocation would be interpreted only in one sense, viz, as a surrender to Jewish agitation. If such an impression were created, not only would more and more shiploads be encouraged to descend upon us, but the political effect in the Middle East would be altogether deplorable.[95]

Churchill's response, on 22 November, was curt: 'As the action has been announced, it must proceed, but the conditions in Mauritius must not involve these people being caged-up for the duration of the war. The Cabinet will require to be satisfied about this. Pray make me your proposals.'[96]

But before the discussion could proceed any further a horrifying piece of news arrived: on the morning of 25 November a gigantic explosion had ripped open the hull of the *Patria* as the remaining passengers from the *Atlantic* were being transferred to it. The death toll was 267. The cause of the disaster was not established immediately, although there were strong suspicions in official circles in both Jerusalem and London that the Zionists had been responsible. The suspicions were accurate: the explosion was the work of *Haganah* saboteurs acting on orders from the leadership of the underground army. The saboteurs had miscalculated the amount of explosive required to disable the ship, with the result that instead of merely damaging it and preventing its departure, they produced an appalling disaster.[97]

The survivors from the *Patria* and the remaining passengers on the *Atlantic* were transferred to the internment camp at Athlit, where the two groups were kept separate. On 27

[95] Lloyd to Churchill, 21 Nov. 1940, PRO PREM 4/51/84 ff.
[96] Churchill to Lloyd, 22 Nov. 1940, PRO PREM 4/51/1/71.
[97] Dinur, *Sefer Toldot Ha-haganah*, vol. III, part I, pp. 152–5.

November Moshe Shertok, head of the Political Department of the Jewish Agency, went to see the High Commissioner. Both men were in a state of some agitation, and the interview was marked by a profound hostility on both sides. Shertok described the meeting in a memorandum:

I opened by saying that the sinking of the *Patria* was a terrible tragedy . . .

The High Commissioner said that it was indeed a tragedy. The fellow who had done it deserved to be hanged sky-high. It was clear that the affair had not been an accident.

I interjected that it certainly did not look like an accident . . .

I asked whether I might know what was the decision with regard to these people [the survivors].

The High Commissioner looked up in surprise, and said that the decision was well-known. It had not been changed, and the people would have to leave Palestine.

I said: 'You mean to say you are going to inflict this on us and on these people after all the ordeals they have been through?'

The High Commissioner replied with some irritation: 'I cannot understand all this talk about inflicting. One might think that the British Government was going to do something inhuman. It is going to do nothing of the sort. These people are refugees, and the British Government is going to take care of them, but not in Palestine. They will probably be much better off in the place to which they will be sent than they have been for years under Nazi rule. To you all this is something purely political.'

I said: 'I beg to disagree. I beg respectfully, but most emphatically to disagree.'

A fierce altercation followed which culminated in a passionate speech by the (normally phlegmatic) Shertok:

His Excellency had said that the sinking of the *Patria* had not been an accident. I agreed. I would go further and say quite frankly that I admitted the possibility of this having been the work of Jews. Possibly of the refugees themselves who had been driven to despair. Possibly with the help of Jews from outside.

After recalling the Government's attempts to prevent illegal immigration by all possible means, Shertok said:

On top of it all there had come that harsh sentence expressing the

Government's intention not to admit these people even after the war—to my mind an entirely superfluous and unwarranted sentence ... It was difficult to exaggerate the provocative effect which this sentence had had upon masses of Jews. It had made the blood of tens of thousands boil ...

I asked: 'Do you realise what it would mean dragging all these refugees back from the Athlit camp, hundreds, and hundreds, and hundreds of them?' I added that I shuddered to think what the reaction of our people would be to this.

The High Commissioner said somewhat whimsically: 'Well, Governments have sometimes to face unpleasant situations.'[98]

In London the Zionists were no less outraged by the Government's apparent intention to persist with the deportations. The *Zionist Review* denounced the policy as an 'act of inhumanity [which] ... mocks at justice, wisdom, and humanity'. The Colonial Office considered this comment 'outrageous'; Sir John Shuckburgh minuted: 'The Jews have no sense of humour and no sense of proportion.'[99] But the Zionists were in no jocular temper. A grim Weizmann was told the news by Lord Lloyd on the telephone on the evening of the disaster. The next day Weizmann went to see Lloyd whom he found 'in a chastened mood'. Lloyd said he had to administer a White Paper which he did not like; he told Weizmann that he now knew who had organized the latest transports of illegal immigrants; they were foul people who had to be stamped out. Weizmann, described by Shuckburgh as being 'in his most agitated mood', complained bitterly of the Government's inhumanity, and threatened to resign his position as head of the Zionist Organisation. He said that the High Commissioner's communiqué announcing that the deportees would never be allowed to enter Palestine was 'beyond endurance', and that co-operation between the Government and the Zionists was now impossible. According to one account of the interview Weizmann 'hinted darkly at the reaction on the Jews in America and on the length of Lord Lloyd's future tenure of his present office'.[100]

[98] L. B. Namier (for Jewish Agency) to Foreign Office, 25 Mar. 1941, enclosing Shertok's memorandum, PRO FO 371/29162 (W 3502/11/48).

[99] *Zionist Review* 29 Nov. 1940; Shuckburgh minute, 5 Dec. 1940, PRO CO 733/430/76021/35/3.

[100] Minutes of meetings of Zionist Executive, London, 26 Nov. 1940, CZA Z4/302/24; Shuckburgh minute, 26 Nov. 1940, PRO CO 733/429/76021/Part II/5; J. M. Martin to

Weizmann also saw the Labour leader, and Lord Privy Seal, Attlee, who, according to Weizmann, 'behaved very much in the manner of Lord Passfield'. (As Colonial Secretary in the second Labour Government from 1929 to 1931, Passfield, previously Sidney Webb, had fallen out with the Zionists.) In an interview with the Foreign Secretary, Lord Halifax, Weizmann denounced once again the High Commissioner's proclamation, which, he maintained, 'was not carrying out the law; it was an act of vindictiveness'. He warned Halifax that now that the immigrants were on shore in Palestine 'two policemen would be required to carry each on again to any ship'; the depth of the Zionist leader's feeling was indicated by his statement that 'he would fight this thing until they sent him to a concentration camp'.[101]

When the Cabinet considered the matter on 27 December it became clear that Weizmann's representations had had some limited effect. Some ministers expressed objection to the terms of the High Commissioner's proclamation that the deportees would never be permitted to enter Palestine. According to the Cabinet minutes 'it was urged [by an unnamed minister] that the Proclamation should not have taken away from these people the right to take their chance with other applicants of obtaining entry to Palestine in a legal way'. It was also suggested that the proposal to intern the refugees in Mauritius was 'perhaps unduly severe'. Lloyd again referred to the danger of enemy agents being present among the illegal immigrants, and argued 'that it was impossible to put large numbers of aliens, many of them enemy aliens, in a British Colony in wartime without making arrangements for their due surveillance'. He promised, however, that everything possible would be done to ensure that they received humane treatment. Objecting to a suggestion that the *Patria* survivors be allowed to remain in Palestine, Lloyd said that 'if this were allowed, he feared that it was only too likely to encourage further acts of sabotage by other illegal immigrants, in order to obtain a similar concession'. The Cabinet eventually decided that the illegal immi-

Churchill, 26 Nov. 1940, PRO PREM 4/51/1/53. Weizmann's prophecy proved to have a melancholy accuracy: Lloyd died five weeks later.

[101] Minutes of meeting of Zionist Executive, 28 Nov. 1940, CZA Z4/302/24; note by Halifax, 27 Nov. 1940, PRO FO 371/25242/406 (W 12506/38/48).

grants who had been saved from the *Patria* should be allowed to remain in Palestine 'as a special act of clemency, having regard to the sufferings which these immigrants had undergone in the s.s. *Patria*'. This was, however, to be 'the only exception made to the policy of the [High Commissioner's] Proclamation, and . . . in future all other illegal immigrants attempting to enter Palestine should be diverted to Mauritius or elsewhere'. Finally, the Cabinet decided that 'measures should be taken with a view to making the conditions of internment in Mauritius as little burdensome as possible'.[102]

In British politics Cabinet decisions are normally the final word on any point of government policy. But on this occasion the Cabinet decision was challenged. On 30 November the Secretary of State for War, Anthony Eden, received the following 'most immediate' cable from the British Commander-in-Chief in the Middle East, General Wavell:

Have just heard of decision re *Patria* immigrants. Most sincerely trust you will use all possible influence to have decision reversed. From military point of view it is disastrous. It will be spread all over Arab world that Jews have again successfully challenged decision of British Government and that policy of White Paper is being reversed. This will gravely increase prospect of widespread disorders in Palestine, necessitating increased military commitments, will greatly enhance influence of Mufti, will arouse mistrust of us in Syria and increase anti-British propaganda and fifth column activities in Egypt. It will again be spread abroad that only violence pays in dealing with British. If present decision stands must withdraw recommendation . . . of 26 Nov. to open Basra-Baghdad road, as certain result will be great increase of anti-British feeling and action in Iraq. Please exert all your influence. This is serious.[103]

Eden circulated the telegram to the Cabinet without comment, but it was placed on the Cabinet agenda for early discussion on 2 December. Meanwhile Wavell's view found general support in the Colonial Office and in the Foreign Office.[104] The Cabinet decided, however, to reaffirm their previous decision. After a discussion (described by Sir Alexander Cadogan, who was

[102] Cabinet minutes, 27 Nov. 1940, PRO CAB 65/10.
[103] Wavell to Eden, 30 Nov. 1940, PRO PREM 4/51/2/116.
[104] See minutes by C. W. Baxter, 2 Dec. 1940, and T. M. Snow, 3 Dec. 1940, PRO FO 371/25242/247 (W 11766/38/48).

present, as 'heated'[105]) it was decided that, while the High Commissioner's proclamation of 20 November should stand, no further official reference should be made in public to the perpetual exclusion of the deportees from Palestine.[106] Churchill meanwhile pronounced his opinion emphatically in a personal telegram to Wavell:

Cabinet felt that in view of the sufferings of these immigrants and the perils to which they had been subjected through the sinking of their ship, that it would be necessary on compassionate grounds not to subject them again immediately to the hazards of the sea. Personally I hold it would be an act of inhumanity unworthy of the British name to force them to re-embark. On the other hand Cabinet agreed that future consignments of illegal immigrants should be sent to Mauritius provided that tolerable conditions can be arranged for them there . . . I wonder whether the effect on the Arab world will be as bad as you suggest. If their attachment to our cause is so slender as to be determined by a mere act of charity of this kind it is clear that our policy of conciliating them has not borne much fruit so far. What I think would influence them much more would be any kind of British military success. I therefore suggest that you should reconsider your statement about the Basra-Baghdad-Haifa road when we see which way the compass points. I am sorry you should be worrying yourself with such matters at this particular time, and I hope at least you will believe that the views I have just expressed are not dictated by fear of violence.[107]

Wavell accepted the Cabinet decision, although in reply to Churchill he again stressed that 'experience of Palestinian affairs and in Middle East generally has shown me deep-rooted suspicion throughout Arab world that our publicly announced policy is liable to reversals in favour of Jews and that our word and fairness are no longer trusted'. He added, with a strained attempt at humour (of which perhaps Sir John Shuckburgh would have approved): 'Agree that if compass points due west it may divert Arabs from any undue desire [pro] "Patria mori"'[108]

[105] Sir Alexander Cadogan, *The Diaries of Sir Alexander Cadogan O.M. 1938–1945*, ed. David Dilks, London 1971, p. 338 (entry dated 2 Dec. 1940).
[106] Cabinet minutes, 2 Dec. 1940, PRO CAB 65/10.
[107] Churchill to Wavell, dictated on 1 Dec. (i.e. before the Cabinet meeting), dispatched on 2 Dec. 1940, PRO PREM 4/51/2/112–13.
[108] Wavell to Churchill, 3 Dec. 1940, PRO PREM 4/51/2/109.

This was not quite the end of the *Patria* affair, to which there was a dismal conclusion. Although the Cabinet had decided that the survivors of the *Patria* disaster should be permitted to remain in Palestine, the decision was interpreted strictly so as to exclude those passengers on the *Atlantic* who had not been transferred to the *Patria* at the moment of the explosion. The Jewish Agency pleaded with the Government to permit the *Atlantic* passengers to remain in Palestine: in a memorandum submitted by Berl Locker and Lewis Namier, the Jewish Agency again offered its 'friendly cooperation' with the government in arranging for the diversion to a British colony of any future boatloads of illegal immigrants. But it specified:

If refugee boats have to be diverted, every effort must be made to intercept them before they sight Palestine. For a distinction must be made between Jewish refugee boats within the sight of Palestine and those intercepted on the high seas. This may not be logical, but it is human. To turn back these sufferers and wanderers after their relatives and friends have seen them, puts a great strain on human feelings . . . Jewish refugees diverted to a British colony should be treated as eligible candidates for immigration certificates to Palestine. The knowledge of this being so will remove to a very high degree the sting of the diversion and temporary deportation, and make the passengers on the refugee boats less desperately keen to escape interception by British boats . . . Representatives of the Jewish Agency for Palestine should be invited on to boats intercepted at sea, and should further be invited, in the places of temporary refuge assigned to these illegal immigrants, to cooperate in looking after their welfare, vocational training, etc.[109]

This Zionist overture, like Weizmann's earlier offer, was spurned. One reason was a fear, expressed in Foreign Office minutes, that it would be impossible to take action against illegal immigrant ships on the high seas without even the pretext (a threadbare one in international law) of acting under the extra-territorial law of Palestine regarding illegal immigration.[110] But that was not the main reason. Lying behind the

[109] Memorandum dated 4 Dec. 1940 enclosed with Locker to G. H. Hall, 9 Dec. 1940, PRO FO 371/25242/435 ff. (W 12715/38/48). It is noteworthy that the letter accompanying this memorandum was signed by Locker, who had earlier opposed Weizmann's offer of such co-operation to the Government.

[110] Foreign Office minutes, 26 Dec. 1940–11 Jan. 1941, PRO FO 371/433/25242/433 (W 12715/38/48).

British refusal to consider such offers was the fear that acceptance would entail the reception of large numbers of Jewish refugees in some place other than Palestine. A telegram from the British Embassy in Bucharest in mid-December warned that a BBC broadcast in Roumanian had indeed 'been interpreted by local Jews to mean that they will all be immediately received [in] some British colony for duration of war'.[111] The primary British object was to prevent, not to stimulate, such an exodus: that was why the Jewish Agency proposal could not be contemplated.

The deportation of 1,580 out of the passengers on the *Atlantic* was a sordid affair. The High Commissioner described it as 'a carefully planned joint operation successfully carried out by the naval, military, and police personnel concerned'. But he continued: 'Certain initial resistance was dealt with by uniformed policemen calling in the military forces held in reserve.'[112] In fact, the deportation was accomplished only by repressing a considerable display of passive resistance by the refugees. On 9 December the Athlit camp was surrounded by military vehicles and troops, and police made a 'show of strength' (as the Inspector-General of Police described it) within the camp. The refugees had decided to resist by refusing to pack their few belongings and by refusing to dress: both males and females lay down naked on their beds and did not get up. Policemen, armed with sticks, entered the barracks in strength, belaboured some of the men with blows, and carried them naked on blankets to waiting lorries. Some were carried on stretchers. One Jewish eye-witness account stated:

They brought out over a hundred of the first batch of people, all of them wounded, completely naked . . . The remaining young people walked, quite naked, pushed from behind by the British police, until they reached the lorry, and they were then flung into it . . . One immigrant was pushed while he was naked and clasping a fiddle in his hand. . . Many of the old men fell on the ground and kissed it. They pleaded with tears before the police officers . . . to have pity on them, that they had already passed through Dachau and Buchenwald. And

[111] 'Decode of telegram', Bucharest to Foreign Office, n.d. Dec. 1940, PRO FO 371/25242/400 (W 12451/38/48).
[112] High Commissioner to Colonial Office, 10 Dec. 1940, PRO FO 371/25242/148 (W 12160/38/48).

the officers paid no heed to them . . . A British military officer turned very pale, and left the place in anger.[113]

Several other accounts by witnesses and by the victims themselves told similar stories. A report by the Inspector-General of Police, while denying the allegations of police brutality as being based on 'false testimony', admitted that there had been considerable resistance and that the operation had been a 'distasteful task'.[114]

The refugees, among whom were 621 women and 116 children, were taken to the port in Haifa. There their belongings were subjected to a customs examination, and 'tins, bottles, razor blades, cigarettes, knives, utensils and any other articles which looked suspicious' were confiscated and dumped in the sea. Other items, including cameras, which had been confiscated at an earlier stage, were sold, the proceeds being retained by the Government of Palestine. Subsequent claims for restitution by the refugees were met by a government refusal to admit liability. However, in mid-1944, when there appeared to be a threat of unfavourable publicity being given to the matter in the U.S.A., a Colonial Office official minuted: 'I think it might be best to "come clean" about it.'[115] An *'ex gratia'* payment of £3,000 (about eighteen per cent of the amount claimed) was made in April 1945.[116] But the loss of their property was not the worst that befell the refugees: some lost their lives. Typhoid had been diagnosed among the passengers on the *Atlantic* when the boat was towed into Limassol on the way to Palestine. Some infected refugees were allowed to stay in Palestine when the remainder of the passengers were deported. Sir Harold Mac-Michael was advised that there was no means of ascertaining whether any of the deportees was in the incubation stage of the disease until the fever occurred. The incubation stage of typhoid lasts between ten and twelve days. But the Government did not wait until it was clear that the disease had subsided. On the way to Mauritius an epidemic broke out

[113] 'Evidence of an eye-witness' (translated from Hebrew), PRO CO 733/445/76021/31.

[114] Inspector-General of Palestine Police to Chief Secretary, 18 Feb. 1941, PRO FO 371/29162 (W 4838/11/48).

[115] C. G. Eastwood minute, 27 June 1944, PRO CO 733/466/76021/30B.

[116] Zwergbaum, 'Exiles in Mauritius', p. 203.

aboard ship. It continued to rage after the arrival of the deportees on the island. Twenty-two died of typhoid, and a further
nineteen perished 'due to the privations suffered in the early
stages of the voyage'.[117] In Mauritius the deportees were held in
confinement in what were at first squalid conditions. A string of
protests by Jewish organizations, by the internees themselves,
by the Czechoslovak Government-in-exile (which objected that
many of its citizens were held in detention without having been
charged with any offence), and by the German Government
(which appears not to have realized that the internees were
Jewish) failed to move the British Government. A few were
released to join the Czech armed forces: the dependants of
those so released remained under detention. In 1945 the 1,310
surviving detainees were asked where they wanted to go:
eighty-one per cent chose Palestine. The perpetual exclusion
decree having at last been lifted, they finally returned to Haifa
in August 1945.[118]

The survivors of the *Atlantic* thus reached their destination
five years after the beginning of their odyssey: other refugee
voyages had a less happy ending. In December 1940, as the
Atlantic passengers awaited deportation in the Athlit camp, a
further illegal immigrant ship set out for Palestine from the
Bulgarian Black Sea port of Varna. This was the s.s. *Tzar Krum*,
which was renamed for the voyage *Salvador*; displacing 130
tons, the ship flew the Panamanian flag, and carried between 350
and 380 passengers. The ship was unseaworthy and was in-
adequately provided with life-saving apparatus. The passengers
included Bulgarian Jews, as well as Jewish refugees from central
European countries, who were being deported by the Bulgarian
authorities.[119] The passports of all the passengers were confiscated by the Bulgarian police before the ship left port, apparently with the intention of preventing their return to Bulgaria.
The British Ambassador in Sofia had protested in vain to the
Bulgarian Prime Minister against the departure of the ship.[120]

[117] Foreign office to Swiss Legation, 15 Aug. 1941, PRO CO 73/499/P5/1/63.

[118] Zwergbaum, 'Exiles in Mauritius', p. 255.

[119] Frederick B. Chary, *The Bulgarian Jews and the Final Solution 1940–1944*, Pittsburgh 1972, pp. 35–6.

[120] Rendel (Sofia) to Foreign Office, 6 Dec. 1940, PRO FO 371/25242/73 (W 11091/38/48); Rendel to Bogdan Filoff, 30 Nov. 1940, PRO FO 371/25242/422 (W 12674/38/48).

The British ambassadors in Athens and Ankara were instructed by the Foreign Office to take whatever action possible to prevent the passage of the ship through the Straits and the Aegean. To Ankara it was suggested that the Turks might be invited to 'take delaying action on sanitary grounds'.[121] But by the time the telegram reached Ankara it had been rendered superfluous.

The *Salvador* was wrecked in the Sea of Marmara on 12 December, and over two hundred of the passengers drowned. Among the dead were seventy children. The head of the Foreign Office Refugee Section, T. M. Snow, commented:

There could have been no more opportune disaster from the point of view of stopping this traffic.[122]

The callousness of the Bulgarian Government, it was generally agreed in the Foreign Office, was the primary cause of the disaster, and the Bulgarian Minister in London was summoned to an interview with the head of the Foreign Office, Sir Alexander Cadogan, who gave vent to his deep indignation at the Bulgarian 'connivance in the ship's departure'.[123]

The fate of the *Salvador* was widely publicized by the British Government in broadcasts to south-east Europe specifically in order to deter Jewish refugees from seeking to leave for Palestine.[124] By early 1941 the flow of illegal immigrants was diminishing; the news of the *Patria* and *Salvador* disasters probably deterred some Jews from attempting to escape from Europe by sea; but more important was the fact that by this time the German policy of encouraging the emigration of Jews was beginning to change; impediments to travel were further increased by the steady growth of German influence in Roumania and Bulgaria, which led Britain to break off relations with Bucharest in February and with Sofia in March. Yet the increasingly desperate position of the Jews in Europe still led some to grasp any means of escape. Hence the extraordinary story of the *Darien II*.

[121] Foreign Office to Knatchbull-Hugessen (Ankara), 14 Dec. 1940, PRO FO 371/25242/375 (W 12432/38/48).
[122] Snow minute, 17 Dec. 1940, PRO FO 371/25241/389 (W 12451/38/48).
[123] Foreign Office to British Embassy, Washington, 11 Feb. 1941, PRO FO 371/25242/432 (W 12674/38/48).
[124] Foreign Office note, Dec. 1940, PRO FO 371/25242/393 (W 12451/38/48).

This four-hundred-ton vessel had been purchased in Greece in the spring of 1940 by agents of the *Mossad Le-aliyah* (literally translated, 'institution for immigration'), the arm of the Jewish Agency which organized much of the illegal Jewish immigration to Palestine. The ship was sent to Roumania in the summer of 1940 to take on board a party of Jewish refugees. But meanwhile the *Haganah* sold the ship to the British security services in the area (with whom they had been co-operating in undercover intelligence and sabotage activities in the Balkans, most notably in an attempt to block the Danube to German oil supplies from Roumania). The central authorities of the *Haganah* ordered the *Mossad* to hand the *Darien II* over to the British security services for use in sabotage operations. However, although the *Mossad* was under the command of the *Haganah* chiefs, its representatives in Istanbul refused to comply with the order, arguing that the saving of refugees' lives must take precedence over any other consideration. A long quarrel ensued, in which Weizmann (who normally held aloof from such matters) intervened: in a letter to Moshe Shertok on 3 January 1941 Weizmann urged that the *Mossad* agents be induced to obey their orders to turn the ship over to the British. He warned that if the ship were used to transport illegal immigrants 'this would immediately be seized upon by hostile forces as an excuse for ordering a complete break-off of our relations with them' [British intelligence].[125] But even Weizmann's authority failed to persuade the *Mossad* agents to yield up the ship. On 19 February 1941 the boat left Constanza loaded with Jewish refugees; more were taken on at Varna and at Istanbul, until there was a total of eight hundred on board. Among the passengers were reported to be some of the survivors from the *Salvador* (whom the Palestine Government had refused to admit after the sinking of their ship).[126] As usual the British Ambassador in Turkey was instructed to ask the Turkish Government to bar passage through the Straits to the ship; however, the Turks refused. The *Darien II* reached Haifa on 18 March, and it was decided that the passengers should be sent to Mauritius in accordance with the policy laid down by the Cabinet after the

[125] Weizmann to Shertok, 3 Jan. 1941, WA.
[126] Namier (for Jewish Agency) to Lord Moyne, 24 Mar. 1941, PRO CO 733/445/76021/28.

Patria explosion. But the High Commissioner was advised by the British naval authorities that even if the *Darien II* were properly ballasted and supplied with life-saving apparatus she could take at most one hundred out of the eight hundred passengers on to Suez for further transport to Mauritius. After holding the passengers on the ship for a week, the High Commissioner reluctantly decided to allow them to land, since no alternative ship was available to take them to Mauritius. They were interned at Athlit to await deportation. Shipping difficulties, however, prevented the Government from implementing its policy. The refugees therefore remained in the internment camp until the summer of 1942 when they were released and allowed to remain in Palestine.[127]

The *Darien II* was the last major illegal immigrant vessel to run the gauntlet successfully during the early part of the war; paradoxically the illegal immigration organizers, whose involuntary contacts with the Gestapo had aroused so much suspicion in British official circles, thus achieved this final success partly as a result of their contacts with *British* security organs in the eastern Mediterranean. Between the spring of 1941 and mid-1944 the flow of illegal immigrants reaching Palestine virtually dried up, as the German grip on southeast Europe was tightened, and as German policy switched from extrusion to extermination. British officials, however, remained haunted throughout the war by the spectre of a resumption of a massive traffic in illegal immigrants, possibly under Gestapo auspices. In May 1941, in the wake of the pro-Nazi Rashid 'Ali Gailani coup in Iraq (in which the Mufti of Jerusalem played a prominent role), Colonial Office officials again considered drastic expedients to counter a potential 'flood of Jewish refugees by means of wholesale expulsions'. One measure which received serious consideration was a proposal that the policy, abandoned in 1939, of firing on illegal immigrant ships in order to drive them away from Palestinian ports should be revived. J. S. Bennett minuted: 'It is an ugly business having to fire at a ship load of "refugees". But the present serious state of the war in the Middle East justifies

[127] Dinur, *Sefer Toldot Ha-haganah*, vol. III, part 1, pp. 158–9; David Hacohen, *Et Lesaper*, Tel Aviv 1974, pp. 138 ff; Bauer, *From Diplomacy to Resistance*, pp. 116–8; High Commissioner, Jerusalem, to Colonial Office, 26 March 1941, PRO CO 733/446.

strong measures.' Sir John Shuckburgh concurred in the suggestion, although he pondered:

What is to happen to these wretched creatures when they are driven back into the open seas, it is rather difficult to imagine. They must go somewhere, but I can think of nobody who would be in the least likely to take them in. However, these are days in which we are brought up against realities and we cannot be deterred by the kind of pre-war humanitarianism that prevailed in 1939.[128]

It was not, however, found necessary to adopt such extreme solutions, for the official apprehensions of a renewed 'flood' of Jewish refugees proved to be premature. From mid-1941 the escape routes from south-east Europe to Palestine were effectively barred by the Germans and their allies to all save a handful of intrepid or fortunate refugees.

The British Government thus found itself superseded by the Germans from 1941 onwards as the major agency preventing Jewish escape from Europe to Palestine. During the early part of the war, when the German Government openly tried to dispatch large numbers of Jews beyond the borders of the Reich, every practicable tactic was employed by the British Government to prevent significant numbers of Jews reaching Palestine (or, indeed, anywhere else in the Empire, including, as will be seen, Britain itself). Only the restraining influences of Churchill, of American Jewish opinion, and of potential Jewish unrest in Palestine stopped the policy being enforced even more stringently. As the escape routes were sealed so too was the fate of the majority of the Jews imprisoned in Nazi Europe.

[128] Minutes by Bennett, 4 May, and Shuckburgh, 6 May 1941, PRO CO 733/449/P1/0/20.

3

The Home Front

IMMEDIATELY UPON the outbreak of the war the British Government took steps to halt immigration to Britain from Germany and German-occupied territories. All visas granted to enemy nationals prior to the outbreak of war automatically ceased to be valid at 11.00 a.m. on 3 September 1939. The Home Office noted that 'apart from the practical difficulties of making contact between the refugee in enemy territory and the refugee organizations in the United Kingdom which are likely to be almost insuperable, it would be necessary for us to proceed with the utmost caution having regard to the possibility that enemy agents might by this means be introduced into this country'. Certain exceptions were, however, made. Some refugees who were in possession of visas but had been unable to reach British ports before 3 September were nevertheless admitted to Britain. The Home Office declared itself willing to consider the possibility of admitting relatives of refugees already in Britain, as well as a limited number of refugees from Germany who had already reached neutral territory: 'transmigrants' who wished to proceed overseas via the United Kingdom might also enter for 'a very short period'.[1]

As a result of the implementation of this policy the numbers of Jewish refugees entering the country declined sharply. Until the summer of 1940 there remained some possibility of escape from German-occupied territory to Britain, but with the fall of France and the occupation of Norway, Denmark, and the Low Countries the movement of refugees dwindled to a trickle. A small number succeeded in reaching Britain by way of Sweden or the Iberian peninsula. Some Polish Jews arrived in units of the Polish Army stationed in Britain after 1940. No precise figure is available of the number of Jewish refugees admitted to

[1] E. N. Cooper (Home Office) to A. W. G. Randall (Foreign Office), 18 Sept. 1939, PRO FO 371/24100/120 ff. (W 13792/3231/48).

Britain during the war. It is certain, however, that the Jewish proportion of total immigration was much smaller in the war years than during the period 1933 to 1939. A reliable estimate is that the net increase in the Jewish refugee population of the country between 1939 and 1945 was no more than 10,000.[2]

With the outbreak of the war it became clear that the Jewish refugee organizations were no longer able to honour the commitment given to the Government in 1933 that all Jewish refugees would be maintained 'by the Jewish community without ultimate charge to the state'. That undertaking had been given on the basis of an estimate that the number of Jewish refugees coming to Britain 'might be as many as 3,000 to 4,000'.[3] By 1939 some 55,000 had arrived (about 50,000 from the expanded Reich, 5,000 from elsewhere) at a cost to the Jewish community of more than £3,000,000.[4] Even before the outbreak of war the refugee organizations had decided it would be necessary to halt the influx because of their severe shortage of funds.[5] After September 1939 the number of refugees requiring financial assistance greatly increased; by December 13,300 were being maintained by the voluntary organizations; among these were about 3,000 domestic servants who had lost their employment since the beginning of the war.[6] It was now impossible for the voluntary organizations to continue, and they therefore turned to the Government for help. The Home Office was at first reluctant to abandon the long-established principle of voluntary maintenance. The Cabinet Committee on

[2] *Report of the Anglo-American Committee of Inquiry regarding the problems of European Jewry and Palestine*, Cmd. 6808, London 1946, p. 59. The Anglo-American Committee's estimate was based on figures supplied by Jewish organizations in Britain (see Schiff to Brodetsky, 29 Jan. 1946, BD C2/2/5/4). There was substantial re-emigration of refugees from Britain during the war: the peak year was 1940 when over 6,000 left, mainly for the U.S.A.; in succeeding years the numbers of those leaving declined (Norman Bentwich, *They Found Refuge*, London 1956, pp. 115–16). In June 1944 the Foreign Office stated that 60,000 alien refugees had been admitted to the United Kingdom between May 1940 and December 1943 (memorandum dated 21 June 1944 submitted to Cabinet Committee on Refugees, PRO CAB 95/15/181 ff.). This figure did not include Allied forces in Britain.

[3] Memorandum by Home Secretary, 7 Apr. 1933, quoted in Sherman, *Island Refuge*, p. 30.

[4] Bentwich, *They Found Refuge*, p. 41; Sherman, *Island Refuge*, p. 271.

[5] Home Office memorandum, 20 Sept. 1939, PRO FO 371/24078/233 (W 14035/45/48).

[6] Memorandum by Home Secretary for Cabinet Committee on the Refugee Problem, n.d., Dec. 1939, PRO CAB 98/1/262.

Refugees, which considered the problem in December 1939, was informed that

the heads of the Jewish Organisation had been reminded of the appalling consequences which must follow if their Organisation collapsed and if some 13,000 Jewish refugees were left to be maintained out of public funds. It was inevitable that in such circumstances anti-Semitic tendencies in the country would be strengthened.[7]

Rather than allow the full cost of refugee maintenance to fall on public funds, the committee endorsed a proposal by the Home Secretary that the Government should henceforth pay half the cost of maintenance of destitute refugees, the remainder of the burden to be borne as before by the voluntary organizations. On this basis the Government granted £533,000 to the Central Council for Jewish Refugees in 1940.[8] A public appeal in early 1940 raised a further £380,000 for the Central British Fund for Jewish Relief and Rehabilitation.[9] In the course of the war, as refugee unemployment decreased, expenditure on refugee maintenance decreased. However, the Government share of the cost was increased: in 1941 the Government paid £264,000 out of a total expenditure by the Central Council of £302,000. By 1945 the Government was paying the entire cost of maintenance amounting in that year to some £140,000.[10]

Before the war the Government had decided that there should be no immediate general internment of aliens in Britain at the outbreak of hostilities. Aliens of enemy nationality would be subject to restrictions on their movement, and possession of arms, cameras, and motor vehicles would be prohibited. However, a sub-committee of the Committee of Imperial Defence on 'Control of Aliens in War' had reported on 1 April 1939 that although it was 'not proposed to undertake automatic internment of male enemy aliens immediately on an outbreak of war', the sub-committee nevertheless concurred 'in the Home Office view that some measure of general internment would become inevitable at a very early date'. The full Committee of Imperial

[7] Minutes of meeting of Cabinet Committee on the Refugee Problem, 8 Dec. 1939, PRO CAB 98/1/92 ff.

[8] Bentwich, *They Found Refuge*, p. 120.

[9] *Central British Fund for Jewish Relief and Rehabilitation Report for 1933–1943*, London 1944, p. 5.

[10] Bentwich, *They Found Refuge*, pp. 46 and 120.

Defence had accepted the sub-committee's report on 6 April, and had approved 'the action taken by the War Office in earmarking accommodation for 18,000 civilian internees'. Secret 'Administrative Instructions for Internment Camps' issued on 25 August 1939 had designated a number of sites for the proposed camps: among these were Northolt Park Racecourse, Butlin's holiday camps at Clacton and Dovercourt, and the Kitchener Camp at Richborough, Kent, which was already occupied by refugees. A telegram to the Dominions Governments on 31 August suggested that general internment of Germans in Britain might become necessary during a war 'in view of public opinion'. In the event of general internment it was proposed that refugees be segregated from other enemy aliens and interned under less severe conditions. Women would not normally be interned, and certain classes of aliens such as doctors and chemists would be exempt from detention provided they were known to be friendly to Britain.[11] Foreign Office minutes on the cable noted that difficulties might arise 'in distinguishing the sheep from the goats', and in explaining the policy to the American Government and public which might be expected to take an interest in the matter.[12]

On 4 September 1939 the Home Secretary, Sir John Anderson, announced to the House of Commons 'an immediate review of all Germans and Austrians in this country'. He outlined the procedure to be adopted:

I am asking a number of men with legal experience to assist me in this matter. These examiners will sit not only in London but in the provinces, and each of them will examine all cases in the district assigned to him with a view to considering which of these can properly be left at large and which should be interned or subjected to other restrictions. I am also arranging for a similar review by special tribunal of all Czecho-Slovaks.[13]

Confidential instructions issued by the Home Office to the

[11] Sub-committee report, 1 Apr. 1939, Home Office papers 144/21262 (700470/2); extract from minutes of Committee of Imperial Defence meeting, 6 Apr. 1939, ibid.; Secret 'Administrative Instructions for Internment Camps, 25 Aug. 1939, Home Office papers 144/21258 (700463/39); circular telegram from Dominions Office to Dominions Governments, 31 Aug. 1939, PRO FO 371/24100/112 ff. (W 12851/3231/48).

[12] Minutes by D. P. Reilly, 28 Aug., and F. R. Cowell, 29 Aug. 1939, PRO FO 371/24100/107 (W 12851/3231/48).

[13] HC, vol. 351, col. 367, 4 Sept. 1939.

one-man tribunals laid down that the proceedings were not to be held in public and that the aliens might not employ a barrister although they might bring a friend; the tribunals were not to be regarded as courts of law but as administrative bodies. Members of the tribunals were reminded:

Germans and Austrians in this country, being nationals of a state with which His Majesty is at war, are liable to be interned as 'enemy aliens', but most of the Germans and Austrians now here are refugees from the regime against which this country is fighting, and many of them are anxious to help the country which has given them asylum . . . It would therefore be wrong to treat all Germans and Austrians as though they were 'enemies'.[14]

The main task of the tribunals was to divide the enemy aliens into three categories: 'A' (to be interned); 'B' (exempt from internment but subject to restrictions); 'C' (exempt from internment and from restrictions).

The tribunals set to work immediately and carried out the reviews with dispatch. About a hundred tribunals were established (seven sat in the Richborough Camp alone), and by 28 October over 13,000 enemy aliens had been examined: of these only 186 were interned, while 3,189 were placed under restrictions, and 9,656 were exempt from internment and restrictions.[15] The operation was virtually completed by January 1940: by then a total of 528 aliens had been interned, and 8,356 subjected to restrictions, while the remainder (some 60,000) were left at liberty. In the anti-climatic atmosphere of the 'phoney war' these restrained measures seemed to reflect the public mood, and there was at first relatively little demand for the extension of internment to the large numbers of aliens in categories 'B' and 'C'.

However, the work of the tribunals aroused some criticism. This derived in large part from a secondary task assigned to them. In addition to deciding whether aliens were to be interned, restricted, or left at liberty, the tribunals were required to determine whether the aliens were friendly or hostile to Britain;

[14] 'Home Office Memorandum for the Guidance of Persons Appointed by the Secretary of State to Examine Cases of Germans and Austrians', n.d., Sept. 1939, ISA 2 D/38/41.
[15] Home Office memorandum, 20 Sept. 1939, PRO FO 371/24078/233 ff. (W 14035/45/48); *Jewish Chronicle*, 13 Oct. and 10 Nov. 1939.

a subsidiary division was accordingly made into 'refugee' and 'non-refugee' categories. A certain inconsistency soon became apparent in the findings of the tribunals, for a large number of those categorized as 'refugees' were interned or restricted, while the majority of those declared to be 'non-refugees' were placed in category 'C' and therefore freed.[16] This curious discrepancy led to expressions of disquiet from various quarters. A representative of M.I.5. told the Foreign Office

that the procedure of the tribunals which were deciding whether enemy aliens were or were not refugees from Nazi oppression was so diverse that their decisions could not be taken as in all cases reliable. In consequence, a number of people might be placed in the category of refugees who would elect to remain in this country but of whom M.I.5. would wish to get rid.[17]

On the other hand, the fact that some of those categorized as 'friendly enemy aliens' (as the jargon of the time had it) were restricted or interned led to complaints, particularly when it was discovered that fighting had broken out in camps between Nazis and Jews who (contrary to the original intention) had been interned together.[18]

In the spring of 1940 a change in the public mood was discerned. On 2 March Sir John Anderson, in a letter to his father, noted:

The newspapers are working up feeling about aliens. I shall have to do something about it, or we may be stampeded into an unnecessarily oppressive policy. It is very easy in wartime to start a scare.[19]

The end of the 'phoney war', with the invasion of Denmark and Norway in April 1940, and of the Low Countries and France in early May, produced a sudden intensification of anti-alien feeling in Britain. One pro-refugee activist, describing the heightened public animosity to aliens in mid-1940, wrote: 'The passing attitude may be described by reversing the Latin

[16] Home Office to Foreign Office, 20 Jan. 1940, PRO FO 369/2563/49 (K 2809/2757/701).

[17] Minute by F. M. Shepherd, giving account of telephone call from G. Liddell of M.I.5, 16 Nov. 1939, PRO FO 369/2549/323 (K 16963/14958/270).

[18] *Jewish Chronicle*, 22 Dec. 1939 and 12 April 1940.

[19] John W. Wheeler-Bennett, *John Anderson, Viscount Waverley*, London 1962, p. 239.

adage: "Nothing alien do I regard as human."[20] A Mass Observation survey at the end of April reported that anti-alien sentiment was pronounced among 'the middle and upper classes'; the report continued:

There is as yet no sign that the press campaign for internment has fully registered on the masses, but there is every sign that the situation is developing, and especially that it is becoming the socially done thing to be anti-refugee.

A common characteristic of anti-foreigner scares, the exaggeration of numbers, was noted by the same survey; in reply to the question, 'How many refugees do you think there are?', one man 'put the number at a couple of million, and another at four million'. The interviewers remarked that 'the tone of voice did not indicate that those persons were being facetious'.[21] Parliamentary opinion now began to echo the demands in the press for firmer action by the Government. Lieutenant-Colonel Acland-Troyte, Conservative M.P. for Tiverton, observed: 'You cannot trust any Boche at any time.'[22] Colonel Henry Burton, Conservative M.P. for Sudbury, suggested: 'Would it not be far better to intern all the lot and then pick out the good ones?'[23]

The alarming events in Europe in May and June, which created widespread apprehension of an imminent invasion of Britain, gave rise to an irresistible wave of anti-alien feeling, which bordered on mass hysteria, and to which the Government felt bound to respond. Even newspapers hitherto notable for their championing of the refugee cause now demanded mass internment: 'No half-measures will do!', declared the *Manchester Guardian*.[24] One of the first actions of the new government formed by Churchill on 11 May 1940 was to declare the establishment of a 'protected' area along the eastern and southern coasts, within which all male Germans and Austrians between the ages of sixteen and sixty were to be rounded up and interned.

[20] Norman Bentwich, 'England and the Aliens', *Political Quarterly*, XII, 1, Jan.–Mar. 1941, p. 90.
[21] Quoted in 'Judex', *Anderson's Prisoners*, London 1940, pp. 101–9.
[22] Ibid., p. 104.
[23] HC vol. 360, col. 33, 23 Apr. 1940.
[24] Quoted in Wheeler-Bennett, *Anderson*, p. 241.

The Government was spurred into further action by reports from the Netherlands suggesting that the swift German victory there was to be explained in large part by the subversive activities of a German 'fifth column' which had paved the way for the invading forces. The notion was given credibility by a memorandum on the 'Fifth Column Menace' written by the British Minister at the Hague, Sir Neville Bland, and circulated in Whitehall. Bland cited a number of hair-raising instances of fifth-column activity in the Netherlands, including that of 'a female German, recently in service in the Hague' who had been 'dropped by parachute with a party of men whom she was to guide to a certain house'. The memorandum warned that 'the paltriest kitchen-maid' with German connections 'not only can be, but generally is, a menace to the safety of the country'. In urgent tones Sir Neville pressed that the lesson of Holland be taken to heart:

Every German or Austrian servant, however superficially charming and devoted, is a real and grave menace, and we cannot conclude from the experiences of the last war that 'the enemy in our midst' is no more dangerous than it was then. I have not the least doubt that, when the signal is given, as it will scarcely fail to be when Hitler so decides, there will be satellites of the monster *all over the country* who will at once embark on widespread sabotage and attacks on civilians and the military indiscriminately. We cannot afford to take this risk. *All* Germans and Austrians, at least, ought to be interned at once.[25]

This memorandum created a widespread impression in official circles. Sir Robert Vansittart, Chief Diplomatic Adviser to the Foreign Office, criticized the Home Office for having interned only males: 'This is just silly. The females are often quite as dangerous; sometimes more dangerous. Experience in Holland showed that.'[26]

The reports from the Netherlands tallied with other information reaching the Foreign Office and the security services in early 1940. The British Consul-General in Zurich reported that a German contact had warned him 'that we must not trust too much the German Jewish refugees in England'. The German had said that 'in some cases the Gestapo still had a hold on these people through their relatives still in Germany and he cited

[25] Memorandum dated 14 May 1940, PRO FO 371/25189/462 (W 7984/7941/49).
[26] Minute dated 20 May 1940, PRO FO 371/25189/425 (W 7984/7941/49).

cases to prove his point'.[27] The British Embassy in Madrid informed the Foreign Office:

A head of a mission, who is on intimate terms with the German Embassy here, but is well disposed, told me that the Germans were jubilant over their successes and were now talking quite openly about the methods they had employed. It was evident that the new weapon was the fifth column and that the basis of the fifth column everywhere except in the Iberian peninsula was Jewish refugees from Germany and Austria. It seemed that they had been approached individually in Scandinavia and the Low Countries and told that if they would work for Germany they would be allowed to return after the war and their relatives would be released forthwith. Otherwise they would be put on the black list. The Minister said that he had noticed that 3,000 refugees had been detained in England but England would not be safe until the whole 80,000 had been placed in concentration camps.[28]

On 16 May the Joint Intelligence Committee urgently recommended that the limited internment measures applied to the coastal belt be extended to 'all enemy aliens, both male and female, between the ages of 16 and 70' throughout the country. They further urged that 'special measures should be taken for the control of non-enemy aliens'.[29] These recommendations were endorsed by the Chiefs of Staff. The Prime Minister, probably on the basis of information received from the security services, appears to have taken the fifth column threat seriously; Churchill was later to write in his memoirs: 'There were known to be twenty thousand organised German Nazis in England at this time.'[30] In the second half of May all category 'B' enemy aliens (hitherto restricted but not interned) throughout the country were interned. Women were included. *The Times* reported:

At one of the London receiving centres, there were young nuns, babies only a few weeks old, and boys and girls. One group of young women were fashionably dressed, and each had a fur coat. Several of the older women were in tears. All carried gas masks.[31]

[27] Memorandum by J. E. Bell, 6 Feb. 1940, PRO FO 371/24388/210 (C 2578/6/18).
[28] Yencken to Foreign Office, 21 May 1940, PRO FO 371/25189/421 (W 7958/7941/49).
[29] J.I.C. memorandum, 16 May 1940, PRO FO 371/25189/439 (W 7984/7941/49).
[30] Churchill, *Second World War*, I, p. 313.
[31] Quoted in 'Judex', *Anderson's Prisoners*, p. 7.

The Government was supported and stimulated to further action by an excited press and public opinion. The *Daily Herald* pronounced the 'country saved from fifth-column stab'.[32] In the *Sunday Chronicle*, on 26 May 1940, Beverley Nichols speculated on 'The Fifth Column: And What about the Spies Here?' Sir Neville Bland created a stir on 30 May with a wireless broadcast in which he repeated the substance of his secret memorandum on the fifth column menace.[33] A report by Mass Observation noted the change in public feeling:

The always latent antagonism to the alien and foreigner began to flare up. Nearly everyone, as previous research has shown, is latently somewhat anti-semitic and somewhat anti-alien. But ordinarily it is not the done thing to express such sentiments publicly. The news from Holland made it the done thing all of a sudden . . . Sir John Anderson's new restrictions on aliens corresponded with this feeling and were therefore widely welcomed.[34]

In late May, before the round-up of category 'B' Germans and Austrians was complete, and before the entry of Italy into the war, all Italians in Britain were interned. Explaining the latter development, the Chairman of the Joint Intelligence Committee wrote:

I have been told that the wholesale internment of Italians before that of the more dangerous Boches had been completed was due to the matter having been mentioned to the Prime Minister, who said 'Collar the lot', whereupon, somewhat in the same manner as the henchmen of King Henry II rushed to slaughter Thomas à Beckett, orders were given to M.I.5., the police etc., to arrest all Italians, with the result that restaurant keepers, some of whom had been here for 30 years and had fought for us in the last war, were cast into jail . . . whilst a large number of dubious Huns remained at large.[35]

The final stage was reached in June when it was decided to intern all 'C' category Germans and Austrian males. Within a few weeks some 30,000 persons were detained in makeshift camps in various parts of the country, most notably the Isle of Man.[36]

[32] Quoted in Wheeler-Bennett, *Anderson*, p. 241.

[33] F. Lafitte, *The Internment of Aliens*, London 1940, p. 173.

[34] Quoted in 'Judex', *Anderson's Prisoners*, p. 110.

[35] V. Cavendish-Bentinck minute, 29 July 1940, PRO FO 371/25248/366 (W 8972/7848/48).

[36] Bentwich, *They Found Refuge*, p. 117.

In the weeks of tension following the Dunkirk evacuations it is hardly surprising that the fifth column panic gained such wide currency and respectability. In fact, however, it was misconceived. There had been no appreciable subversive pro-German activity aiding the German advance into the Netherlands.[37] As for the danger of German agents operating in England it appears that the estimate of 20,000 supplied to Churchill was wildly exaggerated. The German espionage network in Britain in 1940 was small, rudimentary, and amateurish. Moreover it was soon penetrated by the British security services, and eventually run entirely under British control in the service of the British war effort as the famous 'double-cross system'.[38] No extensive plans for the employment of German refugees in underground activity in England seem to have been seriously contemplated by the German security agencies. The strong suspicions apparently entertained by the British counter-espionage service of the sympathies of German domestic servants in England were probably somewhat misplaced: the only such agent ever unearthed was a cook in Manchester. As for the Italians, Count Ciano wrote in his diary on 11 September 1940: 'It seems incredible, but we do not have a single informant in Great Britain.'[39]

The hasty mass internments of mid-1940 produced a number of bizarre episodes and not a few absurdities. Presumably acting on the 'known haunts' theory, a group of C.I.D. men walked into Hampstead Public Library at 1.30 p.m. on 13 July and asked all Germans and Austrians to leave with them. Internationally known anti-Nazi propagandists such as Franz Borkenau were interned.[40] The Hungarian editor of the popular weekly news magazine, *Picture Post*, Stefan Lorant, was deprived of his car and bicycle; he avoided further harassment only by emigrating to the U.S.A. But that option was open only to a few. The pianist duo, Rawicz and Landauer, who had lived in Britain since 1935, were interned. German socialist politicians, former inmates of concentration camps, an official of the Dutch Government, and a Norwegian general

[37] See Louis de Jong, *The German Fifth Column in the Second World War*, London 1956.
[38] See J. C. Masterman, *The Double-Cross System in the War of 1939–1945*, London 1972.
[39] Quoted in de Jong, *The German Fifth Column*, pp. 208–9.
[40] Lafitte, *The Internment of Aliens*, p. 76 ff.

were all arrested. Twenty German announcers and translators employed by the B.B.C. were arrested; those who remained behind were forbidden wireless sets. Galician Jews long resident in Britain were interned on the ground that Galicia had formed part of the Austrian Empire before 1918. In Tyneside a man was interned who had lived in Britain since the age of three.[41]

Although the great majority of those interned in the spring and summer of 1940 were Jewish refugees, the initial reaction of the established Anglo-Jewish community was somewhat muted. In an editorial on 17 May, the *Jewish Chronicle* expressed approval of the extension of internment, declaring that the argument in its favour could not 'be resisted, least of all at this juncture when the very life of the nation is at issue'. In its issue of 24 May, indeed, the *Jewish Chronicle* contributed to the 'fifth column' panic by publishing on its front page a report from its Amsterdam correspondent which stressed the supposed role of fifth columnists in the German conquest of the Netherlands and vehemently urged that 'the most rigorous steps' be taken against all refugees in Britain. The defensive reaction of the Anglo-Jewish community is reflected in a draft circular prepared by the Jewish refugee organizations in May 1940 for circulation to German Jewish refugees in England: the recipients were warned not to speak German in public, not to push in queues, and not to tell Englishmen that things were done better in Germany.[42] The Chairman of the Defence Committee of the Board of Deputies of British Jews expressed strong concern at what he described as 'the thoughtless behaviour of so many of them [the refugees] in areas where they are concentrated, namely Golders Green, Hampstead, North London etc.'.[43] Fear of anti-Semitism in areas of high refugee concentration probably lay behind the policy of dispersal of refugees which was pursued by the Jewish refugee organizations.[44]

[41] 'Judex', *Anderson's Prisoners*; Lafitte, *The Internment of Aliens*; J. G. Ward minute, 25 July 1940 and L. Collier minute 27 July 1940, PRO FO 371/25248/365 ff. (W 8972/7848/48); memoranda on internment of long-resident aliens, BD C2/3/5/40/5; *Jewish Chronicle*, 18 Oct. 1940.

[42] BD C2/3/3/10/2. A similar circular entitled 'Helpful Information and Guidance for Every Refugee' had been issued in January 1939 by the German Jewish Aid Committee and the Board of Deputies of British Jews (Sherman, *Island Refuge*, pp. 218–19).

[43] M. Gordon Liverman to A. G. Brotman, 14 May 1940, BD C2/3/3/10/2.

[44] See Secretary, Jewish War Refugees Committee to Mrs Davis of London E.1., 25

The nervousness of the Jewish community reflected a common opinion that anti-Semitic feeling in Britain was increasing at this time. There were allegations that the resignation in January 1940 of Leslie Hore-Belisha, the Jewish Secretary of State for War, had been produced in part by anti-Semitic prejudice against him; the Foreign Secretary, Halifax, expressed the view that the fact that Hore-Belisha was a Jew rendered him unsuitable for appointment as Minister of Information. The Permanent Under-Secretary at the Foreign Office, Sir Alexander Cadogan, was of the opinion 'that Jew control of our propaganda would be [a] major disaster'.[45] Numerous complaints were voiced about alleged anti-Semitic outbursts in Polish Army camps in Britain.[46] A Foreign Office official commented that 'it seems quite on the cards that anti-semitism is in fact fairly rife in the Polish army' although allowance must be made for what was termed 'mess-room exuberance'.[47] Another official remarked: 'I shouldn't be much surprised if there was a good bit of anti-Semitism in the British army.'[48] In April 1940 there was some discussion in the Foreign Office about priorities for Jewish immigration to Palestine. One official suggested that immigrants from Holland and Belgium should have priority on the ground that

our policy of cancelling visas upon the outbreak of war has left Holland at least saddled with a number of refugees who morally belong to us but whom the Home Office for one reason or another very comprehensibly refuses to admit. The admission of a few thousand of the unassimilable and otherwise unemigrable Jewish refugees from the Low Countries to Palestine would make a very great difference to anti-Semitism in those countries and would accordingly be a considerable setback to the development of the local Nazi parties—a development full of danger for us.

June 1940, thanking her for her offer of accommodation for two refugees but declining it 'owing to the fact that refugees are not permitted to be billeted in the East End' (BD B4/ROS 9).

[45] Austin Stevens, *The Dispossessed*, London 1975, pp. 247–9; A. J. P. Taylor, *English History 1914–1945*, p. 460; *Cadogan Diaries*, pp. 241–2 (entry dated 1 Jan. 1940).

[46] D. N. Pritt M.P. to R. A. Butler, 2 April 1940, PRO FO 371/24481/40 (C 5143/5143/55); *Jewish Chronicle*, 26 July and 16 Aug. 1940.

[47] R. M. Makins (Foreign Office) to Colonel Gubbins (War Office), 13 Apr. 1940, PRO FO 371/24481/43 (C 5143/5143/55).

[48] Minute dated 11 Apr. 1940, PRO FO 371/24481/38 (C 5143/5143/55).

However, another official disagreed because

I am inclined to think that the danger of anti-Semitism in this country is as great as in Holland and Belgium. The hatred of the Jews amongst the middle and lower strata of London's population has increased greatly since the influx of German Jewish refugees. I think that the U.K. should take first place in the order of preference.[49]

Government sensitivity to the danger of anti-alien feeling in Britain was similarly reflected in remarks by Osbert Peake, a junior Home Office minister, who told a deputation from the Parliamentary Committee for Refugees that mass internment was necessary because, if German bombing raids occurred, 'the anger of the local population might be vented on the innocent heads of these aliens, who would inevitably be accused of showing a light or some other offence'.[50] That this fear was not altogether idle is demonstrated by a complaint by Alderman F. W. Dean of the London County Council:

We are told to avoid careless talk, yet there is very useful information to be obtained in the Civil Defence services where aliens are employed. Moreover, the idea of Germans taking charge of Britons in an air raid is grotesque, particularly as it is ten chances to one that the man dropping bombs is his cousin or some relative. Can you imagine a Briton being allowed to take part in Berlin's civil defence measures? These people are nationals of an enemy country, however much they may dislike the government now in power, and deep down they must have a love of their native land.[51]

Although there appears to have been general public support for the mass internment of enemy aliens (a Mass Observation survey in early July reported that 55 per cent of those questioned approved of the internment of all enemy aliens, while 27 per cent favoured interning only those regarded as dangerous),[52] there were some critical voices. The Archbishop of Canterbury, the Warden of Toynbee Hall, Professor Gilbert Murray, and other notables protested against the policy of

[49] Minutes by R. T. E. Latham, 4 Apr. 1940, and by J. E. M. Carvell, 8 Apr. 1940, PRO FO 371/25240/1 ff. (W 2812/38/48).

[50] Note on interview of Osbert Peake M.P., Parliamentary Under-Secretary at Home Office, with deputation from Parliamentary Committee for Refugees, 24 June 1940, BD C2/3/3/10/2.

[51] *Jewish Chronicle*, 10 May 1940.

[52] 'Judex', *Anderson's Prisoners*, p. 111.

wholesale internment. Murray condemned what he termed the 'public hysteria' over the issue:

This is the reaction of the average ignorant and unthinking man, who can see no difference between one German and another, or, if it comes to that, 'between one foreigner and another'. Oppressor and victim, Fascist and anti-Fascist, are all the same to him . . . Let our rulers listen to every word which comes from Scotland Yard or the responsible Intelligence Services . . . but I tremble for any democracy which yields either to party faction or to mob hysteria.[53]

Such views were not limited to unofficial, liberal 'do-gooders'. R. T. E. Latham, a barrister, and fellow of All Souls, who was serving as a temporary clerk in the Refugee Section of the General Department of the Foreign Office, roundly condemned the 'pathetic policy of interning all male enemy aliens', which he argued had been adopted by the Home Office under pressure from the military and security services. In a minute urging the establishment of an advisory committee on the problem (with both official and non-official members) Latham wrote:

M.I.5., the department of the security service charged with the examination of the loyalty of individuals to the Allied cause . . . is under the stress of recent currents in public opinion, and, under the influence of high authority in the War Office, has adopted the rule of thumb that any person of foreign nationality is to be presumed (almost, it would seem, irrebuttably presumed) to be hostile . . . Under the influence of propaganda by the actual Fifth Column designed to convince the public and the military authorities that the real Fifth Column consists not of themselves but of refugees from Nazi oppression, the Home Office machinery for classifying persons of enemy nationality into categories according as they were friendly, doubtful, or hostile to the Allied cause has, *de facto* though not *de jure*, broken down. The machinery was in fact faulty from the start.[54]

The proposal for the creation of new machinery for dealing with the alien problem evoked considerable support, and at the end of July the War Cabinet decided to establish a small advisory committee and a larger Advisory Council to assist the Government in dealing with the aliens problem.[55]

[53] Ibid., p. 112; Stevens, *The Dispossessed*, p. 189; *Jewish Chronicle* 8 July 1940.

[54] Latham minute, 27 June 1940, PRO FO 371/25253/140 (W 8686/8686/48).

[55] Extract from War Cabinet Conclusions, 22 July 1940, PRO FO 371/25248/411 (W 9808/G).

Criticism of the Government's policy towards enemy aliens gathered force in the course of the summer as the Government decided to go beyond mass internment and enforce large-scale deportation of aliens. In a minute to the Cabinet Secretary on 3 June, Churchill wrote:

Has anything been done about shipping 20,000 internees to Newfoundland or St Helena? Is this one of the matters that the Lord President has in hand? If so, would you please ask him about it. I should like to get them on the high seas as soon as possible, but I suppose considerable arrangements have to be made at the other end. Is it all going forward?[56]

Churchill told the House of Commons the next day:

I know there are a great many people affected by the orders which we have made who are the passionate enemies of Nazi Germany. I am very sorry for them, but we cannot, at the present time, and under the present stress, draw all the distinctions which we should like to do.[57]

As a result of the deportation order, some eight thousand aliens were sent overseas, mainly to Canada and Australia. The deportations produced a host of difficulties, and some minor scandals which soon led to the abandonment of the entire enterprise. 2,400 aliens who were transported to Australia on the troopship *Dunera* were robbed and maltreated by soldiers on board. The commanding officer and two N.C.O.s were court-martialed for these offences and severely disciplined, and compensation was paid by the British Government to the victims, but the incident provoked public disquiet.[58] When 1,714 aliens (mainly in the 'B' and 'C' categories) arrived in Quebec aboard the *Ettrick* in July 1940, they were searched by British and Canadian soldiers, and a great part of their baggage was stolen.[59] There were complaints from both Canada and Australia that Nazis and anti-Nazis were being housed in camps together, and that there had been trouble between the two groups.[60] Considerable offence was given by an order

[56] Churchill, *Second World War*, III, p. 561.

[57] HC vol. 361, col. 794, 4 June 1940.

[58] War Office to Foreign Office, 31 July 1941, PRO FO 916/90/19; *Jewish Chronicle* 28 Feb. 1941; K. G. Loewald, 'A *Dunera* Internee at Hay, 1940–1941', *Historical Studies*, XVII, 69, Oct. 1977.

[59] Report on civilian internees sent from U.K. to Canada in 1940, July 1941, Home Office papers, 45/23515 (GEN 200/117/163).

[60] *Jewish Chronicle* 22 Nov. 1940 and 28 Feb. 1941.

issued by the office of Internment Operations in Canada that orthodox Jews in the internment camps there must work on Saturdays; in reply to complaints from Jewish organizations, the Director of Internment Operations wrote that he suspected that many of the internees were 'using their Sabbatarian principles as a means of avoiding work'. The order was withdrawn, but the incident provoked further unfavourable publicity.[61]

In response to such criticisms the British Government dispatched H.M. Commissioner of Prisons, Alexander Paterson, to Canada in November 1940 to investigate the circumstances of the deportation and internment of aliens there. Paterson remained in Canada until the summer of 1941: his report, presented to the Home Secretary in July 1941, substantiated many of the internees' complaints. Most of the internees sent to Canada turned out to be Jewish refugees rather than Nazi agents. The internees were subjected to anti-Semitic insults and petty persecution by their guards until, at the behest of Paterson, an order was issued forbidding such behaviour. The Director of Internment Operations was reported by Paterson to be thoroughly unsympathetic towards the internees: 'He disliked, despised, and distrusted them. They were just a lot of "sick headaches" to him, and, during the war, any time spent on them was a waste.' In meetings with Paterson, the Director was apt to indulge 'in a tirade against refugees, Jews, and voluntary agencies'. As a result of Paterson's recommendations, the conditions of internment in Canada were eased, and some refugees were permitted to return to Britain: by June 1941, 891 had already returned from Canada.[62] Eugen Spier, a German Jew resident in Britain since 1922, who had been interned in 1939 and deported to Canada in 1940, was one of those permitted to return to Britain in the summer of 1941 as a result of Paterson's visit to Canada. In his memoirs Spier recorded his bemusement, upon his arrival in London after having travelled 5,300 miles to and fro across the Atlantic at the Government's expense, to find himself confronted with a

[61] Director of Internment Operations, Department of State, Canada, to Saul Hayes, Executive Director, United Jewish Refugee and War Relief Agencies, 8 Feb. 1941, BD C2/3/5/50/5; *Jewish Chronicle* 31 Jan., 7 Feb., 7 Mar. 1941.

[62] Report on civilian internees sent from U.K. to Canada in 1940, July 1941, Home Office papers 45/23515 (GEN 200/117/163).

Ministry of Information hoarding which inquired: 'Is Your Journey Really Necessary?'[63] A Home Office minute on Paterson's report commented: 'In one sense it is a pity that the report is written in such an enjoyably racy style. It can never be published!'[64] The Home Secretary, Herbert Morrison, noted: 'With reluctance I agree that we cannot publish at this stage Mr Paterson's brilliant report. It is a great human document and really a great State Paper also.'[65]

Apart from the deportations to the Dominions, the Government wished to encourage aliens to proceed under their own steam to the U.S.A. Several thousand who were able to satisfy American immigration regulations did so, but further large-scale movement to the U.S.A. was rendered difficult by an American insistence that the aliens be provided with a guarantee by the British Government that they would be permitted to return to Britain not later than six months after the end of the war. This condition led to a wrangle between the Home Office and the security services. The Home Office was anxious to promote the departure of as large a number of aliens as possible. But M.I.5. objected to a return visa being issued to such emigrants, and the fear was expressed that such a procedure 'might open a channel for instructing agents who, after a short visit to the United States, would return to this country'.[66] Failure to resolve this difficulty prevented much progress being made in alien emigration to the U.S.A.

The turning-point in public attitudes to the aliens problem, and in government policy, came in July 1940 as a result of the *Arandora Star* disaster. This Blue Star liner had been placed at the disposal of the War Office for the transportation of enemy aliens to Canada. The ship sailed on 30 June; on board were 473 Germans and 717 Italians who had been hastily selected for deportation by the security authorities. At 6.00 a.m. on 2 July the ship was struck by a torpedo fired by a German submarine

[63] Eugen Spier, *The Protecting Power*, London 1951, p. 251.

[64] Minute by F. A. Newsam dated 21 Aug. 1941, Home Office papers 45/23515 (GEN 200/117/163).

[65] Minute by Morrison, 4 Sept. 1941, ibid.

[66] Minutes of meetings of Overseas Travel Committee, 28 Oct. 1940, PRO FO 371/25253/57 (W 11716/8261/48); sim., 29 Nov. 1940, PRO FO 371/25252/198 (W 10429/8261/48); Lothian (Washington) to Foreign Office, 11 Sept. 1940, PRO FO 371/25252/192 (W 10429/8261/48).

and sank off the west coast of Ireland. Of the passengers 146 Germans and 453 Italians were drowned. The disaster provoked outspoken criticism of the Government's internment policy. It was widely alleged that a number of the victims had not been Nazi or Fascist sympathizers but refugees mistakenly selected for deportation. Statements by the Minister of Shipping and the Secretary of State for War that all the Germans on board had been category 'A' internees failed to dispel the criticism. Under pressure it was admitted by the Government that 53 of the 'A' category passengers had claimed to be refugees, and the Government's critics argued that in several cases the victims had wrongly been placed in the 'A' category.[67] Among the cases cited was that of a Jewish refugee, one Mr Bloch, aged forty, unmarried, a former concentration camp inmate. After imprisonment and torture by Spanish fascists in Spanish North Africa, Bloch had settled at Lagos, whence he had been deported to Britain with Nazis from West Africa at the outbreak of the war. Classified 'A' he was sent to the internment camp at Paignton, where he was selected for inclusion on the *Arandora Star* deportation list.[68] Allegations that a number of genuine refugees had met their deaths in the disaster led the Government to establish a judicial inquiry under Lord Snell. The inquiry concluded that all the Germans and Austrians on board the ship had been 'persons who could properly be regarded as coming within category "A"', and Lord Snell therefore 'saw no reason to question the decision that they be deported'. In the case of the Italians, however, he concluded that there had probably been about a dozen errors by the security authorities.[69] Although the findings of the report broadly vindicated the Government, the report had little effect on public opinion because it was not published until December 1940 (and then in a somewhat truncated form). By then public and official opinion had turned irreversibly against both deportation and mass internment.

In the Jewish community doubts about the policy had begun to surface before the disaster. The first hint of criticism in the

[67] Lafitte, *The Internment of Aliens*, pp. 123–43; 'Judex', *Anderson's Prisoners*, pp. 82–3.

[68] 'The Internment Policy: Statement of Facts', unsigned memorandum, 19 Aug. 1940, BD C2/3/5/40/5.

[69] *Summary of the Arandora Star Inquiry*, Cmd. 6238, London 1940.

Jewish Chronicle was to be detected in the issue of 31 May. By 21 June the paper was arguing:

No one, indeed, quarrels with steps that have been taken to ensure the safety of the country against the possible machinations of any ill-disposed among them, however few. But such steps cannot be the last word on the matter of a humane country like this. Internment is, at best, an irksome and wearing, if not sometimes demoralising experience.

On 19 July the paper condemned the 'cruel, indiscriminate, and wasteful round-ups of men whose *bona fides* had been scrutinised again and again and who had always been vindicated'. Later issues spoke of '"Gestapo" methods in Britain' and of 'a spirit of ugly treachery in certain quarters, treachery which rejoices as much in inflicting misery upon Hitler's refugee enemies as in damaging the interests of this country'.[70] Nathan Laski, a leading Manchester Jew, who had been a prominent supporter of Churchill in his successful campaign for election as Liberal M.P. for North-West Manchester in 1905–6 (when Churchill put up spirited opposition to the Aliens Bill directed primarily against the immigration of Russian Jews), wrote to the Prime Minister in early August drawing attention to the harm that the internment policy was causing to Britain's reputation in the U.S.A., and protesting against 'the tragedies that the War Office and the Home Office have brought about to inoffensive and loyal people'.[71] The refugees themselves voiced fearful objections; one group in the 'Central Promenade Camp' at Douglas on the Isle of Man expressed their 'great alarm' at 'the prospect of being packed away like cattle and sent to another continent and the frightful aspect of becoming completely segregated from our wives and children'.[72] A letter to H. W. Butcher M.P. (Secretary of the Parliamentary Committee on Refugees), written by a woman refugee, and forwarded to the Foreign Office, produced what was for a communication of this sort an unusual impact on Foreign Office opinion. In the letter, Mrs Theresa Steuer wrote:

[70] *Jewish Chronicle*, 2 Aug. and 26 July 1940.
[71] N. Laski to Churchill, 9 Aug. 1940, BD C2/3/3/10/2. On Laski, Churchill, and the 1906 election, see Randolph S. Churchill, *Winston S. Churchill*, II, London 1967, p. 81 ff.
[72] H. A. Goodman to Board of Deputies of British Jews, 25 June 1940, enclosing refugees' protest, BD C2/3/5/20/5.

Out of the chaos of Nazi Austria, my husband and I saved only each other. Country, home, family, friends, career, books, income, everything was lost, but my husband and I clung to each other resolutely, through grave dangers, and together finally reached this country and refuge . . . We refugee wives were proud and satisfied when our men volunteered for admission into the army. These applications were rejected . . . On June 25th, my husband, an Austrian of Polish birth and parentage, was arrested. I have heard nothing of him since, have still, after two long weeks, no idea where he is. All I definitely know is that German and Austrian internees of category "C" were drowned in the Atlantic.[73]

After the *Arandora Star* catastrophe there was a marked reversal in public opinion on the aliens question. In the House of Lords the Bishop of Chichester and Viscount Cecil were among those who condemned the policy of wholesale internment,[74] Lord Newton denounced it as a 'huge and stupid mistake'.[75] The *Evening Standard*, in a leader headed 'SHAME', declared:

We are locking up our friends, some who are skilled, all who are ready to work . . . It is worse than folly. It is sabotage against the war effort. It is a damnable crime against the good name of England.[76]

H. G. Wells, in an article in the *Reynolds News*, went even further:

This is not a case of administrative stupidity; that is my point; it is a case of 'doing Goebbels's work', of enemy activity entrenched in our midst . . . While these pro-Nazi officials remain at their posts, Britain will be fighting with one arm tied behind her back . . . I myself think they ought to be shot or hung out of hand, but maybe I am taking this war too seriously.[77]

By the first week in August a Mass Observation survey concluded that only one third of those interviewed now felt that all aliens should be interned (as against 55 per cent who had held this view a month earlier).[78]

The change in opinion was by no means universal. In the

[73] Mrs Theresa Steuer to H. W. Butcher M.P., 8 July 1940, PRO FO 371/25248/331 (W 8962/7848/48).
[74] HL vol. 116, cols. 875–80, 10 July 1940; vol. 117, cols. 120–7, 6 Aug. 1940.
[75] Quoted in *Jewish Chronicle*, 12 July 1940.
[76] Quoted in *Jewish Chronicle*, 26 July 1940.
[77] Quoted in *Jewish Chronicle*, 2 Aug. 1940.
[78] 'Judex', *Anderson's Prisoners*, p. 112.

House of Lords the Duke of Devonshire justified the deportations as 'desirable both to husband our resources of food and to get rid of useless mouths and so forth'.[79] Everard Gates, Conservative M.P. for Middleton and Prestwich, in a memorandum on internment, argued that it would be too costly to investigate aliens' cases individually. He added that he had 'gained the impression that the majority of my correspondents, in pleading the cause of a friend, acquaintance, or employee, have allowed their kind hearts to run away with them . . . We are a waywardly sentimental people.'[80] K. W. M. Pickthorn, Conservative M.P. for Cambridge University, announced: 'If an archangel appeared before all the members of the War Cabinet at once and said, "There is one red-headed man in England who, unless care is taken, will do something to injure the State", I think it would be the duty of the War Cabinet to see that all red-headed men were interned.'[81] Notwithstanding such picturesque arguments, the tide of anti-alien sentiment receded in the course of the summer and autumn as the invasion threat appeared less imminent and the 'fifth column' danger more remote.

The new mood in the press, Parliament, and the general public was reflected in official and ministerial circles. In the Foreign Office, in particular, vehement criticism was expressed of the security services and the Home Office over the issue. On the orders of the Parliamentary Under-Secretary, R. A. Butler, an 'indictment' was prepared of the departments responsible for mass internment and deportations.[82] The memorandum, prepared by R. T. E. Latham, constituted a chapter-and-verse philippic directed against M.I.5. and the Home Office. Latham argued that the mass internment policy had induced among German and Austrian refugees in Britain a 'loss of faith in all values, worse in its way than the demoralisation caused by German concentration camps, with which I am acquainted'. He added that the policy meant that the Government had 'quite gratuitously (a) harried the nationals of our Allies, the

[79] HL vol. 117, col. 137, 6 Aug. 1940.

[80] Undated memorandum, *c.* Aug. 1940, BD C2/3/3/10/2.

[81] Quoted in Maximilian Koessler, 'Enemy Alien Internment with Special Reference to Great Britain and France', *Political Science Quarterly*, LVII, 1, March 1942, p. 107.

[82] R. A. Butler minute, 12 July 1940, and R. T. E. Latham minutes, 10 and 16 July 1940, PRO FO 371/25248/330 ff. (W 8962/7848/48).

Belgians, the Dutch and the Norwegians, thereby severely trying their allegiance, and (b) rubbed up the Americans the wrong way, and given actual offence to the Japanese, Hungarians, and Swiss'. The 'scandalous' administration of the internment camps, and the 'almost criminally haphazard and unthinking' selection of deportees, Latham continued, had 'provided the Germans with a fine line of propaganda ("The Liberals and the Jews are the enemies of every nation: even the English have to put the Jews into concentration camps") for consumption at home and in Central Europe which is unanswerable as propaganda and almost unanswerable in reasoned discourse.' The most damning of Latham's strictures were reserved for M.I.5. whom he accused of lack of experience, lack of political judgement, stupidity, and poor organization. As a consequence of M.I.5.'s 'incompetence and meddling', he asserted, the Home Office had been 'placed in the anomalous and humiliating position of having to administer and to acknowledge as its own a policy which it did not desire, and details of which it did not frame . . . Inefficient administration by the Home Office is a natural consequence of this situation.' Latham urged that the Foreign Office should consider

what effect it will have on (a) neutral judgement of our present claim to represent the cause of oppressed peoples throughout Europe, and (b) our ultimate attempts to raise revolt in German-occupied territories, if we appear to be permanently unable or unwilling to discriminate between our friends and our enemies among the people from German-occupied countries and from neutral states who are in our midst.[83]

Latham's indictment aroused general support in the Foreign Office. J. G. Ward declared the affair 'a terrible page in the administration of this country' and expressed the view that 'the fatal step was putting "MI5" under military control, which meant giving it as chiefs long-retired army officers regarding whose capacities the less said the better'.[84] The Chairman of the Joint Intelligence Committee, V. Cavendish-Bentinck, attempted a partial rebuttal of Latham's charges. He declared himself 'not ashamed, but extremely glad, that the J.I.C. took

[83] Memorandum on 'Aliens Policy' by R. T. E. Latham, 19 July 1940, PRO FO 371/25248/369 ff. (W 8972/7848/48).

[84] Minute dated 25 July 1940, PRO FO 371/25248/365 (W 8972/7848/48).

part in pushing the Home Office into a policy of ordinary prudence and common sense'. He admitted that M.I.5. had its faults, but argued that this was because it had been starved of funds for years, whereas 'the Gestapo has reached its present admirable pitch of efficiency as a result of 7 years' work'. He stressed that the trigger for the mass internment policy had been 'the invasion of Holland, when we had seen the Fifth Column really working efficiently'.[85] This evoked a savage riposte from Latham alluding to the 'dunderheaded attitude of "the military"' and 'incompetence in M.I.5 as the cause of our recent crude, cruel, and foolish treatment of every kind of alien'.[86]

The sudden shift in public and official attitudes led to a swift reversal of policy. Deportations of aliens to the Dominions diminished to a trickle after the *Arandora Star* episode, and by 1941 the flow of traffic was reversed, as some of the deportees were permitted to return to Britain. By September 1941 it was reported that about 900 of the deportees sent to Canada had already returned, and many of those remaining were anxious to return and prevented from doing so only by lack of shipping space.[87] Conditions in the internment camps in Britain (and in the Dominions) gradually improved as the improvised confusion of the summer of 1940 gave way to more ordered procedures. Complaints of friction between Nazis and anti-Nazis in the camps died away by early 1941.[88] Some of the more rigorous restrictions on the inmates were removed: they were permitted to listen to the wireless;[89] the procedure under which internees were made to sign a declaration binding themselves not to reveal any details of conditions in the camps was dropped after publicity was given to the matter in the *News Chronicle*;[90] restrictions on access to newspapers and books were eased after having been subjected to some ridicule when it was revealed that the forbidden literature included such publications as *The*

[85] Minute dated 29 July 1940, PRO FO 371/25248/366 (W 8972/7848/48).

[86] Minute dated 1 Aug. 1940, PRO FO 371/25248/367 (W 8972/7848/48).

[87] Minutes of meetings of Aliens Committee of Board of Deputies of British Jews, 12 Feb. and 2 Sept. 1941, BD C2/1/6.

[88] *Jewish Chronicle*, 22 Nov. 1940 (on such friction in an Australian camp), 28 Feb. 1941 (on similar trouble in a camp in Canada), 10 and 24 Jan., 28 Feb., and 7 March 1941 (on trouble in the internment camp at Huyton).

[89] *Jewish Chronicle*, 31 Jan. 1941.

[90] 'Argus', 'Friendly Enemy Aliens', *Contemporary Review*, Jan. 1941, p. 58.

Times, the *Jewish Chronicle*, the *New Statesman*, and, most remarkably, the *Oxford Book of English Verse*. (It was alleged in the House of Commons that the latter work had been confiscated from an internee on the ground that it was 'unsuitable'.)[91] Action was taken against the Commandant of the Bromley (Kent) internment camp, who was found guilty of theft of internees' property, including Italian, Swiss, Turkish, and South African banknotes and coins, as well as a hundred gold sovereigns, a typewriter, and 1,040 safety razor blades.[92] On the Isle of Man (where the largest concentration of internment camps was situated) there was some apparent hostility between internees and the local population. Rev. John Duffield, a vicar on the island, found it necessary to reprove some of his parishioners who, it was said, regarded his activities on behalf of the internees as tantamount to hobnobbing with the enemy.[93] The local newspapers were accused of unfriendliness towards the internees when they published reports that relatives of those interned—German Jewesses—were taking up aeroplane places which might otherwise have been used by other travellers.[94] However, as the number of aliens interned diminished such reports too died away.

The turn-about in government policy was so rapid that less than a month after the order had been issued for the wholesale internment of all category 'C' males, the Home Secretary announced that he was considering the release of certain classes of internees. A White Paper issued at the end of July specified these classes: they included 'persons under 16 and over 70 years of age'; 'the invalid or infirm'; 'persons who occupied key positions in industries engaged in work of national importance'; 'scientists, research workers and persons of academic distinction for whom work of national importance in their special fields is available'; 'Doctors of Medicine and dentists'; 'internees who are accepted for enlistment in the Auxiliary

[91] Lafitte, *The Internment of Aliens*, p. 108; *Jewish Chronicle* 21 June 1940; 'Judex', *Anderson's Prisoners*, p. 76.

[92] *Jewish Chronicle* 4 April 1941; 'note of deputation from the Refugee Joint Consultative Committee received by Mr Osbert Peake M.P.', 11 Aug. 1941, Home Office papers 45/23514 (GEN 29/3/438).

[93] *Jewish Chronicle* 22 Aug. 1941.

[94] Memorandum referring to reports in the *Isle of Man Daily Times* 17 Oct. 1941, and the *Isle of Man Examiner* 17 Oct. 1941, BD C2/3/5/50/5. See also 'Report on visit to Isle of Man Internment Camps', n.d., *c*. Nov. 1940, BD C2/3/5/20/5.

Military Pioneer Corps'; 'persons about to embark for emigration overseas'; and 'special cases of extreme hardship, e.g. where a parent, wife or child is dangerously ill'. The White Paper laid down that release of persons within any of these classes might be refused on security grounds.[95] Although the White Paper represented something of a retreat by the Government, it aroused criticism from opponents of the Government's policy. The *Manchester Guardian* pointed out that 'two thirds of the White Paper . . . simply said that the Government was prepared to release individuals who, according to their instructions ought never to have been arrested'.[96]

Under some public pressure the Government gradually widened the categories of internees eligible for release. A meeting of the Aliens Advisory Committee in November 1940 was informed that

the Home Office in common with the other Departments had given further consideration to this matter, particularly in the light of the views of G.H.Q. that all coastal areas were now equally vulnerable to invasion. In addition, weight must be given to the criticisms directed against the restrictions on aliens in a recent debate in the House. It appeared to the Home Office important to arrive at some logical policy which could be explained and defended in simple terms.

Accordingly, the committee recommended the release of certain further classes of internees, including

Persons who have since early childhood or for at least twenty years lived continuously or almost continuously in the United Kingdom and who have long severed connections with their country of nationality; whose interests and associations are British and who are friendly towards this country. (The Committee felt that the mere fact that an enemy alien had a son or sons serving in His Majesty's Forces was not in itself sufficient to justify exemption but that it should count in an alien's favour if he substantially complied with the above conditions.)[97]

In fact, the release of internees was pursued, if not with the same energetic zeal which had accompanied the initial round-

[95] *German and Austrian Civilian Internees: Categories of Persons Eligible for Release from Internment*, Cmd. 6217, London 1940.
[96] Quoted in 'Judex', *Anderson's Prisoners*, p. 92.
[97] Minutes of meeting of Aliens Advisory Committee, 22 Nov. 1940, PRO FO 371/25249/58.

up, at least with considerably greater liberality than might have been permitted by a rigorous interpretation of the still stringent regulations. By January 1941 it was reported to the Prime Minister that 4,610 aliens had now been enlisted in the Pioneers (as well as some in other military units).[98] Churchill had earlier expressed some reservations in the matter:

I presume that this Corps will be most carefully scrubbed and re-scrubbed to make sure no Nazi cells develop in it. I am very much in favour of recruiting friendly Germans and keep them under strict discipline, instead of remaining useless in concentration camps, but we must be doubly careful we do not get any of the wrong breed.[99]

However, he appeared to be satisfied with an assurance that M.I.5. was keeping the matter under careful surveillance. Churchill's attitude to the question of mass internment appears, indeed, to have undergone something of a change about this time (again rather after the fashion of Henry II), for on 25 January he wrote to the Foreign and Home Secretaries:

I have heard from various quarters that the witch-finding activities of M.I.5 are becoming an actual impediment to the more important work of the Department . . . I have no doubt that there is a certain amount of risk that some bad people may get loose, but our dangers are so much less now than they were in May and June. The whole organisation of the country, the Home Guard and so forth, is so much more efficient against Fifth Column activities, that I am sure a more rapid and general process of release from internment should be adopted.[100]

This proved to be the cue for a hastening of the process of release. By March 1941 Lord Lytton was able to announce in a broadcast to the U.S.A. and Canada that some 12,500 internees had already been freed.[101] By April the figure had risen to 14,250, and by August to 17,745.[102] On 28 August the Chairman of the Jewish Refugees Committee, Otto Schiff, was able to report that there were only two internment camps left on the

[98] E. F. Jacob to Prime Minister, 13 Jan. 1941, PRO PREM 3/42/2/2.
[99] Churchill minute, 3 Jan. 1941, PRO PREM 3/42/2/3.
[100] Churchill minute, 25 Jan. 1941, PRO PREM 4/39/3. Letters on aliens policy sent to Churchill by Lords Lytton and Beaverbrook appear to have been instrumental in changing his view.
[101] *Jewish Chronicle*, 14 March 1941.
[102] *Jewish Chronicle*, 25 Apr. and 22 Aug. 1941.

Isle of Man (as against nine in November 1940), and that only about 1,300 refugees were still interned in Britain. By July 1942 the figure had been reduced to 300–400, and by April 1944 to twenty-five. At that time there were sixty-eight refugees still interned in Australia, and none in Canada.[103]

The relaxation and eventual termination of the mass internment of aliens facilitated their rapid integration into British society during the later years of the war. But the change in the Government's policy towards refugees already resident in Britain was not accompanied by any easing of its policy of strict exclusion of any further refugees emanating from Germany or German-occupied territory. No refugees who arrived were sent back (although some were interned as 'illegal immigrants'[104]) but everything possible was done to prevent the arrival even of the trickle of refugees who might somehow succeed in escaping from Axis-controlled Europe. As T. M. Snow, head of the Foreign Office Refugee Section, put it in December 1940: 'The Security Services and the H[ome] O[ffice] concur in refusing, on security and social grounds, to admit a single further refugee here.'[105]

The question was not an academic one, as was demonstrated by the British response to an approach in December 1940 from the Foreign Minister of the Government-in-Exile of the Grand Duchy of Luxemburg. The Luxemburg Government's note stated that two thousand Jews resident in Luxemburg had been told by the German occupation authorities to leave as soon as possible. Failing departure they would be deported to Poland. Some 150 had already reached Portugal where they were trying to secure visas for overseas countries. A further 300 had left Luxemburg on 11 November in a sealed train accompanied by Gestapo agents. On arrival at the Portuguese frontier they had been refused admission and sent back *via* Spain to occupied France where they were now 'in the most tragic and miserable circumstances'. The Luxemburg Government had applied to

[103] 'Report on visit to Isle of Man Internment Camps', n.d. [Nov. 1940], BD C2/3/5/20/5; O. Schiff to A. Brotman, 28 Aug. 1941, BD C2/3/5/50/5; minutes of meetings of Aliens Committee of Board of Deputies of British Jews, 7 July 1942 and 4 Apr. 1944, BD C2/1/6.

[104] Minutes of meetings of Aliens Committee of Board of Deputies of British Jews, 8 Feb. and 4 Apr. 1944, BD C2/1/6.

[105] T. M. Snow minute, 11 Dec. 1940, PRO FO 371/25243/593 (W 12102/7614/48).

the United States, Brazilian, and Belgian Congo authorities for entrance visas on behalf of those possessing Luxemburg nationality, but only a few had received visas. The Luxemburg Government was therefore turning to the British Government for help, and asked whether the Jews might not be admitted to Tanganyika?[106] In conversation with the British Chargé d'Affaires, the Foreign Minister explained that

he had suggested the possibility of these Jews going to the Tanganyika Territory only because he understood that visas were being given for that country. He was, however, sure that any destination in the British Empire that might be decided upon would be a paradise compared to what these people could expect if transported to Poland.[107]

The immediate reaction of the Foreign Office was negative; R. T. E. Latham minuted:

I am afraid there is next to nothing we can do. They are covered by the Home Office prejudice . . . against people from enemy-occupied territory; and in any case we simply cannot have any more people let into the United Kingdom on merely humanitarian grounds . . . Furthermore these particular refugees, pitiable as is their plight, are hardly war-refugees in the sense that they are in danger because they have fought against the Germans, but simply racial refugees.[108]

After further discussion the Foreign Office dispatched a reply on 13 January which reflected this negative conclusion. It was explained that no visas were available for refugees to enter Tanganyika, and that it was 'not possible in existing circumstances for the United Kingdom to admit refugees whether of Allied or of other nationality, on compassionate grounds alone'. On the suggestion of Latham it was added that some Luxemburg citizens 'possessed of technical skill which would constitute a valuable contribution to the war effort may in certain circumstances be admitted to the United Kingdom upon examination of their credentials by His Majesty's Passport Control Officer in Madrid or Lisbon'. The possibility of affording asylum to allied citizens in the British Empire was

[106] Luxemburg Foreign Minister to British Chargé d'Affaires, 16 Dec. 1940, PRO FO 371/25254/490 (W 12667/12667/48).

[107] Chargé Aveling to Halifax, 17 Dec. 1940, PRO FO 371/25254/489 (W 12667/12667/48).

[108] Latham minute, 24 Dec. 1940, PRO FO 371/25254/487 (W 12667/12667/48).

being studied, but the British Chargé was instructed 'to avoid raising any false hopes' on this account.[109] The correspondence was not pursued further. Many Luxemburg Jews survived the war in hiding in France and the Iberian peninsula, and 104 were able to secure admission to the United States in 1941–2. But 512 Jews were deported from Luxemburg to Poland in late 1941, and a further group reached Treblinka in March 1943. Only four or five hundred Jews were found alive in Luxemburg at the end of the war.[110]

In the autumn of 1942 the question of admission of Jewish refugees to the United Kingdom arose again in a different form. In July 1942 the Vichy regime agreed to hand over to the Germans 10,000 foreign Jews in the unoccupied zone; they were to be deported to Poland.[111] This decision, coming soon after the mass deportations of Jews from Paris, aroused fear of imminent death among all Jews in unoccupied France, whether French or foreign. Thousands attempted to flee to Switzerland, but the Swiss Government closed its frontiers to all except certain restricted categories of refugees (excluding the majority of Jews). Some refugees who had crossed into Switzerland illegally were taken to the border and forced to cross back into France.[112] There was a great deal of public pressure in favour of admission of refugees, and the deportations were discontinued, but military measures to prevent illegal entry to Switzerland were stepped up.[113] The Minister of Justice estimated that about 100,000 people were trying to enter the country, and announced, 'It is impossible for us to accept them.'[114] The Chief of the Justice Department said 'We cannot turn our country into a sponge for Europe, and take in, for example, eighty or ninety per cent of the Jewish refugees.'[115] A public

[109] Snow to Aveling, 13 Jan. 1941, PRO FO 371/25254/496 (W 12667/12667/48).

[110] *American Jewish Year Book*, vol. 45, Philadelphia 1943/5704, p. 589; G. Reitlinger, *The Final Solution*, London 1968, p. 539; L. Dawidowicz, *The War Against the Jews 1939–1945*, London 1975, p. 366.

[111] Robert O. Paxton, *Vichy France: Old Guard and New Order, 1940–1944*, New York 1972, p. 182.

[112] Millard (Foreign Office) to Thornley (Colonial Office), 4 Sept. 1942, PRO FO 371/32683 (W 12276/4993/48); R. Lichtheim (Geneva) to Jewish Agency, Jerusalem, 28 Aug. 1942, CZA L22/34.

[113] Harrison (Berne) to State Dept., Washington, 5 Sept. 1942, USNA 840.48 Refugees 3070.

[114] *Jewish Chronicle*, 25 Sept. 1942.

[115] Harrison to State Dept., 5 Sept. 1942, USNA 840.48 Refugees 3070.

statement by Laval that it was his intention to 'cleanse France of its foreign Jewry' did not increase optimism regarding the fate of refugees in unoccupied France, and their plight aroused some sympathy in Britain and the U.S.A.[116] Under pressure the State Department agreed in early September to admit 1,000 Jewish children from France to the U.S.A., and the President of the Dominican Republic announced his readiness to admit more to his territory (although the sincerity of this offer was regarded with some scepticism in American government circles).[117]

The question of admitting refugees from unoccupied France to Britain was discussed at a meeting of officials from the Home and Foreign Offices with Sir Herbert Emerson on 7 September 1942. The meeting was informed that the Home Secretary might be prepared to allow the entry of children and old people.[118] Foreign Office minutes were not enthusiastic: it was pointed out that the scheme seemed to involve 'giving priority in the grant of U.K. visas to Jews over all other categories of Allied nationals', and it was felt that this would 'be resented by the Allied governments'. The fear was expressed that, as the British had tried to dissuade the Free French authorities from encouraging volunteers to leave France save in special cases, 'if they now hear that we are promising visas to aged Jews, they will probably be indignant'. At a meeting on 8 September Sir Herbert Emerson told the Home Secretary, Herbert Morrison, that French exit visas could be obtained for Jews under fourteen and over sixty, and suggested that the British Government might admit up to 1,000 in the hope that this good example would be followed by the U.S.A. and perhaps by South American countries. Morrison 'saw considerable difficulty' but eventually agreed to 'consider first of all a limitation of the suggestion to children, one or both of whose parents had been admitted to this country as refugees'. The Foreign Office representative at the meeting expressed doubt as to the effect on American policy, and urged that priority should be given to children

[116] Statement by Laval on 10 Sept. 1942, quoted in A. Rhodes, *The Vatican in the Age of the Dictators 1922–45*, London 1973, p. 316.

[117] *The War Diary of Breckenridge Long*, ed. Fred L. Israel, Lincoln, Nebraska, 1966, p. 282 (Diary entry dated 12 Sept. 1942).

[118] Minute by A. W. G. Randall, 7 Sept. 1942, PRO FO 371/32683 (W 11681/4993/48).

of Allied nationality as 'it would be very difficult to justify to our Allies the grant of visas to enemy aliens, however sound our humanitarian reasons'.[119] These doubts were echoed in further Foreign Office minutes; Sir Alexander Cadogan concluded, 'It seems to me wrong to support bringing children to this country at present.'[120]

The Chairman of the Jewish Refugee Committee, Otto Schiff, visited the Home Secretary and suggested that children and old people with close relatives in Britain might be admitted from unoccupied France. He calculated that (on a narrow interpretation of 'close relatives') 'the total number of such children and such persons over 60 would not exceed 300 or 350'. The Jewish Refugee Committee offered to guarantee that 'there would be no question of any such children or persons over 60 becoming a charge on public funds'. Presenting the matter to the Cabinet in a memorandum on 23 September, Morrison outlined the suggestions made by Emerson and Schiff, but reiterated that

the general policy has been not to admit during the war additional refugees to the United Kingdom unless in some quite rare and exceptional cases it can be shown that the admission of the refugee will be directly advantageous to our war effort. Any departure from this rigid policy is liable to lead to fresh claims and additional pressure for the admission to the United Kingdom of persons who are in danger or distress, and I am convinced that it would not be right to make any general departure from the principle that the United Kingdom is unable during the period of the war at any rate, to accept additional refugees.

Morrison pointed out that there was the danger that any relaxation of British policy might merely encourage the Vichy Government to deport Jewish parents if it were known that Britain 'would allow children who are stranded as a result of this policy to be dumped here'. He added that public opinion was not wholly enthusiastic about the large number of refugees already in Britain and that further arrivals might 'stir up an unpleasant degree of anti-semitism (of which there is a fair amount just below the surface), and that would be bad for the country and

---

[119] Minutes by F. K. Roberts, R. L. Speaight, and A. W. G. Randall, 8 Sept. 1942, ibid.

[120] Minutes by Cadogan and others 8 Sept. 1942, ibid.

the Jewish community'. In spite of these misgivings, Morrison suggested that the plight of the refugees might 'make a very strong appeal to the humanitarian feelings of large numbers of our people, including no doubt many M.P.s, and in some individual cases at any rate it may be extremely difficult for the Government to maintain what would appear to be a hard-hearted rigidity'. He therefore 'inclined to think that the balance of advantage would lie in acceding to the request of the Jewish Refugee Committee', provided that it were agreed that there would be no further concessions whatsoever.[121]

On 28 September the Cabinet decided that admission of refugees from unoccupied France should be limited to children who had a parent or parents already in the country; the Home Secretary was given discretion also to admit orphan children who had a near relative in Britain. However, on 2 October the Home Secretary submitted a second memorandum to the Cabinet in which he explained that it had now been discovered that

The cases in which a child is in Unoccupied France and a parent is in this country are exceptional . . . the number will be very small, perhaps not more than 20. . . No representations have as yet been made to the Home Office about orphan children with near relatives in this country. Most orphan children are believed to be in institutions and their position will not be affected by the deportation policy of the Vichy Government . . . The children whose position is most pitiful are those who become in effect orphans as the result of the deportation of their parents. The fate of their parents will often be uncertain and as a result of the Cabinet decision it will be necessary to refuse to admit such children unless evidence is forthcoming that both of the parents have perished.

The Home Office evidently balked at such a macabre requirement, and Morrison therefore suggested that the Cabinet decision might be amended so as to include 'de facto orphans in France' who had near relatives in Britain.[122] This was agreed, and it was further decided that 1,000 Jewish orphans from unoccupied France might be admitted to Palestine.[123]

[121] Morrison to War Cabinet, 23 Sept. 1942, CAB 66/29/18.
[122] Morrison to War Cabinet, 2 Oct. 1942, CAB 66/29/98.
[123] Eden to Winant, 14 Oct. 1942, USNA 840.48 Refugees 3190.

At a meeting on 28 October with a pro-refugee deputation, Morrison explained the background to the Government's policy regarding refugee immigration. He said that the Government 'did not under-estimate the magnitude of the horrors which Vichy were committing or the difficulties of the unfortunate refugees'. But he reminded his hearers of the large contribution which Britain had made to the solution of the refugee problem since 1933. Britain had been blitzed, there were accommodation problems, the threat of invasion remained, and there was the possibility that the country might be the jumping-off point for offensive operations on the continent. In the face of all these difficulties it would have been open to the Government to say that it could do nothing: but it had done otherwise. Morrison stressed that the solution of the problem did not rest with the British Government. Hitler could always create more victims than Britain could absorb. All Britain could do was to mitigate the horrors, and that Britain had done. The general body of public opinion was broadly sympathetic towards refugees, but Morrison warned that there was also a body of opinion which was 'potentially anti-semitic'. He asked the deputation not to ignore the existence of that feeling. They must look at the problem realistically. He said he could offer no hope of any relaxation of the Government's policy. It was, of course, open to the Members of Parliament present to raise the matter in the House of Commons, but he invited them to consider whether public controversy in the House or in the press might not prove damaging to the interests of foreigners and Jews.[124]

In the event the negative tone of these remarks proved to be appropriate, for even the limited concession made by the Government over the admission of 'de facto orphans' was never implemented. The Vichy Government did not take swift action to grant exit permits to the children. On 8 November 1942 the 'Operation Torch' landings of Allied Troops in North Africa began, and this proved the signal for the Axis occupation of the rump hitherto administered by the Vichy regime. These events marked the end of any realistic hope of evacuating the children to Britain. On 8 December 1942 Otto Schiff reported to the Aliens Committee of the Board of Deputies

[124] Note of meeting on 28 Oct. 1942, PRO FO 371/32681 (W 14673/4555/48).

of British Jews that 'it had not been possible to bring one child here'.[125]

The attitudes revealed by the Luxemburg and French orphan episodes remained the basis of official policy towards Jewish immigration to Britain throughout the war. In December 1942 the Government came under renewed public pressure in favour of the admission of refugees after news of the German campaign of mass murder of Jews was published by the governments of Britain, the U.S.A., and the U.S.S.R.[126] At a meeting of the newly established Cabinet Committee on the Reception and Accommodation of Jewish Refugees on 31 December 1942, Herbert Morrison stated that

the Home Office would not refuse to take a limited number of refugees say, from 1,000 to 2,000, but certainly not more . . . on the condition that they were sent to the Isle of Man and stayed there as long as he thought it necessary. He could not, however, agree that the door should be opened to the entry of uncategorised Jews. It should be borne in mind that there were already about 100,000 refugees, mainly Jews, in this country.

The Home Secretary stipulated that the possible admission of '1,000 to 2,000 refugees' was contingent upon 'the firm understanding that the United States and the Dominions would accept proportionate numbers'. Morrison said that he 'deprecated the tendency to regard the United Kingdom as the sole repository for refugees', and he added a warning that

there was considerable anti-Semitism under the surface in this country. If there were any substantial increase in the number of Jewish refugees or if these refugees did not leave this country after the war, we should be in for serious trouble.[127]

The latter point appears to have weighed heavily in Morrison's mind, for, in the face of urgent public demands in early 1943, led by the Archbishop of Canterbury, that the British Government 'give a lead to the world' by providing 'an immediate refuge in territories within the British Empire' for Jews threatened with death, Morrison repeated his fear of the danger

[125] Minutes of meeting of Aliens Committee, 8 Dec. 1942, BD C2/1/6.
[126] See pp. 172–3.
[127] Minutes of meeting, PRO CAB 95/15.

of stimulating anti-Semitism which, he said, was 'always under the pavement'.[128]

The argument deserves serious consideration. Morrison, perhaps more than any other member of the Cabinet, was 'in tune' with the fears and prejudices of the 'man on the Clapham omnibus', and his assessment of the state of public feeling cannot be dismissed lightly. A lifelong supporter of Zionism, Morrison was outspoken in his public condemnations of anti-Semitism, which he regarded as a real danger and no mere political 'bogey'.[129] Morrison was not alone in detecting a significant undercurrent of anti-Semitic feeling in Britain at this time. The *Jewish Chronicle* on 26 February 1943 warned of a 'noticeable extension of the anti-Jewish campaign in this country'. The view that anti-Semitism was increasing in early 1943 was shared by such figures as Lord Melchett, Sir Wyndham Deedes, and Anthony de Rothschild.[130] The Board of Deputies of British Jews was sufficiently concerned to send a delegation to discuss the matter with the Minister of Information, Brendan Bracken, who agreed that 'it was correct to say that there had been an increase in anti-semitic activity recently', although it seemed 'to be organised very largely by cranks'.[131]

There is a large body of evidence suggesting that, even after the 'fifth column' scare of 1940 had died away, a sizable residue of anti-alien and anti-Jewish feeling remained 'under the pavement'. Wartime anti-Semitism in Britain was not (except in the case of a lunatic fringe) akin to the ideological racialism of the Nazi doctrine. It should be seen rather as an outgrowth of the habitual island xenophobia stimulated by the heightened fears and resentments of the war. Its nature, of course, varied from one man to the next. But that it attained considerable

[128] Statement by Archbishops of Canterbury, York, and Wales, 15 Jan. 1943, BD C11/2/38; note by M. Rosetté on meeting of Morrison with a deputation from his constituency, 29 Jan. 1943.

[129] See B. Donoghue and G. W. Jones, *Herbert Morrison: Portrait of a Politician*, London 1973; Lord Morrison of Lambeth, *Herbert Morrison: An Autobiography*, London 1960; for Morrison's views on anti-Semitism in the East End of London in 1936 see note of a conversation of Morrison with Neville Laski (President of Board of Deputies of British Jews) and Harry Pollitt (leader of the Communist Party of Great Britain) on 14 Oct. 1936, ed. Colin Holmes, in *Bulletin of Society for the Study of Labour History*, no. 32, Spring 1976, pp. 26–33.

[130] Minutes of meetings of Zionist Executive, London, 21 Jan. 1943, (CZA Z4/302/26), 22 Feb. 1943 (CZA Z4/302/27), and 19 Apr. 1943 (CZA Z4/302/27).

[131] Note on interview, 29 Apr. 1943, BD C11/7/1/5.

dimensions during the war as a general prejudice cannot be doubted. There were criticisms of Jewish behaviour in the Blitz: it was alleged that Jews were crowding into the tube stations during air raids;[132] when a mass stampede into a tube station during an air raid on 3 March 1943 led to a terrible disaster (with 173 deaths) in Bethnal Green it was said that a panic by Jews was responsible.[133] The columnist 'Cassandra' in the *Daily Mirror* attacked malpractices by Jewish traders.[134] A circular by the 'Economic League' in February 1941 reported that Jews were going round farms buying chickens and eggs which they then sold in London. It further alleged that Jews were evading military service, and added that 'should anyone doubt the accuracy of this statement they would do well to visit the Thé Dansant at the Café de Paris any Saturday [*sic*] after-noon between 4.30 and 5.30 p.m.'[135] Even an outspoken champion of Jewish claims in Palestine, such as Oliver Harvey (Eden's Private Secretary), remarked in his diary in August 1941 that there was increased feeling against the Jews who, as he wrote, were 'their own worst enemy by their conduct in cornering foodstuffs and evacuating themselves to the best billets'.[136]

Quasi-scientific notions about Jewish origins seem to have been making the rounds of the London clubs about this time. Harvey noted that Sir Leonard Woolley, the distinguished archaeologist, had told him over dinner that 'the Jews of Cen-tral Europe were not real Jews, but a Mongoloid race converted to Judaism in early times; hence their distinctive Mongoloid appearance'.[137] In June 1942 the former Colonial Secretary, Lord Moyne, told the House of Lords: 'It is very often loosely said that the Jews are Semites, but anthropologists tell us that, pure as they have kept their culture, the Jewish race has been much mixed with Gentiles since the beginning of the Diaspora. During the Babylonian captivity they acquired a strong Hittite

[132] Ibid.; *Jewish Chronicle*, 11 and 25 Oct. 1940.

[133] G. F. Vale, *Bethnal Green's Ordeal 1939–1945*, London 1945; interview of Prof. S. Brodetsky et al. with Brendan Bracken, Minister of Information, 29 Apr. 1943, BD C11/7/1/5.

[134] See Andrew Sharf, *The British Press and Jews Under Nazi Rule*, London, 1964, p. 178.

[135] Circular dated 11 Feb. 1941, BD C11/2/35/1.

[136] Diary of Oliver Harvey, entry dated 7 Aug. 1941, BL 56398.

[137] Ibid., entry dated 29 Jan. 1941, BL 56387.

HOW THE BEASTLY BUSINESS BEGINS

Evening Standard 18 June 1943

Reproduced by permission of the Low Trustees and the London *Evening Standard*

admixture, and it is obvious that the Armenoid features which are still to be found among the Sephardim have been bred out of the Ashkenazim by an admixture of Slav blood.'[138]

In the later years of the war anti-Semitism does not appear to have diminished. The view of one unsentimental observer, George Orwell, in an article written in early February 1945, was that 'it is generally admitted that antisemitism is on the increase, that it has been greatly exacerbated by the war, and that humane and enlightened people are not immune to it'.[139] The effects were particularly noticeable in the retail trade. In August 1943 the Hampstead Chamber of Commerce passed a resolution declaring that it viewed 'with great concern the granting of licences to persons of other than British nationality under both the local Food Committees of the Ministry of Food and the Location of Retail Businesses Order', and demanding 'that all such licences be reviewed within six months of the cessation of hostilities'.[140] The later years of the war were punctuated with allegations of Jewish black market activity.[141] The matter was raised in the House of Commons, evoking a gleeful diary comment from Dr Goebbels: 'A frontal attack on black markets was made in the House of Commons. No bones are made about the fact that Jews were chiefly implicated in profiteering in the food market. Heading the procession were the Jewish immigrants who went from Germany to England.'[142] Rattled leaders of the Jewish community in Britain laid part of the blame at the doors of some of their co-religionists. John Goodenday, Chairman of the Textile Section of the Trades Advisory Council (originally a sub-committee of the Defence Committee of the Board of Deputies of British Jews, operating from 1940 as an autonomous body under the aegis of the board, its main aim being the removal of friction in industry, trade and commerce where good relations between Jews and Gentiles were threatened), incurred much odium in

[138] HL, vol. 123, col. 198, 9 June 1942.

[139] George Orwell, 'Anti-Semitism in Britain' in Sonia Orwell and Ian Angus, eds., *The Collected Essays, Journalism and Letters of George Orwell, vol. III As I Please 1843–1945*, New York 1968, pp. 332–40.

[140] *Jewish Chronicle*, 22 Oct. 1943.

[141] See e.g. *Jewish Chronicle*, 17 July 1942; minutes of meeting at Foreign Office, 12 April 1944, PRO FO 371/42725/14 (W 6380).

[142] *Jewish Chronicle*, 20 March 1942; Louis P. Lochner (ed.), *The Goebbels Diaries*, London 1948, p. 73 (entry dated 6 March 1942).

the columns of the *Jewish Chronicle* for referring at a public
meeting to 'many weak and wicked Jewish traders attracted to
the black market'.[143] Otto Schiff forwarded to the Board
of Deputies a report on increased anti-Semitism in Cardiff.
Schiff's Cardiff correspondent remarked that 'from the sparse
contact I have had with my co-religionists in Cardiff, I must
admit that the majority of them are not a very likable lot', and
stressed the 'typically continental and Jewish outlook' of many
Jewish refugee employers in the area.[144]

That all this could not be dismissed merely as a series of
sporadic outbursts was demonstrated by reports on the state of
public feeling throughout the country which were compiled by
the Home Intelligence Unit of the Ministry of Information.
One such report, in January 1942, stated that while there was
'no indication of any feeling that as a nation we are "Jew-led"
on the lines suggested by enemy propaganda', it appeared that
anti-Semitism was 'latent . . . in most districts'. There were
widespread reports of a general belief that black markets were
largely run by Jews. A 'continuous simmering of anti-Jewish
feeling' was reported from Leeds and Sheffield. Jews were
accused of evasion of military service and Civil Defence duties
(the latter complaint was particularly pronounced in Sheffield). It was said that Jews were being evacuated to the safest
areas. There was criticism of Jewish ostentation, and Jews were
sighted eating in expensive restaurants.[145]

The most important manifestations of war-time anti-
Semitism in Britain, both as regards their impact on Jewish
refugees in the country and in their international implications,
were, however, of a quite different type: they concerned not the
indigenous population (although there appears to have been a
certain 'spill-over' effect) but the large numbers of Polish
troops stationed in Britain. Complaints of anti-Semitism
among Polish officers in Britain were voiced as early as
December 1939.[146] These allegations persisted throughout the

[143] *Jewish Chronicle*, 31 July 1942.
[144] Schiff to Brotman, 4 May 1943, BD C2/2/5/1.
[145] Report dated 15 Jan. 1942, BD B5/3/6. See also note of interview with R. H.
Parker, Director of Home Intelligence Division of Ministry of Information, 12 Feb.
1943, BD C11/7/1/5.
[146] Minutes of meeting of Aliens Committee of Board of Deputies of British Jews,
4 Dec. 1939, BD C2/1/6.

war and greatly inflamed relations between Polish army authorities and the Jewish community in Britain. The British Government found itself dragged into the controversy, and, in its later stages, the Soviet Government found the matter an opportune propaganda stick with which to beat the Polish Government-in-Exile in London.

The problem was first raised at the official level in April 1940 by the left-wing Labour M.P., D. N. Pritt, who wrote to R. A. Butler at the Foreign Office quoting from a speech allegedly delivered by a Polish captain to his troops in which the officer had declared that when they returned to Poland they would slaughter the Jews.[147] The matter was referred for comment to the British Embassy to Poland (at that time situated with the Polish Government at Angers in France), and to the War Office. For the Embassy, Frank Savery, wrote to the Foreign Office stating:

As regards the present attitude of the Poles, and especially of those now in foreign countries, towards Jews and the Jewish question we must not forget that in September last the Jewish population in the provinces occupied by the U.S.S.R., notably in Eastern Galicia, with the exception of the wealthy Jews who had much property to lose, sided in the main with the Russian invaders. According to recent reports which have passed through my hands the Jews in those parts of Poland are still the main support of the Bolshevik regime.[148]

The reply from the War Office was similar in tone: 'The Jews' behaviour in Poland during the Russian advance must clearly have caused a feeling of animosity in Army circles which I think justified.'[149]

With the removal of the Polish Government to London upon the fall of France in the summer of 1940 the continuing complaints of Polish anti-Semitism became a matter of more immediate concern to the British Government. A draft letter to Pritt prepared for Butler at the Foreign Office on 27 July conceded that 'there had undoubtedly been a certain amount of anti-Semitic feeling in the Army' but stressed that 'the official attitude of the Polish authorities was beyond reproach in this

[147] Pritt to Butler, 2 Apr. 1940, PRO FO 371/24481/40 (C 5143/5143/55).
[148] Savery to Makins, 25 Apr. 1940, PRO FO 371/24481/57 (C 6231/5143/55).
[49] Wilkinson to Makins, 6 May 1940, PRO FO 371/24481/60 (C 6231/5143/55).

respect'.[150] This position was strengthened by an order of the day issued on 5 August 1940 by General Sikorski, in which the Polish Commander-in-Chief declared:

Particularly on the ground of the Army there must prevail an unanimity and brotherhood in arms undisturbed by any quarrels. My point of view is that a soldier who has taken up arms for his country has thereby proved that he is a Pole without regard to his race or religion.[151]

This attitude was consistently maintained by Sikorski and by the Polish Government throughout the war, and a number of further statements of this sort were issued (although the fact that they were regarded as necessary may be significant). When the matter was taken up with Sikorski by the British Ambassador in September 1940, the General stated that the trouble was mainly caused by members of a right-wing extremist party, who had contributed anti-Semitic articles to a Polish weekly in England, called *Jestem Polakiem* ('I am a Pole'). The General said he intended to take 'energetic measures regarding their activities and proposed in a broadcast to the Polish people to condemn any tendencies of this nature'. The effect of this statement was, however, somewhat tarnished by the fact that, after this exchange had taken place on the steps of the headquarters of the Polish General Staff, the Ambassador accompanied Sikorski into the lobby of the hotel occupied by the Poles, where it was discovered that a news vendor was selling copies of *Jestem Polakiem*. The Ambassador reported that Sikorski, 'with great indignation, gave instructions that this paper was no longer to be sold on the premises'.[152]

Although Sikorski's attitude towards the Jews was apparently beyond reproach, the same could not be said of all of his colleagues in the Polish Government. Two ministers of his government, Dr Marian Seyda and General Jozef Haller, were described in a Foreign Office minute as having been 'rather notorious for their anti-Semitic tendencies'. The subject was discussed in August 1940 between the head of the British

[150] Butler to Pritt (draft), 27 July 1940, PRO FO 371/24481/48 (C 5143/5143/55).

[151] Quoted in Savery to Roberts, 19 Aug. 1940, PRO FO 371/24481/62 (C 8802/5143/55).

[152] Sir H. Kennard to Halifax, 20 Sept. 1940, PRO FO 371/24481/72 (C 10125/5143/55).

Military Mission attached to the Polish Forces and the Polish Director of Military Intelligence, Colonel Mitkiewicz; the British officer reported that Mitkiewicz had assured him that 'the policy of General Sikorski's Government was to be entirely fair and unbiassed towards all Polish citizens'.

He could not, however, forbear from referring to the undesirable Jewish Communist elements in Poland, and declared that, although there were a few good Jews in the Polish Army, all those deserters from the Polish Forces in this country and practically all those who now refused to join it were Jews. He thus gave himself away. . .[153]

Such opinions seem to have been widespread at all echelons in the Polish Army; even Generals Sikorski and Anders were not immune from them as is apparent from the minutes of an unusually cordial Russo-Polish exchange which took place in Moscow in December 1941:

General Anders 'I am counting on 150,000 people, that is eight divisions, together with the army's maintenance forces. Perhaps there are even more of our people, but among them there is also a great number of Jews who do not want to serve in the army.'

Stalin 'Jews are poor warriors.'

General Sikorski 'Many from among the Jews who reported are speculators or those who have been punished for contraband; they will never make good soldiers. Those I don't need in the Polish Army.'

General Anders '200 Jews deserted from Buzuluk upon hearing the false report on the bombing of Kuibyshev. More than sixty deserted from the 5th Division a day before the distribution of arms to the soldiers was made public.'

Stalin 'Yes, the Jews are bad warriors.'[154]

In the light of the above, it is perhaps not surprising that there was discussion among the Polish military authorities of the possibility of introducing a *numerus clausus* for Jews in the Polish army.[155] A further indication of attitudes to the Jewish question among senior Polish politicians is to be found in a conversation between a deputation of the Joint Foreign Committee of the

[153] Minute by F. K. Roberts, 13 May 1941, PRO FO 371/26769 (C 4878/4655/55); Charles Bridge to F. Savery, 21 Aug. 1940, PRO FO 371/24481/64 (C 8923/5143/55).

[154] *Documents on Polish-Soviet Relations 1939–1945 vol. I 1939–1943*, London 1961, p. 241.

[155] Kot to Mikolajczyk, 11 Oct. 1941, in Stanislaw Kot, *Conversations with the Kremlin and Dispatches from Russia*, London 1963, p. 62.

Board of Deputies and the Anglo-Jewish Association and Professor Stanislaw Kot, a Minister of the Polish Government, at Angers in April 1940. Kot (who was not regarded as an anti-Semite) argued that the most likely 'solution' to the Jewish problem in Poland after the war would involve mass emigration, perhaps to the Odessa region.[156] The notion that such mass emigration would be required after the war was widely held in Polish Government circles (at any rate until the fate of the Jewish population of Poland became known), and it aroused some sympathetic comment in the British Foreign Office, although this was tempered by concern lest the destination of the emigrants should prove to be Palestine rather than Odessa.[157]

Against the background of such equivocal attitudes in the senior ranks of the Polish military and official community in England, the public statements repudiating anti-Semitism which were issued from time to time by the Polish authorities had a rather hollow ring, and did little to restrain what was sometimes virulent anti-Jewish prejudice among lower ranks. The affair of *Jestem Polakiem* provided an illustration of this. In spite of Sikorski's condemnation of the paper it was still appearing in the spring of 1941, and occasioned protests by Jewish organizations.[158] Questions were asked in the House of Commons, and there were demands that the British Government ban the offending journal. These were rejected, although the Government promised to keep an eye on the publication.[159] That the paper's backers were not all Polish became apparent when it was reported by the Ministry of Information that there was reason to believe that *Jestem Polakiem*'s source of newsprint (a scarce commodity in war-time) was the *Catholic Herald*, an

[156] Note of meeting between Kot and Prof. S. Brodetsky L. J. Stein, and A. Brotman, 6 Apr. 1940, BD C11/2/34; see also note of Brotman meeting with H. L. Baggallay at the Foreign Office, 30 Apr. 1940, ibid.

[157] Minute by F. K. Roberts, 13 May 1941, PRO FO 371/26769 (C 4878/4655/55); minute by C. W. Baxter, 22 Apr. 1941, PRO FO 371/26737/35 (C 3836/815/55).

[158] Note by R. A. Butler on meeting on 26 May 1941 between Eden and Lady Reading and Sidney Silverman M.P. (representing the British Section of the World Jewish Congress), PRO FO 371/26769 (C 4878/4655/55). Dr. I. Schwarzbart to Joint Foreign Committee of Board of Deputies and Anglo-Jewish Association, 7 and 22 May 1941, YV M 2/486.

[159] Waclaw Jedrzejewicz (ed.), *Poland in the British Parliament 1939–1945* (3 vols., New York 1946–62), vol. I, pp. 459–62.

English Catholic newspaper with a long history of hostility to the Jews.[160] The rumour of a 'Catholic connection' was strengthened by a report that, although formally banned in the Polish Army, the paper had been secretly distributed by Catholic priests.[161] Although the paper was independent, the Foreign Office considered taking the matter up with Cardinal Hinsley's secretary.[162] Soon afterwards the paper seems to have died.

Jestem Polakiem was, however, a minor irritant compared with the most intractable subject of controversy involving Poles and Jews in England during the Second World War: this was the issue of Polish recruitment of Jewish refugees who were Polish citizens for service in the Polish armed forces. There was a general reluctance among Polish Jews to serve under the Polish flag; the cause was not lack of anti-fascist zeal, but a widespread suspicion that there existed among Polish soldiers and officers a certain sympathy with the anti-Jewish aims of the Nazis; the behaviour of the Polish troops to their Jewish comrades-in-arms often lent colour to these suspicions. Typical of the accusations levelled against Polish troops were a series of incidents recounted in a memorandum prepared by the Board of Deputies of British Jews. It was alleged, for example, that, at a meeting of Polish officers, the A.D.C. to the Polish Commander-in-Chief, had announced that such Jews as remained in Poland after the war should be killed. At a similar meeting, General Paszkiewicz was reported to have said that the Polish Army did not require recruits in England because the Polish emigration in the country was predominantly Jewish. A Polish army chaplain was said to have declared that a total British victory in the war might not be desirable because it would leave power in the hands of the Jews and the Church of England. At Edinburgh University, where a number of Polish soldiers were studying in the Faculty of Medicine, Jewish students were said to have been compelled by their non-Jewish fellow-students to sit at separate tables (as had formerly been the practice in Polish universities). Further examples of petty

[160] Minute by F. K. Roberts, 19 April 1941, PRO FO 371/26737/34 (C 3836/815/55). On the *Catholic Herald*, see Sharf, *The British Press*, *passim*.

[161] Dr. I. Schwarzbart to Joint Foreign Committee of Board of Deputies and Anglo-Jewish Association, 22 May 1941, YV M2/486.

[162] A. W. G. Randall minute, 21 Apr. 1941, PRO FO 371/26737/34 (C 3836/815/55).

persecution and insults were cited.[163] The Foreign Office, although regarding the matter as something of a nuisance, considered that there was some substance to the complaints, and several M.P.s took the affair up.[164] Several of the latter supported the demand that Polish Jews in Britain be accorded the option of serving either in the Polish or the British forces.[165]

The problem came to a head in 1941 when it became known that the Polish Government in London had been 'conscripting' Polish refugees on British soil, and had arrested some recalcitrants on charges of desertion. When the issue was raised in Parliament by Sidney Silverman M.P., the Government admitted that some such cases had occurred and stated that an order had been given that the men should be released immediately unless they were willing to serve in the Polish Army.[166] A bill clarifying the status of the Polish Army in Britain was eventually passed in 1942, but in the interval controversy continued. The Government had hoped that when it had been established by law that Poles in Britain had the right to opt to serve in either the Polish or the British armies that would end the matter. But in the summer of 1943 there were further complaints by Sidney Silverman and other M.P.s who asserted that threats by the Polish authorities that any Poles who failed to answer their call-up notices would be shot hardly reflected the spirit of the 'option' arrangement.

In early 1944 the problem turned from a parliamentary squabble into a public scandal. In January a group of sixty-eight Jewish soldiers in the Polish Army deserted complaining of anti-Semitism among Polish troops. Particular offence had been taken at the anti-Jewish behaviour of Poles captured while fighting for the Germans in Tunisia who had subsequently been permitted to join the Polish Army in Britain. The deser-

---

[163] Board of Deputies memorandum sent to Dr. I. Schwarzbart (Jewish member of Polish National Council), Sept. 1943, BD C 11/7/1/6.

[164] See e.g. D. Allen minute, 15 Feb. 1944, PRO FO 371/39480 (C 1906/918/55); Tom Driberg M.P. to R. Law, 12 Feb. 1944, PRO FO 371/39480 (C 2243/918/55); R. R. Stokes M.P. to Eden, 7 Feb. 1941, PRO FO 371/26440 (C 12454/125/62).

[165] Eleanor Rathbone M.P. to R. Law, 1 Nov. 1941. PRO FO 371/26440 (C 12778/125/62); R. R. Stokes M.P. to Eden, 25 Nov. 1941, PRO FO 371/26440 (C 12454/125/62); Jedrzejewicz, *British Parliament*, p. 452.

[166] Jedrzejewicz, *British Parliament*, vol. I, p. 453; Silverman to Schwarzbart, 31 Dec. 1940, YV M2/461; *Jewish Chronicle*, 14 March 1941.

ters claimed that they had been told that when the Second Front was opened they would be shot in the back, and that all the Jews left in Poland at the end of the war would be massacred. The soldiers addressed themselves to Jewish organizations and to sympathetic Labour M.P.s., threatening hunger strikes and suicides unless they were transferred to the British Army. In February a second group, numbering 134 men, deserted and made similar complaints and demands.[167] The main concern of the British Government appears to have been to avoid unfortunate publicity. When Sir Owen O'Malley, British Ambassador to the Polish Government, discussed the problem with the Polish Foreign Minister, Tadeusz Romer, he discovered that the Polish authorities, while anxious to settle the dispute, had come to the conclusion 'that these men were reluctant to fight and were nothing but an incubus in the Polish Army'. They would therefore 'very gladly be rid of them if any means could be found of achieving this'.[168] The British were prepared to arrange for the transfer of the first group of deserters to the Pioneer Corps, but after the desertion of the second group the War Office began to 'fear a landslide'. D. Allen of the Foreign Office Central Department, while convinced 'that a good deal of very undesirable anti-Semitic behaviour has been going on in the Polish Forces', seems to have inclined to the view that 'these Polish Jews are shirkers and of little military use anyway'. The danger of publicity (which, it was feared, might be exploited by the Soviet Government to the detriment of the London Poles) therefore suggested compliance with the deserters' demands; but the threat of wholesale defections from the Polish forces led some officials to urge that the Poles be encouraged to enforce strict discipline against any further deserters, while being warned to curb anti-Semitic tendencies.[169]

When several further groups of Polish Jews deserted in March 1944 the patience of all concerned snapped. The War Office and the Foreign Office agreed that 'the rot must be

[167] Conflicting accounts are given of the numbers involved; estimates of the size of the first group range from 50 to 100. Jedrzejewicz, *British Parliament*, vol. II, pp. 422–5; PRO FO 371/39480 (C 1087/918/55) *passim*.

[168] D. Allen (Foreign Office) to Major Dru (War Office), 24 Jan. 1944, PRO FO 371/39480 (C 1087/918/55).

[169] Minutes by D. Allen *et al.*, 23 & 24 Feb. 1944, *ibid*.

stopped even at the cost of some public discussion'.[170] It was decided that the deserters would be tried by court-martial, and that no further transfers to the British Army would be permitted.[171] At this point the Labour M.P.s who were concerned about the matter decided to raise it in the House of Commons. When Tom Driberg M.P. put down a question on the subject, Dr Ignacy Schwarzbart (the sole Jewish member of the Polish National Council) telephoned him urging him to withdraw it (and so avoid giving publicity to the matter).[172] Driberg ignored the advice and went ahead with the support of other left-wing M.P.s. He later commented:

The odd thing was that we had pursued this matter in the House against the advice—the almost lachrymose pleading—of the official spokesmen of the Jewish community in Britain. They felt that any publicity about this might lead to more anti-Semitism, perhaps directed against their own flock.[173]

At a public meeting at the Stoll Theatre in London on 14 May, Driberg, George Strauss, and Michael Foot made speeches of protest against Polish anti-Semitism and against the courts-martial of the deserters.[174] A newspaper campaign against the Polish Government gathered steam. *The Observer* pronounced that the time had arrived 'for both the British Government with righteous indignation, and the Polish Government with patriotic wisdom, to say uncompromisingly that "This must stop" '.[175] The *Manchester Guardian* echoed these sentiments. (The *Catholic Herald*, however, saw in 'Those Anti-Jewish Charges: A Conspiracy to Malign Poles'.[176]) Whatever their initial hesitations about the value of publicity, the Jews now pulled few punches. There was a demonstration in Downing Street. The President of the Board of Deputies of British Jews,

---

[170] Dixon (Foreign Office) to Redman (War Office), 19 March 1944, PRO FO 371/39481 (C 3386/918/55); Redman to Dixon, 22 March 1944, PRO FO 371/39481 (C 3843/918/55).

[171] A. Brotman notes of interview with D. Allen, 4 and 7 Apr. 1944, BD C11/11/2.

[172] D. Allen minute, 4 Apr. 1944, PRO FO 371/39481 (C 4570/918/55).

[173] Tom Driberg, *Ruling Passions*, London 1977, pp. 202–3; Mary Stocks, *Eleanor Rathbone: A Biography*, London 1950, p. 303.

[174] M. McLaren (Political Warfare Executive) to F. K. Roberts, 15 May 1944, PRO FO 371/39484 (C 6589/918/55).

[175] Quoted in Sharf, *The British Press*, pp. 118–19.

[176] Quoted ibid.

Professor Selig Brodetsky, had an acerbic interview with the Polish Prime Minister, Mikolajczyk.[177] The *Jewish Chronicle* published a series of outspoken leaders and reports under headlines such as 'Anti-Semitism in Polish Army: Shocking Revelations in Parliament: 3,000 Ex-Hun Soldiers in Polish Ranks?'[178] Two posters were stuck on the door of the Polish Consulate-General in Portland Place; one read: 'Warning: The imprisonment of Jewish-Polish soldiers will be avenged. Irgun Zvai Leumi—Jewish National Military Organisation.'[179]

The Polish Government appears to have regarded itself as the victim of Soviet propaganda, although the Polish Ambassador, Count Raczynski, admitted in his diary: 'We have handled the matter clumsily, and played into the hands of our enemies.'[180] Substance was given to the latter point on 24 April when *Pravda* published a Tass message from London on the court-martial of thirty Jewish deserters.[181] Raczynski, who was 'enraged by the hypocrisy of our press and Parliamentary critics' and agitated by the 'witch-hunt against Polish anti-Semitism', wrote: 'Nobody ventures to suggest that our Jewish soldiers might be to blame for deserting their units on the eve of battle.'[182] At lunch with Churchill, Raczynski defended the conduct of the Poles, and complained of discrimination by the B.B.C. over the matter.[183] Churchill appears to have been impressed for he wrote to the Foreign Secretary:

What is this amnesty that is to be made by the Poles? Is it about Jewish deserters? If so, I do not think we should press them beyond what they have done. I do not like people who desert on the eve of battle, and I believe there has been some Communist intrigue behind all this to discredit the Polish division.[184]

In reply Eden explained that the amnesty in question related

[177] Note of interview (by A. G. Brotman), 24 Apr. 1944, BD C11/11/2.

[178] *Jewish Chronicle*, 14 Apr. 1944; see also issues dated 28 April, 5, 12, 19, and 26 May 1944.

[179] Count Edward Raczynski, *In Allied London*, London 1962, pp. 203–4 (Raczynski diary entry dated 29 April 1944).

[180] Ibid, pp. 201–13; Jedrzejewicz, *The British Parliament*, vol. II, pp. 422–5.

[181] Sir A. Clark Kerr (Moscow) to Foreign Office, 26 April 1944, PRO FO 371/39483.

[182] Raczynski, *In Allied London*, p. 213 (diary entry dated 20 May 1944).

[183] Ibid, p. 206.

[184] Churchill to Foreign Secretary and C.I.G.S., 23 May 1944, PRO PREM 3/352/14A.

not to the Jewish deserters but to Poles who had served under compulsion in German forces; this appears to have satisfied the Prime Minister.[185] Notwithstanding Eden's minute, the affair was apparently resolved by an amnesty to the offenders, who were discharged from the Polish Army 'with a view to enrolment as miners'.[186]

The Polish army controversy echoed ominously the similar disputes during the First World War over whether Jewish refugees from Russia who lived in England should be compelled by the British Government to serve in the Tsarist armed forces.[187] On that occasion the reluctance of Jews to fight for the Emperor, from whose anti-Semitic tyranny they had fled, had stimulated some hostility to Jews in general, and had provided a handle for anti-Semitic agitation. The sensitivity of the Government and of the Anglo-Jewish community to the similar problem during the Second World War should be seen against this background. Nevertheless, the 'spill-over' from Polish to indigenous anti-Jewish activity turned out to be very small. The episode may perhaps be said to provide an indication both of the potential danger and of the shallowness of anti-Semitic feeling in Britain during the war.

In fact, Herbert Morrison was probably over-cautious in his view that the admission of further Jewish refugees during the war would be likely to provoke dangerous outbreaks of anti-Semitism. In spite of the undercurrent of anti-Jewish and anti-alien feeling which clearly existed, there are no recorded instances of serious anti-Jewish violence during the war. The British Union of Fascists, which had played a prominent role in such activity before the war, was a spent force; even after its leader, Sir Oswald Mosley, was released from detention by Morrison in 1943, the right-wing fringe made no headway. The identification of anti-Semitism with Nazism and Fascism during the war may have helped to discredit manifestations of anti-Jewish sentiment.[188] That there was a significant seg-

[185] Eden to Churchill, 25 May 1944, ibid.

[186] A. G. Brotman note of interview at Foreign Office with F. K. Roberts, 18 Aug. 1944, BD C11/11/3/2.

[187] Leonard Stein, *The Balfour Declaration*, London 1961, pp. 488–90; for a compilation of documents on this matter, see Zosa Szajkowski, *Jews and the French Foreign Legion*, New York 1975, pp. 230–49.

[188] Angus Calder, in *The People's War: Britain 1939–45*, p. 498, argues, however, that

ment of public opinion sympathetic to refugees is indicated by a Gallup poll taken in February 1943 on the question of admitting to Britain Jews threatened with death in Europe. Of those questioned 78 per cent supported admission (40 per cent specified that asylum should be given only until the refugees could be settled elsewhere; 28 per cent approved of admission until the end of the war; and 10 per cent favoured the granting of refuge for an indefinite period).[189] The Government, however, made no attempt during the war to build a more generous policy towards refugees on these elements in public opinion. Even in May 1945, Morrison remained 'seriously alarmed regarding the possibility of anti-Semitism in this country'. Indeed he appears to have regarded it as a greater danger in Britain than in Germany, for he told the Cabinet Committee on refugees that

as regards such persons [refugees] in the United Kingdom he was clear that we ought to act on the assumption that those who had come here had done so temporarily, and that they should eventually go back whence they came. It was often said that the Jewish refugees in this country were terrified of returning to Germany. We should not be influenced by this attitude. It was possible that post-war Germany would abandon anti-Semitism altogether. If the Jews were allowed to remain here they might be an explosive element in the country, especially if the economic situation deteriorated.[190]

The British record regarding refugees on the 'home front' during the Second World War should not be judged in isolation. Other countries (most notably France) interned large numbers of Jewish refugees. The United States interned its own citizens of Japanese origin. After the 'fifth column' panic of 1940 had ebbed, the British Government released the majority of internees within a few months, and most were soon integrated into British society. If the British war-time record in the admission of Jewish refugees seems ungenerous, the same might be said of most of Britain's allies (many of whom participated in the struggle against Nazism for a much shorter

'the connection between Nazism-Fascism and anti-Semitism was not widely grasped'. See also George Orwell's essay, 'Anti-semitism in Britain', in *Collected Essays of George Orwell, vol. III As I Please*, pp. 332–40.

[189] *Jewish Chronicle*, 2 Apr. 1943.

[190] Minutes of Cabinet Committee on Refugees. 16 May 1945, PRO CAB 95/15.

period). It has been estimated that approximately 70,000 Jewish refugees entered the U.S.A. between 1940 and 1944.[191] But of these more than 50,000 were admitted in the years 1940 and 1941, before the U.S.A. entered the war; thereafter refugee immigration to the U.S.A. dwindled to a trickle.[192]

But if the British record appears a little more impressive in the light of such international comparisons, it is perhaps most properly assessed on the basis of the official British attitude to non-Jewish refugees. In this connection it is illuminating to note that in the spring of 1940, at a time when the Home Office considered it inopportune to admit any further Jewish refugees from Germany, official arrangements were said to have been made 'to receive in this country up to 300,000 Dutch and Belgians . . . after the invasion of these countries has taken place'.[193] Only a small fraction of this number of citizens of the Low Countries in fact arrived in England (among them a few Jews); but the empty places were not taken up by Jewish refugees from Central Europe (nor by those from France and Luxemburg whose cases are discussed above). The reason was less a matter of deliberate anti-Jewish prejudice than of the limited horizons of bureaucratic thinking. In the government departments concerned no general effort of sympathetic imagination appears to have been made to understand the peculiar predicament of the Jews as a distinct persecuted group. In the official mind German and Austrian Jews tended to be regarded merely as enemy aliens. Even when Jews were allied citizens, as in the cases of the French and Luxemburg Jews, their claims to attention were weighed against the overriding claims of the war effort of each of the allies involved. The fact that Jews were subject to special dangers figured little in official consideration of such matters as immigration to Britain or the British Empire. Thus 'technicians' and military personnel could be admitted to

[191] Malcolm Proudfoot, *European Refugees 1939–1952: A Study in Forced Population Movement*, London 1957, p. 75.

[192] Tartakower and Grossmann, *The Jewish Refugee*, p. 346. On American immigration policy see also pp. 196–7.

[193] J. E. M. Carvell minute, 6 May 1940, PRO FO 371/25243/253 (W 7614/7614/48).

For official discussion of the question of Belgian and Dutch refugees see report by Aliens Advisory Committee to Civil Defence Committee of War Cabinet, 29 Feb. 1940, PRO HO 45/20733, and memorandum submitted to the War Cabinet by the Home Secretary, 19 May 1940, PRO MH 79/50.

Britain; but, as we have seen, merely to be what was described as a 'racial refugee' was not, in general, regarded as a sufficient qualification for entry. This reluctance to recognize the Jews as a distinct allied nation permeated British policy on all aspects of the Jewish problem during the war. At a time when Jews were being persecuted as a distinct entity the attitude was probably unrealistic. Both at home and abroad it helped to prevent Britain giving effective succour to the Jews of Europe.

4

The 'Final Solution'

AS EARLY as January 1939 Hitler had made a public 'prophecy' that he would bring about 'the end of the Jews in Europe'.[1] At that time the Führer had stated plainly: 'We are going to destroy the Jews. They are not going to get away with what they did on 9 November 1918. The day of reckoning has come.'[2] A series of official decisions from the spring of 1941 onwards laid the bureaucratic basis for the systematic organization of the mass murders.

On 13 March 1941 Hitler dictated 'Instructions on Special Matters attached to Directive No. 21 (Barbarossa)', laying down 'certain special tasks within the operations zone of the army' to be carried out by *Einsatzgruppen* murder squads. Subsequent written orders issued to the *Einsatzgruppen* specified that among those to be executed summarily were 'Jews in the service of the Party or the State'. These were supplemented by verbal orders to squad commanders that *all* Jews were to be shot. A report by *Einsatzgruppe* A on 15 October 1941 stated that 'the cleansing operations being carried out by the security police, in accordance with basic instructions, have as their objective the total elimination of the Jews'. By 1942 the massacres of Jews in Poland and in the occupied regions of the U.S.S.R. had already claimed the lives of an estimated 1,400,000 Jews.[3]

Decisions taken from the summer of 1941 onwards accelerated the process. On 31 July 1941 Hermann Göring, in his capacity as Controller of the Four-Year Plan of the Reich, addressed a memorandum to the Chief of the Security Police,

[1] Speech by Hitler to Reichstag, 30 Jan. 1939, quoted in Krausnick and Broszat, *Anatomy of the SS State*, p. 62.
[2] Note on conversation of Hitler with Czechoslovak Foreign Minister, Chvalkovsky, 21 Jan. 1939, quoted ibid. *Einsatzgruppen* orders and reports, ibid., pp. 78–81.
[3] Hilberg, *Destruction of European Jews*, p. 256.

Reinhard Heydrich. The memorandum ordered Heydrich to prepare 'in the near future an overall plan of the organisational, functional, and material measures to be taken in preparing for the implementation of the aspired final solution of the Jewish question'.[4] In November 1941, in response to a query as to whether Jews were to be killed irrespective of economic considerations (including labour requirements), the head of the Political Department of the Reich Ministry for the Occupied Eastern Territories wrote that economic considerations were 'to be regarded as fundamentally irrelevant in the settlement of the problem'.[5] In December 1941, Hans Frank, Governor-General of Poland, explained to his officials:

I ask nothing of the Jews except that they should disappear. They will have to go. I myself have been involved in the business of deporting them to the East. A full-scale conference on this subject is taking place in Berlin in January . . . The least we can expect is that a large-scale Jewish migration will begin. But what is going to happen to the Jews? Do you really believe they are going to be quartered in settlers' villages in the Ostland? In Berlin people have said to us: why do we go to all this trouble? There is nothing we can do with them in the Ostland or in the *Reichskommissariat* either—let the dead bury their dead! Gentlemen, I must ask you to arm yourselves against all considerations of pity. We must destroy the Jews wherever we meet them, and whenever opportunity offers, so that we can maintain the whole structure of the Reich here.[6]

In late 1941 the construction began in Poland of camps, distinct from the concentration camps and ghettos already in existence in that the primary purpose of the new installations was not mere confinement but mass murder. At Chelmno, near Lodz, in December 1941, at least 152,000 were killed by means of mobile gas chambers. In March 1942 a camp equipped with permanent gas chambers was established at Belzec. Later that year similar camps were opened at Sobibor, Treblinka, and Majdanek, all in the Lublin region. The largest such centre

[4] Text in Raul Hilberg, ed., *Documents of Destruction: Germany and Jewry 1933–1945*, London 1972, pp. 88–9.
[5] Memorandum by Otto Bräutigan, [Nov.] 1941, quoted in Jeremy Noakes and Geoffrey Pridham, eds., *Documents on Nazism 1919–1945*, London 1974, p. 487.
[6] Quoted in Krausnick & Broszat, *Anatomy of the SS State*, p. 111.

was constructed at Birkenau, attached to the Auschwitz (Oswiecim) concentration camp in Upper Silesia. In the course of 1942 increasing numbers of Jews were 'deported' to meet their deaths in these places.

On 20 January 1942, Heydrich, under the authority conferred on him by Göring's memorandum of July 1941, convened a meeting in the Berlin bureau of Interpol at 56/8 Grosse Wannsee. The 'Wannsee Conference' was attended by representatives of various ministries, security organs, and party offices. Heydrich was in the chair, and the minutes of the meeting were taken by Adolf Eichmann. Delivering a speech prepared for him by Eichmann, Heydrich stated:

Instead of emigration, there is now a further possible solution to which the Führer has already signified his consent—namely deportation to the east. Although this should be regarded merely as an interim measure, it will provide us with practical experience which will be especially valuable in connection with the future final solution.

It was estimated that about eleven million Jews in Europe (excluding those of Britain, and of neutral states such as Sweden and Switzerland) would be 'involved in this final solution'. According to the minutes of the meeting, Heydrich explained what this would entail as follows:

In pursuance of the final solution, special administrative and executive measures will apply to the conscription of Jews for labour in the eastern territories. Large labour gangs of those fit to work will be formed, with the sexes separated, which will be directed to these areas for road construction, and undoubtedly a large part of them will fall out through natural elimination. Those who remain alive—and they will certainly be those with the greatest powers of endurance—will be treated accordingly. If released, they would, being a natural selection of the fittest, form a new cell from which the Jewish race could again develop. (History teaches us that.) In the course of the practical implementation of the final solution, Europe will be combed from west to east.[7]

At the conclusion of his speech, Heydrich answered a few questions and secured general agreement from the fourteen officials present. The formal part of the proceedings over,

[7] Text in Hilberg, *Documents*, pp. 89–99; see also Krausnick and Broszat, *Anatomy*, pp. 100–3.

Eichmann (according to his testimony at his trial in Jerusalem in 1961) stopped taking minutes, as butlers served liquor, and the officials stood around 'in small groups to discuss the ins and outs of the agenda . . . they spoke about methods for killing, about liquidation, about extermination'.[8] The measures decided upon at the Wannsee Conference were in full accord with Hitler's genocidal obsession. Writing in his diary in February 1942 Goebbels noted:

The Führer once more expressed his determination to clean up the Jews in Europe pitilessly. There must be no squeamish sentimentality about it. The Jews have deserved the catastrophe that has now overtaken them. Their destruction will go hand in hand with the destruction of our enemies. We must hasten this process with cold ruthlessness. We shall thereby render an inestimable service to a humanity tormented for thousands of years by the Jews.[9]

By the time these words were written official decisions were being translated into deeds of murder on a vast scale.

In October 1941 mass deportations of Jews from Germany to the ghettos in the east began. The first transports of Jews direct from Slovakia to Auschwitz and Majdanek left Bratislava in March 1942. In July the process accelerated with the start of deportations from the Netherlands and Occupied France. Meanwhile the liquidation of the Polish ghettos proceeded. Between late July and mid-September more than 300,000 Jews from the Warsaw ghetto were sent to be killed in Treblinka, Majdanek, and elsewhere. Some seventy thousand Jews remained in the ghetto for use as slave labour. Instrumental in the organization of the machinery of mass murder was section IV B 4 (Jewish Affairs and Evacuation) of the Reich SS Security Department; the section was headed by Adolf Eichmann, formerly in charge of the Reich Central Office for Jewish Emigration . While the system of deportations and murder camps came into operation, massacres of Jews by German military and para-military units continued as before, particularly in the Baltic states, the U.S.S.R., and Yugoslavia.

The Germans were aided in their task by anti-Semitic elements of other nationalities. Slovak border guards shot Jews

[8] Extracts from Eichmann trial testimony, 23 and 26 June, 24 July 1961, in Hilberg, *Documents*, pp. 99–106.

[9] Lochner, Goebbels Diaries, pp. 48–9 (entry dated 14 Feb. 1942).

seeking to escape across the frontier to Hungary.[10] French police collaborated in the round-up of Jews in Paris, and the Vichy regime acquiesced in German demands that it hand over non-French Jews from the unoccupied zone for deportation to the east.[11] In Poland an officer of the underground Home Army noted in 1942:

The peasants, fearing German reprisals, are hunting down the Jews in the countryside; they bring them to the towns or sometimes they kill them on the spot. Generally speaking, Jews are treated as if they were wild animals; the people here are driven into a kind of psychosis, and disinhibited by the German example, they forget that the Jews are human beings; they treat them like rabid dogs, rats, or other vermin, which have to be exterminated in any way possible.[12]

In Croatia and in the Ukraine local fascists joined in massacres of Jews. The worst atrocities committed by non-Germans were probably those carried out by Germany's ally in the war against Russia, Roumania. In the autumn of 1941, 185,000 Roumanian Jews were deported to camps in the Roumanian-occupied area of the U.S.S.R., known as Transnistria. This area and the camps in it were under direct Roumanian (not German) control: by May 1942 two thirds of the Transnistrian Jews were dead. When Roumanian forces occupied Odessa in October 1941, 19,000 Jews were driven into the harbour area, and concentrated in a square enclosed by a wooden fence. They were then shot by the Roumanians and their bodies burned. Another 40,000 Jews were transported outside the city and shot by the Roumanians in anti-tank ditches.[13]

Collaboration in the massacres was not universal throughout Europe. Even Laval balked at attempts to deport Jews of French nationality (inducing irritated German officials to annotate memoranda from Laval with remarks such as 'the fox' and 'where insolence becomes a method').[14] Fascist Italy resisted German pressure for the deportation of Jews from Italy and from the Italian-occupied portion of south-east France.

[10] R. Lichtheim (Geneva) to Jewish Agency, Jerusalem, 13 May 1942, CZA L22/134.
[11] Paxton, *Vichy France*, pp. 181–5.
[12] Extract dated 26 Nov. 1942 from diary of Dr Zygmunt Klukowski, quoted in S. Krakowski, 'The Slaughter of Polish Jewry—A Polish "Reassessment"', *The Wiener Library Bulletin*, 1972/3, vol. XXVI nos. 3/4, new series nos. 28/9, pp. 13–20.
[13] Hilberg, *Destruction of European Jews*, pp. 201 and 493 ff.
[14] Paxton, *Vichy France*, p. 185.

Another provoked German official in July 1943 pronounced the attitude of the Italians 'incomprehensible', and added: 'The Italian military authorities and the Italian police protect the Jews by every means in their power. The Italian zone of influence, particularly the Côte d'Azur, has become the Promised Land for the Jews in France.'[15] There were protests by churchmen in France and the Netherlands against the deportations of Jews. A few brave German churchmen made lonely gestures of opposition. The extraordinary case of Kurt Gerstein shows that some resistance to the process of mass murder was possible even within the ranks of the SS.[16] In Hungary the regime of Admiral Horthy, although it promulgated anti-Jewish discriminatory legislation, rebuffed German pressure to yield up its Jews. In a talk with Hitler in April 1943 Horthy inquired what he was expected to do with the Jews, who had already been deprived of their livelihoods—'he could not after all kill them'. To this Hitler replied (according to the official German transcript):

If they couldn't work they had to perish. They had to be treated like tuberculosis germs which could infect a healthy body. That was not cruel if one remembered how even innocent creatures like hares and deer were being killed in order to prevent damage. Why should these beasts who wanted to bring us Bolshevism be spared any more? Nations which could not defend themselves against the Jews perished.[17]

But the Hungarian, Italian, and Vichy regimes were effective only in delaying not in preventing the extension of the anti-Jewish terror into their territories. As each was engulfed by German military occupation the capacity to oppose German designs diminished. In Western Europe large numbers of Jews owed their survival to the shelter offered by resistance groups and civilians. But in central and eastern Europe, where popular anti-Semitism was a widespread and potent force, the number of Jews saved from death by such means was minuscule.

In spite of the German effort from 1941 onwards to seal off all

---

[15] Roethke to Schmidt, 21 July 1943, quoted in Leon Poliakow & Jacques Sabille, eds., *Jews under the Italian Occupation*, Paris 1955, pp. 104–6.

[16] Saul Friedländer, *Counterfeit Nazi: The Ambiguity of Good*, London 1969.

[17] Transcript of Hitler-Horthy- Ribbentrop discussion, 17 Apr. 1943, in Braham, *Destruction of Hungarian Jewry*, pp. 218–28.

escape routes for Jews from Nazi territory, small groups of Jewish refugees succeeded in making their way into relatively friendly states. Hundreds of thousands of Jews in the Baltic states and in the area of Poland occupied by the U.S.S.R. in 1939 had been fortuitously saved from the Nazis by being deported to the eastern provinces of the Soviet Union in the course of 1940 and 1941; many of these were sent to Russian prison or labour camps, but others survived the war. Following the German attack on the U.S.S.R. in June 1941 there was a further massive movement of Jews to the interior of the Soviet Union.[18] As the German armies swept across Europe neutral states such as Turkey, Switzerland, Spain, and Portugal, became increasingly uneasy about offering shelter to Jewish refugees for fear of giving offence to the Germans. The closure of the railway to Lisbon, the high price of trans-Atlantic tickets, the reluctance of the Portuguese to admit refugees who did not have visas and tickets to final destinations, and the entry of the U.S.A. to the war in December 1941 (which made it almost impossible for prospective emigrants in Europe to obtain United States entry visas), all rendered exit through the Iberian peninsula increasingly difficult during late 1941 and 1942. Nevertheless, the pressure of Nazi persecution was such that refugees continued to cross the Pyrenees, often by illegal means, in the hope that they would somehow be able to reach friendly territory. The Spanish authorities interned some of them in a camp at Miranda del Ebro; the camp had originally been designed to accommodate about seven hundred people, but by early 1943 there were more than 3,000 inhabitants in what the British Ambassador described as this 'veritable Noah's Ark of every species of refugee'.[19] In addition, there were several thousand more refugees living semi-legally in Spanish cities. The British and American embassies in Madrid, with the assistance of voluntary relief organizations, gave some succour to the refugees. Some were enabled to leave for North America: between December 1941 and May 1942 fourteen boats carrying an estimated 5,000 refugees left Lisbon for the

[18] Tartakower and Grossmann, *The Jewish Refugee*, pp. 46–8 and 265–8.
[19] 1st Viscount Templewood [Sir Samuel Hoare], *Ambassador on Special Mission*, London 1946, pp. 232–3; see also Carlton J. H. Hayes, *Wartime Mission in Spain 1942–1945*, New York 1945, pp. 112–24.

U.S.A.[20] But shipping difficulties and American immigration regulations prevented many from leaving, and the residue in Spain and Portugal increased. As prospects of legal departure from Europe receded, desperate refugees resorted to other means of escape. Forged passports, spurious visas, questionable baptismal certificates fed the refugee traffic which, with the aid of humanitarian sympathizers and underworld racketeers, flowed out of south European ports. In the winter of 1941–2 the voyages of two ships laden with refugees with no legal destination impelled the British Government into decisions which aroused widespread criticism and cast a lurid light on British policy towards refugees. These were the cases of the *Alsina* and the *Struma*.

The s.s. *Alsina* had left Marseilles on 1 January 1941 bound for Brazil. On board were reported to be 570 passengers of at least twenty nationalities; travelling third-class was the ex-President of the Spanish Republic, Alcalá Zamora, who was said to have lost most of his luggage and to be almost penniless. Forty-four passengers had visas for the United States; the remainder had been issued with visas for Brazil by the Brazilian Consul in Marseilles, but the Brazilian Government refused to accept these as satisfactory.[21] Under Vatican pressure Brazil had, in fact, offered in June 1939 to admit three thousand 'German Catholic non-Aryans'; but the offer was hedged with reservations and eventually withdrawn. Further Vatican representations had merely evoked the comment from the Brazilian Ambassador to the Holy See that the Jews who had arrived hitherto had made the worst possible impression, and that very many of them seemed to have been baptized only in 1939.[22] From 1941 even 'capitalist' visas, hitherto obtainable upon deposit of $12,500 per family in a Brazilian bank, became difficult to obtain.[23] The *Alsina* stopped *en route* at Dakar in French West Africa. The pro-Vichy authorities there detained the ship for four months, while the Vichy régime asked the

[20] Mark Wischnitzer, *To Dwell in Safety*, Philadelphia 1948, p. 237.

[21] U.S. Consul, Dakar, to State Dept., 25 Mar. 1941, USNA 840.48 Refugees 2491; *Daily Herald*, 1 July 1941; British Embassy, Buenos Aires, to Foreign Office, 8 Oct. 1941, PRO FO 371/29220 (W 12001/570/48).

[22] *VAT*, vol. 6, docs. nos. 34, 42, 46, 70, 111, 120, 128, 163, 184, 208, 304, and 396; *VAT*, vol. 8, docs. nos. 202 and 205.

[23] Tartakower and Grossmann, *The Jewish Refugee*, p. 316.

American Government whether the passengers might be admitted to the U.S.A. In the absence of a positive response the boat sailed in early June for Casablanca. There most of the passengers were put in a concentration camp, while arrangements were made for their onward voyage.[24]

In October 1941 the British Embassy at Buenos Aires reported that, having been refused admission to Brazil, they had arrived at Buenos Aires in a Spanish boat. The report continued:

They were not permitted to land here, and may on return to Spanish concentration camps, be handed over to the Nazis. They have therefore appealed to be allowed to land at Trinidad where the ship will touch on its way to Spain. Appeal seems to me justified at least in the case of the Polish, Czech, and Belgian refugees.[25]

Although the number of refugees involved appears to have been reduced to about eighty-five Jews (the remainder, mainly non-Jews, having disembarked at earlier stages of the odyssey), the acting Governor of Trinidad rejected the appeal, and his decision was endorsed by the Colonial Office.[26] Forced to move on from Argentina, the party found temporary refuge at Curaçao, but the Netherlands Government-in-exile specified that they must not remain there permanently. When the possibility was mooted that they might be admitted to Britain, A. W. G. Randall of the Foreign Office Refugee Department minuted: 'We could not possibly have these people in the United Kingdom. The Home Office and the Ministry of Food would be adamant.'[27] The Dutch Government remaining insistent that the refugees must not stay in Curaçao, the American Jewish Joint Distribution Committee finally intervened, and eventually arranged for their dispersal to the U.S.A. and other destinations.[28] The saga had had a relatively fortunate ending, but it had demonstrated again the extreme reluctance of the British Government (a reluctance shared with most of its allies and

[24] Foreign Office minutes, 7 and 8 July 1941, PRO FO 371/29220 (W 8197/570/48).

[25] British Embassy, Buenos Aires, to Foreign Office, 8 Oct. 1941, ibid.

[26] Officer Administering Government of Trinidad to Colonial Office, 9 Oct. 1941; Colonial Office to Foreign Office, 11 Oct. 1941, PRO FO 371/29220 (W 12001/570/48).

[27] Minute dated 8 Nov. 1941, PRO FO 371/29220 (W 13209/570/48).

[28] Netherlands Minister to Eden, 2 Dec. 1941; Foreign Office to Netherlands Minister, 8 Dec. 1941, PRO FO 371/29220 (W 14404/570/48); Kullmann to Randall, 10 Dec. 1941, PRO FO 371/29220 (W 14820/570/48).

with neutral states) to admit refugee Jews to any of its territories.

The case of the *Struma* had a very different *dénouement*, and, as a result of the widespread publicity which it attracted, marked a crucial stage in British policy towards Jewish refugees. The s.s. *Struma*, an ancient converted yacht of 240 tons,[29] left Constanza on 12 December 1941 under the command of a Bulgarian captain G. T. Gorbatenko, flying the Panamanian flag, and carrying 769 Jewish refugees. The violent anti-Semitic persecutions unleashed in Roumania in the autumn of 1941 had produced an atmosphere of terror among Roumanian Jews; the only solution, in the view of the American Minister in Bucharest in November 1941, seemed to be 'a refuge abroad . . . to which these unfortunate people would be able to emigrate, probably with no worldly possessions whatsoever'.[30] It was against this background that a Greek ship-owner, Yanaki Pandelis, possibly in concert with Revisionist Zionists, had offered for sale to Bucharest Jews tickets to Palestine aboard the *Struma*. The tickets were not accompanied by Palestine immigration certificates.[31] British security organs had learnt of the ship's imminent voyage before it set sail, and the Foreign Office had pressed the Turkish Government to bar the *Struma* passage through the Straits.[32] The initial Turkish response was that the Montreux Convention prevented their taking effective action.[33]

The *Struma* arrived off Istanbul after a three-day voyage, but was unable to proceed into the Sea of Marmara because her engine had broken down. The Turkish authorities refused to allow the passengers to land while repairs were being effected; the boat therefore remained anchored offshore with the passengers on board. Conditions on the ship were described in a

---

[29] The *Struma* was built in 1867 at Newcastle. She first appears in Lloyd's Register in 1874 under the name *Xantha*. In 1895 she is included in the Yacht Register under the name *Sea Maid*. In 1902 her name changes to *Kaphireus*, and she switches from the British to the Greek flag. By 1934 (the last year in which she appears in the Register) her name is *Esperos* and her flag Bulgarian; no name of owner is given.

[30] Gunther (Bucharest) to State Dept., Washington, 4 Nov. 1941, *FRUS 1941 vol. II*, pp. 871–4.

[31] Statement of David Ben Yakov Stolar to Palestine C.I.D., Jaffa, 3 May 1942, PRO CO 733/446 (76021/42/26–7); Dinur, *Sefer Toldot Ha-haganah*, vol. III, part I, p. 159.

[32] High Commissioner, Jerusalem to Colonial Office, 9 Oct. 1941, PRO FO 371/29163 (W 12180/11/48); Foreign Office to Angora, 11 Oct. 1941, ibid.

[33] Angora to High Commissioner, Jerusalem, 16 Oct. 1941, PRO FO 371/29163 (W 12180/11/48).

British naval intelligence report as 'appalling'.[34] According to the Jewish Agency there was only one lavatory on board, and one small kitchen; there were no provisions and no fresh water whether for drinking or washing. Air in the hold was foul, but passengers could breathe fresh air only by taking turns as there was no room for all of them on the deck even if they stood jammed together. There were numerous cases of dysentery, and two or three of mental illness; there was no separate accommodation for the sick. Although the authorities prohibited any contact between ship and shore, some members of the Istanbul Jewish community managed to send food to the ship. Hot meals were served by turns once a week. Under this regimen the passengers were reported to have fallen into a state of general enfeeblement.[35] They remained on the immobile ship in these conditions for more than two months, while efforts were made to repair the engine, and while the world considered their fate.

On 20 December the British Ambassador in Ankara, Sir Hughe Knatchbull-Hugessen, discussed the problem with the Assistant Secretary-General of the Turkish Ministry of Foreign Affairs. Sir Hughe was told that while the Turks believed that they could do nothing to stop the passage of the ship through the Straits without breaching the Montreux Convention, they were nevertheless considering whether to send her back into the Black Sea on the ground that she might founder in the Sea of Marmara. The Turkish diplomat stated that his government wished at all costs to avoid such a disaster because the survivors might then be left in Turkey. The implication, left unsaid, was that a similar catastrophe in the Black Sea, which, unlike the Sea of Marmara, was not completely surrounded by Turkish territory, would not be regarded with equal apprehension by the Turkish Government. The official added, however, that if His Majesty's Government would promise to admit the refugees to Palestine, the Turks would allow the ship to proceed, and even assist it. In reply, Sir Hughe said that His Majesty's Government 'did not want these people in Palestine' and that they 'had no permission to go there'. He added that

---

[34] S.O. (I.) to Admiralty, 5 Feb. 1942, PRO FO 371/32661/28 (W 2093/652/48).

[35] M. Shertok to J. Macpherson (Chief Secretary of Government of Palestine), 13 Feb. 1942, PRO CO 733/446 (76021/42/55).

from a humanitarian point of view he did not like the Turkish proposal to send the ship back into the Black Sea. 'If the Turkish Government must interfere with the ship on the ground that they could not keep the distressed Jews in Turkey, let her rather go towards the Dardanelles. It might be that if they reached Palestine, they might despite their illegality receive humane treatment.'[36]

Sir Hughe's report on this conversation was received with dismay in London. In particular, his unauthorized suggestion that the passengers might 'receive humane treatment' if they arrived in Palestine without certificates gravely disturbed the Colonial Office. S. E. V. Luke minuted: 'This is the first occasion on which . . . the Turkish Government has shown any signs of being ready to help in frustrating these illegal immigrant ships, and the Ambassador then goes and spoils the whole effect on absurdly misjudged humanitarian grounds.'[37] Endorsing Luke's view, E. B. Boyd added: 'Sir H. Knatchbull-Hugessen had a heaven-sent opportunity of getting these people stopped at Istanbul and sent back to Constantsa, and has failed to avail himself of it.'[38] The Colonial Office's annoyance was given authoritative expression in a letter of protest against the Ambassador's statement, written by the Colonial Secretary, Lord Moyne, to Richard Law, Parliamentary Under-Secretary at the Foreign Office. Moyne declared:

The landing [in Palestine] of seven hundred more immigrants will not only be a formidable addition to the difficulties of the High Commissioner . . . but it will have a deplorable effect throughout the Balkans in encouraging further Jews to embark on a traffic which has now been condoned by His Majesty's Ambassador. We have good reason to believe that this traffic is favoured by the Gestapo, and the Security Services attach the very greatest importance to preventing the influx of Nazi agents under the cloak of refugees. As to Knatchbull-Hugessen's humanitarian feelings about sending the refugees back to the Black Sea countries, it seems to me that these might apply with equal force to the tens of thousands of Jews who remain behind and who are most eager to join them. I find it difficult to write with moderation about this occurrence which is in flat contradiction of

[36] Angora to Foreign Office, 20 Dec. 1941, PRO CO 733/449 (P3/4/30).
[37] S. E. V. Luke minute, 23 Dec. 1941, ibid.
[38] E. B. Boyd minute, 23 Dec. 1941, ibid.

established Government policy, and I should be very glad if you could perhaps even now do something to retrieve the position, and to urge that [the] Turkish authorities should be asked to send the ship back to the Black Sea, as they originally proposed.[39]

Lord Moyne's view was reinforced by a cable from the High Commissioner, Sir Harold MacMichael, who insisted that it was 'most important both from policy and security points of view that these illegal immigrants should be prevented from coming to Palestine'. Sir Harold added that he thought there was much substance in the fear expressed by the Turkish Foreign Ministry that the ship might founder during the onward voyage to Palestine.[40]

The British Embassy in Ankara was accordingly instructed to correct the false impression of British policy which appeared to have been conveyed to the Turks. On 27 December the Turkish Foreign Ministry was therefore informed that 'His Majesty's Government saw no reason why the Turkish Government should not send [the] *Struma* back into the Black Sea if they wished'.[41] The Turks, however, discovered that they faced three obstacles to their sending the ship back, or indeed moving it at all. In the first place the Roumanian Minister in Ankara told the Turkish Government that the passengers on board the *Struma* had left Roumania illegally and that there could be no question of their being allowed to return.[42] It thus seemed that in whichever direction the ship sailed it would lack a destination. Secondly, all attempts by Turkish engineers to mend the ship's engine proved fruitless; it appeared to be damaged beyond repair. The third obstacle took the form of a letter written to the Istanbul Port Captain on 10 January 1942 by the captain of the *Struma*. In this communication Captain Gorbatenko pointed out that his ship was registered under the Panamanian flag, and asserted that the recent entry of Panama into the war (Panama had declared war on Germany on 12 December 1941—the day the *Struma* left Constanza) rendered it dangerous for the ship to proceed unless escorted by a Turkish

[39] Moyne to Law, 24 Dec. 1941, ibid.
[40] High Commissioner, Jerusalem, to Colonial Office (for repetition to Angora), 22 Dec. 1941, PRO CO 733/449/P3/4/30.
[41] Angora to Foreign Office, 29 Dec. 1941, PRO PREM 4/51/1/40.
[42] Angora to Foreign Office, 27 Feb. 1942, PRO CO 733/446 (76021/42/98).

warship. He added that, Bulgaria being at war with Britain, and he being a Bulgarian citizen, he considered it his duty to return to Bulgaria with his crew. In any case, he maintained, the condition of the ship and of the passengers had deteriorated so far that he was unable to take responsibility for continuing the voyage. He ventured the opinion that the only solution to the problem was the disembarkation of the passengers and their continuation of the voyage on another boat.[43]

During the two months that the *Struma* stood off Istanbul, the Jewish Agency pleaded with the British and Palestine Governments to admit the refugees to Palestine. In Jerusalem Moshe Shertok disputed the notion that the *Struma* might be used by the Nazis to smuggle agents into Palestine. He pointed out that, notwithstanding repeated objections of this nature to immigration from Europe, not a single case had come to light of any Jewish refugee acting as an enemy agent in Palestine.[44] (It was, incidentally, an illuminating sidelight on the degree of Zionist knowledge of British security arrangements in the Middle East, that Shertok was able to make this—accurate—statement with confidence.) In London Lewis Namier informed the Colonial Office that the American Jewish Joint Distribution Committee had offered to contribute £6,000 towards the absorption of the refugees in Palestine.[45] Chaim Weizmann, lunching with Eden's Principal Private Secretary, Oliver Harvey, told him flatly that Jewish emigration from Eastern Europe could not be prevented; the Jews would swim to Palestine whatever the British did.[46] All this, however, failed to move the Colonial Office or the High Commissioner. Meanwhile the Turkish Government announced to the British Ambassador that as no solution could be found it was intended to send the ship and passengers back in the direction from which they had come; action would be taken on about 16 February.[47]

On 11 February, five days before this deadline, a minute by Oliver Harvey struck a new note. Commenting on a telegram

[43] Captain G. T. Gorbatenko to Port Captain, Istanbul, 10 Jan. 1942, in Daphne Trevor, *Under the White Paper*, Jerusalem 1948, p. 23.

[44] Shertok to Macpherson, 13 Feb. 1942, PRO CO 733/446 (76021/42/55).

[45] Namier to Moyne, 18 Feb. 1942, PRO CO 733/446 (76021/42/120).

[46] Oliver Harvey diary, BL 56398 (entry dated 29 Jan. 1942).

[47] Angora to Foreign Office, 9 Feb. 1942, PRO FO 371/32661/27 (W 2083/652/48).

from Ankara reporting the Turkish intention to send the ship back, Harvey wrote: 'Can nothing be done for these unfortunate refugees? Must H.M.G. take such an inhuman decision? If they go back they will all be killed.'[48] Harvey's inclination in favour of some concession to the refugees was not, however, shared by most of his Foreign Office colleagues. C. W. Baxter argued that 'if we were to accept these people, there would, of course, be more and more shiploads of unwanted Jews later! . . . Personally, I feel strongly that it would be unwise for us to intervene, and that our intervention would only mean more shiploads later and more suffering.'[49] A. W. G. Randall concurred, but suggested rather half-heartedly the idea of diverting the ship to Cyprus where the refugees might be interned temporarily pending the provision of a ship to take them to Mauritius. He suggested that Eden might discuss the problem with Moyne.[50] Harvey was deputed by Eden to speak to Moyne's private secretary, and after doing so he wrote to Eden:

I have spoken to Lord Moyne's private secretary and represented to him your feelings about the decision that these refugees should be sent back again from Turkey to the Black Sea. He will speak to Lord Moyne about it at once and let us know his views. He pointed out, however, that in the summer it had been decided that such refugees should be refused admission. I understood, however, that the Prime Minister's heart had also been stirred by these latest telegrams.

Harvey disputed Baxter's opinion that it would be unwise for the Foreign Office to intervene at all:

I am inclined to think that we should press the Colonial Office very strongly to admit them to Cyprus *pro tem* . . . After all, these unfortunate people are on our side. The exodus could hardly assume very great proportions, and it should be possible to sort out the enemy agents.[51]

But the reply from the Colonial Office was predictably negative. On 13 February, three days before the Turkish deadline, Eden, in a minute to the Prime Minister, summed up what was evidently the joint view of the Foreign and Colonial Offices. He

[48] O. Harvey, minute, 11 Feb. 1942, PRO FO 371/32661 (W 2083/652/48).
[49] C. W. Baxter minute, 12 Feb. 1942, ibid.
[50] A. W. G. Randall minutes, 12 Feb. 1942, ibid.
[51] Harvey to Eden, 12 Feb. 1942, ibid.

said that he had consulted Moyne who had informed him that it had been learnt from secret sources that the *Struma* was the first of several ships which were being chartered in order to carry illegal immigrants from south-east European ports to Palestine. Moyne had declared it impossible to send the boat to Cyprus because the island was on a war footing and no accommodation for the refugees would be available there. Moyne therefore felt that there was 'nothing for it but to carry out the last Cabinet instruction on the subject'.[52] This was the decision of 27 November 1940 (immediately after the *Patria* explosion) that 'illegal immigrants attempting to enter Palestine should be diverted to Mauritius or elsewhere'.[53] This Cabinet ruling would, of course, have left open the possibility of the refugees on the *Struma* being permitted to continue their voyage provided it were to a destination other than Palestine. However, the question was never put to the Turks whether they would permit the boat to continue on that basis. Nor was any alternative destination found. The interpretation put upon the Cabinet decision by the Foreign and Colonial Offices was, in any case, much more restrictive: their understanding was that the ruling required that the British Government encourage the Turks to turn the *Struma* back into the Black Sea. The possibility of diversion 'to Mauritius or elsewhere' arose only if an illegal boat succeeded in reaching Palestinian territorial waters and thereby became an inescapable British concern. Eden, in his minute to Churchill, did not explain this restrictive interpretation of the Cabinet ruling. But he concluded the minute by expressing agreement with Moyne's view of the matter:

I feel, too, that there is, alas, no other choice. But I thought you should know.

P.S. I should add that we have reason to believe that, now that these countries are under enemy control, suspected persons on whose relatives the enemy may have a hold will be infiltrated into these parties.[54]

The purpose of this minute appears to have been to shelter behind a reference to the Cabinet ruling of 27 November 1940 in order to secure the Prime Minister's acquiescence to the

[52] Eden to Churchill, 13 Feb. 1942, PRO FO 371/32661/25 (W 2093/652/48).
[53] Cabinet minutes, 27 Nov. 1940, PRO CAB 65/10.
[54] Eden to Churchill, 13 Feb. 1942, PRO FO 371/32661/25 (W 2093/652/48).

policy (not spelt out in the minute) of pressing the Turks to turn the boat back. Churchill, however, does not appear to have been satisfied, and gave notice that he intended to raise the matter in Cabinet on 16 February.[55] This was the deadline originally set by the Turks, after which the boat would be sent back. At this eleventh hour the High Commissioner relented slightly. In a cable to the Colonial Office, he announced: 'It has been decided to admit to Palestine children from the *Struma* between the ages of eleven and sixteen years . . . No repeat no adults can be accepted.'[56] In the discussion in Cabinet on 16 February, the *Struma* was mentioned in the course of a consideration of what should be done with previous illegal immigrants (from the *Darien*) now interned in Palestine. Churchill advocated their release. Moyne used the case of the *Struma* to illustrate his argument that 'any weakening of our attitude in this matter would afford encouragement to the very undesirable trade in illegal immigration into Palestine'. Consideration of the *Struma* case was delayed pending a report on the *Darien* internees from the Minister of State in Cairo. No immediate decision was reached by the Cabinet.[57] The existing policy (as interpreted by the responsible departments) therefore stood.

In the event, the Turks did not send back the *Struma* into the Black Sea on 16 February as they had threatened, but allowed the boat to remain moored off Istanbul for a further week while discussions continued. The High Commissioner, however, made it clear that he was not prepared to countenance any further concession. In a long cable to the Colonial Office on 17 February he defended his position:

My advisers again endorsed the general security objection . . . on account of the risk of leakage into the Middle East of persons working in Axis interests. In the particular case of Rumanians [the] objection [is] now reinforced by report (unquotable) of negotiations between Rumanian Jews and the Germans. Information which has recently come to light shows that illegal immigration on the *Atlantic, Milos*, and *Pacific* in 1940 was directly engineered by the Gestapo. There has been [a] specific report of Nazi agents on the *Struma*.

[55] Harvey to Eden, 15 Feb. 1942, PRO CO 733/446 (76021/42/124).

[56] High Commissioner, Jerusalem, to Colonial Office, 15 Feb. 1942, PRO FO 371/32661/53 (W 2483/652/48).

[57] Extract from War Cabinet Conclusions, 16 Feb. 1942, PRO CO 733/446 (76021/40/1942).

MacMichael again stressed the difficulty of identifying and verifying the *bona fides* of the passengers. He added that a further objection lay in the fact that the passengers were in the main professional people and would therefore, if admitted to Palestine, constitute an addition to 'the unproductive element in the population'.[58]

Even the decision to admit to Palestine children on board the *Struma* aged between eleven and sixteen was not implemented. The reason for this was the adamant refusal of the Turkish Government to permit the children to travel overland across Turkey in order to reach Palestine. The Ministry of Foreign Affairs told the British Ambassador that the children could be allowed to proceed to Palestine only if the British sent a boat to take them there by sea.[59] The Foreign and Colonial Offices agreed in finding the Turkish refusal to allow overland transit for the children unreasonable.[60] Harvey thought the Foreign Office 'should keep up stiff pressure on the Turks over this'.[61] But a sense of despair now pervaded official discussion of the matter. On 19 February A. W. G. Randall wrote:

I see no way of ending the deadlock except by either the Turks sending the ship back, or sending the ship on for such action as may be authorised against it, or finally, our pressing the Turks to reconsider their decision against letting the children travel overland. Even if we get the Turks to agree I should imagine that the process of selecting the children and taking them from their parents off the *Struma* would be an extremely distressing one. Who do you propose should undertake it, and has the possibility of the adults refusing to let the children go been considered?[62]

Pressure on the Turks to relent over the question of transit for the children across Turkey proved unsuccessful.[63] On 23 February the British Passport Control Officer at Istanbul reported that preparations were being made to tow the *Struma* (her engine still unrepaired) 'towards the Black Sea where

[58] High Commissioner, Jerusalem, to Colonial Office, PRO FO 371/32661/56 (W 2483/652/48).

[59] Angora to Jerusalem, 18 Feb. 1942, PRO FO 371/32661/53 (W 2483/652/48).

[60] Randall minute, 19 Feb. 1942, PRO FO 371/32661/49 (W 2483/652/48).

[61] Harvey minute, 20 Feb. 1942, ibid.

[62] Randall to Boyd, 19 Feb. 1942, PRO FO 371/32661/57 (W 2483/652/48).

[63] Foreign Office to Angora, 20 Feb. 1942, PRO FO 371/32661/59 (W 2483/652/48), unsigned memorandum headed 's.s. Struma', PRO CO 733/446 (76021/42/105).

she would doubtless be cast adrift outside Turkish territorial waters.'[64] This message evoked an immediate Foreign Office telegram to the British Embassy in Ankara instructing that urgent representations be made to the Turkish Government asking that the action should at least be postponed while the question of the children was reconsidered.[65] But by the time this message arrived it was too late.

A single minute sheet in the Foreign Office files, containing two minutes by A. Walker of the Refugee Department, poignantly records the outcome. The first minute, dated 24 February, reads: 'The Black Sea is rough at this time of year and the *Struma* may well founder. I do not at all like the idea that we may be acting as accessories in bringing about the death of these miserable people.' The second minute is dated 25 February: 'The ship is today reported as having sunk with all on board.'[66] According to the account of the solitary survivor of the disaster, David Stoliar, Turkish police had suddenly arrived on board the *Struma* in force and informed the passengers that they must leave Turkey and return to Roumania. Stoliar's account, made in a deposition to the Palestine Police in May 1942, continued:

None of us could resist but some of the passengers objected and came to blows with the police, but the police overpowered them and there were some 100 to 200 policemen. They took the ship some ten kilometres from the coast and left us. This was at night, and early in the morning when I was still asleep an explosion occurred . . . When the ship started to sink, I was together with the second Captain [i.e. the ship's mate]. We both jumped into the sea; he was near me. As he told me, the explosion was caused by a torpedo which he saw. The explosion occurred about ten kilometres from the Turkish coast. I saw the coast and I believed that the same [i.e. the ship] could be seen from the coast. Nobody came to our help from ashore. The second Captain who was with me in the sea disappeared about a quarter of an hour before the saving boat arrived.[67]

Stoliar said that after some twenty-four hours in the sea he was rescued by a Turkish motor launch and taken to hospital in Istanbul where he remained for two weeks. Upon discharge

[64] Angora to Foreign Office, 23 Feb. 1942, PRO FO 371/32661/77 (W 2810/652/48).
[65] Foreign Office to Angora, 24 Feb. 1942, PRO FO 371/32661/79 (W 2810/652/48).
[66] A. Walker minutes, 24 and 25 Feb. 1942, PRO FO 371/32661/75 (W 2810/652/48).
[67] Statement to Jaffa C.I.D., 3 May 1942, PRO CO 733/446 (76021/42/26–7).

from the hospital he was consigned to prison.[68] There is independent evidence to support Stoliar's account of the sinking of the ship. A naval intelligence report stated that the *Struma* was torpedoed.[69] A report from the British Ambassador in Ankara said that the possibility of her having been torpedoed was not ruled out.[70] According to one account the torpedo may have been fired in error by a Soviet vessel.[71] The possibility that the boat struck a mine or that the rotten, overcrowded, engine-less hulk sank as a result of the rough weather cannot, however, be excluded.

If the immediate cause of the disaster is likely never to be ascertained, the ultimate responsibility can be analysed. The root of it was the German anti-Jewish terror in Europe; but the responsibility was not exclusively German. The Germans indeed played little or no direct part in the sequence of events which led to the catastrophe. Apart from the alleged presence of Gestapo agents aboard the ship, which so greatly concerned Moyne and MacMichael, there is only one item of evidence suggesting direct German involvement. This is an American intelligence report claiming that the German Government had exerted pressure on the Turks to 'have the ship driven from Istanbul, hoping that subsequent developments would cause adverse reactions in England and the United States'.[72] British sources, however, stated that the report could not be confirmed.[73] A major share of the responsibility must be assigned to the Roumanian Government. The victims of the disaster were Roumanian citizens who fled Roumanian persecution and whom the Roumanian Government refused to allow back into the country. But some share also rests with the Turkish Government whose primary concern throughout appears to have been unwillingness to take any responsibility for the fate of the passengers on the ship. However, the Foreign Office was in 1942 trying to entice a neutral Turkey into the war on the Allied

[68] Ibid.

[69] Beyoglu to Admiralty, 27 Feb. 1942, PRO CO 733/446 (76021/42/105).

[70] Angora to Foreign Office, 8 Mar. 1942, PRO CO 733/446 (76021/42/88).

[71] Jürgen Rohwehr, *Die Versenkung der jüdischen Flüchtlings-transporter Struma und Mefkure im Schwarzen Meer (Februar 1942, August 1944)*, Frankfurt/Main 1965.

[72] H. Schantz (U.S. Embassy, London) to A. W. G. Randall, 4 Mar. 1942, PRO FO 371/32662 (W 3401/652/48).

[73] See Foreign Office notes, ibid.

side, and was therefore concerned that 'no reflection must be cast on the Turks'.[74] Little stress was therefore laid by the British Government on the Turkish role in the affair; *The Times*, reflecting this concern, concluded on 27 February: 'The responsibility for this tragedy rests entirely on the Roumanian Government which drove away these unfortunates.'

What of the British role? There is no doubt that the catastrophe evoked a distinct sense of moral disquiet in certain quarters of Whitehall and Westminster. Although the full horror of the Jewish fate in Europe was not yet appreciated in official circles in February 1942, Oliver Harvey's view that 'if they go back they will all be killed' had not been contradicted by any of his colleagues. The chain of official communications on the *Struma* provides some indication of where the key British decisions were made. The Prime Minister, overwhelmingly preoccupied with the disastrous surrender of Singapore to the Japanese (on 15 February), could not give the matter full attention, although his sympathy for the refugees had been aroused. The Foreign Secretary, apparently influenced by his private secretary, Harvey, seems at first to have leant towards a similarly lenient view; later he changed his mind. But the Foreign Office was not the dominant force in the making of the vital decision to press the Turks to turn the boat back. The primary role was that of the Colonial Office, strongly supported by the Government of Palestine. The central figures were clearly Lord Moyne and Sir Harold MacMichael: they were the chiefs of the two departments most directly concerned; they took an active personal interest in the matter; they played crucial roles in pressing for the decisions which were ultimately adopted.

The bitter debates over responsibility for the tragedy, which continued for several years, proved to be a running sore in relations between the British and the Zionists. More than any other single event of the war years the *Struma* episode aroused Palestinian Jewish hostility to the British and Palestine Governments. The disaster may, indeed, have marked a psychological watershed for the *Yishuv*, destroying the last vestiges of the special relationship between Britain and Zionism inaugurated by the Balfour Declaration. Followed closely by news of the full

[74] Randall minute, 26 Feb. 1942, PRO FO 371/32661/89 (W 2906/652/48).

horror of the 'Final Solution' in Europe, the story of the *Struma* was to fester in Jewish minds for years as an example of British callousness and inhumanity. Embroidered accounts of the tragedy were to provide part of the ideological justification for the terrorist movements which emerged among the *Yishuv* in the later years of the war.[75] Among the targets for terrorist attack were to be Sir Harold MacMichael, who escaped an assassination attempt in August 1944, and Lord Moyne, assassinated in Cairo in November 1944.

In Britain the sinking of the *Struma* led to strong criticism of the Government's policy. The *Manchester Guardian* inquired, 'Need this have happened?', and in a leader insisted:

The admission of refugees should be treated not with niggling statecraft but with generous humanity and common sense ... It is said that some refugees might be Axis agents. Any refugees from any Nazi country may conceivably be spies. We have taken the risk here and have not suffered for it. In Palestine itself, since the war began, several thousand refugees have been admitted and it is not suggested that Axis agents have been found among them ... The Administration is now readmitting to Palestine former supporters of the Mufti of Jerusalem. It is prepared, apparently, to go bail for them. If so, it passes understanding why the victims of Axis brutalities, the shattered fugitives from butcher-States like Rumania, should be thrust back from safety in the home of their race.[76]

But the *Manchester Guardian* was a long-standing sympathizer with Zionism and champion of Jewish refugees, and its views could to that extent be discounted by the Government, as could those of prominent parliamentary pro-Zionists, who were taken to task in a *Daily Telegraph* editorial:

There can hardly be a more flagrant abuse of the freedom of Parliamentary debate than occurred yesterday when the question of our policy in Palestine was raised in the House of Lords. Lord Davies thought it a fitting time to launch a violent attack upon the Palestinian administration ... Lord Wedgwood came to his support with

[75] See e.g. Arthur Koestler, *Promise and Fulfilment: Palestine 1917–1949*, London 1949, pp. 62–3; & Menachem Begin, *The Revolt*, 5th ed. Jerusalem 1972, p. 35. Mr Koestler states: 'Indirect evidence suggests that the Palestine Government never informed the Turks of its willingness to take care of the children.' As has been shown this allegation is incorrect. Mr Begin alleges that the *Struma* 'arrived off the coast of Eretz Israel' whence it was sent back to Roumania. This too is embroidery.

[76] *Manchester Guardian*, 26 Feb. and 2 Mar. 1942.

yet wilder accusations of anti-Semitism on the part of the Palestine authorities.[77]

The sympathy for Jewish refugees evoked in Britain (mainly in predictable quarters) by the *Struma* disaster was soon swallowed up in the welter of war news, which, with the continued German and Japanese victories, prevented all save enthusiasts (and those directly involved) from considering the Jewish refugee problem as a vital and immediate British concern.

In the aftermath of the disaster the High Commissioner in Jerusalem manifested no sign of second thoughts. In a cable to the Colonial Office he maintained: 'The fate of these people was tragic, but the fact remains that they were nationals of a country at war with Britain, proceeding direct from enemy territory. Palestine was under no obligations towards them.'[78] Sir Harold MacMichael stuck to the principle of non-obligation a few weeks later when the question arose of admitting to Palestine a group of twenty refugees stranded in Turkey, among them the imprisoned David Stoliar, and another former passenger on the *Struma*; the latter was a woman who had been allowed to leave the ship because she was pregnant; her husband had died when the boat sank, and her newborn child had died in an Istanbul hospital. MacMichael ruled against their admission to Palestine, insisting that the 'basic principle that enemy nationals from enemy or enemy-controlled territory should not be admitted to this country during the war applies to all immigrants'. He added that admission of these immigrants would be likely to 'open the floodgate and completely undermine our whole policy regarding illegal immigration'.[79] MacMichael was, however, overruled on the admission of the two *Struma* survivors by Moyne's successor as Colonial Secretary, Lord Cranborne. In a cable to the High Commissioner, explaining the decision to admit the two survivors 'on humanitarian grounds as an act of clemency', Cranborne pointed out that refusal of admission 'could only have exacerbated [the] intense feeling of resentment which [the] *Struma* disaster has aroused in Jewish

[77] *Daily Telegraph*, 11 Mar. 1942.

[78] High Commissioner, Jerusalem, to Colonial Office, 1 Mar. 1942, PRO CO 733/446 (76021/42 (1942)/1).

[79] High Commissioner, Jerusalem, to Colonial Office, 19 Mar. 1942, PRO CO 733/446 (76021/42 (1942)/62).

and pro-Jewish circles in this country and [the] United States'.[80]

Under Cranborne, indeed, a new and somewhat more compassionate spirit was infused into Colonial Office policy on the question of illegal immigration to Palestine. In an interview with Weizmann, the new Colonial Secretary declared himself 'personally determined to see that there should be no similar disaster in the future if it could in any way be avoided'.[81] On Cranborne's instructions the Colonial Office prepared a memorandum for submission to the Cabinet, urging a liberalization of policy towards illegal immigration to Palestine. Such a modification was hardly welcome to the department, although, as Sir Cosmo Parkinson, the Permanent Under-Secretary, reflected, there was 'at least the hope that under War conditions the number of illegal immigrants who are likely to reach Palestine, whatever impetus there may be from the enemy in occupied territory, will not be great'.[82] In his Cabinet memorandum, Cranborne stated that the White Paper policy must stand, but argued that there might be 'modifications which could usefully be made in its practical application'. He pointed out that the *Struma* disaster had 'greatly shocked public opinion both in this country and the United States, and that it seemed certain that the fate of the *Struma* would lead to renewed pressure on the Government 'both by Jews and pro-Jews, and by purely humanitarian persons, to modify the present ban on illegal immigration'. There were, the memorandum continued, two practicable alternatives: the Government might 'stand pat . . . and refuse to budge'; or they might 'agree to admit illegal immigrants, so long as their numbers were deducted from the annual quota, and so long as under no circumstances did they exceed that quota'. Cranborne went on:

My own preference, after careful consideration, inclines slightly to the second. The fate of those miserable people who do succeed in leaving enemy countries is so terrible, if we refuse them entry into Palestine, that I cannot feel that it is right to abandon them in their extremity.

[80] Colonial Secretary to High Commissioner, Jerusalem, 21 Mar. 1942, PRO CO 733/446 (76021/42 (1942)/61).
[81] Note by Cranborne on conversation with Weizmann, 18 Mar. 1944, PRO CO 733/444.
[82] Sir C. Parkinson minute, 1 Mar. 1942, PRO CO 733/445 (76021/41).

Cranborne stated that the practical effect of his proposal would be as follows:

A shipload of immigrants would arrive at a Palestinian port, and would immediately be put into a detention camp. While there, each immigrant would be subject to close scrutiny by the Palestine authorities on security grounds, and a decision would be reached, in consultation with the Jewish Agency, on the application of the principle of economic absorptive capacity to each of them. Those who passed through these two sieves would be admitted to the country—the remainder would be taken elsewhere, to Mauritius or wherever it might be. In practice, of course, nearly all the immigrants would be admitted, for the Jewish Agency would see that jobs were available for them. But the fact that we were maintaining the main provisions of the White Paper might be used as an argument to rebut subsequent Arab criticism.[83]

When the proposal was discussed in the Cabinet on 5 March, however, Cranborne's suggestion was subjected to much criticism from his colleagues, and was not approved. In the Cabinet discussion it was pointed out that it was the policy of the Roumanian Government to expel Jews from the country; there was, therefore, 'a grave risk that if we agreed to admit to Palestine illegal immigrants fleeing from enemy oppression, even if subject to the conditions suggested by the Colonial Secretary, the influx would soon reach large proportions'. The shortage of shipping, it was further argued, made difficult the sending of Jewish refugees to alternative destinations such as Mauritius. On the other hand, 'an awkward issue' would arise 'when the next shipload of illegal immigrants reached Istanbul and we were asked whether we would agree to the ship proceeding to Palestine'. In the light of these considerations, the Cabinet decided that

All practicable steps should be taken to discourage illegal immigration into Palestine. Any illegal Jewish immigrants who, notwithstanding these steps, reached Palestine should be treated with humanity. They should be kept in internment camps unless and until arrangements could be made for them to be shipped off to some other destination; e.g. technicians might be sent to Eritrea, where useful employment could be found for them; and opportunities might be found to send others to Mauritius.

[83] Cranborne to Cabinet, 4 Mar. 1942, PRO CAB 66/22.

The Cabinet invited the Colonial Secretary to raise the matter again 'on the next occasion when a shipload of refugees from enemy-occupied territories reached Istanbul and we were asked whether we would agree to let them into Palestine'. But Cranborne was warned that 'nothing should be said in the meantime to encourage the view that such a request would be granted'.[84]

Two weeks later the news arrived that another boat, the *Mihai*, carrying 1,400 Jewish refugees, had reached Istanbul. Cranborne, anxious to avoid a repetition of the *Struma* tragedy, approached the Foreign Office with the urgent request that the British Ambassador in Turkey should do everything possible to prevent the newly-arrived ship being towed back into the Black Sea. After a discussion between Cranborne's Private Secretary and Oliver Harvey, instructions to that effect were sent to Knatchbull-Hugessen.[85] On reading the telegram, however, Eden complained that its text went beyond his instructions, to which he had 'reluctantly agreed'. The immediate crisis passed when it turned out that the *Mihai* had on board 14 and not 1,400 passengers. However, Cranborne felt it necessary 'to be prepared for the appearance of fresh shiploads on a scale comparable with that of the Struma', and therefore set about making contingency arrangements. In a letter to the Secretary of State for War he took up the proposal that refugees be sent to Eritrea.[86] A copy of the letter was forwarded to the Foreign Office, and Harvey passed it to Eden with the comment, 'You may wish to support this.' But Eden's response was, 'No! I think that Lord Cranborne is going to land us with a big problem, and that it would be more merciful to send these ships back.'[87] The general Foreign Office opinion was hostile to the Eritrean proposal, for as one official remarked, 'to put these Jews . . . amidst a hostile Tigrean population would be a jump from the frying-pan into the fire, notwithstanding their previous hardships, and would bring nothing but odium upon H.M. Govt. and no comfort to the wretched Jews'. The alternative idea was floated of sending the refugees to live among 'their

[84] Extract from Cabinet Conclusions, 5 Mar. 1942, PRO CO 733/445 (76021/41).

[85] Foreign Office to Angora, 19 Mar. 1942, PRO FO 371/32662/174 (W 4351/652/48).

[86] Cranborne to Grigg, 28 Mar. 1942, PRO FO 371/32663/132 (W 5318/652/48).

[87] Undated notes by Harvey and Eden, PRO FO 371/32663/131 (W 5318/652/48).

co-religionists . . . the Falasha Jews in Abyssinia'.[88] However, objections were soon discovered to both the Eritrean and the Ethiopian proposals, and they were dropped.

In April it was learnt that three further small boats, carrying a total of sixty-six refugees had reached Istanbul. Further reports from 'secret sources' indicated that 'some thousands of Jews' were congregating at the port of Constanza seeking a means of escape from Roumania. Cranborne felt that the time had now come 'when the problem must be frankly faced'.[89] Taking advantage of the visit to London for consultations of Sir Harold MacMichael, Cranborne set about trying to hammer out a modification of the illegal immigration policy. MacMichael did not appear to be in a conciliatory mood towards the Zionists. He told Cranborne that the Jewish Agency was 'professionally engaged in pulling the two races apart', and that the Jewish National Home, in its present form was based on a 'highly developed national-socialist system'. When Harold Macmillan (the junior minister at the Colonial Office at this time) suggested that, at any rate after the war, the settlement of the Jewish problem in Europe would bring about 'a vital need for generous emigration opportunities to Palestine', the High Commissioner demurred, opining that 'provided conditions in Europe were at all tolerable, there would probably be a substantial exodus of Jews from Palestine to Europe after the war'.[90] Turning to the immediate problem, Cranborne stressed the Government's concern 'that every possible step must be taken to avoid the occurrence of another "Struma" disaster'. The High Commissioner remarked that 'the danger of a Jewish insurrection arising out of this question could not be ignored.' MacMichael said 'it was a matter of fundamental importance that nothing should be done which could be interpreted in any way as facilitating their journey to Palestine'. At the same time he was prepared to agree to a concession:

Those Jews who might succeed in reaching the country would be placed in a detention camp on arrival and would only be released subject to a careful security check and the overriding principle of

[88] G. Mackereth minute, 13 Apr. 1942, PRO FO 371/32663/129 (W 5318/652/48).
[89] Cranborne to Cabinet, 15 May 1942, PRO CO 733/445 (76021/41); High Commissioner, Jerusalem to Colonial Office, 17 Apr. 1942, ibid.
[90] Minutes of meeting on 23 Apr. 1942, PRO FO 371/31338 (E 3121/49/65).

economic absorptive capacity. Jews thus released would be set off against the quota.[91]

A proposal to this effect was put to the Cabinet by Cranborne on 15 May. Cranborne emphasized that his proposal meant 'in practice, that no facilities should be granted to Jewish refugees who may become stranded in Turkey in attempting to enter Palestine illegally from enemy-occupied territories, even though the deportation of such persons from Turkey back to those territories as a result of our refusal to intervene may be represented by the Jewish Agency as likely to create future incidents comparable to the *Struma* disaster'.[92] The modification of policy was approved by the Cabinet on 18 May, and it was decided that the same procedure would be applied to the detainees from the *Darien* who were still interned in Palestine awaiting deportation. No publicity was to be given to the new arrangements, although 'private explanations' might be given to the Zionists.[93] At a meeting with Jewish Agency representatives on 20 May, Cranborne explained the new procedures, and was accorded a favourable reception. Mrs Dugdale 'expressed her appreciation of what she described as a miracle'. However, when pressed by Professor Namier to concede to refugees reaching Turkey the right to apply for Palestine immigration certificates, Cranborne replied that 'the Government, which was not anti-Jewish, had gone as far as possible'.[94]

The implementation of the modified policy was facilitated by the fact that by the spring of 1942 Jewish escape from Europe had become virtually impossible. The total number of immigrants to Palestine (both legal and illegal) in 1942 was 3,038, the lowest figure for any year of the war. Foreign Office fears that rumours of the modification of immigration policy might result in a mass exodus of Jews from Europe were not fulfilled. The handful of Jews now arriving in Turkey were in several cases admitted to Cyprus. By September 1942 it was agreed between the Foreign and Colonial Offices that the British Ambassador in Ankara should be instructed to ask the Turkish Government to notify him immediately any Jewish refugee

[91] Extract from note of discussions, 23 Apr. 1942, PRO CO 733/445 (76021/41).
[92] Cranborne to Cabinet, 15 May 1942, PRO CO 733/445 (76021/41).
[93] Extract from Cabinet Conclusions, 18 May 1942, PRO CO 733/445 (76021/41).
[94] Minutes of interview, 20 May 1942, PRO CO 733/445 (76021/41).

vessel was wrecked in Turkish waters. He was further to request that he be informed before any action was taken to send the refugees back to Roumania, so that the British Government might 'have an opportunity of considering the position which has arisen'. A Colonial Office official noted that the instruction had 'embarrassing implications', but added that the British Government had by now accepted in effect a responsibility for the fate of Jewish refugees reaching Turkey.[95]

The logical extension of this recognition of British responsibility was the decision taken by the Cabinet on 2 July 1943 that all Jewish refugees who succeeded in reaching Turkey would be regarded 'as eligible for onward transport to Palestine' where they would be treated in the same manner as illegal immigrants.[96] This decision, on the face of things a considerable reversal of the British attitude at the time of the *Struma* incident, was, however, more apparent than real. When the change in policy was revealed in confidence to the representatives of the Jewish Agency, a Colonial Office official admitted that the total number of Jews who had succeeded in escaping to Turkey in the sixteen months since the *Struma* disaster was only 184.[97] The change in policy (approved only with some reluctance by the High Commissioner in Jerusalem) meant that this small trickle of refugees would henceforth be diverted to Palestine. The cosmetic nature of the decision was underlined by A. Walker of the Foreign Office Refugee Department who noted:

If we can show that a number [of refugees] are in fact, while getting out 'under their own steam', being let into Palestine, it may draw off to some extent the ire of the 'pressure groups'. Should the Bulgarian Government and/or the Roumanian Government prove unexpectedly amenable and allow Jews to [leave] their territories, this present concession could be withdrawn since it is not to be made public.[98]

The total number of Jewish refugees (from Hungary, Bulgaria, and Roumania) who passed through Turkey to Palestine during 1943 was 1,200 (the figure included both legal and illegal immigrants).[99] When, in the autumn of 1944, the number of

[95] E. B. Boyd to A. W. G. Randall, 18 Sept. 1942, PRO FO 371/32666.
[96] Extract from Cabinet Conclusions, 2 July 1943, PRO FO 371/36680.
[97] Note of meeting at Colonial Office, 9 July 1943, CZA Z4/302/27.
[98] Minute by A. Walker, 28 June 1943, PRO FO 371/36680 (W 9840/G).
[99] Conversation of H. Barlas (Jewish Agency representative, Istanbul) with Patrick

such refugees began to increase, Walker's reassurance that the concession could always be withdrawn if it produced a large-scale migration proved to be prophetic.[100] That the apparent concession was made at all in July 1943 was a sign less of a fundamental change in Government policy than of its need to make some gesture to an influential body of public opinion which since the autumn of 1942 had become greatly aroused by reports of the real nature of the German 'final solution' of the Jewish problem in Europe.

That the German atrocities against the Jews had greatly intensified since the beginning of the war was a fact of which the British Government (and to a lesser extent the public) had been aware since September 1939. Indeed, shortly after the beginning of the war the Government had published a White Paper 'Concerning the Treatment of German Nationals in Germany 1938–1939'.[101] The choice of title (eschewing any explicit reference to the Jews) was not accidental; it reflected a reluctance, which endured in official circles throughout the war, to single out for special attention German atrocities against the Jews. This reluctance was founded partly on principle and partly on political calculation: the former in that it was often felt that to single out the Jews would involve, as it were, a spiritual surrender to German racialism; the latter in that excessive emphasis on German treatment of the Jews might give a handle to German propaganda themes stressing 'the Jewish war'; recognition that German treatment of the Jews fell into a special category might also be construed to carry with it the embarrassing corollary that the problem required a special solution—with unfortunate consequences for British policy in Palestine. In general, the element of political calculation was more prominent in official thinking than that of liberal principle.

This is evident in Foreign Office discussion of the proposal to issue the White Paper on German atrocities in the autumn of 1939. The idea originated in reaction to a series of German propaganda broadcasts in Afrikaans in which South African

Malin (Vice-Director, Inter-Governmental Committee), 23 March 1944, minutes in Barlas, *Hatzalah Bimei Shoah*, pp. 276–7.
[100] See p. 340.
[101] Cmd. 6120, London 1939.

wireless-listeners were urged to revolt and asked whether they intended to submit to the rule of those who put powdered glass in the food of children in concentration camps in South Africa during the Boer War.[102] In view of this 'shameless propaganda', Ivone Kirkpatrick, head of the Foreign Office Central Department, proposed that the British should publish some of their consular dispatches describing conditions in German concentration camps.[103] The idea was supported by the Ministry of Information, but it encountered some reservations from Kirkpatrick's colleagues. The Permanent Under-Secretary, Sir Alexander Cadogan, pointed out that the British consuls in Germany had derived most of their information 'from persecuted Jews, who are not, perhaps, entirely reliable witnesses'. He added:

And the Germans will only say that this is further proof that the British Empire is run by international Jewry. And I am not sure that sympathy with the Jews hasn't waned very considerably during the last twelvemonth.[104]

Published in spite of such reservations, the White Paper unreservedly denounced German behaviour as 'reminiscent . . . of the darkest ages in the history of man'. Details were given of German anti-Semitic outrages, but much prominence was also given to other aspects of the Nazi terror, notably the persecution of the churches (to which theme the first four consular dispatches quoted in the White Paper were devoted). In retrospect the White Paper was not regarded by the Foreign Office as having been a success. It was held to have misfired particularly in its effect on neutral opinion, and 'was largely criticised as being merely stale and tendentious propaganda on our part'.[105]

The anxiety not to give special prominence in British propaganda to German atrocities against the Jews was reflected in a Ministry of Information circular listing 'Propaganda Themes for the Middle East': among the themes considered undesirable

[102] *The Times*, 28 Sept. 1939.

[103] Memorandum by Kirkpatrick, 16 Oct. 1939, PRO FO 371/23105/14 (C 16788/16776/18).

[104] Minute by Cadogan, 16 Sept. 1939, PRO FO 371/23105/3 (C 16788/16776/18).

[105] Minute by Sir Orme Sargent, 5 Feb. 1940, PRO FO 371/24422/168 (C 2026/2026/18).

for British use were 'Jewish persecution' and 'atrocity stories which imply Germany's strength and her victim's weakness'.[106] When the Polish Government in early 1940 urged that the British and French Governments join in a declaration condemning German atrocities in occupied Poland, the Foreign Office objected 'to Jews being introduced as the culminating point in the list of German wrongs'.[107] On October 1941 Eden circulated to the Cabinet the draft text of a further declaration to be issued by Allied Governments, which again denounced German actions in occupied territories. The declaration referred to 'acts of undisguised terrorism and murder' and promised a 'sure retribution' for the perpetrators. No reference was made to crimes against the Jews.[108] In January 1942 a conference of allied powers met at St James's Palace in London under the presidency of General Sikorski in order to consider German actions in occupied Europe. The conference issued a declaration enumerating Nazi atrocities against civilian populations; again the Jews were not mentioned. Representations by Jewish organizations produced a reply by Sikorski that 'the enumeration in the preamble to this Declaration is only by way of example and in no respect bears a limitative character'. Explicit reference to the sufferings of the Jews might, argued Sikorski, 'be equivalent to an implicit recognition of the racial theories which we all reject'.[109] The British and United States Governments participated in the St James's Palace Conference only as observers, and not as signatories to the declaration, but the Foreign Office approved of the terms of the declaration and of the absence of any explicit reference to the Jews. F. K. Roberts, for example, wrote that he was 'glad to see that General Sikorski has behaved correctly in this matter', and mentioned that at a recent meeting with the Czech Foreign Minister, Jan Masaryk, the latter, 'whose

[106] Rushbrook Williams (M.O.I.,) to Foreign Office, 25 Nov. 1939, PRO FO 371/24548 (E 297/297/65).
[107] Minute by F. K. Roberts, 8 Apr. 1940, PRO FO 371/24423/297 (C 5475/2026/18).
[108] Eden to Cabinet, 8 Oct. 1941, PRO CAB 66/19/34.
[109] Sikorski to World Jewish Congress, 9 May 1942, WJCL; see also E. Eppler, 'The Rescue Work of the World Jewish Congress during the Nazi Period', *Rescue Attempts During the Holocaust* (Proceedings of the Second Yad Vashem International Conference), Jerusalem 1977, pp. 47–70; and John P. Fox, 'The Jewish Factor in British War Crimes Policy in 1942', *English Historical Review*, XCII, no. 362, Jan. 1977.

humanity is better than his judgement, mentioned to me . . . that he thought that the Jews should also have been represented'.[110]

In the course of 1942, however, as the character of the Nazi 'final solution' gradually became known to the British Government, the refusal to recognize the special character of Nazi anti-Jewish persecutions was modified. The change in official attitudes was slow because, although the Government was provided by several sources with accurate information as to the scale and nature of Nazi actions the reports were not at first believed by British officials. Even when it became clear that they were substantially true, officials remained reluctant to accept the full enormity of the reports. The veracity of reports emanating from Jewish sources was frequently questioned. Apart from this there was a general feeling that atrocity propaganda during the First World War had been shown to be greatly exaggerated and a widespread aversion from falling into the same error again.

Information about the Jewish fate in Nazi Europe reached the British Government from neutral observers, from refugees, from the allied governments-in-exile, from Jewish organizations, and from 'secret sources'. The reports evoked mixed responses in official circles. A press report in October 1939 concerning German treatment of Jews in Poland led H. F. Downie of the Colonial Office to speculate that the 'German proposal to create . . . a territorial reserve exclusively for Jews in which Jews from all over Poland are to be concentrated' might facilitate the handling by the Colonial Office of an application on behalf of certain Jews in Russian-occupied Poland for permission to emigrate to Palestine. Downie surmised that 'the proposed Jewish "state" would apparently offer an alternative refuge for . . . Jews from Russian-occupied Poland and would make it unnecessary for us to consider the request for their immigration to Palestine'.[111] In April 1940 the Foreign Office received an account by two Jewish refugees of conditions in German-occupied Poland. The account was corroborated by other sources, but it was nevertheless received with a certain scepticism. Reginald Leeper commented: 'As a general rule

[110] Minute by Roberts, 16 Aug. 1942, quoted in Eppler, op. cit., p. 60.
[111] Downie to Randall, 31 Oct. 1939, PRO FO 371/24085/295 (W 15982/520/48).

Jews are inclined to magnify their persecutions. I remember the exaggerated stories of Jewish pogroms in Poland after the last war which, when fully examined, were found to have little substance.'[112]

Towards the end of 1941 the news from Europe took on an even more gruesome aspect than hitherto. The British Minister in Berne, D. V. Kelly, reported in November 1941 that a Polish informant had told him 'that about 1½ million Jews who were living in eastern (recently Russian) Poland have simply disappeared altogether; nobody knows how and where'. The Netherlands Minister in Berne had told Kelly that fifty per cent of the Dutch Jews sent to German concentration camps were now dead.[113] The British Consul-General in Basle reported in February 1942 on a rumour 'about young Jews taken to Germany for gas experiments'.[114] In late June 1942 the Polish Government reported that more than 700,000 Jews had been murdered by the Germans in Poland since the beginning of the war.[115] In early October the Polish Ambassador at the Vatican gave details of wholesale massacres of the Jews in Poland by means of poison gas.[116]

Such reports were confirmed by more detailed evidence from Jewish sources. In October 1941 the *Jewish Chronicle* reported that thousands had died in pogroms in the Ukraine. In November it reported that one third of all the Jews in Bessarabia had been killed. In January it published a report that poison gas experiments had been conducted at the Mauthausen concentration camp. In the spring and summer of 1942 it carried further detailed reports on German atrocities, including one of the mass murders carried out by mobile gas chambers at Chelmno.[117] In December 1941 a report by the Joint Foreign Committee of the Board of Deputies of British Jews and the Anglo-Jewish Association stated that 52,000 people, Jews and non-Jews, had been murdered by the Nazis after the

[112] Minute dated 21 Apr. 1940, PRO FO 371/24472/11 (C 5471/116/55). See above p. 5.

[113] Kelly (Berne) to F. K. Roberts, 19 Nov. 1941, PRO FO 371/26515 (C 13826/18/18).

[114] Basle to Foreign Office, 18 Feb. 1942, PRO FO 371/30898 (C 2345/29/18).

[115] *Jewish Chronicle*, 3 July 1942.

[116] 'Notes de l'ambassade de Pologne', 3 Oct. 1942, *VAT*, vol 8, doc. no. 497.

[117] *Jewish Chronicle*, 24 Oct and 7 Nov. 1941, 9 Jan., 3 and 24 Apr., 19 June, and 3 July 1942.

German occupation of Kiev (the Babi Yar massacre).[118] In February 1942 the Geneva representative of the Jewish Agency wrote that reports from Germany, Holland, Yugoslavia, and Poland indicated that millions of Jews would be dead by the end of the war.[119] In March he gave details of a 'new wave of persecution sweeping Europe', and in June of deportations from Germany, Austria, and Czechoslovakia.[120] Further reports in September and October spoke of the 'total destruction of the Jewish communities in Belgium and Holland', of the 'extermination [of] Jews following deportation from various countries to Germany or Poland', and of the impending 'complete annihilation' of the Jews of Europe.[121]

The Foreign Office treated these reports with cautious reserve. In August 1942 a report was received from the Geneva representative of the World Jewish Congress, Dr Gerhart Riegner, that a plan was under consideration by the German authorities that all Jews in Nazi Europe were to be deported to the east and exterminated 'at one blow' in order to resolve once and for all the Jewish question in Europe.[122] The first reaction in the Foreign Office was that there was 'no confirmation of this report from other sources, although we have, of course, received numerous reports of large-scale massacres of Jews, particularly in Poland'.[123] On 15 August F. K. Roberts wrote: 'I do not see how we can hold up this message much longer, although I fear it may provoke embarrassing repercussions.'[124] The message was forwarded to the World Jewish Congress representatives in London; Sidney Silverman M.P., the W.J.C. Chairman, told the Foreign Office that he regarded the source as entirely reliable, and asked for permission to convey the message to Rabbi Stephen Wise in New York, and for the

[118] Report dated 17 Dec. 1941, BD C11/2/35/3.

[119] Lichtheim to Lourie (New York), 11 Feb. 1942, CZA L22/134.

[120] Lichtheim to Linton (London), 16 Mar. 1942, WJCL; Lichtheim to Goldmann (New York), 15 June 1942, BD C11/7/2/6.

[121] Lichtheim to Linton, 26 and 29 Sept. 1942, CZA L 22/134; Lichtheim to Grünbaum (Jerusalem), 8 Oct. 1942, CZA L22/3; Lichtheim to Lauterbach (Jerusalem), 26 Oct. 1942, CZA L22/3.

[122] Norton (Berne) to Foreign Office containing message from Dr. G. Riegner to S. S. Silverman M.P., 10 Aug. 1942, PRO FO 371/30917 (C 7853/61/18).

[123] D. Allen minute, 14 Aug. 1942, ibid.

[124] F. K. Roberts minute, 15 Aug. 1942, ibid.

Foreign Office's views as to whether the report should be publicized. D. Allen commented:

We have also received plenty of evidence that Jews deported from other parts of Europe have been concentrated in the Government-General, and also that Jews once there are being so badly treated that very large numbers have perished: either as a result of lack of food or of evil conditions e.g. in the Warsaw ghetto, or as a consequence of mass deportations and executions. Such stories do provide a basis for Mr Riegner's report but they do not, of course amount to 'extermination at one blow'. The German policy seems to be rather to eliminate 'useless mouths' but to use able bodied Jews as slave labour . . . I do *not* think we should be wise to make use of this story in propaganda to Germany without further confirmation . . . We should *not* help matters by taking any further action on the basis of this rather wild story.[125]

In early September 1941 a report from a representative in Switzerland of the *Agudas Yisroel* (an organization of orthodox Jews) stated that the deportation and murder of the Jews in the Warsaw Ghetto was proceeding. It continued: 'The corpses of the victims are used for the manufacture of soaps and artificial fertilisers.'[126] The Foreign Office reaction was that the story should be treated 'with the greatest reserve' until corroborated.[127] F. K. Roberts wrote: 'The facts are quite bad enough without the addition of such an old story as the use of bodies for the manufacture of soap.'[128]

However, by the autumn of 1942, the weight of the evidence from all sources confirming the Nazi massacres of the Jews compelled the British Government to shift from its previous position of studious avoidance of any explicit reference to the matter. In a statement in the House of Lords on 7 October, announcing the establishment of a United Nations Commission for the Investigation of War Crimes, the Lord Chancellor, Lord Simon, made a brief reference to the persecutions of the Jews.[129] In a Cabinet memorandum on 'Enemy Breaches of the Rules of Warfare', prepared in early November by the Lord

[125] D. Allen minute, 10 Sept. 1942, ibid.; see also Eppler, 'Rescue Work', pp. 56–7; and Fox, 'Jewish Factor', pp. 91–2.

[126] Cable received by World Jewish Congress on 4 Sept. 1942, WJCL.

[127] Minute by A. David, 11 Sept. 1942, quoted in Fox, 'Jewish Factor', pp. 94–5.

[128] Minute by F. K. Roberts, 12 Sept. 1942, quoted ibid.

[129] HL vol. 124, cols. 577–87, 7 Oct. 1942.

Privy Seal, Sir Stafford Cripps, reference was made (although in a comparatively inconspicuous position in the paper) to the execution of large numbers of Jews by poison gas, and to the slaughter of the Jewish populations in Kiev and other cities in the occupied area of the Soviet Union.[130]

The Government now came under increasing pressure from Jewish organizations, from the Polish Government, and from sections of public opinion, to take up a more explicit stance on the matter, and to consider whether any means of affording succour to the victims of Nazi persecution was available. The *Manchester Guardian* commented on 27 October on a speech by Hitler which had threatened the annihilation of the Jews of Europe:

It is easy to take such a passage when first read as just another wild and whirling threat, but it would be a mistake. Hitler means what he says. He aims literally at the 'extermination' of the Jews in Europe in so far as his hand can reach them, and for weeks past reports from country after country have shown that the policy is being carried out with every circumstance of cruelty.[131]

An emergency meeting of representatives of several of the major Jewish organizations in Britain on 3 December considered various forms of action 'to meet the situation'. The President of the Board of Deputies, Professor Brodetsky, said that 'one of the main difficulties of the situation was that public opinion is little informed of the extent of these horrors, and many good people find it extremely hard to believe that such bestiality is possible. In addition to various other forms of action it was therefore agreed to intensify pressure on the Government to issue a declaration 'covering specifically the extermination and persecution of the Jews'.[132] On 2 December, the Soviet Ambassador in London, Ivan Maisky, told Eden that he had been approached by a Jewish deputation who had asked that the U.S.S.R. associate itself with such a declaration. Maisky said that although he had received no instructions on the subject from his government he considered personally that a three-power declaration on the massacres of the Jews was

[130] Cripps to Cabinet, 3 Nov. 1942, PRO CAB 21/1509.
[131] Quoted in Sharf, *The British Press*, p. 99.
[132] Note on meeting, BD C 11/7/2/6.

desirable and 'might give the unhappy Jews some comfort'.[133] On 7 December, the American Ambassador in London, J. G. Winant, cabled to the State Department:

Two or three times I have been approached by committees of British Jews asking for intercession in their behalf because of informations which have been received from their representative in Geneva in regard to a plan by Hitler to totally exterminate all Jews under his military control. Each time I have brought the matter to the attention of Mr Eden as I was requested to do . . . Last week I was asked to petition my government to intervene. Hitler's last speech has intensified this feeling of an impending mass attack and there have been requests to Eden, Maisky, and myself that we ask our three governments to take a joint stand in protesting against German terrorism and to make it clear that punishment will be meted out to those responsible for Jewish atrocities. Eden looked favourably on this plan as did Maisky, and I would like to give it my support.[134]

To the support of the two ambassadors was added that of the Archbishop of Canterbury and of significant elements of public opinion.[135]

Opinion in the Foreign Office and in the State Department, both still somewhat sceptical as to the accuracy of the reports, acquiesced only reluctantly to the proposal for a declaration. F. K. Roberts of the Foreign Office considered on 27 November that there was still 'no actual proof of these atrocities', but he added, 'their probability is sufficiently great to justify action'.[136] R. B. Reams of the State Department, in a memorandum on 9 December, objected to the draft declaration in the following terms:

While the statement does not mention the soap, glue, oil, and fertiliser factories, it will be taken as additional confirmation of these stories and will support Rabbi Wise's contention of official confirmation from State Department sources. The way will then be open for further pressure from interested groups for action which might affect the war effort.[137]

[133] See Fox, 'Jewish Factor', p. 101.

[134] Winant to State Dept., 7 Dec. 1942, USNA 740.00116 European War 1939/660.

[135] See Fox, 'Jewish Factor', p. 101; and Winant to State Dept., 8 Dec. 1942, USNA 740.00116 European War 1939/663; Eden to Prime Minister (draft not sent), 14 Dec. 1942, PRO FO 371/30924/106 (C 12313/61/18).

[136] Minute by Roberts, 27 Nov. 1942, quoted in Fox, 'Jewish Factor', pp. 99–100.

[137] Quoted in Arthur D. Morse, *While Six Million Died*, London 1968, p. 33.

On 10 December the Foreign Office circulated a long dispatch from the Polish Ambassador, Count Raczynski, drawing attention to 'fully authenticated information received from Poland during recent weeks' which indicated that 'the German authorities aim with systematic deliberation at the total extermination of the Jewish population of Poland and of the many thousands of Jews whom the German authorities deported to Poland'. The dispatch gave details of the liquidation of the Warsaw ghetto, and of the massacres of tens of thousands of Jews in other Polish cities; it stated that an exact estimate of the number of victims was impossible but that all reports agreed that 'of the 3,130,000 Jews in Poland before the outbreak of the war, over a third have perished during the last three years'. The Polish Government urged the 'necessity of not only condemning the crimes committed by the Germans and punishing the criminals, but also of finding means offering the hope that Germany might be effectively restrained from continuing to apply her methods of mass extermination'.[138] On seeing this dispatch, Churchill asked the Foreign Office to provide further information.[139] The Polish Government memorandum and Churchill's expression of interest appear to have removed the lingering doubts of the Foreign Office and State Department as to the need for a declaration. On 14 December 1942 Eden told the War Cabinet

that, while there was no direct confirmation of these reports so far as concerned the methods used, there were indications that large-scale massacres of Jews were taking place in Poland. It was known that Jews were being transferred to Poland from enemy-occupied countries, for example, Norway; and it might well be that these transfers were being made with a view to wholesale extermination of Jews.

On this basis the War Cabinet approved the terms of the proposed declaration.[140]

Issued in the name of eleven Allied Governments and of the French National Committee, the declaration was made on behalf of the British Government by Eden in the House of Commons on 17 December in reply to a question put by Sidney

[138] Raczynski to Eden, 9 Dec. 1942, PRO FO 371/30924/121 (C 12313/61/18).
[139] F. K. Roberts minute, 14 Dec. 1942, PRO FO 371/30924/105 (C 12313/61/18).
[140] War Cabinet minutes, 14 Dec. 1942, PRO CAB 65/28.

Silverman M.P. It stated that the attention of these governments had been drawn to

numerous reports from Europe that the German authorities, not content with denying to persons of Jewish race in all the territories over which their barbarous rule has been extended the most elementary rights, are now carrying into effect Hitler's oft-repeated intention to exterminate the Jewish people in Europe.

The declaration continued:

From all the occupied countries Jews are being transported in conditions of appalling horror and brutality to Eastern Europe. In Poland, which has been made the principal Nazi slaughterhouse, the ghettos established by the German invader are being systematically emptied of all Jews except a few highly skilled workers required for war industries. None of those taken away are ever heard of again. The able-bodied are slowly worked to death in labour camps. The infirm are left to die of exposure and starvation or are deliberately massacred in mass executions. The number of victims of these bloody cruelties is reckoned in many hundreds of thousands of entirely innocent men, women and children.

After condemning 'this bestial policy of cold-blooded extermination', the declaration concluded with an affirmation of the 'solemn resolution' of the United Nations Governments 'to ensure that those responsible for these crimes shall not escape retribution, and to press on with the practical measures to this end'.[141] The effect of the declaration on the House of Commons was considerable. Sir Henry ('Chips') Channon, Conservative M.P. for Southend West, commented in his diary:

An extraordinary assembly today in the august Mother of Parliaments. It was sublime. Anthony read out a statement regarding the extermination of Jews in East Europe, whereupon Jimmy de Rothschild [Liberal M.P. for the Isle of Ely] rose, and with immense dignity, and his voice vibrating with emotion, spoke for five minutes in moving tones on the plight of these peoples. There were tears in his eyes, and I feared that he might break down; the House caught his spirit and was deeply moved. Somebody suggested that we stand in silence to pay our respects to those suffering peoples, and the House as a whole rose and stood for a few frozen seconds. It was a fine moment, and my back tingled.[142]

[141] Hansard, House of Commons, 17 Dec. 1942.
[142] R. Rhodes James, ed., *Chips: The Diaries of Sir Henry Channon*, London 1970, pp. 423–4.

Eden, writing in his diary, noted: 'It had a far greater dramatic effect than I had expected . . . Lloyd George said to me later: "I cannot recall a scene like that in all my years in Parliament." '[143]

The declaration was given wide publicity both in the press and on the air. On the evening of 17 December the Polish Ambassador broadcast a 'postscript' after the nine o'clock radio news in which he spoke on the persecution of the Jews in Poland. A few days later he spoke at a meeting of protest organized by the Board of Deputies of British Jews.[144] A central directive issued by the Political Warfare Executive for the week beginning 10 December ordered that wireless broadcasts and leaflets to occupied Europe 'should coldly and factually establish Hitler's plan to exterminate the Jews in Europe . . . Anti-Semitism was a potent weapon of Nazi political warfare. The time has now come to use it against them.' The directive for the following week recommended that 'main languages should include this week at least one message of encouragement to the Jews'. For the week beginning 24 December the directive stated:

The sufferings of the Jews should now be merged in the wider picture of Nazi persecutions . . . We should bear in mind (i) the Jewish persecution has in all countries been the prelude to the persecution of other sections of the population; (ii) that apart from its physical brutality, it is a subtle form of political warfare aimed at breaking human ties between different groups and individuals in all countries and destroying any feeling of common citizenship where persecution of the Jews is set on foot.[145]

Thus, for the first time in the war, the Nazi persecution of the Jews was made a central theme of British propaganda to Europe.

The international effect of the declaration was mixed. In the United States it was reported to have had a much smaller impact on public opinion than in Britain.[146] The declaration was published by the Soviet Government in the press, but its

[143] The Earl of Avon (Sir Anthony Eden), *The Eden Memoirs: The Reckoning*, London 1965, p. 358.
[144] Raczynski, *In Allied London*, p. 127.
[145] P. W. E. Central Directives, PRO FO 898/289.
[146] See pp. 186–7.

effect on public opinion in the U.S.S.R. was impossible to gauge: it did not appear to weaken the propensity of anti-Semitic elements in the occupied areas to collaborate with the Germans in the murder of Jews. A P.W.E. surmise that the declaration had 'discomfited' the Germans was perhaps borne out by an irritated diary comment of Goebbels commenting on the scene in the House of Commons:

[Rothschild] delivered a flood of sob-stuff bemoaning the fate of the Polish Jews. At the end of the session the House observed a minute of silence ... That was quite appropriate for the British House of Commons which is really a sort of Jewish exchange. The English, anyway, are the Jews among the Aryans. The perfumed British Foreign Minister, Eden, cuts a good figure among these characters from the synagogue. His whole education and entire bearing can be characterised as thoroughly Jewish.[147]

The Pope in his Christmas broadcast on 24 December made reference to 'hundreds of thousands who, without personal guilt, sometimes for no other reason but on account of their nationality or descent, were doomed to death or exposed to a progressive deterioration of their condition'.[148] However, the British Minister to the Holy See, after an audience with the Pope in which the broadcast was discussed, reported to the Foreign Office:

The reaction of some at least of my colleagues was anything but enthusiastic. To me he claimed that he had condemned the Jewish persecution. I could not dissent from this, though the condemnation is inferential and not specific, and comes at the end of a long dissertation on social problems.[149]

Mussolini's comment on the broadcast was contemptuous: 'This is a speech of platitudes which might better be made by the parish priest of Predappio [Mussolini's native village].'[150] Efforts by the British, United States, and Polish Governments to persuade the Vatican to take a more explicit position evoked

[147] P. W. E. Central Directive for week beginning 31 Dec. 1942, PRO FO 898/289; Lochner, *Goebbels Diaries*, p. 190 (entry dated 19 Dec. 1942).
[148] Quoted in Günter Lewy, *The Catholic Church and Nazi Germany*, London 1964, p. 299.
[149] Osborne to Foreign Office, 31 Dec. 1942, quoted in *VAT*, vol. 9, p. 71.
[150] M. Muggeridge, ed., *Ciano's Diary*, London 1947, p. 538 (entry dated 24 Dec. 1942).

the familiar response that only general condemnations of atrocities could be issued by the Pope. A suggestion by the Archbishop of Canterbury that the Pope might recommend 'courses of action to the Roman Catholics in Germany' did not alter the Vatican's view.[151]

The shocked horror which the declaration induced in British public opinion was naturally felt most deeply among the Jewish community. The Chief Rabbi had declared a day of fasting and mourning for the victims of the Nazis on 13 December. The *Jewish Chronicle* on 11 December appeared with a black border: it gave details of the Nazi massacres, and urged vigorous action by the Government, including the formation of a Jewish Army, free immigration to Palestine, broadcasts and leaflets to Germany, and warnings of retribution to war criminals. Following the declaration Jewish organizations made urgent representations to the Government demanding that some effort should be made to offer relief and refuge to the Jews of Europe. On 23 December a Jewish deputation, including Lord Samuel, James de Rothschild M.P., and Professor Brodetsky, met Eden at the Foreign Office and put forward a number of specific requests. Eden said that an effort would be made to get refugee Jews out of Spain, and that a declaration might be made by the United Nations to neutral states promising that refugees would not be left on their hands at the end of the war. Eden further promised that money and food might be provided for refugees reaching neutral countries, and that an approach would be made to the Vatican. Samuel suggested that some alteration might be made to the arrangements for granting visas to Britain; Eden replied that one of the difficulties was that the U.S.A. had not done anything about liberalizing her immigration procedures.[152] At a meeting with Colonial Office officials on 28 December, a Zionist deputation headed by Moshe Shertok demanded a relaxation of the ban on Palestine immigration certificates for refugees reaching Istanbul. Shertok also asked that the similar ban on certificates for Jews in enemy-occupied territory should be removed, that a further attempt should be made to secure

[151] Osborne to Foreign Office, 5 Jan. 1942, quoted in *VAT*, vol. 9, p. 71; Friendländer, *Pius XII*, pp. 132–4; Archbishop of Canterbury to Cardinal Hinsley, 27 Jan. 1943, and reply from Hinsley, 29 Jan. 1943, quoted in *VAT*, vol. 9, p. 136.

[152] Account of meeting by Brodetsky in minutes of Zionist Executive, 23 Dec. 1942, CZA Z4/302/26.

the emigration of Jewish children from France, and that the internees in Mauritius should be permitted to go to Palestine.[153] At an interview with Richard Law (junior minister at the Foreign Office) on 30 December, Professor Brodetsky pressed for at least a token intake of refugees to Britain and to the Dominions, for warnings to be issued in leaflets and broadcasts to Europe, and for the establishment of United Nations refugee camps.[154] A memorandum by the British Section of the World Jewish Congress urged that an approach should be made to Germany by the British Government demanding that the Jews be allowed to leave occupied territory; it also suggested the consideration of 'ever possible method of exchange'.[155]

The Jewish organizations were not alone in pressing that the declaration should be followed by effective government action. There was much support for their demands in Parliament, the press, the churches, and among the allied governments-in-exile. Eleanor Rathbone M.P. circulated a memorandum arguing 'the case for an offer to Hitler'.[156] In a letter to *The Times* on 22 December, Sir Neill Malcolm, former League of Nations High Commissioner for Refugees, suggested that the allied declaration, although valuable so far as it went, should be followed by the admission of Jewish refugees to Britain, the colonies, and Eire. Lord Cranborne tried to persuade Malcolm not to send his letter but without success. The Foreign Office News Department then persuaded *The Times* 'not to follow up' the letter as 'in present circumstances demands put forward in public are not only an embarrassment but provide enemy propaganda with material'.[157] A deputation of the Council of Christians and Jews, including the Archbishop of Canterbury and the Moderator of the Free Churches, met Richard Law on 16 December. Law commented:

In spite of the fact that the deputation expressed great appreciation of my alleged sympathetic attitude, I don't think that I gave anything

[153] Account of meeting by Shertok in minutes of Zionist Executive, 28 Dec. 1942, ibid.

[154] Note on interview, 30 Dec. 1942, BD C 10/2/8/20/2.

[155] Memorandum dated 21 Dec. 1942, WJCL.

[156] Memorandum dated 7 Jan. 1943, BD C11/7/1/5.

[157] Record of interview between Cranborne and Malcolm in Lord Privy Seal's Office to Oliver Harvey, 18 Dec. 1942, PRO FO 371/32682 (W 17575/4555/48); minute by A. W. G. Randall, 22 Dec. 1942, ibid.

away. I was very much impressed by their anger against the Home Secretary, which quite clearly has not abated, and I feel very doubtful myself whether we shall be able to stand much longer on the very strict line that the Home Office is adopting. It has always seemed to me that the apprehensions of the Home Office have been exaggerated and that it would be very difficult for us to go on confining ourselves to denunciation of the German action while refusing to take any alleviating action ourselves. I did not give the deputation any idea that this was my view.[158]

The Government was slightly taken aback by the public response to the allied declaration. Doubts as to the accuracy of the reports of Nazi persecution and as to the efficacy of the declaration subsisted after December 1942. The scale of the Nazi holocaust was such that many British officials until the end of the war remained dubious of reports from Jewish sources and unable to grasp the magnitude of the tragedy. Even in January 1945 an official of the (relatively well-informed) Refugee Department of the Foreign Office wrote:

Sources of information are nearly always Jewish whose accounts are only sometimes reliable and not seldom highly coloured. One notable tendency in Jewish reports on this problem is to exaggerate the numbers of deportations and deaths.[159]

The allied declaration, while promising retribution for the crimes committed against the Jews, had carefully avoided any suggestion that the Allies might offer refuge or relief to those threatened by the Germans. When the suggestion had been made in the House of Commons immediately after the declaration that some steps might be taken to evacuate Jews from Nazi Europe to allied or neutral territory, Eden had replied:

Certainly we should like to do all we possibly can. There are, obviously, certain security formalities which have to be considered. It would clearly be the desire of the United Nations to do everything they could to provide wherever possible an asylum for these people, but the House will understand that there are immense geographical and other difficulties in the matter.[160]

The wave of public indignation which followed the declaration

---

[158] Note by Law, 16 Dec. 1942, PRO FO 371/32682 (W 17401/4555/48).
[159] I. L. Henderson minute, 11 Jan. 1945, PRO FO 371/51134 (WR 89/14/48).
[160] HC vol. 385, cols. 2082–3 (17 Dec. 1942).

forced the Government to consider whether it should do more than give vague assurances. A. W. G. Randall of the Foreign Office wrote on 29 December that 'the exceptional pressure on H.M.G. by refugee sympathisers stimulated by the Allied declaration on Germany's extermination measures' could 'only be met by a new policy, or modification of the present one'. He suggested consideration of a 'generous gesture' by the British Government in the hope of bringing about similar action by the U.S.A. and neutral governments.[161] When a telegram arrived at the Foreign Office from the British Embassy in Ankara, reporting that there was a prospect of the resumption of large-scale emigration from Roumania by as many as 70,000 Jews, A. Walker of the Refugee Department minuted: 'This is a frightful prospect but is one which will have to be faced, I think. This is not the moment to raise objections of any kind to facilitating the escape of refugees, unless we are prepared to risk further archiepiscopal reproaches.' H. M. Eyres added: 'The risk has been in our minds all the time and I think it was agreed that we must take it rather than risk the possibility of another "Struma" incident. There can hardly be enough shipping in Roumania to carry 70,000 persons except over a period of years.'[162] The threatened mass exodus did not, however, transpire.

The Government had been conscious, even before the parliamentary exchanges on 17 December, that a declaration unaccompanied by any concrete action by the Government might have a hollow ring. Responding, therefore, to a suggestion made by the Jewish Agency, the Colonial Secretary, Oliver Stanley, suggested to Churchill that 4,500 children from Bulgaria, with five hundred accompanying adults, might be admitted to Palestine within the White Paper quota. In a minute to Churchill, Stanley wrote that there were indications that anti-Semitic persecutions were about to be intensified in Bulgaria, and that the Jewish Agency had pleaded that if no concession could be made in respect of the adults at least the children might be saved. Stanley continued:

Public opinion has been much aroused by recent reports of the

[161] A. W. G. Randall minute, 29 Dec. 1942, PRO FO 371/36648 (W 121/49/48).

[162] Angora to Foreign Office, 23 Dec. 1942; minutes by Walker and Eyres, 28 Dec. 1942, PRO FO 371/32668 (W 17422/652/48).

systematic extermination of the Jews in Axis and Axis controlled countries. Nothing can be done by us for the great mass of those who may still survive, but this would seem an opportunity for showing our willingness to help where conditions do permit. So long as the proposal is limited to a definite number of children I do not think it presents any serious dangers from our point of view.[163]

Sir Harold MacMichael had opposed the Jewish Agency's original plea that adults be admitted from Bulgaria on the ground that 'the door would then be thrown open to any number and condition of Jews whom any Axis country felt disposed to get rid of', but his acquiescence to the more limited proposal was obtained.[164] Churchill's response to the proposal was enthusiastic. 'Bravo!', he replied to Stanley. 'But why not obtain, as you will, the hearty endorsement of the War Cabinet.'[165] Cabinet approval was obtained, and the proposal relayed to the Bulgarian Government through the Swiss embassy in Sofia.

The scheme, potentially the most substantial British measure to flow from the allied declaration, came to nothing. On 3 February 1943 Stanley announced the plan publicly in the House of Commons, adding that apart from the 4,500 persons from Bulgaria, a further five hundred children from Roumania and Hungary would be admitted to Palestine. Provided transport became available, larger numbers of children with some accompanying adults up to the maximum quota still available under the White Paper of 29,000 might be admitted to Palestine. However, he warned that 'the practical difficulties involved' even in the limited initial phase of the project were 'likely to be considerable'.[166] The difficulties forecast by Stanley proved formidable. First, the Turkish Government made difficulties regarding the transit of the refugees through Turkey (whose limited railway system was already fully stretched). Then the Bulgarian Government, under pressure from the Germans who accused the Bulgars of having come to a secret arrangement with the British, closed their border with Turkey

[163] Stanley to Churchill, 9 Dec. 1942, PRO PREM 4/51/2/121.
[164] High Commissioner, Jerusalem, to Colonial Office, 9 Nov. 1942, PRO FO 371/32698 (W 15197/15197/48); Foreign Office minutes, 7 and 8 Dec. 1942, PRO FO 371/32698 (W 16004/15197/48).
[165] Note by Churchill, 11 Dec. 1942, PRO PREM 4/51/2/123.
[166] HC vol. 386, col. 865 (3 Feb. 1943).

to Jewish emigrants. Efforts by the British Embassy in Ankara to negotiate through the Turks for the charter of two Roumanian luxury liners to take the children to Palestine by sea ended in failure. At the behest of the Foreign Office the Ministry of War Transport made available a British ship for the emigrants. But the Roumanians and Bulgars refused to permit Jews to depart. In the summer of 1943 the German Government intimated that it might be prepared to allow the departure of the Jews from Bulgaria on condition that they were exchanged for an equal number of German prisoners-of-war and provided that the emigrants were sent to Britain rather than Palestine (the latter condition apparently being a gesture of friendship to the Mufti of Jerusalem). This transparent political warfare manoeuvre was rejected on the ground that alien civilians could not be given priority over British soldiers in any prisoner-of-war exchange.[167] Oliver Stanley pursued the scheme for the emigration of the Bulgarian children energetically, fearing, as he wrote to Eden in April 1943, that unless it were pushed through 'the only practical proposal we have yet been able to make for the assistance of the Jews will prove to be a damp squib'.[168] But by the autumn of 1943 it was plain that there was no hope of success.

The declaration of December 1942 was not, in retrospect, regarded by the Foreign Office as having been a success. It was concluded that the pronouncement had done nothing to mitigate the harshness of German treatment of the Jews. The identification of the Jews in the declaration as special targets of the Nazi terror was not regarded as setting a precedent by the Foreign Office, which, as one official noted in October 1943, continued to 'hold the view that it is desirable as a general practice to regard Jews primarily as being nationals of the countries to which they belong, and not to treat them as a separate category. The Allied declaration of 17 December 1942 about German crimes against the Jews in Europe was to some

[167] Foreign Office note to Cabinet Committee on Refugees, 18 Feb. 1943, PRO CAB 95/15; British Embassy in Ankara file, PRO FO 195/2478 *passim*; O. Stanley Cabinet memorandum, 26 June 1943, PRO FO 371/36680 (W 9840/G). I. L. Henderson minute, 15 July 1943, ibid; A. W. G. Randall to E. A. Armstrong (War Cabinet Office), 16 July 1943, PRO FO 371/36712 (W 9966/1499/48); Chary, *The Bulgarian Jews and the Final Solution*.

[168] Stanley to Eden, 14 Apr. 1943, PRO FO 371/36678 (W 6426/80/48).

extent an exception to this general practice, which we felt to be justified by the special circumstances.'[169] Jewish and other bodies urged during 1943 and 1944 that further similar declarations should be issued by the Government. Eden, however, remained sceptical as to their value, arguing that 'these repeated threatenings debase the currency, and that so far as Germany is concerned a new declaration would have little effect'.[170] He noted that the most apparent effect of the declaration of December 1942 had been to stimulate complaints that the Government's efforts to save the threatened victims of Nazi persecution were inadequate. Such criticism of the Government, loudly voiced in the immediate aftermath of the declaration, placed on the official agenda the question of whether the British Government should make some more tangible response to the Jewish holocaust in Europe.

[169] J. D. Greenway (Foreign Office) to Office of High Commissioner of South Africa, Oct. 1943, PRO FO 371/34374 (C 12031/31/62).
[170] Eden to Cabinet Committee on Refugees, 10 Mar. 1944, PRO CAB 95/15/138.

5

The British Response

THE WAVE of public sympathy in Britain for the victims of Nazi persecution, following the United Nations declaration of 17 December 1942, impelled the British Government to seek some means of giving effective succour to the Jews of Europe. The public response impressed on the official mind that, as Sir Herbert Emerson put it, the declaration 'if not followed by such action as practicable to save persons is a mockery'.[1] A Cabinet Committee on the Reception and Accommodation of Jewish Refugees was established, and held its first meeting on 31 December with Eden in the chair. The committee was told by the Home Secretary, Herbert Morrison, that he could not agree to the admission of more than 1,000 to 2,000 refugees to Britain.[2] The Colonial Secretary, Oliver Stanley, suggested that no distinction should be made between Jewish and non-Jewish refugees: the word 'Jewish' was consequently deleted from the name of the committee. There was some consideration of the position of the refugees streaming into Spain. A suggestion by the British Government that the refugees might be evacuated to North Africa had been rejected by the American Government 'on military grounds'. Stanley said that 'there could be no question of Palestine accepting Jews either direct from Spain or through North Africa', and he reminded the meeting 'that there was already an acute Jewish problem in North Africa which was giving the Americans some concern'.[3] At its second meeting on 7 January 1943 the committee was joined by the Dominions Secretary, Attlee, who reported that Canada had already taken five hundred refugees and could take no more; Australia

---

[1] U.S. Embassy, London, to State Dept., Washington, 28 Dec. 1942, enclosing message from Emerson to Myron Taylor, USNA 840.48 Refugees 3557.
[2] See p. 115.
[3] Minutes in PRO CAB 95/15.

and New Zealand were too far away to offer refuge; South Africa had already given shelter to Jewish and non-Jewish children from Poland, and in addition was accommodating prisoners of war; as for Eire, she was unable to feed refugees without British help 'which it would be undesirable to give'.[4] After these rather negative statements, it was agreed that a further approach should be made to the U.S.A. in order to try to resolve by joint action the particularly pressing refugee problem in Spain.[5]

In accordance with this decision a lengthy memorandum was prepared for transmission to the State Department, setting out British views on the refugee problem, and inviting the United States to consider 'the expediency of a private and informal United Nations conference' to discuss possible solutions. The memorandum, sent to the State Department on 20 January 1943, began by setting forth 'certain complicating factors' which appeared to the British Government to emphasize the necessity for a 'joint effort in dealing with the problem':

(a) The refugee problem cannot be treated as though it were a wholly Jewish problem which could be handled by Jewish agencies or by machinery only adapted for assisting Jews. There are so many non-Jewish refugees and there is so much acute suffering among non-Jews in Allied countries that Allied criticism would probably result if any marked preference were shown in removing Jews from territories in enemy occupation. There is also the distinct danger of stimulating anti-semitism in areas where an excessive number of foreign Jews are introduced.

(b) There is at present always a danger of raising false hopes among refugees by suggesting or announcing alternative possible destinations in excess of shipping probabilities.

(c) There is a possibility that the Germans or their satellites may change over from the policy of extermination to one of extrusion, and aim as they did before the war at embarrassing other countries by flooding them with alien immigrants.

However, the document continued, in spite of these complications, the British Government found it 'impossible to make a merely negative response to a growing international problem, disturbing the public conscience and involving the rescue of

---

[4] Minutes of meeting on 7 Jan. 1943, PRO CAB 95/15.
[5] Ibid.; and Eden to Cabinet Committee on Refugees, 9 Jan. 1943, PRO CAB 95/15.

people threatened by Germany's extermination policy'. After giving details of the contributions made by Britain and the Colonial Empire to the solution of the problem, and paying tribute to 'the generous reception by the United States accorded to many thousands of refugees', the memorandum inquired 'whether, taking all factors into consideration, food potentialities, housing accommodation, and the absorptive capacity of the United States on the one hand, and the margin for free action within the immigration quota on the other, the United States Government would still find it possible to offer, as part of an international effort, homes for a proportion of adult refugees now reaching neutral countries'. While it was unlikely 'that any but a very limited number of refugees could in future be accepted into the United Kingdom', the British Government suggested that if an Anglo-American understanding on the problem could be attained, the way would be open for approaching other allied governments, particularly those of Latin America and the British Dominions. Finally, attention was drawn to the pressing nature of the refugee problem in Spain, and the British offered to 'take their share' in administering the reception of 'a substantial proportion of the refugees from Spain and Portugal' in North Africa.[6]

This memorandum, one of the fullest and most considered British statements of policy on the refugee problem, was designed to provide the framework within which the proposed United Nations conference might consider further action. In several respects the 'complicating factors' and reservations thus stressed at the outset by the British delimited the scope and nature of Anglo-American efforts to resolve the problem in the course of the following year. Most notable was the ready acceptance by the British Government that there was no prospect of any modification of American immigration quotas; implicit was the expectation that the American Government would be no less complaisant regarding immigration to Britain and to Palestine; 'for the convenience of the Department of State' a copy of the 1939 White Paper on Palestine was helpfully enclosed with the British memorandum.[7]

[6] British Embassy, Washington, to State Dept., 20 Jan. 1943, *FRUS 1943* vol. I, pp. 134–7.
[7] Ibid.

The American Government took some time to reply to the British approach. Meanwhile public demands for urgent action by the British Government did not abate. Sir William Beveridge (whose reputation was at this time at its height) wrote an article on 'The Massacre of the Jews' in *The Observer*.[8] In the House of Commons on 3 February 1943, Sir Richard Acland, Common Wealth M.P. for Barnstaple, asked: 'Do not the claims of humanity come before your quota restrictions? Why not take all [the refugees] you can under all conditions?' These sentiments were echoed by Eleanor Rathbone, Sidney Silverman, Commander Locker-Lampson, and others. Oliver Stanley (although by no means unsympathetic to the refugees—as his action over the Bulgarian children had shown) reminded the House: 'Winning the war is the most important thing of all.'[9] Jewish organizations pressed the Government to take effective action immediately.[10] Eva, Marchioness of Reading, President of the British Section of the World Jewish Congress wrote to Churchill: 'In other days I would have come to you in sackcloth and ashes to plead for my people . . . Some can still be saved if the iron fetters of the red-tape can be burst asunder.'[11] The Archbishops of Canterbury, York, and Wales issued a statement 'in the name of the whole Anglican Episcopate' calling on the British Government to give a lead by providing a sanctuary for the victims of Nazi persecution.[12] The British Embassy in Washington told the Foreign Office that the delay in securing an American response was due to 'lack of appreciation of the real urgency of the problem', and disputes over which U.S. government agency was primarily responsible; it was noted that there was 'a striking difference between the intensive propaganda campaign regarding Hitler's Jewish victims carried on here and the apparently negligible publicity in

[8] *The Observer*, 7 Feb. 1943.

[9] HC vol. 386, col. 866 (3 Feb. 1943).

[10] Minutes of meeting of Zionist Executive, London, 17 Feb. 1943, CZA Z4/302/26; Report of Joint Foreign Committee of Board of Deputies and Anglo-Jewish Association, 17 Feb. 1943, BD C11/2/38; Note on interview of Prof. S. Brodetsky and A. G. Brotman with Richard Law at Foreign Office, 28 Jan. 1943, BD C11/7/1/5; World Jewish Congress, British Section, draft memorandum on measures for the rescue of European Jewry, 28 Jan. 1943, BD C11/7/1/5.

[11] Lady Reading to Churchill, 16 Jan. 1943, PRO PREM 4/51/8/556. Churchill sent a sympathetic reply on 21 Feb. 1943, WJCL.

[12] *The Times*, 25 Jan. 1943.

the United States'.[13] After a month had passed without an American reply, Richard Law (junior minister at the Foreign Office) told the American Embassy 'that while, much to his regret, he was not sure that much practical help could be given these unfortunate people, public opinion in Great Britain [was] rising to such a degree that the British Government [could] no longer remain dead to it'. Law added: 'The temper of the House of Commons is such that the Government will be unable to postpone beyond next week some reply to the persistent demands to know what it is doing to help the Jews.'[14] On 22 February Eden told the Cabinet that 'it was becoming difficult to hold the Parliamentary position on the basis that we were engaged in international negotiations when in fact the United States Government had shown no readiness to discuss the matter'.[15] Meanwhile parliamentary uneasiness increased, with Sidney Silverman, Sir Percy Hurd, and other M.P.s pressing the Government to announce action in favour of refugees.[16]

The long-awaited American response finally arrived at the end of February. It dwelt at length on what the United States had already done for refugees. The State Department suggested that existing machinery was adequate to tackle the refugee problem. However, the American reply acceded to the British suggestion of a meeting to consider further action. The British Government was greatly embarrassed by the fact that the American reply (unlike the original British memorandum) was published by the United States Government. This led to an abrasive telephone conversation between Sir Ronald Campbell, of the British Embassy in Washington, and Sumner Welles, the acting Secretary of State. Campbell protested that the publication of the American document had 'made it appear that [the United States] Government had taken the initiative whereas the British Government had actually done so'. Welles made no apology and declared that he 'had been regretfully forced to the conclusion for some time past by many incidents that the British Government was permitting the impression to

[13] Foreign Office note to Cabinet Committee on Refugees, 18 Feb. 1943, PRO CAB 95/15.

[14] Matthews (London) to State Dept., Washington, 20 Feb. 1943, USNA 840.48 Refugees 3609.

[15] Cabinet minutes, 22 Feb. 1943, PRO CAB 95/15.

[16] HC vol. 387, cols. 143–6 (24 Feb. 1943).

be created that it was the great outstanding champion of the Jewish people . . . and that it was being held back in its desire to undertake practical steps to protect the Jews in Europe and elsewhere . . . by the unwillingness of this Government to take any action for the relief of these unfortunates beyond words and gestures'.[17] Ruffled American sensibilities were eventually smoothed over in the course of a visit to Washington by Eden at the end of March. Eden discussed the refugee problem with Roosevelt, Hull, and Welles on 27 March. The Americans raised the question of the Jews reported to be 'threatened with extermination unless we could get them out' of South-East Europe, and they 'very urgently pressed Eden for an answer to the problem'. Eden declared that it was necessary 'to move very cautiously about offering to take all Jews out of a country', and pointed out:

If we do that, then the Jews of the world will be wanting us to make similar offers in Poland and Germany. Hitler might well take us up on any such offer, and there simply are not enough ships and means of transportation in the world to handle them.

Eden said the British would admit a substantial number of Jews to Palestine, but he stressed shipping difficulties and security risks, adding that 'the Germans would be sure to put a number of their agents in the group'.[18] It was finally agreed that an Anglo-American Conference on refugees would meet at Bermuda.

The Bermuda Conference opened on 19 April 1943. By one of the savage ironies of history this date coincided with the first night of the Jewish Passover festival (when the exodus of Hebrews from slavery in Egypt is commemorated) and with the beginning of the doomed revolt of the remnants of the Jewish ghetto in Warsaw. The convening of the conference raised hopes that some effective Anglo-American action would at last be taken to give substance to the sympathy expressed in the declaration of December 1942. But the conference turned out to be as much of a disappointment to the advocates of such action

[17] Welles to Matthews (London), 6 Mar. 1943, *FRUS 1943* vol. I, pp. 144–6.
[18] Note on conversation by Harry Hopkins, 27 March 1943, *FRUS 1943* vol. III, pp. 38–9. According to Hopkins's account, Eden said Britain would admit 'about 60,000 more Jews to Palestine'. It is, however, unlikely that Eden mentioned such a figure, as this would have breached the White Paper limit.

as had been the Evian Conference of 1938. The Canadian Government having rejected an earlier proposal that the meeting take place at Ottawa,[19] the British and American delegates gathered on the island of Bermuda in the 'Horizons Hotel': the name, however, was soon belied in the sessions of the conference, as the prospect of havens for large numbers of refugees receded from sight. Even before the conference opened the Foreign Office view was clear as to the limited scope of possible action. On 16 April, A. W. G. Randall wrote: 'It is time that the idea of "measures of rescue" . . . was shown up as illusory.'[20] Jewish organizations pleaded with the Government to notify Germany that places would be found for all Jews who wished to leave Axis territory.[21] But such suggestions were rejected. I. L. Henderson minuted: 'We have already opposed the idea of a general appeal to the German Government suggesting that they should unload all Jews under their control on to the Allies. German acceptance would raise insuperable difficulties connected with transport, supply, passage through neutral countries, security considerations etc.'[22]

The American delegation at Bermuda was headed by Harold Dodds, President of Princeton University, and included Senator Scott W. Lucas of Illinois and Representative Sol Bloom of New York; R. Borden Reams of the State Department was the Secretary to the delegation. The composition of the delegation had caused some difficulty for the State Department: three nominees as head of the delegation withdrew, and there was a protest from (the Zionist) Rabbi Stephen Wise against the inclusion of (the non-Zionist) Bloom on the ground that he was not 'a representative of Jewry'; Wise was told that Bloom was 'a representative of America'.[23] The British Embassy in Washington considered the appointment of Bloom 'a sop to Jewish opinion'.[24] However, the Foreign Office noted

[19] A. Walker minute, 10 Apr. 1943, PRO FO 371/36658 (W 5749/49/48).

[20] Randall minute, 6 Apr. 1943, PRO FO 371/36658 (W 5559/49/48).

[21] Note by William Strang (Foreign Office) on talk in Washington with Nahum Goldmann, Moshe Shertok, and Rabbi Maurice Perlzweig, 24 March 1943, in the course of which Goldmann made an 'impassioned appeal' for such an Allied communication to Germany, PRO FO 371/36658 (W 5684/49/48).

[22] Minute dated 15 Apr. 1943, *ibid.*

[23] Israel, *Diary of Breckenridge Long*, p. 306 (entry dated 3 Apr. 1943).

[24] Halifax (Washington) to Foreign Office, 7 Apr. 1943, PRO FO 371/36658 (W 5534/49/48).

that Bloom, who was Chairman of the Foreign Affairs Committee of the House of Representatives, 'though Jewish and representing a largely Jewish district of New York, plays no part in Zionist affairs . . . does not even sign their frequent manifestos (which is remarkable independence in the circumstances) and does not appear to belong to any Jewish organisation'. The note added that Bloom was *very* friendly, rather touchy, and should not be underestimated'.[25] The inclusion of Bloom encouraged demands by British Jews that there should be a Jewish member of the British delegation. But these were rejected on the ground that 'to admit a Jewish representation would open the door to a request for similar favours from other interested parties'; efforts by Jewish organizations to secure independent Jewish representation at the Conference were equally unsuccessful.[26] The British delegation was headed by Richard Law, and included Osbert Peake (Under-Secretary of State at the Home Office) and G. H. Hall (Financial Secretary to the Admiralty, and previously junior minister at the Colonial Office). A. W. G. Randall of the Foreign Office Refugee Department was Secretary to the British delegation.

The directions prepared for the British delegation to the conference clearly delimited the scope for manoeuvre at the meeting. It was laid down that the problem was 'not confined to persons of any particular race or faith', and that 'in view of transport limitations refugees shall be housed as near as possible to where they are now or to their homes'. Plans were to be made for maintaining refugees in neutral countries in Europe. The possibility of asylum in allied countries 'should be investigated, taking account of availability of shipping, food and accommodation'. The directions recalled that 'although it is not denied that America has done a great deal for refugees in the way of refuge and supplies, the greater part of the burden, both political and financial, has been borne by His Majesty's Government'. The British delegates were instructed to seek to secure from the U.S.A. assistance in arranging for refugee accommodation in North Africa, and in persuading Latin

[25] Note by Foreign Office for Cabinet Committee on Refugees, 31 Mar. 1943, PRO CAB 95/15.
[26] Minutes by A. Walker, 11 Apr. 1943, PRO FO 371/36659 (W 5962/49/48 and W 6301/49/48); minute by A. W. G. Randall, 5 Apr. 1943, PRO FO 371/36657 (W 5657/49/48).

American countries to be more liberal in their policy regarding refugee immigration. After an inter-departmental meeting in Whitehall, the delegation was further advised that if the United States delegation were to offer (though this was considered improbable) to take into the U.S.A. several thousand refugees from Spain on condition that the United Kingdom and colonies took the rest, this 'embarrassing development' should be dealt with by reminding the Americans 'of the limits we have reached in the African colonies' and by giving them 'a warning that the neutral Spanish Government would be embarrassed by such a sweeping offer, and a cautious promise to look into the United Kingdom and non-African colonial possibilities'.[27]

When the British delegates reached Bermuda they found that their American counterparts appeared to be 'men who had no knowledge of and no public responsibility for the problem under discussion'. Dr Dodds, the chief American delegate, was said to have 'cheerfully admitted that he had had such little warning of his appointment that he knew nothing about refugees until after he had arrived'. However, the British delegates reported that the State Department officials soon 'took the delegates in hand', and 'excellent relations' were established between the two delegations. The American delegates had been accompanied to Bermuda by several non-officials, including a number of journalists, whom the British were anxious to exclude from the discussions; in this the Americans obliged. The British representatives 'soon found that, although not under such intense and widespread pressure as we, they [the Americans] were anxious to resist obviously impracticable or undesirable suggestions made by extremist groups.'[28]

The conference decided to begin with an effort to 'deal with the demands put forward by refugee organizations, and in particular attempt to dispose of those which were generally considered Utopian and impracticable'.[29] The first such proposal was that for an approach to be made to Hitler to release Jews in Nazi-occupied countries. Dodds said that this would involve negotiating with Hitler and that was definitely against

[27] Foreign Office note to Cabinet Committee on Refugees, 25 Mar. 1943, PRO FO 371/36657/93 (W 5336/49/48).

[28] United Kingdom Delegates to the Bermuda Conference to Eden, 28 June 1943, circulated to Cabinet, PRO PREM 4/51/3.

[29] Minutes of first discussion at conference, 19 Apr. 1943, PRO FO 371/36725.

United States policy. Law agreed: the only terms of negotiating with Hitler were unconditional surrender. Peake said that there were thirty or forty million people of whom Hitler would be glad to be rid, as they made no contribution to the war effort. 'If we approached Hitler he might offer to release forty million whom we could not possibly handle, and we should then look ridiculous. He might only let "useless mouths" go. If he made such an offer there would be a large section of people both in the U.K. and the U.S.A. who would say that we must try to take them and to attempt this would gravely hinder our war effort.' The only dissenting voice was that of Bloom who said that he thought it 'a mistake to close the door definitely to this proposal'.[30] The British delegates reported that Bloom 'doubtless with a view to quieting his Jewish conscience, was inclined to make difficulties, but he was firmly overruled by Dr Dodds and the State Department officials, who were even more emphatic than ourselves in rejecting these particular extreme suggestions from the "pressure groups"'.[31] In the final report signed by the two delegations, the proposal for an approach to Germany was stated to be 'directly contrary to the settled policies of the two Governments concerned', although 'it was felt that the question might be borne in mind in case conditions altered at a later date'.[32]

Other 'Utopian' schemes were similarly discarded. A proposal 'that we should exchange Nazi internees and prisoners of war against Jewish people in occupied Europe' was agreed by all to be impracticable, and unlike the first suggestion was not 'left open'.[33] A third proposal, that food should be sent through the Allied blockade to help feed the Jews of Europe, was considered to involve questions of blockade policy 'which were . . . outside the terms of reference of the conference. But it was agreed that to supply food to Jews in Europe would be impossible except as part of a general proposal to feed all the oppressed nationalities under Nazi control.'[34] Both the British and the Americans were pleased that

[30] Minutes of discussion on 20 Apr. 1943, PRO FO 371/36725.

[31] U.K. delegates to Eden, 28 June 1943, PRO PREM 4/51/3.

[32] Bermuda Conference Report, 29 Apr. 1943, circulated to War Cabinet 4 May 1943, PRO CO 733/449 (76208/2).

[33] Minutes of discussion on 20 Apr. 1943, PRO FO 371/36725.

[34] Bermuda Conference Report, PRO CO 733/449 (76208/2).

the 'many illusions [which] had been fostered regarding the scope and possibilities of our discussions' had thus been quickly swept away.[35]

Law next proposed that 'they should define the problem positively, that is, in terms of possible solutions'.[36] A lengthy discussion of the availability of shipping for refugees ensued: according to the British delegation, the Americans at this point 'introduced their shipping expert, an official from the State Department, who, in an exhaustive survey, demolished one by one any hopes we might have had for the use of Allied ships for refugees, and dismissed as quite out of the question for reasons of "turn around" and security the proposal that ships under the control of the Allies should wait at any Allied controlled port to take anyone on board other than prisoners of war, wounded and fighting personnel.'[37] It was decided that 'the only hope at present of obtaining transportation for the refugees to overseas destinations was neutral shipping'; the conference agreed that 'detailed decisions and arrangements on this point should normally be left to the Inter-governmental Committee' and to the two governments concerned.[38]

The conference then began to consider certain specific categories of refugees. There was, first, the question of some 40,000 Polish civilian refugees in Persia whose presence was stated to be 'highly inconvenient as Persia was rapidly developing into an important military area'. Some 1,700 Jews among them had been or would be moved to Palestine. Arrangements had been made for 21,000 to be taken to East Africa, and 5,000 to India. Asylum for the remaining 12,300 had been offered in Mexico, Southern Rhodesia, and South Africa, but there were shipping and other difficulties which 'should be referred to the Inter-governmental Committee'. The problem of Greek refugees was similarly dispatched with surprising ease: some 16,500 Greeks were said to have escaped from the islands after the German occupation in 1941. Of these, 3,000 had been admitted to the Belgian Congo, 4,650 to Cyprus, 200 to Palestine, and 2,000 to Syria.[39] The Polish and Greek problems

[35] U.K. delegates to Eden, 28 June 1943, PRO PREM 4/51/3.
[36] Minutes of discussion on 20 Apr. 1943, PRO FO 371/36725.
[37] U.K. delegates to Eden, 28 June 1943, PRO PREM 4/51/3.
[38] Bermuda Conference Report, PRO CO 733/449/76208/2.
[39] Minutes of discussion on 20 Apr. 1943, PRO FO 371/36725.

(both predominantly non-Jewish) having thus been disposed of with relatively little difficulty, the conference turned to the more complex problem of the refugees in Spain. These fell under three headings. First, there were the French citizens, numbering about 14,000; for these a country of destination existed in North Africa. Secondly, there were 'Allied nationals who had been accepted for service in the armed forces of their respective countries'; these could travel to the United Kingdom and North Africa. Finally, there were the remaining 6,000 to 8,000 refugees, 'largely, though not exclusively, Jews from Central Europe'. In contrast to the swift resolution of the problems of disposing of the much larger numbers of refugees under other categories and headings, this provoked some argument.

Law urged that the American military authorities should be asked to reconsider the possibility of these refugees being sent to camps in North Africa. However, the American delegates objected. Reams said 'that there would be an adverse Arab reaction in North Africa if they sent Jewish refugees there. The American troops would not tolerate that any country occupied by them should put Jewish refugees in concentration camps.' Dodds said that the General Staff was 'diametrically opposed to receiving refugees in North Africa'. Bloom said that 'it would annoy the Arabs to bring in Jews and they must think of how it would affect the war'. He feared that if they put refugees in concentration camps there 'they might cause an explosion: this they could not risk'. In reply to these American objections Peake said 'that he had had experience of running an internment camp in the Isle of Man. They had taken two villages and wired them round, and the conditions were not unpleasant; the internees had a certain amount of liberty and were contented.[40] The Americans were reluctant to enter into any engagements regarding camps in North Africa until they had consulted the State Department, and it was agreed that the British delegation should put forward a formal proposal on the matter for American consideration.

The suggestion that camps should be established in North Africa was not, however, welcomed in the State Department.

---

[40] Bermuda Conference Report, PRO CO 733/449(76208/2); and minutes of discussions on 21 Apr. 1943, PRO FO 371/36725.

Assistant Secretary of State Breckenridge Long noted in his diary:

To put them in Moslem countries raises political questions which immediately assume a paramount military importance—considering that of the population of 18 million behind our long lines 14 million are Mohamedans. The whole Mohamedan world is tending to flare up at indications that the Allied forces are trying to locate Jewish people under their protection in Moslem territory . . . Altogether it is a bad tendency.[41]

However, the American delegation at the conference, evidently persuaded by the arguments of their British colleagues, sent a series of messages to the State Department urging that a concession be made to the British on the point. Dodds, in a personal message to Long stressed that:

The impression created by the removal from Spain [of] all refugees but Jews would be unfortunate and would furnish ammunition for the pressure groups and even friendly Jewish organizations and humanitarian groups.[42]

Eventually the State Department authorized the American delegates to agree that the American Government would 'take all practical steps' to establish the camps, provided that a *quid pro quo* were forthcoming from the British.[43] The latter therefore agreed that in return for the American concession regarding Morocco (where the Americans recognized the administration of General Giraud), the British would 'press General de Gaulle for more generous offers over Madagascar'. The British further agreed to 'put forward the question of receiving refugees in Cyrenaica'.[44]

While the bargaining over the North African camps proceeded behind the scenes, the formal sessions of the conference continued to discuss other aspects of the refugee problem. The next item on the agenda was that of 'Jewish refugees from the

---

[41] Israel, *Diary of Breckenridge Long*, p. 309 (entry dated 22 Apr. 1943).

[42] U.S. Consul General at Hamilton, Bermuda, to State Dept., enclosing Dodds to Long, 24 Apr. 1943, *FRUS 1943* vol. I, p. 164. Previous messages from Dodds, ibid., pp. 157–163.

[43] Secretary of State Hull to Dodds, 28 April 1943, *FRUS 1943* vol. I, p. 172.

[44] U.K. delegates to Eden, 28 June 1943, PRO PREM 4/51/3.

Balkans and the obstacles in the way of removing them to Palestine'. The British delegates later commented:

In approaching the subject of Palestine we felt we might have some embarrassment. The United States Government had, we knew, been under considerable pressure from Jewish organisations; there had also been elaborate advertisements, summaries of which were telegraphed to us by His Majesty's Ambassador, denouncing the Bermuda Conference, and urging the opening up of Palestine. . . We began by explaining what Palestine had done in regard to Jewish immigration, and for refugees generally, and we repeated the offer of the Secretary of State for Colonies to take large numbers of Jewish children from South-Eastern Europe. . . Mr Sol Bloom was inclined to press us for some assurance regarding admissions after the expiry of the White Paper period, if the numbers announced had not by then been received. But we declined to discuss this hypothesis, and the other American delegates said they were not empowered to discuss British policy in Palestine. Mr Dodds, indeed (following, it seemed clear, the State Department's directive, for a similar statement was made even more emphatically by the Secretary of the American Delegation), said that they were too much aware of difficulties confronting us to wish to force the Jewish issue.[45]

The implicit agreement whereby the Americans would show understanding of the British position regarding Palestine, provided that the British behaved similarly over the question of immigration to the U.S.A., was fully honoured by both delegations. An immigration official from the State Department presented to the conference a survey of United States immigration policy. He was introduced by Dodds who reminded the meeting that 'administrative changes could only be made by the consent of Congress, and at the present time it would not be possible to make such changes in their system. At the present moment it might result in disaster should two or three saboteurs manage to come in with the refugees.'[46] The immigration official then presented an exposition of American immigration policy, in the course of which he claimed that the U.S.A. had issued 547,000 visas to persons from Axis-controlled countries since 1933.[47] As the British delegates commented in their report to the Foreign Office, 'It would be

[45] Ibid.; minutes of discussion on 21 Apr. 1943, PRO FO 371/36725.
[46] Minutes of discussion on 24 Apr. 1943, PRO FO 371/36725.
[47] Ibid.

possible for an exacting critic to pick holes in the statement . . .
regarding admissions to the United States. The imposing total
of visas given since 1933 impresses rather less if one realises that
it must include a considerable number of people who were not
refugees.'[48] The number of refugees admitted to the U.S.A. was
probably less than half that of the number of visas issued. When
the larger figure was cited by Assistant Secretary Breckenridge
Long in a Congressional hearing in November 1943, the discrepancy was revealed and became the subject of intense public
criticism in the U.S.A.[49] The British delegates at Bermuda
forbore from challenging the Americans on this point. They
did, however, press the Americans gently on a specific aspect of
their immigration policy: the fact that even the limited numbers permitted to enter the U.S.A. under the quota regulations
were not being filled. The German-Austrian quota theoretically permitted the entry of 27,370 persons per annum: in 1939
and 1940 the quota had been almost completely filled; but in
1941 it was only 47.7 per cent full, and in 1942 17.8 per cent.[50]
The State Department expert admitted that the quotas had not
been filled, but Senator Lucas said that the refugees in Spain
included a great number who 'would not be desirable and
would not qualify' for admission to the U.S.A. Law then
inquired whether, 'if the ships could be found and a thousand
or more could qualify, would the U.S. take them?' The pill was
sweetened for the Americans when Peake asked 'if the U.K.
said they would take in several hundreds of refugees from
Spain, would it be embarrassing to the U.S. Government? Mr
Bloom said that the U.K. could just go right ahead and embarrass the U.S. Government'.[51]

This hint of a concession regarding immigration to Britain
was given in spite of a statement by Peake which stressed the
limited capacity of the country for further refugees. Peake said:

At one time they had been told that there were 20,000 children in
Vichy France, but in the present overcrowded state of the U.K.,
difficulties of transport, food, and accommodation, such a number

[48] U.K. delegates to Eden, 28 June 1943, PRO PREM 4/51/3.
[49] Henry L. Feingold, *The Politics of Rescue: The Roosevelt Administration and the Holocaust
1938–1945*, New Brunswick N.J. 1970, pp. 230–37.
[50] David S. Wyman, *Paper Walls: America and the Refugee Crisis 1938–1941*, Amherst
Mass. 1968, pp. 220–2.
[51] Minutes of discussion on 24 Apr. 1943, PRO FO 371/36725.

could not be contemplated. It would be embarrassing to the war effort of both the U.S.A. and the U.K. There was a vociferous minority of people in the U.K. who wanted H.M.G. to do this, but the majority there thought that quite as many refugees as they could cope with in war circumstances had been admitted.[52]

The British delegation secured Cabinet approval for a British offer to take in several hundred refugees from Spain with the stipulation that the U.S.A. should do the same. However, the final conference report signed by the two delegations merely stated that Britain was 'prepared, in association with other nations, to assume a further responsibility for giving temporary refuge to persons whose numbers under war conditions must necessarily be limited'.[53] Peake said that 'the generosity of the U.S. immigrant policy was not fully known in the U.K., but he imagined that they had better not put anything in the report as to what each country had done or they might be accused of handing bouquets to each other.'[54] The American delegates were less squeamish on this point, and the final report gave full details of the refugee policies of the two countries, shown in the most favourable possible light.

The other sessions of the conference were mainly occupied with discussions of the position of refugees in neutral countries, particularly Switzerland, with the proposed reactivation of the Inter-Governmental Committee on refugees, and with the potential reception of refugees in such areas as Latin America, the British Empire and Angola. Randall said that the Swiss Legation in London had indicated 'that the question of food and finance for the refugees in their country did not worry the Swiss Government so much as the fact that they did not know whether there would be any limit to the number of refugees they were taking in. . . . The uncertainty of what was going to happen to these refugees after the war was a major worry to the Swiss Government. Many of them would wish to stay in Switzerland.' The British delegation suggested that the problem might be solved by means of a United Nations declaration that all refugees admitted to neutral countries during the war would return to their homes after the conclusion of hostilities. The

---

[52] Ibid.
[53] Bermuda Conference Report, PRO CO 733/449 (76208/2).
[54] Minutes of discussion on 24 Apr. 1943, PRO FO 371/36725.

Americans raised certain difficulties: Reams, for example, pointed out 'that from a propaganda point of view it might be dangerous to announce that the Jews were going to be re-instated in Germany'. But these difficulties were ironed out, and agreement was secured on a draft declaration to be issued by all the European Allied Governments as well as the United States. The draft paid tribute to the 'humanitarian contributions made toward the solution of the refugee problem' by the neutral states, and stated that all the signatories would, after the war, 'ensure such conditions' in their territories as to enable the return of all of their nationals displaced by the war into other countries.[55]

The reactivation of the Inter-Governmental Committee, which had been dormant since the outbreak of the war, was a cardinal point in the minds of the Americans. The British delegates privately deprecated the American 'habit of putting on the Inter-governmental Committee difficult or disagreeable tasks which the United States Government was clearly unwilling to carry out alone', and they remarked that the Americans 'made frequent references to that body as if it were a kind of *deus ex machina*, to be produced on the stage whenever any apparently insoluble questions of finance, shipping, or politics confronted us'.[56] However, in deference to the Americans, the British agreed to the resuscitation of the Committee, under a new mandate (to include responsibility for refugees other than those from Germany, Austria, and the Sudetenland to which its work had previously been limited), with an enlarged membership (to include the U.S.S.R., Poland, Greece, and Yugoslavia), and with an expanded organization and a much larger budget (from both public and private sources).[57]

On possible destinations for refugees in Latin America or the British Empire the conference discussions made little progress. Law asked whether the U.S.A. might approach Latin American governments on the point: Dodds said that would be 'impracticable'. Senator Lucas asked about possibilities in British Honduras: the British replied that there were twenty refugees and two internees there, and no room for further

[55] Minutes of discussions on 23 Apr. 1943, PRO FO 371/36725.
[56] U.K. delegates to Eden, 28 June 1943, PRO PREM 4/51/3.
[57] Bermuda Conference Report, PRO CO 733/449/76208/2.

'Europeans unaccustomed to manual labour in a tropical climate'.[58] Note was taken of the failure of the refugee settlement in the Dominican Republic, and of the obstacles in the way of a refugee influx to British Guiana.[59] The Americans raised the question of Angola, and handed to the British a memorandum 'recounting the history of attempts for many years back to encourage a large Jewish settlement' there. A new approach to the Portuguese Government was urged by the American delegates. They explained, however, that the United States Government 'would not wish to approach the Portuguese Government alone, or even together with ourselves, but would strongly support the suggestion that the Inter-governmental Committee should do so'.[60]

The final action of the conference was to agree that its recommendations were to remain secret until mutual agreement between the two governments had been reached 'to make certain items public, at intervals'.[61] The final communiqué issued to the press by the two delegations stated that the conference had agreed 'on a number of concrete recommendations' but these were not specified. A lengthy report was agreed upon for transmission to the two governments. This summarized the proceedings of the conference and made thirteen recommendations. Of these several referred to the proposal for an expanded and revivified Inter-Governmental Committee. The remainder included suggestions for the dispersal of the refugees in Spain, with the removal of some 'to temporary residence in North Africa, subject to military considerations', and 'further limited admissions' to Britain and the U.S.A. The British authorities were to consider admitting refugees to Cyrenaica, and the French National Committee was to be invited to offer refuge in Madagascar. Appended to the report was the text of the proposed United Nations declaration to neutral states on the post-war return of refugees to their homes.[62]

The British delegates privately admitted the insubstantial

[58] Minutes of discussion on 24 Apr. 1943, PRO FO 371/36725.
[59] Bermuda Conference Report, PRO CO 733/449 (76208/2).
[60] U.K. delegates to Eden, 28 June 1943, PRO PREM 4/51/3.
[61] U.S. Consul General, Hamilton, Bermuda, to State Dept., enclosing Dodds to Long, 28 Apr. 1943, *FRUS 1943* vol. I, pp. 172–3.
[62] Bermuda Conference Report, PRO CO 733/449 (76208/2).

nature of the conclusions of the conference. In their private report to the Foreign Office they wrote that 'so far as immediate relief to refugees is concerned, the conference was able to achieve very little'. 'Limiting factors', they continued,' are bound to be serious and disappointments frequent, as long as the war continues and shipping and food supply present such difficulties, so long as too, we might add, the present combination, in so many countries, of pity for Jews under German control and extreme reluctance to admit further Jews into their borders persists.' However, the delegates observed, the 'ten agreeable days of discussion' in Bermuda had not been wasted, as they had dispelled the 'note of asperity, jealousy, and suspicion of His Majesty's Government in certain American official circles' and 'laid a foundation of mutual understanding and co-operation' concerning the refugee issue.[63]

In a letter to Eden (which was circulated to the Cabinet), the head of the British delegation, Law, reflected on the results of the conference. He drew attention to the differences in the internal pressures on the British and American Governments on the refugee question:

We are subjected to extreme pressure from an alliance of Jewish organisations and Archbishops. There is no counter-pressure as yet from the people who are afraid of an alien immigration into the country because it will put their livelihood in jeopardy after the war. I have no doubt in my own mind that that feeling is widespread in England, but it is not organised so we do not feel it. In the United States, on the other hand, there is added to the pressure of the Jewish organisations the pressure of that body of opinion which, without being purely anti-Semitic, is jealous and fearful of an alien immigration *per se*. And in contradistinction to the position at home, that body of opinion is very highly organised indeed. The Americans, therefore, while they must do their utmost to placate Jewish opinion, dare not offend 'American' opinion.

Law believed that the American Government was genuinely anxious to play its part in the solution of the refugee problem, but he warned that 'if, however, it came to a show-down, Jew and Gentile, I am satisfied that their internal position is such

[63] U.K. delegates to Eden, 28 June 1943, PRO PREM 4/51/3.

that they would have to tell the Jewish organisations to go to hell'. He added:

Before we condemn them too much for their callousness we should remember (a) that we have not got a general election advancing inexorably upon us in a comparatively short time, and (b) that we have the same kind of selfishness at home, only it is latent and still unorganised. (But, personally, my feeling is that we ought not to ignore it altogether, and we must not make some magnificent gesture to the Archbishops now only to find that in twelve or eighteen months' time the average man, *moyen sensuel*, turns and rends us.)

Law hoped that Eden was 'not disappointed by the results of our endeavours', which, he wrote, 'could never be anything but meagre'.[64]

The meagre results of the conference, although obscured at first by the secrecy over what had transpired in Bermuda, aroused public criticism on both sides of the Atlantic. The American Vice-Chairman of the Inter-Governmental Committee, Myron Taylor, commented: 'The Bermuda Conference was wholly ineffective, as I view it, and we knew it would be.'[65] Congressional advocates of swift American action on behalf of refugees were disappointed: Representative Emanuel Celler said the Conference had 'dismally failed'; Representative Samuel Dickstein said it had ended 'the hopes of millions of people'.[66] Similar dissatisfaction was expressed in Britain. The *Jewish Chronicle* commented on 23 April (while the conference was still in session): 'Even the most irrepressible optimists can scarcely fail to experience a rapid chilling of their hopes for refugees of all kinds as they read the reports of the Bermuda Conference.' After the conclusion of the conference the paper declared the results 'not impressive' and continued:

And so the greatest tragedy in modern history must go on ... Already, even under the stress of the present emotion, the ghost of Evian walks abroad. A distressing *non possumus* is being uttered with almost indecent haste in country after country.[67]

[64] Law to Eden, circulated to Cabinet, 3 May 1943, PRO FO 371/36731 (W 6933/6933/48).
[65] Quoted in Feingold, *The Politics of Rescue*, p. 213.
[66] Quoted in Roland Young, *Congressional Politics in the Second World War*, New York 1956, p. 190.
[67] *Jewish Chronicle*, 7 May 1943.

Jewish disappointment with the results of the conference was also reported from Palestine.[68]

In view of parliamentary feeling the Government felt obliged to hold a debate on its refugee policy. Concerned lest the critics of the Government monopolize the debate, the Cabinet decided on 10 May that 'in view of the risk that a disproportionate number of speeches might be by Members holding extreme views in favour of the free admission of refugees to this country, the Whips were invited to arrange that some Members would intervene in the debate who would put a more balanced point of view'.[69] The Cabinet's concern proved to be justified, for when the debate in the House of Commons (meeting as the Supply Committee) took place on 19 May, the Government was subjected to a series of attacks, spearheaded by Eleanor Rathbone, Independent M.P. for the Combined Universities (and guiding spirit of the National Committee for Rescue from Nazi Terror).[70] Only four speakers in the debate supported the Government's policy, and three of these expressed reservations. The fourth, W. A. Colgate, Conservative M.P. for the Wrekin, gave whole-hearted support to the Government but in a form which can have given little satisfaction to the whips:

MR COLEGATE (Wrekin): 'Honestly, I think that the Jews today are suffering from the over-zealousness of their friends. Some of the propaganda simply repels me and puts me absolutely against the Jews, although I have many good and dear Jewish friends and no feeling of anti-Semitism. Some of the propaganda and some of the things that are being done are really dangerous. Let me give . . . a direct instance from my own constituency which does tend to bring about anti-Semitism [sic]. In an agricultural county like Shropshire there are very few Jews, but there is one hostel for Jews who have come here as refugees. They were asked to do agricultural work . . . The Jews in that hostel had been received handsomely, they have been fed and housed and clothed, but they refused to milk cows after four o'clock on Friday. (AN HON. MEMBER: 'That is their Sabbath.') 'Yes, but let me finish. Agricultural labourers who had been working hard had to go in and do their work.'

[68] *Jewish Chronicle*, 14 May 1943; *New York Times*, 23 May 1943.
[69] Extract from minutes of War Cabinet, 10 May 1943, PRO CO 733/449 (76208/2).
[70] Miss Rathbone had shortly before published a pamphlet entitled *Rescue the Perishing* in which she called for a large-scale programme of succour for Jews threatened with death in Europe.

After a series of exchanges on the intricacies of Sabbath obser-
vance and the milking of farm animals it was left to Eden to
reply to the debate. His speech combined apparent enthusiasm
for doing what was possible to help refugees with scepticism
that anything at all substantial was possible. Responding to
one member who had pointed out that some thirty thousand
places for immigrants to Palestine still remained unused from
the White Paper quota, Eden said:

The honourable Member says, 'Why limit them to thirty thousand?' I
would be quite willing and eager to discuss that if there was the
slightest prospect of the thirty thousand vacancies being filled . . . I
know that some Members think that the Government are insensitive
in this matter. I can assure them that we are not. . . . I do not know
whether Ministers can contribute to the problem if they wear their
hearts on their sleeves for the daws to peck at . . . We shall do what we
can, but I should be false to my trust if I raised the hopes of the
Committee because I do not believe that great things can be achieved.
I do not believe it is possible to rescue more than a few until final
victory is won.[71]

The debate did little to dissipate the gloom of the pro-refugee
lobby. On 30 June Rathbone, accompanied by Lord Perth,
Lord Samuel, David Grenfell M.P., and Quintin Hogg M.P.
met Richard Law at the Foreign Office. Samuel complained
that 'since the Declaration of December 17th last, practically
nothing had been done'. The Foreign Office note on the discussion recorded that

Towards the end . . . Lord Samuel raised with some bitterness the
question of admission to the United Kingdom, and guarantee of visas
for people who were still in enemy-occupied territory. He said that
several well-vouched-for cases he had submitted to the Home Office
had been turned down, and he suggested that a three-cornered conference—Foreign Office, Home Office, and their deputation—might
be arranged to deal with this particular aspect of the problem. He was
not encouraged to think that this was possible.[72]

However, in spite of the generally negative reaction to the
Bermuda Conference among Jewish and pro-refugee groups,
public interest in the fate of European Jews, which had been

[71] HC vol. 389, cols. 1117–1204, 19 May 1943.
[72] Note by A. W. G. Randall, 1 July 1943, PRO CO 733/446 (76021/45).

intense at the beginning of 1943, appears to have diminished by the middle of the year. The Government was consequently able to proceed on the basis of the conference's recommendations without paying heed to critics who urged a more liberal policy.

The Government's reaction to the Bermuda Conference was one of general satisfaction. Eden told the Cabinet that it had been a 'marked success'. The conference report was approved, with special emphasis being laid on the declaration to be made to neutrals, the establishment of a camp in North Africa, and the revival of the Inter-Governmental Committee. In the Cabinet discussion, however, reference was made to 'signs of increasing anti-Semitic feeling in this country', and it was agreed that no public statement would be made regarding the number of refugees who might be admitted to Britain 'at any rate until a decision had been reached on the question of a temporary camp in North Africa'.[73] The Government's general policy towards Jewish refugees during the ensuing year followed the lines laid down at Bermuda: there would be no 'magnificent gesture to the Archbishops', no change in immigration policy to Britain, and no major deviation from the White Paper policy in Palestine; on the other hand, the declaration to the neutrals was to be pressed forward, the Inter-Governmental Committee revived, and the North African camp set up. These palliatives saved some lives: they did not have any significant impact on the process of destruction in Europe.

The most tangible of these palliatives was perhaps the establishment of a refugee camp in North Africa, although even this was not achieved without lengthy resistance by the American military authorities, necessitating the intervention of Churchill with Roosevelt. The British regarded it as a high priority, not merely because of its direct effect on the refugee problem in Spain, but because they were anxious to keep open escape routes for British airmen and other military personnel. The matter had come to a head at the end of March 1943 when the Spaniards had closed the Pyrenean frontier to refugees, and ordered that foreigners entering Spain clandestinely were to be sent back to France where they would be handed over to the

[73] Extract from Cabinet minutes, 10 May 1943, PRO CO 733/449 (76028/2).

Germans. Immediate representations were made to the Spanish Government by the British and American Ambassadors, and the Spaniards assured the British Ambassador, Sir Samuel Hoare, that refugees and escaping prisoners of war would not be surrendered to the Germans; the frontier, however, remained officially closed. On 7 April Churchill called in the Spanish Ambassador in London and submitted him to a stiff lecture. The Prime Minister warned him 'that if the Spanish Government went to the length of preventing these unfortunate people seeking safety from the horror of Nazi domination, and if they went further and committed the offence of actually handing them back to the German authorities, that was a thing which would be the destruction of good relations'. The Spanish Ambassador said 'that his Government were very apprehensive of the embarrassment to which they might be exposed by the mass of influential refugees helped by foreign Embassies', but Churchill insisted 'that it was for the Germans to regulate this and to patrol their side of the frontier. If they could not do this effectively, it was certainly not up to the Spanish to reject these unfortunate people and there could not be reprisals by the Germans for accepting them.'[74] Similar representations were made by the American and Portuguese Governments, and (at the behest of the Americans) by the Argentinian Ambassador and by the Vatican Nuncio in Madrid.[75] These protests had the desired effect, but German counter-pressure on the Spanish Government remained strong, and the British were anxious to clear all refugees out of Spain, in order that the Spaniards should have no excuse for closing the frontier again. Hoare outlined the delicate diplomatic position in a letter to Eleanor Rathbone in early May:

The problem of refugees in Spain is inextricably connected with the problem of escaped prisoners of war, and with many of the secret activities of this Mission. The Gestapo is around us at every turn, complicating and attempting to frustrate our efforts, and the Spanish

[74] *Aide-mémoire* from British Embassy, Washington, to State Dept., 16 Apr. 1943, USNA 840.48 Refugees 3868.
[75] State Dept. memorandum, 19 Apr. 1943, USNA 840.48 Refugees 3862; memorandum on meeting of Breckenridge Long with Spanish Ambassador in Washington, 26 Apr. 1943, USNA 840.48 Refugees 3866; Haim Avni, *Sefarad Ve-ha-yehudim Bimei Ha-shoah Ve-ha-emansipatsia*, Tel Aviv 1975, p. 123.

Government, even when they wish to show good will, are terrified of the German army on the Pyrenees frontier.[76]

At a meeting of the Combined Chiefs of Staff on 30 April the British raised the question of the North African camp, pointing out the military considerations involved. The Americans promised to reconsider the matter, but at a meeting on 4 May, they decided to adhere to their opposition to the scheme.[77] Roosevelt was not enthusiastic about the plan which conflicted with views on the Jewish problem in North Africa which he had formed at the time of the Casablanca Conference in January 1943. He had explained these views in conversation with General Noguès, the formerly pro-Vichy Resident-General in Rabat:

The President stated that he felt the whole Jewish problem [in North Africa] should be studied very carefully and that progress should be definitely planned. In other words, the number of Jews engaged in the practice of the professions (law, medicine etc.) should be definitely limited to the percentage that the Jewish population in North Africa bears to the whole North African population. Such a plan would therefore permit the Jews to engage in the professions, and at the same time would not permit them to overcrowd the professions, and would present an unanswerable argument that they were being given their full rights. To the foregoing General Noguès agreed generally, stating at the same time that it would be a sad thing for the French to win the war merely to open the way for the Jews to control the professions and the business world of North Africa. The President stated that his plan would further eliminate the specific and understandable complaints which the Germans bore towards the Jews in Germany, namely that while they represented a small part of the population, over fifty per cent of the lawyers, doctors, schoolteachers, college professors, etc. in Germany were Jews.[78]

[76] Hoare to Rathbone, 3 May 1943, Templewood Papers, Cambridge University Library, XIII: 5.

[77] Admiral Leahy, for Joint Chiefs of Staff, to Secretary of State, 7 May 1943, *FRUS 1943* vol. I, p. 299.

[78] Note on Roosevelt-Noguès talk, 17 Jan. 1943, *FRUS Casablanca Conference*, pp. 608–9; Roosevelt repeated these opinions in a conversation with General Giraud later the same day, ibid. pp. 609–12. That Winston Churchill had, at one time, subscribed to a view similar to that expressed in the final sentence of Roosevelt's statement quoted above is evident from a letter to Churchill from James de Rothschild on 27 May 1938 which stated: 'When you spoke with such sympathy last week at Cranborne about the Jewish situation in Germany, you mentioned that the number of Jews in the various professions and occupations had been, in the days before Hitler, very high in comparison with the proportion which Jews bore to the total population. The idea that this was so was fostered by Nazi propaganda, and has been widely accepted. I am enclosing an

This remarkable utterance (which may most charitably be explained as an example of the President's tendency to concur with the opinions of his interlocutor of the moment) indicates Roosevelt's feeling as to the sensitivity of American-French relations concerning the Jews in North Africa. Hence his comment in mid-May 1943: 'I agree that North Africa may be used as a depot for those refugees but not a permanent residence without full approval of all authorities. I know, in fact, that there is plenty of room for them in North Africa, but I raise the question of sending large numbers of Jews there. That would be extremely unwise.'[79]

The British, however, were not prepared to let the matter rest. On 19 May Eden cabled to Churchill (who was visiting Washington):

I am dismayed and depressed by the refusal of the United States Chiefs of Staff to agree to our recommendation that a small camp should be established in North Africa into which to draft refugees from Spain. This suggestion has long been pressed forward by us . . . It is our main hope of getting refugees out of Spain and so not only satisfying British and American public opinion, but also keeping open the escape routes from France into Spain which are essential to our military and intelligence services. This is the only remaining way of getting pilots and other prisoners out of France . . . The numbers involved are not large and agreement to open a camp even for one thousand would ease the situation. It is difficult to believe that this would put any particular strain on shipping . . . As for the last objection, namely resentment on the part of the Arabs, this could surely be eliminated by putting the camp in a place sufficiently remote from important Arab centres.

Eden emphasized that failure to remove the 'hard core' of refugees from Spain would lead to 'extremely serious parliamentary criticism', and that 'American military objections' would 'hardly be accepted as plausible'. He urged Churchill to 'put all this personally to the President', stressing that it was 'our last hope of carrying through a modest suggestion to which we attach great political and military importance'.[80] General

article which appeared in the "Manchester Guardian" of 3rd January 1936, which disproves this by official German statistics.' (M. Gilbert, *Winston S. Churchill, Companion vol. 5, The Coming of War*, London 1979).

[79] Roosevelt to Hull, 14 May 1943, *FRUS 1943* vol. I, p. 179.
[80] Eden to Churchill, 19 May 1943, *FRUS Washington Conference 1943*, p. 345.

Ismay, Churchill's Chief of Staff, submitted a memorandum to the Prime Minister on the scheme, and suggested that 'you should now go into action with the President on this matter'.[81] Churchill agreed to do so 'if necessary', and there appears to have been some discussion of the subject over lunch with Roosevelt at the White House.[82] Unfortunately, no record of the discussion was kept, and disagreement developed between the British and the Americans over what had been decided.[83]

The Gordian knot was eventually cut by a cable from Churchill to Roosevelt at the end of June, in which he again commended the scheme to the Americans and requested 'an early practical decision'. Churchill argued that the Allies' 'immediate facilities for helping the victims of Hitler's anti-Jewish drive are so limited at present that the opening of the small camp proposed for the purpose of removing some of them to safety seems all the more incumbent on us'.[84] Roosevelt replied on 8 July promising to instruct Generals Eisenhower and Giraud to make arrangements for a camp in French North Africa for five or six thousand Jewish refugees from Spain 'and others who may be able to escape from Axis territory into Spain'. The cable stressed, however, that the camp was to be 'a place of temporary residence', and Roosevelt added that he was 'in complete accord with the thought of the French military authorities in that area that both for political and military reasons it is essential to transfer the refugees . . . to a place of more permanent settlement for the duration'. Tripolitania, Cyrenaica, and Madagascar were, continued Roosevelt, 'under active discussion', and it was also his 'understanding that a limited number of the refugees may be admitted to Palestine'.[85] Skating lightly over the reservations expressed by Roosevelt, Churchill replied thanking Roosevelt for his 'suggestions which will provide a solution for our difficulties in Spain', and undertook that as soon as he heard that the President had issued directives to

[81] Ismay to Churchill, 21 May 1943, ibid., p. 343; sim., 24 May 1943, ibid., p. 342.

[82] Churchill note for Ismay, 22 May 1943, ibid., p. 344; notes on Roosevelt-Churchill meetings on 17 and 24 May 1943, ibid., pp. 96 and 197; Churchill to Foreign and Colonial Secretaries, 8 June 1943, PRO PREM 4/51/4/219.

[83] Memorandum by Breckenridge Long, 4 June 1943, *FRUS 1943* vol. I, pp. 309–10; memorandum by Cordell Hull, 17 June 1943, ibid., p. 313; Israel, *Diary of Breckenridge Long*, p. 316 (entry dated 23 June 1943).

[84] Former Naval Person to President, 30 June 1943, PRO PREM 4/51/4/215.

[85] Roosevelt to Churchill, 8 July 1943, PRO PREM 4/51/4/211.

Eisenhower and Giraud, he would 'give complementary instructions to our authorities'.[86]

Even these top-level exchanges did not secure immediate results, because of a lengthy delay by the French authorities in North Africa in agreeing to the scheme. When they finally did so, it was with a proviso that the occupants of the camps would be subject to restrictions such that they would in effect become prisoners. The Americans refused to accept this and pointed out to the French that 'confinement of the refugees in a camp following their evacuation from Spain where, we believe, they enjoyed some liberty, would cause instant and violent press and public criticism of us and of the French authorities'.[87] The British Minister in Algiers, Harold Macmillan, was instructed to support these representations.[88] The French ultimately gave way, and two refugee camps were established in French Morocco, the first at Fedhala (Camp Maréchal Lyautey), and a second at Philippeville (Camp Jeanne d'Arc). But problems continued to dog the enterprise. It rapidly became apparent that there was little enthusiasm for the scheme among the refugees themselves. In February 1944 the British Embassy in Madrid reported that many of the refugees feared 'with some reason, that going to Africa will only be falling out of the frying pan into the fire; in other words, they suspect that a French camp would be only one degree worse than their present life of uncertainty in Spain where they live in fear of being thrown into prison at any moment'.[89] The refugees' fears were such that by March 1944 the United States Government endorsed a policy of 'involuntary removal' of refugees from Spain to North Africa, with the proviso that it be 'explained' to the deportees that their speedy departure from Spain was necessary in order to facilitate the entry to the country of further refugees.[90] Movement of refugees into the camps began in May 1944, but by this time the scheme had lost much of its *raison d'être*. The refugee position in Spain had by now been somewhat eased by the departure of

[86] Former Naval Person to President, 10 July 1943, PRO PREM 4/51/4/208.

[87] State Dept. to Robert Murphy (Algiers), 15 Oct. 1943, USNA 840.48 Refugees 4537.

[88] Foreign Office to U.S. Embassy, London, 28 Oct. 1943, USNA 840.48 Refugees 4711.

[89] British Embassy, Madrid, to Foreign Office, 19 Feb., 1944, PRO FO 371/42751/118 (W 2925/83/48).

[90] Hull (Washington) to Hayes (Madrid), 23 March 1944, *FRUS 1944*, vol. I, p. 1013.

large groups of refugees for Palestine and North America.[91] In the event, the number of refugees evacuated to French North Africa was far fewer than the five or six thousand discussed at Bermuda and sanctioned by Roosevelt. According to one estimate, no more than 630 Jewish refugees were transported to Fedhala, and most of these were soon moved elsewhere.[92] By the end of 1944 Fedhala appears to have been empty, being 'held in reserve' in case Philippeville should be filled to capacity.[93] A Foreign Office minute in February 1945 stated that Philippeville was being used 'as a dump for Fedhala'. The Foreign Office had at last become disillusioned with the scheme to the sponsorship of which it had devoted such energetic but unproductive efforts. The head of the Refugee Department, Paul Mason, candidly admitted: 'I have never liked the Philippeville plan very much: it has always struck me as a rather obvious piece of window dressing, and, while the alternative courses at the time were not easy to find, I should not be sorry for a decent excuse to bury it.'[94]

The elephantine diplomatic process of conception of the North African camps plan thus gave birth belatedly to an insignificant mouse. The idea, which even in its original form had been characterized by Eden as 'modest', made little effective contribution to a solution to the Jewish refugee problem. It may have helped a little to persuade the Spanish Government to keep open its border to refugees from Nazi-occupied territory. But by early 1944 the flow across the Pyrenees had in any case dwindled to a trickle; escape from France had developed into a high-priced racket, and there were complaints by the British intelligence service that Jewish refugees were outbidding Allied military personnel in the market for Spanish guides through the mountains.[95] By the middle of 1944 the changing

[91] M. Wischnitzer, *To Dwell in Safety*, Philadelphia 1948, p. 254; M. Wischnitzer, *Visas to Freedom: The History of HIAS*, Cleveland 1956, p. 189; Avni, *Sefarad Ve-ha-yehudim*, p. 137.

[92] Avni, *Sefarad Ve-ha-yehudim*, p. 142.

[93] Allied Force Headquarters, Mediterranean, to War Office, 4 Dec. 1944, PRO FO 371/42825 (WR 1951); E. Rhatigan (U.N.R.R.A.) to Foreign Office, 1 Dec. 1944, PRO FO 371/42853/59 (WR 1931/26/48).

[94] Minute dated 3 Feb. 1945, PRO FO 371/51111/120 (WR 275/4/48).

[95] Hayes (Madrid) to State Dept., 28 Feb. 1944, *FRUS 1944* vol. I, p. 996; Note on interview of G. H. Hall with S. S. Silverman M.P. and A. L. Easterman, 5 July 1944, PRO FO 371/42807/23 (WR 18/3/48).

tide of fortune in the war was in any case dictating to the Spanish Government a course of prudent compliance with Anglo-American desires in most matters, including the refugee issue. The opening of the camps probably made no difference to the numbers of refugees entering Spain.

The success with which Franco-American resistance rendered the British-sponsored Moroccan scheme nugatory had a mirror-image in the similar Franco-British resistance to tentative plans agreed upon at Bermuda whereby in return for the Moroccan camps the British undertook to investigate the possibility of more permanent refugee settlements in Libya and Madagascar. The latter territory (to which Hitler too had at one time considered dispatching large numbers of Jews from Europe)[96] was soon dismissed from serious consideration. A telegram from the British Consul-General on the island on 2 June 1943 reported that the French Governor-General had stated that the French National Committee had decided not to pursue the project on the ground that the British Government's terms were 'too onerous'. The consul added: 'Governor-General does not want Jewish elements. He (and not he alone) dislikes prestige lowering innovation of Europeans doing agricultural work of type hitherto exclusively done by natives.'[97] No more was heard of the project.

The possibility of establishing a Jewish refugee settlement in Libya received much more serious consideration, but it foundered on the rock of British military opposition, similar to that of the Americans in Morocco. The suggestion that refugees might be sent to Cyrenaica had first been made by the Greek Government in January 1943. It had been rejected at that time because of opposition by the British Commander-in-Chief in the Middle East, General Alexander, who was supported by the War Office; it had then been held that settling Greeks in the area would antagonize the Arabs and prejudice military operations.[98] As a result of the Bermuda Conference, however, the matter was re-opened with the Americans urging that Jews be settled there in order to ease pressure on the proposed camp in

[96] See p. 43.

[97] Consul-General, Antananarivo, to Foreign Office, 2 June 1943, PRO FO 371/36708/100 (W 8423).

[98] Eden to Churchill, 15 June 1943, PRO PREM 4/51/4/217.

Morocco. Churchill discussed the idea with Roosevelt, and remarked later that there did 'not seem to be any objection on political grounds to their being accommodated during the war without prejudice to the more permanent policy'. Eden noted that 'the difficulties with the Arabs emphasized by the Military Authorities in regard to temporary Greek settlement would seem to apply with even greater force to Jewish settlement', and he pointed out that any alternative destination to Palestine for Jews would be likely to encounter opposition from the Zionists. But he concluded that 'on a long view . . . neither objection is necessarily insuperable'.[99] The long view was not shared by the other bodies concerned. Lord Moyne, the Deputy Minister of State in the Middle East, cabled to the Foreign Office that, after discussion with the military authorities, he had reached the conclusion 'that admission of Jews to Cyrenaica would be disastrous'. The scheme, he felt, 'would have the worst possible effect on [the] Senussi and [would] gravely complicate the whole *status quo* of [the] Arab problem'.[100]

The Foreign Office was not prepared to leave the matter there. It was felt that the concession made by the Americans regarding Morocco required some equivalent gesture by the British in Libya. A. Walker of the Refugee Department minuted:

The Americans have made it clear that they expect us to do our part and provide a reception area in Cyrenaica and Tripolitania as a *quid pro quo* for the assistance the Americans are affording us in North Africa to liquidate our refugee problem. I think, therefore, we should make this clear and inform the military authorities and the Minister of State that unless they can produce chapter and verse for their professed belief that the admission of Jews (under proper safeguards and established in proper camps) to the territories in question will prove disastrous (to what?) they had better consider seriously the practical measures and give effect to our views.[101]

A further telegram in these terms was dispatched to Cairo, but this evoked the response that, apart from the political objections, the project 'would lock up British troops on internal

---

[99] Churchill to Foreign and Colonial Secretaries, 8 June 1943, PRO PREM 4/51/4/219; Eden to Churchill, 15 June 1943, PRO PREM 4/51/4/217.

[100] Moyne to Foreign Office, 8 July 1943, PRO FO 371/36714 (W 9992/1731/48).

[101] Minute dated 20 July 1943, PRO FO 371/36714 (W 9992/1731/48).

security duties and create demands for major works services which could only be fulfilled to the detriment of military operational requirements'. Instead of Libya it was suggested that the possibilities of setting up camps for Jewish refugees in British Somaliland, Kenya, or Northern Nigeria should be examined.[102] It was only after these alternatives had been dismissed by the Foreign Office, and the proposal again put to Cairo for 'an unobtrusive camp for a few hundred at least in Tripolitania' (where the political objections were held to be weaker than in Cyrenaica), that the local authorities gave their blessing to the establishment of 'a camp for a thousand persons'.[103]

The obstructive resources susceptible of deployment by the War Office were, however, no less impressive than those of the Pentagon. In spite of the reluctant concurrence with the scheme of the military and civil authorities in the Middle East, the War Office clung to the view that 'operational commitments and the difficulties of accommodation and supply rule out the proposal for the present, while the political, racial, and economic objections will always exist'.[104] Repeated attempts by the Foreign Office in the autumn of 1943 to shift the War Office from this position failed to yield results.[105] In the spring of 1944 the Americans renewed pressure on the British to set up a camp in Libya, and the Foreign Office again put the proposal to the War Office, only to receive a further rebuff. As American pressure persisted, it was decided to put the matter to the Cabinet for a decision. A Foreign Office memorandum emphasized that in Bermuda 'a bargain' had been struck with the Americans, whereby they had agreed to a camp in Morocco which was now 'on the point of receiving its first contingent of about five hundred refugees . . . on the understanding that H.M.G. admitted refugees from Italy into Cyrenaica or

[102] Foreign Office to Deputy Minister of State, Cairo, 22 July 1943, PRO FO 371/36714 (W 9992/1731/48); Minister of State, Cairo, to Foreign Office, 4 Aug. 1943, PRO FO 371/36714 (W 11368/1731/48).

[103] Foreign Office to Minister of State, Cairo, 20 Aug. 1943, PRO FO 371/36714 (W 11368/1731/48); Minister of State, Cairo, to Foreign Office, 26 Aug. 1943, PRO FO 371/36714 (W 12387/1731/48).

[104] P. J. Grigg (Secretary of State for War) to Clement Attlee, 23 July 1943, PRO FO 371/36714 (W 10927/1731/48).

[105] War Office to Foreign Office, 7 Oct. 1943, PRO FO 371/36714 (W 14309/1731/48); sim., 5 Nov. 1943, PRO FO 371/36714 (W 15550/1731/48).

Tripolitania'. The memorandum stressed 'the great and increasing interest taken in this matter and in general in the solution of the refugee problem at the highest levels in the United States, in particular by the President and by the Secretary of the Treasury, Mr Morgenthau'. It further argued: 'If we do not meet the United States Government's wishes in this matter we may find the United States Government uncooperative in the later and undoubtedly complex phase which the international refugee problem will enter after the end of the war.'[106] Cabinet approval for the plan was at last obtained but it was specified that the camp was to be for no more than 1,000 to 1,500 refugees, and that it was for 'Yugoslavs only'.[107] The latter included a substantial proportion of non-Jews. In this case, as in that of the Moroccan camps, the amount of diplomatic argumentation required to initiate the project was out of all proportion to the diminutive contribution made to a solution to the Jewish refugee problem.

The remaining positive recommendations of the Bermuda Conference suffered similar fates. The proposed declaration by Allied governments, guaranteeing to neutral states that all refugees received by them in the course of the war would be repatriated at the end of hostilities, was the subject of prolonged and complex negotiation during the year following the Bermuda meeting. The formula drawn up at Bermuda was amended, and the concurrence of all the proposed signatories, except one, was received. The exception was the U.S.S.R.: apparently because of its differences with the Polish Government in London (which was also a proposed signatory), the Soviet Government failed to respond to Anglo-American overtures concerning the declaration.[108] Since a large number of the refugees concerned were Polish or Russian citizens the declaration would have had little value without the signatures of those

[106] Foreign Office memoranda, unsigned, undated (May 1944), on 'plan to establish a camp for refugees in Tripolitania', PRO FO 371/42729/48–50; State Dept. to Chapin (Algiers), forwarding War Refugee Board to Murphy, 27 May 1944, *FRUS 1944* vol. I, p. 1052; Eden to Cabinet, 19 May 1944, PRO CAB 95/15/149.

[107] Minutes by I. L. Henderson, 8 June, and Sir A. Cadogan, 13 June 1944, PRO FO 371/42741 (W 9035/21/48); Winant (London) to State Dept., 7 June 1944, *FRUS 1944* vol. I, p. 1058; Foreign Office to Washington, 22 July 1944, PRO CAB 95/15/201.

[108] A. W. G. Randall to Sir H. Emerson, 27 Mar. 1944, PRO FO 371/42751/146–9; Winant (London) to State Dept., 20 Oct. 1943 (and succeeding documents), *FRUS 1943* vol. I, pp. 214 ff.

governments; it was therefore not issued. However, the primary purpose underlying the proposal, the provision of some reassurance to neutrals that they would not be left with sole post-war responsibility for refugees whom they admitted to their territories, was partially achieved by means of direct approaches to neutral governments by Britain and the U.S.A. These fell short of the original conception, in that no guarantee was offered as to the post-war disposition of the refugees. But the Allies offered the neutral states financial assistance, and some easing of blockade restrictions in order to encourage them to take in refugees.[109] These moves had some effect. After the fall of Mussolini in Italy, there was a sudden influx of more than twenty thousand refugees into Switzerland.[110] On this occasion (by contrast with their behaviour at the time of the deportations of Jews from Unoccupied France in the summer of 1942[111]) the Swiss Government pursued a relatively liberal admissions policy towards these refugees. By December 1943 the total number of refugees (including escaped prisoners-of-war) in Switzerland exceeded 64,000, with large numbers being accommodated in some thirty-eight temporary camps.[112] Of these about 10,000 were Jews.[113] In October 1943 German threats to deport the Jews of Denmark to death in Poland led the Swedish Government to permit nearly the entire Jewish community of Denmark (numbering some eight thousand persons) to be smuggled to Sweden in small boats with the help of Danish resistance groups. At the end of 1943 there were reported to be 53,800 refugees in Sweden, of whom 11,600 were Jews.[114] In the final stages of the war both Switzerland and Sweden admitted further groups of Jewish refugees freed from concentration camps by the Germans.[115] These were relatively substantial admissions figures for these small states, comparing

[109] R. K. Law to Cabinet Committee on Refugees, 2 Dec. 1943, PRO CAB 95/15/119 ff.

[110] *Jewish Chronicle*, 8 Oct. 1943; Harrison (Berne) to State Dept., 30 Sept. 1943, *FRUS 1943* vol. I., p. 359.

[111] See p. 110.

[112] R. K. Law to Cabinet Committee on Refugees, 2 Dec. 1943, PRO CAB 95/15/119 ff.; Tartakower and Grossmann, *The Jewish Refugee*, p. 297.

[113] Proudfoot, *European Refugees*, pp. 76–7.

[114] Johnson (Stockholm) to State Dept., 15 Feb. 1944, USNA 840.48 Refugees 5189, referring to a report on refugee numbers on 1 Jan. 1944.

[115] See pp. 341–2.

favourably with the numbers admitted by other neutrals, and indeed with refugee immigration to Britain and the United States during the war. The diplomacy of the Allies played some part in determining Swiss and Swedish government policies towards refugees; but public opinion in both countries was probably the more important influence in shifting these governments to a more liberal stance.

Unlike the proposal for an Allied declaration to the neutrals, the Bermuda decision to resuscitate the Inter-Governmental Committee on Refugees was implemented. But here too the effectiveness of the decision turned out in practice to be very limited. After the Bermuda Conference Law had warned that if the I.G.C.R. were to be rendered effective it would require an expanded and more efficient organization: 'so long as you limit it to one full-time director and a few stuffed-shirts whose function is really little more than that of patrons of a charity matinée it will command no confidence'.[116] Efforts to breathe new life into the I.G.C.R. began immediately after the Bermuda Conference.[117] Sir Herbert Emerson was retained as Director, and an American, Patrick Malin, was appointed Vice-Director. On 4 August 1943 a meeting was convened in London of the Executive of the Committee, attended by representatives of Britain, the U.S.A., Argentina, Brazil, the Netherlands, and the French National Committee. It was agreed that the U.S.A. and Britain would jointly underwrite the expenses of the body.[118] Membership of the Committee was expanded to include the U.S.S.R. The Foreign Office regarded the reconstitution of the I.G.C.R. as the most important achievement to flow from the Bermuda Conference. A Foreign Office memorandum in September 1943 noted with satisfaction that efforts 'to get Jews and enthusiasts like Miss Rathbone appointed to the Committee' had been successfully scotched, and that there appeared to be 'a good prospect of ensuring loyal American support in steering the Inter-Governmental Com-

[116] Law to Eden, circulated to Cabinet by Eden, 3 May 1943, PRO FO 371/36731 (W 6933/6933/48).

[117] Hull to Winant, 15 May 1943, *FRUS 1943* vol. I, pp. 180–1; Winant to Hull, enclosing Eden to Winant, 17 May 1943, ibid., pp. 181–2.

[118] Foreign Office memorandum on 'The Refugee Situation', 3 Sept. 1943, PRO FO 371/36666/43 (W 12841/49/48); Winant to Hull, 4 Aug. 1943, *FRUS 1943* vol. I, pp. 199–200.

mittee free from Jewish influence and intrigue in connection with Palestine'.[119] But in spite of an expanded membership, an enlarged budget, and increased staff, the Committee failed to acquire sufficient independent authority to play any significant role in the succour of refugees from Nazi Europe; it remained a bureaucratic monument to the spirit of futility at Evian where it had been born.

The air of well-meaning ineffectiveness which suffused all the doings of the I.G.C.R. was exemplified by the activities of its representative in Italy, Sir Clifford Heathcote-Smith. The former British Consul-General in Alexandria, Heathcote-Smith had been sent to Naples in early 1944 in order to organize aid to refugees (including many Jews) who streamed into the Allied zone of occupation in the south of the country after the German occupation of the remainder of Italy in the autumn of 1943. Soon after his arrival, Heathcote-Smith greatly disturbed the Foreign Office by seeking to arrange for the transfer to Palestine of several hundred Jewish refugees from Italy. With the White Paper quota now nearly full, apprehension was aroused in Whitehall that what was termed 'a fearful dust-up with the Arab world' might result from Heathcote-Smith's 'unwittingly Zionist enthusiasm'.[120] He was warned that his actions must conform with British policy regarding immigration to Palestine. Having thus given offence to the Foreign Office by apparent sympathy for Zionism, Heathcote-Smith achieved the remarkable feat of provoking fierce Zionist complaints about his 'wickedness'. According to a Zionist account, he appeared before a group of Jewish refugees, and pronounced Palestine a mere 'handkerchief' which was too tiny to accommodate all Jews who wanted to go there; by way of graphic illustration he was reported to have taken his handkerchief out of his pocket, waved it in the air, and inquired of his audience, 'Can this be made into a blanket to cover yourself with?' A protest against this 'offensive illustration' was lodged with the British Government by the American

Jewish Conference.[121] Sir Clifford's indiscretions reached their nadir in the eyes of the Foreign Office when, tiring of what he regarded as the ineffectiveness of British policy towards refugees, he issued a series of urgently phrased but somewhat imprecise memoranda pressing for immediate action to save Jewish lives in Nazi-occupied Europe. He urged 'particularly an UNREMITTING, INTENSIVE campaign, until Germany's collapse, of propaganda, warnings, threats, dramatic and reasoned statements to the actual GERMAN PEOPLE'.[122] His superiors took a dim view of his failure to proceed through 'the proper channels', and his proposals were ruled 'impracticable' by Sir Robert Bruce Lockhart, head of the Political Warfare Executive.[123]

The I.G.C.R. never quite shook off the aura of the charity matinée. Its indefatigable Director, Sir Herbert Emerson, continued to produce lengthy memoranda which were generally admired in the Foreign Office but failed to influence policy. In a minor way the Committee performed a useful co-ordinating function between the British and United States Governments, but often it was by-passed or ignored. The most signal achievement of the I.G.C.R. was probably the part it played in arrangements in the summer of 1944 for payments for Jewish relief and rescue in Roumania. At least three hundred thousand dollars allotted for this purpose by the American Jewish Joint Distribution Committee were paid through secret channels; no foreign currency was transferred to Roumania as the credits were to be made good after the war. After the liberation of Roumania by Soviet forces, the I.G.C.R. offered further sums from its own resources for aid to Roumanian Jews.[124] But beyond this the Committee could point to little to justify its existence. In areas still under Nazi occupation, the major agency for international relief was the Red Cross.[125] In areas already

[121] Corporal K. P. Solomon to Harold Laski, 22 Sept. 1944, PRO FO 371/42844/71. (WR 1487/12/48); Louis Lipsky (for American Jewish Conference) memorandum, 25 Sept. 1944, PRO FO 371/42819/46 (WR 1383/3/48).

[122] Memorandum by Sir C. Heathcote-Smith, 24 Oct. 1944, PRO FO 371/42897/7 (WR 1554/1554/48).

[123] Minute by P. Mason, 1 Dec. 1944; minute by Sir R. Bruce Lockhart, 1 Dec. 1944, PRO FO 371/42897/24–5 (WR 1732/1554/48).

[124] 'Draft telegram to Allied Commission of Control', 23 Jan. 1945, PRO FO 371/51169/6.

[125] See pp. 324–5.

liberated that function was performed by the United Nations Relief and Rehabilitation Administration (U.N.R.R.A.).

U.N.R.R.A., which eventually took over much of the role originally conceived for the I.G.C.R. of an effective international refugee relief agency, was primarily an American creation. It was founded in Washington in November 1943, with the participation of forty-three governments. The dynamic spirit of the organization was Herbert Lehman, former Governor of New York State, who was appointed the first Director-General. A United Kingdom contribution to the U.N.R.R.A. budget was made in January 1944, and amounted to eighty million pounds; in March 1944 an American contribution of 1,350,000,000 dollars was authorized.[126] U.N.R.R.A. took over responsibility for refugee relief in Allied-occupied territories in the course of 1944 in co-operation with voluntary relief agencies. By the end of 1944 U.N.R.R.A. was administering refugee camps for tens of thousands of refugees in Italy, Egypt, Morocco (Fedhala and Philippeville), and Palestine. The Foreign Office regarded U.N.R.R.A. with a certain suspicion, and there were repeated complaints of the 'influence within U.N.R.R.A. of some of the chief American representatives, most of whom are believed to be strongly Zionist'.[127] It was said that 'cases had arisen where men of Jewish extraction had had to be recalled [from U.N.R.R.A. posts in the Middle East] not because they had indulged in any Jewish activities themselves, but because they were continually subject to pressure from the Jewish agencies on the one hand or to anti-semitic rumour-mongering on the other'.[128] In April 1944 the matter seemed to have been resolved, as a Foreign Office official noted: 'I think the security people in the Army have intervened and that there is unlikely now to be any substantial number of purely Jewish teams recruited for relief work.'[129] But complaints were still being voiced in November 1944, when an I.G.C.R. representative in the Middle East, in conversation with a Foreign Office official 'violently criticised the "Jewish set-up" of UNRRA in

[126] George Woodbridge, *UNRRA*, 3 vols. New York 1950.

[127] Minute by R. M. A. Hankey, 20 July 1944, PRO FO 371/42810/57 (WR 315/3/48).

[128] W. J. Hasler (Office of War Cabinet) to E. Hall Patch (Foreign Office) 17 Apr. 1944, PRO FO 371/40534/127 (U 3123/41/73).

[129] Hall Patch to Hasler, 18 Apr. 1944, PRO FO 371/40534/128 (U 3123/41/73).

Cairo, whom he accused of sharp practices and dishonesty'.[130] Organized on a much more elaborate scale than the I.G.C.R., U.N.R.R.A. became the major international relief body for refugees in Allied-occupied areas. However, it was unable to offer any help to endangered persons behind enemy lines. By the time U.N.R.R.A. aid arrived most of the Jews in Europe were already dead.

The wave of public sympathy for the Jews of Europe after the declaration of 17 December 1942 therefore bore little fruit in effective action. The terms of reference of the Bermuda Conference probably restricted it from taking any decisions which might have offered any significant relief to European Jewry. 'Utopian' solutions were in any case ruled out at the beginning of the conference. The final decisions at Bermuda appeared to offer some hope of small-scale action on behalf of Jewish refugees; but even these were in practice whittled down to insignificance. The North African camps, established after gargantuan diplomatic labours, never absorbed even the five to six thousand refugees envisaged for them. The search for alternative destinations for Jewish refugees yielded little fruit. The proposed Allied declaration to neutrals was never issued. The I.G.C.R. was resuscitated but to no avail. Meanwhile the Nazi terror continued unabated. By December 1943 British intelligence reports indicated that ninety per cent of the 3,300,000 Jews of Poland were dead.[131] By the spring of 1944 the majority of the Jews of Germany, Austria, Czechoslovakia, the Netherlands, Yugoslavia, and Greece, had been murdered. Substantial communities of Jews in Axis Europe now survived only in France, Hungary, and Roumania. The shadow of death continued to hang over the remnants of European Jewry. The year since the declaration of December 1942 had shown that any reliance which they might place in the efficacy of Allied rescue efforts, short of outright victory, was indeed a 'Utopian' hope.

[130] I. L. Henderson minute, 28 Nov. 1944, PRO FO 371/42840/77 (WR 1902).
[131] M.I. 19 report on conditions in Poland, 29 Dec. 1943, PRO FO 371/39449 (C 869/G).

6

False Hopes

The bermuda Conference's apparently definitive rejection of 'Utopian' schemes for the saving of Jewish lives in Nazi Europe did not prevent Jewish bodies, and others concerned with the problem, from pressing on the British and American Governments further projects with the same end in view. Such pressure continued until the end of the war: although there were some marginal concessions which led directly to the saving of lives, the general response of both governments on the central issues was negative. There could be no significant modification of the stringent immigration provisions applied in Britain, the U.S.A., and Palestine. There could be no question of negotiation with the enemy, no major relaxation of the economic blockade of Nazi Europe, and no action taken which might promote dissension between the western allies and the Soviet Union. Some of the schemes that were put forward fell within these limitations, others on the borderline or beyond; some were realistic, others far-fetched; few succeeded in surmounting the obstacles of official scepticism and political preoccupation with the overriding priority of victory in battle. The proposals for extricating Jews from Nazi Europe, or at least alleviating their lot, fell into three broad categories: first, there were suggestions that Jews be exchanged for German or other enemy nationals in allied hands; secondly, it was urged that some degree of protection might be afforded to Jews in enemy-held territory by neutral governments such as those of Sweden, Turkey, and Spain; thirdly, and most controversially, approaches were received from enemy sources indicating a readiness to contemplate the release of Jews in return for material inducements or other concessions.

Although the Bermuda Conference dismissed out of hand the

suggestion 'that we should exchange Nazi internees and prisoners of war against Jewish people in occupied Europe',[1] a
small number of Jews had, in fact, already been exchanged for
German civilian internees in British hands. The Jews in question were mainly Palestinian women and children (although, as
will be seen, later exchanges were broadened to include men
and non-Palestinians who were Zionist 'veterans' or rabbis or
had relatives in Palestine). The Germans given in return were
mainly members of the community of Templars in Palestine, a
fundamentalist Christian sect who had settled in several colonies in Palestine in the mid-nineteenth century. During the
1930s some of these Germans had participated in Nazi activity
in Palestine, and on the outbreak of the war the members of the
community had been interned in Palestine.[2] Proposals for such
an exchange had been made to the Foreign Office by the Jewish
Agency in December 1939, but, although the German Government had signified its readiness to make an arrangement of
this kind as early as October 1939, negotiations on the subject
(conducted through the United States Embassy in Berlin and
the International Red Cross) were lengthy and tortuous.[3] The
arrangement of the exchange was rendered more difficult by a
decision to transport a large number of the non-Jewish enemy
alien internees in Palestine to Australia, from where the com-
plexities of organizing repatriation to Germany were considerable.[4] In the course of the negotiations the Germans raised
'little difficulties', demanding, for instance, a larger number of
German women and children than they were prepared to give
in return. The Palestine Government did not ease matters by
insisting on stringent proof of Palestinian identity, and by
rejecting applications for exchange of some Jews whom they

[1] See p. 192.

[2] H. D. Schmidt, 'The Nazi Party in Palestine and the Levant, 1932–9', *International Affairs*, vol. XXVIII, no. 4, Oct. 1952, pp. 460–9.

[3] A. S. Eban (for Jewish Agency) to Consular War Dept., Foreign Office, 18 Dec. 1939, and Foreign Office minutes, PRO FO 369/2546/46; Rebecca Sieff (for Women's International Zionist Organisation) to Foreign Office, 3 Apr. 1940, and Foreign Office minutes, PRO FO 369/2565/225; Colonial Office to War Office and Admiralty, 5 Apr. 1940, PRO FO 369/2565/244; I. J. Linton (for Jewish Agency) to Foreign Office, 12 Apr. 1940, PRO FO 369/2565/271; Foreign Office to Colonial Office, 24 Apr. 1940, PRO FO 369/2565/274.

[4] Wadsworth (U.S. Consul General, Jerusalem) to State Dept., 17 Oct. 1940, *FRUS 1940* vol. III, p. 846; Foreign Office to Duke of Alba (Spanish Ambassador in London), 6 Sept. 1941, PRO FO 916/76/15.

refused to recognize as Palestinian citizens.[5] There were delays in communication between London and Jerusalem which led to Foreign Office complaint that the Colonial Office 'certainly take their time'.[6] It was not until December 1941 that the elaborate negotiations finally yielded results. The Turkish Government permitted the exchange to take place on Turkish soil of sixty-five German women and children from Palestine for forty-six Palestinian women and children from Germany.[7] One Palestinian woman, Mrs Eva Okmiansky-Boehm, chose to remain behind in Germany, because, although her name had been approved for inclusion in the exchange, that of her six-year-old son had not.[8]

In May 1942 the German Government proposed a second exchange, whereby all Palestinians in Germany (including men) would be exchanged for some 217 German internees in Palestine. The German proposal was not wholly acceptable to the Palestine Government, and renewed lengthy negotiations ensued through the good offices of the Swiss Government. Agreement was eventually concluded on a second exchange which was to take place on 1 October 1942. However, shortly before this date a hitch occurred, when it was discovered that most of the Germans to be repatriated had been 'interned' (in their own homes) close to the site of a United States Air Force base in Palestine. British military headquarters in the Middle East consequently expressed anxiety that 'the repatriated internees, by virtue of their proximity to the airfields, would be able to communicate to enemy sources within forty-eight hours of their departure from Palestine details regarding the person-nel, numbers and type of aircraft, operational activities, and static anti-aircraft defences'. (No explanation was offered as to how it had come about that the enemy aliens and the air base had been thus juxtaposed.) After further discussions the security authorities relented, and acceded to the exchange on condition

[5] Sir Harold Satow (Foreign Office Prisoners of War Dept.) to J. H. Eddy (British Red Cross), 9 June 1941, PRO FO 916/94/53.

[6] Foreign Office minute, 26 Aug. 1941, PRO FO 916/94/93; Foreign Office to Colonial Office, 2 Sept. 1941, PRO FO 916/96/85.

[7] Sir H. Knatchbull-Hugessen (Ankara) to High Commissioner, Jerusalem, 8 Dec. 1941, PRO FO 916/95/156; High Commissioner, Jerusalem, to Colonial Office (draft dispatch), 9 March 1943, ISA 2/D48/44.

[8] R. Lichtheim (Jewish Agency representative, Geneva) to I. J. Linton (Jewish Agency, London), 22 Dec. 1941, CZA L 22/199/1.

that the Germans were 'removed forthwith from their places of
internment and transferred to some place where they would not
have similar opportunities for observing the military activities'.
They were therefore deposited in the internment camp at Athlit
(hitherto used to accommodate illegal Jewish immigrants) to
await departure for Germany.[9]

Meanwhile, a further potential difficulty arose: the Jewish
Agency pressed the Governments in Jerusalem and London to
broaden the categories of Jews to be included in the exchange.
The Agency urged that in view of the desperate plight of the
Jews in Europe the British should declare their willingness to
include in the exchanges certain borderline cases, such as wives
of as yet unnaturalized legal immigrants who had returned to
Europe before the beginning of the war. The High Commissioner in Jerusalem saw certain difficulties in including these
people in the exchange, and the Foreign Office was reluctant to
re-open the negotiations with the Germans lest the entire
scheme collapse. However, at the suggestion of Lord Cranborne, about fifty names out of over five hundred included in
the Jewish Agency proposal were telegraphed to London by the
High Commissioner for possible inclusion in the exchange.[10]
The results were disappointing. On 6 November 1942 a party of
301 Germans and 4 Italians left Palestine under police escort
and were transported in a special train across Syria to Meidan
Ekbes on the Turkish-Syrian frontier, where they were handed
over to the Turkish police. On 14 November a train carrying
the returning Palestinians arrived at the Syrian frontier. On
reaching Palestine on 16 November the party was taken to the
Athlit camp where they were questioned by the security
authorities, and (except in two cases) released.[11] The party was
found, however, to include far fewer Palestinians than had been
expected: a total of only 137 people arrived, of whom 69 were
Palestinian nationals, 20 British subjects, and 48 Dominions
subjects. The majority of the Dominions subjects were civilians
who had been captured at sea by the Germans shortly before.

[9] High Commissioner, Jerusalem, to Colonial Office (draft dispatch), 9 Mar. 1943, ISA 2/D/48/44.

[10] Ibid; Zionist Executive meeting, London, 1 Oct. 1942, CZA Z4/302/25.

[11] High Commissioner, Jerusalem, to Colonial Office (draft dispatch), 9 Mar. 1943, ISA 2/D 48/44; C.I.D. report, n.d., ibid.; note on interrogation of party of repatriates, 28 Nov. 1942, ibid.

The number of Jews in the party was 78 (10 men, 39 women, and 29 children), and they included people rounded up by the Germans from Poland, Holland, Belgium, France, and Germany itself. The Germans did not appear to have pursued any consistent policy regarding inclusion in the party. But the absence from the group of a considerable number of those whose names had been on the agreed list for exchange was ominous. The sombre conclusions to be drawn from the German failure to produce these people were confirmed by the terrible accounts given by the arrivals in Palestine of the treatment of Jews in Nazi Europe.[12] In February 1943 a further fifteen people reached Palestine after having been released by the Germans 'in completion of the second Palestinian-German exchange', but the only notification received in the cases of most of the remaining persons named on the Palestinian exchange list was a terse note delivered by the Germans to the Swiss Government announcing that the person was 'not to be found at the given address.'[13]

In the course of 1943 efforts were made to secure a further exchange whereby the disparity in the numbers handed over previously by the two sides would be rectified. But both the British and the Germans encountered difficulties in producing the required numbers of people for exchange. In the case of the British, it was reported that many of the German internees in Palestine designated for exchange had 'declined repatriation'.[14] Suggestions that German internees from places other than Palestine might be exchanged for Palestinian Jews in Europe were not at first accepted by the British Government. In response to such a proposal by the Board of Deputies of British Jews, the Foreign Office pointed out 'that we have only a very limited number of internees whom we could exchange, and that it would be impossible for His Majesty's Government to release these to Germany without securing first the return of

[12] Slightly inconsistent figures regarding nationality are given in the sources: High Commissioner, Jerusalem, to Colonial Office (draft dispatch), 9 Mar. 1943, ISA 2/D 48/44; note on interrogation of party of repatriates, 28 Nov. 1942, ibid.; Barlas, *Hatzalah Bimei Shoah*, p. 152.

[13] Ibid.

[14] Secretary of State, Washington, to U.S. Ambassador in Uruguay, 26 May 1944, *FRUS 1944* vol. I, p. 1051; Chief Rabbi Herzog (of Palestine) to Cardinal Maglione (Vatican Secretary of State), 19 July 1943, *VAT* vol. 9, doc. no. 270, p. 403.

the many British women who are suffering increasingly from their captivity in Germany or German-occupied countries'.[15] Little progress towards a third exchange had been made by the spring of 1944, when the British Chief Rabbi, J. H. Hertz, wrote an appeal to the Prime Minister calling for a declaration by the British Government 'that all Jews in enemy territories are British-protected persons' for whom exchanges would be arranged and places of refuge found. The Foreign Office rejected the idea as impracticable, arguing that the suggested proclamation would lead

to a complete misunderstanding about facilities for exchange. We have probably not enough eligible German civilians to exchange for British subjects in German hands, and in any case only some of these British subjects are likely to benefit this year from the very limited shipping facilities available for the purpose of exchange. It will be readily appreciated that we could not give priority to foreign Jews, including presumably large numbers who are 'enemy nationals', over British subjects, and therefore an assurance of facilities for 'exchange and place of refuge' on our part would in fact be of no help to European Jewry.

The matter was placed before the War Cabinet by Churchill on 12 June 1944, and the Foreign Office view was endorsed.[16] Nevertheless, in order to make up a suitable number for a third exchange, some German internees from South Africa were included in the party offered for repatriation to Germany.[17] However, if the British found it difficult to produce candidates for exchange, the Germans, in consequence of their policy of mass murder of Jews, found it almost impossible. A total of some 1,700 names were put forward by the Government of Palestine (in concert with the Jewish Agency) as 'Palestinian and near-Palestinian citizens' to be returned to Palestine. But the overwhelming majority of those named were declared to be untraceable by the German Government: in the event, the

[15] F. K. Roberts (Foreign Office) to A. G. Brotman (Board of Deputies of British Jews), 16 Mar. 1943, BD C 11/2/38.

[16] Hertz to Churchill, 8 May 1944, PRO PREM 4/51/8/443; Dixon (Foreign Office) to J. M. Martin (Prime Minister's Private Secretary), 16 May 1944, PRO FO 371/42725/155; extract from War Cabinet minutes, 12 June 1944, PRO PREM 4/51/8/433.

[17] Government of Palestine minute, 30 May 1944, ISA 2/D/45/44.

Germans were able to produce only 26 Palestinian citizens and five returning residents.[18]

In order to try to expedite the prolonged negotiations, Jewish bodies pressed the British Government to broaden the categories of those whom it was prepared to offer for exchange, and of those whom it was prepared to accept in return. In the case of two suggested categories these Jewish representations met with some success. The first suggestion was that Germans interned in Dutch possessions overseas should be exchanged against Dutch Jews who appeared on lists of 'veteran Zionists' and rabbis prepared by the Jewish Agency. The proposal was designed both to increase the number of candidates for exchange on both sides and to answer the British Government's objection that it could not place a higher priority on the exchange of foreign Jews than on that of its own citizens in enemy hands. The Germans had earlier manifested a tendency to connect the question of Germans interned by the free Dutch authorities with that of the treatment of Dutch citizens in the occupied Netherlands. In 1940 several prominent Dutchmen had been arrested by the Germans as a reprisal for the detention of Germans in the Netherlands East Indies. A message from the Reich Commissar Seyss-Inquart to Ribbentrop in May 1941 discussed further such reprisals to be undertaken if efforts to obtain the release of the internees should be unsuccessful.[19] There was at first some anxiety in Dutch Government circles lest the Germans might agree to the proposed exchange in order to trick Dutch Jews who were in hiding to emerge and report to the authorities.[20] However, instructions not to emerge on any account were sent to Jews in hiding by underground channels, and a list of over 3,000 names of Dutch Jews who were 'veteran Zionists' was furnished to the Dutch Government in the hope that the Germans would be able to produce some of these for exchange from internment camps in the

[18] J. V. W. Shaw (Chief Secretary, Government of Palestine) to Colonial Office, 4 Aug. 1944, PRO FO 916/925; E. A. Walker (Foreign Office) to I. J. Linton (Jewish Agency), 18 Apr. 1944, PRO FO 371/42755/121 (W 5255/91/48).

[19] Sir N. Bland (British Legation to the Netherlands) to Foreign Office, 14 Nov. 1940, PRO FO 371/24462/321 (C 12343/7847/29); Seyss-Inquart to Ribbentrop, 3 May 1941, in *Documents on German Foreign Policy 1918–45, Series D, vol. XII*, doc. no. 445, p. 697.

[20] L. Kubowitski (World Jewish Congress, New York) to A. L. Easterman (World Jewish Congress, London), 12 Feb. 1944, WJCNY, drawer 177A, file 'Alex Easterman Corres. Mar. 1943 to Aug. 1944'.

Netherlands or Germany. The Dutch Government, which had about 1,600 German internees under its control, agreed to make 400 of these available for exchange against Dutch Jews.[21] The Dutch Government communicated the list of proposed exchange candidates to the Germans through the Swedish Government, hoping that even if the Germans did not agree to an exchange, it might at least be possible to save lives by gaining time.[22] The hope was not a totally forlorn one, at least in the cases of those Jews named who had not yet been killed, since it was known that the Germans sometimes refrained from deporting to Poland persons whose names had been communicated to them on proposed exchange lists.[23] Possibly because the Germans did not recognize the Dutch Government in London, no reply was received to the Swedish communication; a further message was therefore sent by the British Government through the Swiss, but again no immediate reply was received.[24]

While these complex diplomatic interchanges proceeded Jewish organizations pressed the British Government to accede to the inclusion in the proposed exchange of a second category of Jews. These were Jews interned by the Germans in camps in France and Germany who were in possession of passports or other identity documents purporting to originate from authorized officials of Latin American governments. In some cases these were legitimate documents issued with the approval of the governments concerned. But more often the documents were forged, or had been issued on the personal initiative of consular agents in Europe, sometimes out of sympathy for the plight of the Jews, frequently in return for cash inducements. Thousands of such documents circulated on the underground black market throughout the war. In January 1941, for example, the United States envoy in Bucharest reported

[21] Minutes of Jewish Agency Political Committee, London, 20 Dec. 1943, CZA Z 4/302/28; memorandum by I. J. Linton, May 1944, WA; G. Riegner (World Jewish Congress, Geneva) to L. Kubowitzki, 14 Mar. 1944, WJCL.

[22] E. F. M. F. Michiels van Verduynen (Dutch Ambassador) to Eden, 24 July 1944, PRO FO 916/927.

[23] R. Lichtheim (Jewish Agency, Geneva) to Zionist Executive, Jerusalem, 8 Mar. 1943, CZA L22/3.

[24] Michiels van Verduynen to Eden, 24 July 1944, PRO FO 916/927; memorandum by I. J. Linton, May 1944, WA.

a most deplorable situation . . . in the consulate of one of the greater South American countries. Shameful advantage is being taken of the necessities of Jewish refugees, and between 200,000 and 300,000 lei are being extorted for residence visas. I have been implored, however, by a leading Jew not to give a hint of this matter to the Minister of the country in question, with whom I am well acquainted, as he might dismiss the guilty parties and thus block this channel of escape for Jews of means.[25]

In general these documents proved of little value to their holders as a means of escape from Nazi Europe, because during the early part of the war they were generally disowned by the countries concerned. But, particularly after the entry of the United States into the war in December 1941 (which was followed, in some cases immediately, in others after an interval, by declarations of war on Germany or statements 'of solidarity' with the U.S.A. by Latin American states), rumours spread that the value of such documents might rise, since their holders might become eligible for exchange against German citizens in South America. The trade in Latin American passports reached such proportions in Switzerland that the Swiss Federal Government was obliged to intervene for fear of diplomatic embarrassments. The consuls in Switzerland of Haiti, Paraguay, and Peru were dismissed. However, the consul of Honduras, dismissed for other reasons in 1942, issued over 400 unauthorized passports after he had lost his exequatur. By February 1944 it was estimated that 4,000 bogus Latin American documents had been issued from Switzerland alone, and that the total number in circulation in Europe might be as many as 10,000.[26]

The behaviour of the German authorities helped to stimulate the bizarre racket, which as a result developed some grotesque ramifications. Emmanuel Ringelblum records the prevalence of such documents even in the Warsaw Ghetto in May 1942:

The South American citizens living in the Ghetto were called to the Pawia Street prison. There they were informed that they would have to leave Warsaw by the 18th inst. for Switzerland, where they will be

[25] Gunther (Bucharest) to State Dept., Washington, 18 Jan. 1941, USNA 840.48 Refugees 2387.

[26] Sir Herbert Emerson (Inter-Governmental Committee) to H. Bucknell Jr. (U.S. Embassy, London), 29 Feb. 1944, PRO FO 371/42755/95.

exchanged for German citizens. But there is still a question as to whether the newly created citizens, i.e. those who bought their citizenship for a price during the war, will be allowed to benefit from this exchange.[27]

The holders of such passports were detained in prison in Warsaw and most survived the first wave of deportations from the ghetto to the murder camps. In May 1943 many foreign passport holders from Warsaw were dispatched to the internment camp at Vittel in eastern France, where the regime was comparatively mild. According to one account, Gestapo agents were to be found at the Hotel Polski in Warsaw in June 1943 selling Latin American papers received from Switzerland.[28] On 26 June 1943 Adolf Eichmann wrote: 'Though it is undesirable that Jews otherwise designated for deportation should acquire such nationalities by legitimate [*read* illegitimate *?*] means, there is nothing we can do about it.'[29] On 11 November 1943 the German Foreign Office informed its delegate in the Netherlands that the possession of Paraguayan papers was no proof of Paraguayan citizenship, but that Jews with such passports must nevertheless be detained for possible exchange against German citizens.[30]

However, the limited nature of the protection afforded by such documents to their possessors soon became apparent. In December 1943 all Jews in the Vittel camp were forced to yield up their identity papers which were never returned to them.[31] This action followed a declaration made by the Spanish Ambassador in Berlin (acting in his capacity as 'protecting power' for Paraguayan interests in Germany) to the effect that Paraguay refused to recognize as valid the supposed Paraguayan passports held by Vittel internees.[32] The seized documents included passports of Chile, Costa Rica, Ecuador, Haiti,

[27] Sloan ed., *Ringelblum Journal*, p. 267.
[28] Nathan Eck, 'The Rescue of Jews with the Aid of Passports and Citizenship Papers of Latin American States', *Yad Vashem Studies*, vol. I, Jerusalem 1957, pp. 136–41.
[29] J. Presser, *Ashes in the Wind: The Destruction of Dutch Jewry*, London 1968, p. 228.
[30] Ibid.
[31] Deposition by Mrs Sophie Skipwith (a British subject interned at Vittel who was later included in a separate exchange agreement whereby British subjects were exchanged for German internees from South Africa), n.d. [c. Sept. 1944], PRO FO 371/42872/57.
[32] Note by Dr. I. Schwarzbart, 29 Dec. 1943, BD C 14/26/1.

Nicaragua, Peru, Venezuela, and other countries.[33] Fearing that the Jews whose documents had been seized might be deported to Poland and killed because their invalid documents might render them worthless in German eyes as potential exchange candidates, Jewish organizations pressed the British and United States governments to ask the Paraguayan and other governments concerned to declare that they would after all recognize the documents of the Vittel internees.[34] On 4 January 1944 the Paraguayan Foreign Office told the British Minister in Asunción that 'in deference to representations made by the Governments of the United States, Poland, and the Netherlands' Paraguay had already notified the Spanish Government that the passports in question would be recognized as valid by the Paraguayan Government.[35] But the message was either not received, not believed, or ignored by the German Government, for on about 20 March the commandant of the Vittel camp informed the internees that the South American papers were not recognized by the various governments, and that in consequence they were not considered as suitable for exchange. The holders of the Latin American documents (including at least 105 'Paraguayans' and 32 holders of Honduras papers) were separated from the rest of the camp and threatened with deportation. News regarding their plight was somehow transmitted to Jewish bodies in nearby Switzerland, and diplomatic efforts were immediately undertaken by the British and United States Governments to secure recognition of the confiscated documents. Most of the Latin American states concerned agreed to recognize the documents (helped by a United States guarantee that none of the states would be obliged actually to admit any of the passport-holders).[36] But the flurry of diplomatic activity was in vain. The

[33] H. Bucknell (U.S. Embassy, London) to Sir Herbert Emerson, 13 Jan. 1944, PRO FO 371/42755/60.

[34] Rabbi S. Schonfeld (for Chief Rabbi's Religious Emergency Council) to Foreign Office, 30 Dec. 1943, PRO FO 371/42755/12; Sir Herbert Emerson to H. Bucknell, 21 Feb. 1944, PRO FO 371/42755/97.

[35] Asunción to Foreign Office, 5 Jan. 1944, PRO FO 371/42755/15.

[36] A. G. Brotman (Board of Deputies of British Jews) to A. W. G. Randall (Foreign Office), enclosing a cable received from Switzerland by the Agudas Yisroel Organisation, 6 Apr. 1944, PRO FO 371/42755/138; Brotman to Randall, 21 Apr. 1944, BD C 14/26/1; I. J. Linton (Jewish Agency) to Brotman, 11 May 1944, ibid.; note by W. Frankel (Board of Deputies), 5 Apr. 1944, ibid.; State Dept., Washington to U.S.

Germans declared that mere recognition of the documents was insufficient, and that definite inclusion in an agreed exchange scheme was required in each individual case. On 17 April a train with boarded windows left Vittel carrying 165 former South-American document-holders, mainly of Polish origin. They were taken to the clearance camp at Drancy, and thence on 29 April 1944 to 'an unknown destination'. It was later learnt that they had perished at Auschwitz. A second group, including most of the remaining 'South Americans' left Vittel in May.[37]

The fate of the internees at Vittel appears to have been a sign less that the Germans were not prepared to recognize South American documents at all, than that they tended to do so only when they considered it to their advantage for exchange purposes. The fate of another group of Latin American 'Austauschjuden' ('exchange Jews' as they were called) illustrates this. Interned in the camp at Bergen-Belsen in Germany in the spring of 1944 were some 1,800 such Jews possessing passports of Latin American or other allied governments and, in many cases, papers signifying that they were on lists of 'veteran Zionists' and others who had been approved for admission to Palestine. These enjoyed slightly better treatment and food than the general population of the camp, from whom they were kept separate. In May 279 of this group were segregated from the others and told that agreement had been secured with the British Government on a third exchange, whereby they were to be sent to Palestine in exchange for Germans. The information was largely correct: the two sides had arranged that an exchange would take place of about 110 Germans for about 280 'Palestinians' (the disparity being accounted for by the difference in the numbers previously exchanged). However, a cruel disappointment awaited fifty-seven of the Bergen-Belsen nominees who were informed on 1 June that they had been excluded from the exchange and were ordered back to hard labour in the general section of the camp. On 13 June the

diplomatic representatives in several South American republics, 11 Apr. 1944, *FRUS 1944* vol. I, p. 1026; British Embassy, Madrid, to Spanish Foreign Ministry, 28 June 1944, PRO FO 371/42871/10.

[37] Lists of deportees in CZA L 22/144; statement by Vittel internee, Apr. 1944, PRO FO 371/42755/251; statement by Sophie Skipwith, n.d. [Sept. 1944], PRO FO 371/42872/57; Serge Klarsfeld, *Le Mémorial de la déportation des Juifs de France*, Paris 1977.

remaining 222 nominees were also ordered back to work, and it appeared that the entire arrangement had collapsed. But suddenly on 29 June the latter group were told that they were to leave immediately. They were medically examined, their luggage was weighed, and finally at 3.00 a.m. they were taken out of the camp to the nearby railway station at Celle:

We could not believe what we saw at Celle Station. A proper train with five wagon-lits, two buffet-cars, and first and second-class compartments had been made ready. The SS and the railway guards were on their best behaviour. When the train started we all burst into *Hatikvah*.[38] Then we stormed into the buffet cars.[39]

The party were taken to Vienna, where they were joined by a contingent of 62 people from Vittel. These had been included at the last moment by the Germans in place of the similar number originally nominated at Bergen-Belsen; the alteration was perhaps a consequence of the diplomatic commotion over the South American internees at Vittel previously sent to Auschwitz. The entire group numbered 283 on departure from Vienna (one Egyptian national was left behind there), of whom 169 were women, and 47 children. Only 26 were Palestinians, and of the remainder at least 100 were Dutch citizens. They continued their journey by train through Hungary, Yugoslavia, and Sofia, reaching Istanbul on 6 July. At Meidan Ekbes on the Syro-Turkish frontier they were exchanged for the party of Germans travelling in the opposite direction. They arrived in Haifa on 10 July.[40]

As soon as the third exchange had been successfully concluded negotiations opened for a fourth. Although agreement in principle on a further exchange was reached very rapidly, the discussion of the detailed arrangements proved even more complex than on previous occasions. One difficulty arose from the Turkish decision in August 1944 to sever diplomatic rela-

[38] The Jewish national anthem.

[39] Quoted in Presser, *Ashes in the Wind*, p. 295.

[40] Statement of Israel Taubes (formerly an Austrian citizen, resident in Amsterdam 1933–1943, then interned at Westerbork and Bergen-Belsen) to Palestine C.I.D., 22 Aug. 1944, PRO FO 371/51115/167; Dutch Ambassador to Eden, 24 July 1944, PRO FO 916/927; J. V. W. Shaw to Colonial Office, 4 Aug. 1944, PRO FO 916/925; Lichtheim (Jewish Agency, Geneva) to Dobkin (Jewish Agency, Lisbon), 7 July 1944, CZA L 22/135.

tions with Germany: this meant that any further exchange would have to take place in Sweden or Switzerland. Another complication arose from the fact that there were now hardly any German internees left in the Near East who could be used by the British for exchange. It was decided that 368 Germans, who had been transported from Palestine to Australia early in the war and interned there, would be brought back for use in the fourth exchange. But shortage of shipping space delayed their departure from Australia. They had still not left in February 1945; by then the prospect of an early end to hostilities in Europe rendered the possibility of their being exchanged remote.[41] An offer by the Belgian Government of seventy-five German internees from the Belgian Congo for exchange against Belgian Jews was accepted by the British Government, but in this case, too, transport difficulties were encountered.[42] Meanwhile the Dutch Government, surprised by the unexpected inclusion of a large number of Dutch Jews in the third exchange, offered to make available six hundred German internees captured in the Netherlands East Indies who were now held in India. However, the Germans failed to respond to an approach on the subject by the British Government.[43] As a result, although some Jews were included in other civilian exchanges contracted between the Allies and the German Government, no fourth exchange of Germans for 'Palestinians' had been concluded by May 1945.

In the arrangement of the exchanges a crucial function had been performed by neutral states, particularly by Switzerland in acting as a post office for messages between the belligerent governments, and by Turkey in permitting the exchanges to take place on her soil. The neutrals were, however, called upon

[41] M. Kahany (Jewish Agency, Geneva) to Leo Kohn, 22 Dec. 1944, CZA L22/135; P. Mason (Foreign Office) to M. Budny (Polish Embassy), 6 Sept. 1944, PRO FO 371/42876/4; A. G. Ponsonby minute, 26 Feb. 1945, PRO FO 371/51176 (WR 398/379/48).

[42] F. K. Roberts (Foreign Office) to Baron Beyens (Belgian Embassy), 28 Aug. 1944, PRO FO 916/928; G. W. Harrison (for F. K. Roberts) to Beyens, 2 Oct. 1944, ibid.; Colonial Office to Foreign Office, 18 Oct. 1944, ibid.; Swiss Federal Political Dept., Foreign Interests Division, to British Legation, Berne, 25 Oct. 1944, ibid.

[43] Dutch Ambassador to Eden, 24 July 1944, PRO FO 916/927; A. G. Ponsonby minute, 26 Feb. 1945, PRO FO 371/51176 (WR 398/379/48); Colonial Office to Foreign Office [11] Oct. 1944, PRO FO 916/927; Foreign Office to Swiss Legation, London, 16 Oct. 1944, ibid.

to co-operate in a much more direct manner in the second broad category of schemes designed to assist Jews in Axis Europe. These schemes invited neutrals to act not merely as go-betweens but as protecting powers in their own right either by extending consular protection or by affording refuge to Jews threatened by the Nazis. During the early part of the war neutral states (with varying degrees of reluctance) had, as we have seen, admitted refugee Jews to their territories, in some cases in substantial numbers. But as the war spread, and as it became increasingly difficult for Jews to escape from enemy-controlled territory, the numbers reaching neutral countries diminished to a small trickle. During the later part of the war, therefore, the emphasis shifted from pleas to neutrals to provide refuge to appeals for consular protection in enemy territory. The two issues were linked, since neutral governments often feared that the granting of consular protection to refugees would be followed inevitably by demands for admission by protected persons. However, these apprehensions were eased by neutral awareness of travel difficulties which would prevent the arrival of large numbers of such protected persons, and in certain cases by a readiness by allied governments to assure neutrals that they would not be obliged to grant permanent sanctuary to refugees to whom they offered such protection. In consequence, some neutral powers were prepared to co-operate in a limited way in a few of the proposals put to them by allied Governments and by Jewish organizations. Among the most striking examples were schemes involving Spain, Turkey, and Sweden.

The most remarkable case was perhaps that of Spain: although a neutral, the Spanish Government had strong ideological and political links with the fascist powers; it owed a historic debt to the German and Italian governments for military aid during the civil war; it sent the 'Blue Division' to fight with the Germans on the Russian front; it insisted that Roman Catholicism was the sole religion of Spain, thus preventing the small Jewish community from acquiring a legal status; it was not free from a tendency to equate Bolshevism with 'the Jews'; its secret police and Falangist bully-boys subjected Jews in Spanish Morocco to a long campaign of persecution and intimidation; and, as has been seen, it displayed considerable hesitancy over the admission of Jewish refugees from Axis Europe. Against this background the readiness of the Spanish Government to undertake any diplomatic activity on behalf of Jewish victims of Nazism could not be confidently expected. Nevertheless, a measure of protection was successfully accorded by Spanish representatives to a small category of Jews: these were a few among the Ladino-speaking Sephardim of south-east Europe (descendants of the expulsions from Spain and Portugal at the end of the fifteenth century) who claimed that they were Spanish 'nationals', and therefore entitled to protection by Spanish consuls. When the Germans occupied northern Greece in April 1941 there were in the area over five hundred Jews under Spanish protection, mostly in Salonica.[44] In March 1943 the deportation of the Jews of Salonica began, and by the middle of May more than 45,000 of the city's 56,000 Jews had been transported to Poland to be killed. With the perverted legalism which characterized their anti-Semitic policies, however, the Germans refrained at first from deporting those Jews recognized by the Spanish Government as its 'nationals'. But on 30 April the German Foreign Ministry informed its embassy in Madrid that the Spanish Government must remove its nationals from Greece by 15 June.

The Spanish Government appears to have been divided over the issue: the British Embassy in Madrid reported that the Spanish Foreign Ministry was 'in principle friendly to the idea of allowing these Jews with Spanish passports to come to Spain from the Balkans as an alternative to being sent to Poland, where they would presumably die in concentration camps and be made into soap'; on the other hand, the security section of the Ministry of the Interior was said to be much cooler towards the idea.[45] The Spanish Government having failed to remove the Spanish Jews from northern Greece by the given date, the Germans rounded them up and dispatched them to the Bergen-Belsen concentration camp on 13 August. After much hesitation the Spanish Government declared its readiness to admit them to Spain, but it insisted that they must not remain

---

[44] H. Avni, 'Spanish Nationals in Greece and their Fate during the Holocaust', *Yad Vashem Studies*, vol. VIII, Jerusalem 1970, p. 38.

[45] British Embassy, Madrid, to Foreign Office, 28 Aug. 1943, PRO FO 371/36666 (W 12950/49/48).

as permanent residents. This modified form of protection was accorded apparently as the result of representations made by the British and American Ambassadors, the Vatican Nuncio, and the representative of the American Jewish Joint Distribution Committee. A total of 365 Jews from Salonica reached Spain from Bergen-Belsen in the spring of 1944. The Spanish Government threatened to imprison them or conscript them for military service if they remained in the country, and they were therefore transferred to the refugee camp at Fedhala.[46] Meanwhile the German occupation of southern Greece (hitherto occupied by the Italians) had led to further deportations of Greek Jews; again the Germans did not kill those Jews who could show some evidence of Spanish nationality. In April 1944 155 such people from Athens were transported to Bergen-Belsen, and the German Government informed Spain that this second group would be permitted to leave for Spain in the same manner as the first. The Spanish Government, again under pressure from the British and Americans and from Jewish organizations, agreed to admit them, but difficulties in transport across France in the summer of 1944 prevented their release. They were not, however, murdered, but remained in Bergen-Belsen until April 1945, when abandoned on a train by their guards they were liberated by the advancing allied forces.[47] The Spanish diplomatic action was therefore effective in saving the lives of over five hundred Greek Jews (as well as a few others from elsewhere) whose claim to Spanish 'nationality' was open to question. Spanish motives seem to have been prudential: the concession might, at little cost to Spain, help to dissociate Spanish fascism in allied eyes from the excesses of its German counterpart. However, there appears to have been some disappointment with the allied reaction. The Spanish Ambassador in London complained in April 1944 that Spain's 'humanitarian and Christian' policy in the matter had 'never

[46] Ibid.; Templewood, *Ambassador on Special Mission*, p. 237; Hayes, *Wartime Mission in Spain*, pp. 123–4; Avni, 'Spanish Nationals', pp. 46–55; Cicognani (Madrid) to Vatican, 24 Aug. 1943, *VAT*, vol. 9, doc. no. 311, p. 447.

[47] Avni, 'Spanish Nationals', pp. 61–5; Avni, *Sefarad Ve-hayehudim*, pp. 179–83; State Dept., Washington, to Hayes (Madrid), 21 Apr. 1944, *FRUS 1944* vol. I, p. 1035; A. Walker to Sir H. Emerson, 15 Dec. 1943, PRO FO 371/36646 (W 16729/46/48); Hoare (Madrid) to Foreign Office, 3 Mar. 1944, PRO FO 371/42764 (W 3467/177/48); Duke of Alba (Spanish Ambassador in London) to B. Rubenstein (World Jewish Congress, London), 12 Apr. 1944, WJCL.

received any recognition', and that on the contrary 'Spain and its present regime' had been made the butt for a 'campaign of falsehoods'.[48]

In early 1944 an analogous situation arose in France where ten thousand 'Turkish' Jews claimed consular protection from the Turkish Government and exemption from the fate of French Jews deported to the east. As in the Spanish case the claim was somewhat doubtful: some of the Jews were Sephardi immigrants from the Balkans or North Africa, areas which had long been under non-Turkish rule. The danger of deportation of these people was brought to the attention of the British and United States Governments by Jewish organizations, which urged that Turkey should be pressed to grant protection to the endangered Jews. Sir Herbert Emerson of the Inter-Governmental Committee was deputed to make semi-official representations to the Turkish Embassy in London; he was, however, fobbed off with a junior official. The American and British ambassadors in Ankara then approached the Turkish Foreign Ministry, and after further delays were told that the problem arose from the fact 'that any Turkish nationals living abroad who had ceased their relations e.g. by means of registration etc. with Turkish Consulates and Missions, for a period of five years, automatically lost their Turkish nationality'. A senior Foreign Ministry official told Sir Hughe Knatchbull-Hugessen that the measure 'was perhaps severe but [the] Turkish Government were very strict on nationality questions and considered that people who did not think it worth while to maintain their Turkish connexion in good times were not worth protecting merely when trouble arose'. The Turks were prepared to recognize the nationality only of those who had conformed strictly to the law.[49] The Foreign Office felt that the matter was one of domestic policy which it was difficult for the British Government to press officially, but the British and American ambassadors in Ankara continued to apply discreet

[48] Duke of Alba to B. Rubenstein, 19 Apr. 1944, WJCL.
[49] Knatchbull-Hugessen to Foreign Office, 22 Feb. 1944, PRO FO 371/42755/100; see also State Dept., Washington, to U.S. Embassy, London, 25 Jan. 1944, *FRUS 1944* vol. I, p. 986; Barlas, *Hatzalah Bimei Shoah*, pp. 306–7. Turkey had, since November 1942 enforced a discriminatory tax law directed against minorities, including Jews. Defaulters were sent to labour camps. See Bernard Lewis, *The Emergence of Modern Turkey*, London 1968, pp. 297–300.

pressure: perhaps as a result the Turks did not apply the policy with great rigour. Some Turkish citizens from France were readmitted to Turkey, and at least seven hundred return visas for Turkish citizens in France were authorized. Some 'Turkish' Jews in France thereby survived, but the limited value of Turkish citizenship to Jews in France is apparent from a perusal of the German deportation lists of Jews from France which record the deportation of large numbers of Jews born in Constantinople, Smyrna, and other parts of Turkey.[50]

The reaction of the Swedish Government to requests that it take diplomatic action on behalf of Jews was rather more generous than the opportunistic attitude of the Spanish regime or the grudging concessions made by the Turks. In April 1943 a proposal was put to the Swedish Government by a representative of the Central British Fund, the principal Jewish refugee relief agency, for the admission to Sweden of twenty thousand Jewish children from Germany and German-occupied countries. It was suggested that the British and American Governments should offer to Sweden an assurance that the children would be removed from Sweden immediately after the war, and that additional foodstuffs would be permitted to enter Swedish ports to help support the children. The initiator of the scheme, Salomon Adler-Rudel, visited Sweden and succeeded in persuading the Swedish Minister for Social Affairs to agree in principle to make an offer to the German Government to provide immediate asylum for twenty thousand children from German-held territory. The Swedish Cabinet confirmed this decision, and the Foreign Minister discussed the scheme with the British Ambassador in Stockholm. The minister said that he considered there was practically no chance of the Germans consenting to the emigration of the children, but that he believed it might help matters if the British and United States Governments could provide some assurance 'that in the event of these children coming to Sweden, arrangements will be made to transport them to Palestine or some other place outside Europe as soon as transport was available after the war'. The

[50] Foreign Office to World Jewish Congress, 29 Mar. 1944, WJCL; Schwartz (Joint Distribution Committee, Lisbon) to Leavitt (J.D.C., New York), 28 Mar. 1944, PRO FO 371/42755/159; A. Walker to A. G. Brotman, 28 Mar. 1944, PRO FO 371/42788/16; editorial note in *FRUS 1944* vol. I, p. 986. Klarsfeld, *Mémorial, passim*; see esp. convoy no. 74.

ambassador replied that it seemed to him possible that many of them 'might be able to return to some place inside Europe'. The minister agreed that this might be so but insisted 'that from the point of view of Swedish negotiations with [the] Germans it might be useful for the Swedish Government to be able to say that they had an assurance that these Jewish children would be settled outside Europe eventually, in view of the German insistence that Europe must in future be free of Jews'.[51]

The British Foreign Office had mixed feelings on the subject. A. Walker of the Refugee Department minuted: 'We cannot give any assurance that we propose to collaborate in the German policy of a "Judenrein" Europe.'[52] However, in late April 1943, while the scheme was being considered, the Bermuda Conference's deliberations were nearing their inconclusive end, and it therefore seemed that the scheme, although impracticable, might nevertheless be helpful to the Foreign Office as a face-saving device for the meagre results of the conference. Walker remarked: 'On general grounds it will be of great advantage if H.M.G. and the international refugee organization to be set up [the I.G.C.R.] can declare themselves the sponsors of the removal of these children to Sweden because it will look as if it is a direct outcome of the Bermuda Conference, the success of which we shall need to "plug" as much as possible if we are to avoid over-much criticism.' J. H. Le Rougetel similarly reflected:

On the face of it we could hardly object to a scheme of this kind . . . It must, however, be admitted at the outset that there is very little prospect of the Germans agreeing to anything of this kind. Its value will therefore be mainly in the nature of propaganda.[53]

The British Embassy in Stockholm was informed that the scheme enjoyed Foreign Office approval: the supply of additional foodstuffs to Sweden (upon which the Swedish Government did not insist as a condition) would be given sympathetic consideration; but the British Government could give no guarantee that the children would be removed to a destination

---

[51] British Embassy, Stockholm, to Foreign Office, 21 Apr. 1943, PRO FO 371/36659 (W 6497/49/48).

[52] Walker minute, 5 May 1943, ibid.

[53] Walker and Le Rougetel minutes, 30 Apr. 1943, ibid.

outside Europe.[54] After some delay the approval of the United States Government was also obtained.[55] However, in December 1943 Richard Law reported to the Cabinet Committee on Refugees that

In the meantime, owing to the deterioration of Swedish relations with Germany, the Swedish Government felt less inclined to press the matter on the German Government, and eventually on the initiative of the United States Government further negotiations were entrusted to the Director of the Intergovernmental Committee. Sir Herbert Emerson accordingly had a long discussion with the Swedish Minister in London, who was sceptical of the value of any approach to the German Government, and doubtful about his Government's willingness to pursue the scheme while they were not in a position to do a similar service for Norwegian child refugees.[56]

An effort was made to revive the scheme in early 1944, when the British and United States Governments made a joint *démarche* to the Swedes, suggesting that notwithstanding the German failure to accede to earlier representations a fresh approach might now be made by the Swedish Government. But the Swedish reply was that while they would be willing to receive the children, they were convinced that a further approach would be 'nothing but an empty gesture'.[57] Attempts to implement the plan by means of an approach through the International Red Cross were no more successful in inducing the German Government to co-operate.

While the scheme for the migration of twenty thousand children turned out to be will-o'-the-wisp, other measures taken by the Swedish Government during the later years of the war were effective in saving the lives of considerable numbers of threatened Jews. Further groups of refugees continued to be admitted to Sweden after the arrival of the Danish Jews in October 1943.[58] The Swedish Government played a prominent role in international efforts to afford succour to the Jews of

[54] Foreign Office to British Embassy, Stockholm, 13 May 1943, ibid.

[55] Foreign Office to British Embassy, Washington, 27 July 1943, ibid.; Law to Cabinet Committee on Refugees, 2 Dec. 1943, PRO CAB 95/15/119.

[56] Ibid.

[57] Lord Selborne and Ware Adams to Swedish Minister, London, 19 Jan. 1944, PRO FO 371/42752/76; Swedish Minister to Lord Selborne, 8 Mar. 1944, PRO FO 371/42752/77.

[58] See p. 216.

Hungary after the start of deportations from there to Auschwitz in the spring of 1944. An appeal by the King of Sweden to the Hungarian Regent, Admiral Horthy, was partly instrumental in securing a halt to the deportations from Hungary in July 1944.[59] During the summer and autumn of 1944 a special Swedish diplomatic emissary to Hungary, Raoul Wallenberg, granted large numbers of protective documents to Hungarian Jews, often persons with little or no previous connection with Sweden. By 9 October a total of some five thousand such passports had been issued by the Swedish Legation. In many cases the holders were gathered together in special houses in Budapest which were placed under Swedish diplomatic protection. The Swedish Government offered to receive all the possessors of such documents in Sweden. The German representatives in Budapest complained about Wallenberg's activities, but the Hungarian Government, after initial hesitations, undertook to honour the Swedish documents and permit the emigration of their holders. Although the majority of them did not leave Hungary, the vigorous Swedish action probably prevented the deportation or persecution of several thousand Hungarian Jews.[60]

The British Government generally encouraged diplomatic action on behalf of endangered Jews by neutral powers such as Spain, Turkey and Sweden (and other countries, most notably Switzerland). However, perennially apprehensive as to the effects of a mass movement of Jews to Palestine, Whitehall tended to look with greater favour on schemes designed to assist the victims of Nazi persecution in their countries of residence rather than projects which involved the emigration of large numbers to unspecified destinations. A similar concern also influenced the British reaction to the third broad category of schemes for preventing Nazi massacre of Jews: these schemes arose out of ransom proposals received from various enemy sources offering to exchange Jews for material compensation. The objections to such offers were clear: they appeared to

[59] Veesenmayer (Budapest) to German Foreign Ministry, 13 July 1944, in Braham, *Destruction of Hungarian Jewry*, p. 449.

[60] Foreign Office memorandum, n.d. [Nov. 1944], 'Swedish Help to Jews in Hungary', PRO FO 371/42823/5; Veesenmayer (Budapest) to German Foreign Ministry, 15 Sept. 1944, in Braham, *Destruction of Hungarian Jewry*, p. 484.

involve negotiation with the enemy, which had been ruled out of account by the allies at Bermuda (although it had been agreed there 'that the question might be borne in mind in case conditions altered at a later date'),[61] such negotiations might, if so much as suggested, compromise relations between the western powers and the U.S.S.R., which was perpetually suspicious of any hint of contact between her allies and Germany; any payment across the fighting lines was in any case quite contrary to the principles of economic warfare to which Britain in particular attached great importance; finally, there was much scepticism about the degree of good faith with which such offers were made, whether by the Germans themselves or by their satellites. For all these reasons such projects were in general discountenanced by the British Government. Two ransom demands of this nature which were forced on the attention of the British Government concerned the Jews of Roumania and Hungary.

On 13 February 1943 the *New York Times* published a report that the Roumanian Government had intimated its readiness to permit the emigration of seventy thousand Roumanian Jews who had been transported in late 1941 to the occupied area of the Soviet Union known as Transnistria. The Roumanian authorities were said to be prepared to allow the Jews to leave by sea in ships flying the Vatican or Red Cross flag, on condition that a departure tax was paid by each emigrant to cover the cost of transport from Transnistria to the final destination. The *New York Times* correspondent responsible for the report told the United States Embassy in London that he did not attach much importance to the proposal, which he considered was probably a Nazi trick.[62] However, the Jewish Agency felt that given the desperate position of the Jews in Europe some response should be made. Weizmann, who was in the U.S.A., spoke to the British Ambassador, Lord Halifax, and later wrote to him:

I would like again to emphasize as I did in my talk with you that it may be a trap on the part of the enemy to embarrass the United Nations by making an offer and hoping that the United Nations

[61] See p. 192.
[62] Matthews (London) to State Dept., Washington, 19 Feb. 1943, USNA 840.48 Refugees 3606.

would not be able to avail themselves of it. But whatever it is, I think that in view of the possibility of saving thousands of lives an attempt should be made to take this offer seriously. I would also beg you to accept my assurance that I am not attempting to utilise a very terrible position in order to bring about a change in the policy of His Majesty's Government. As you well know, I am against this policy, but I would never try to combat it in an oblique way. I hope the time will come when we shall all agree that a revision of the policy is desirable. Far be it from me to force the pace, but I am terribly anxious, in view of the great catastrophe which has befallen European Jewry, to save as many lives as we possibly can. I am quite sure that His Majesty's Government would be inclined to look at the subject in the same light.[63]

The Foreign Office looked at the matter in a different light; its reaction was set forth in a telegram to the Washington Embassy on 26 February:

We have so far no evidence to show whether Roumanian proposal was meant to be taken seriously. But if it was, it was clearly a piece of blackmail which, if successful, would open up endless process on the part of Germany and her satellites in South-Eastern Europe of unloading, at a given price, all their unwanted nationals on overseas countries. In regard to admission of refugees into Palestine, His Majesty's Government have gone to their furthest practicable limits . . . Difficulties of carrying out this scheme are formidable enough and no country would be willing to lay itself open to a continuance of pressure such as is implied in alleged Roumanian suggestion.

His Majesty's Government, in conjunction with Governments of the United Nations will continue to give earnest study to all practical means of alleviating refugee position which are consistent with the fullest war effort, but to admit method of blackmail and slave-purchase would mean serious prejudice to successful prosecution of the war. Blunt truth is that the whole complex of human problems raised by the present German domination of Europe, of which the Jewish question is an important but by no means the only aspect, can only be dealt with completely by an Allied victory, and any step calculated to prejudice this is not in the interest of Jews in Europe.[64]

The gist of this message was transmitted to Weizmann who was told that 'Mr Eden trusts you will appreciate that His

[63] Weizmann (New York) to Halifax (Washington), 16 Feb. 1943, WA.
[64] Foreign Office to British Embassy, Washington, 26 Feb. 1943, PRO FO 371/36676 (W 3019/80/48).

Majesty's Government must proceed along practicable lines, and avoid being drawn into action dictated by an enemy government.'[65]

Towards the end of 1943 the Foreign Office was obliged to reconsider the matter. This was because, although the U.S. State Department had misgivings similar to those of the Foreign Office, the scheme had secured powerful backing in certain quarters in the U.S.A. Particularly energetic in pressing for adoption of a modified version of the scheme were the U.S. Treasury Secretary, Henry Morgenthau Jr., and Rabbi Stephen Wise, President of the World Jewish Congress and a prominent Jewish supporter of Roosevelt. At a meeting with Roosevelt on 22 July Wise secured his approval for a suggestion made by Dr Gerhart Riegner, Geneva representative of the World Jewish Congress, that funds remitted by Jewish organizations in the U.S.A. should be paid into a blocked account in a Swiss bank from which no withdrawals could be made until after the war. Against the credit of these hard-currency blocked funds, Jewish merchants in Roumania would then make available Roumanian currency in order to finance the proposed emigration. It was estimated that on this basis the evacuation of some seventy thousand Jews could be procured at a cost of only 170,000 dollars. The advocates of the scheme emphasized that the total sum involved was comparatively small, and 'that payments should not (repeat not) be regarded as ransom as they involve only a few dollars per head and are required for payment of various expenses such as transportation and clothing'. In spite of State Department opposition Morgenthau authorized the United States Minister in Berne to issue the necessary licence for a preliminary payment to Riegner.[66]

However, the issue of the licence was held up because of strenuous British objections. The Commercial Secretary at the British Legation in Berne, upon being consulted by his American counterpart, observed that the proposed arrangement 'might result in leakage of funds to the enemy' and would be

[65] Sir R. Campbell (British Embassy, Washington) to Weizmann, 4 Mar. 1943, WA.

[66] Stephen Wise, *Challenging Years*, London 1951, p. 193; Morgenthau to Roosevelt, 16 Jan. 1944, in Michael Mashberg, 'Documents Concerning the American State Department and the Stateless European Jews, 1942–1944', *Jewish Social Studies*, vol. XXXIX, nos. 1–2, Winter–Spring 1977, pp. 174–176; Halifax (Washington) to Ministry of Economic Warfare, 24 Nov. 1943, PRO FO 371/36747.

likely to give rise to abuses by 'the type of adventurer who would undoubtedly participate'.[67] The British Embassy in Washington advised acceptance of the proposal in view of the strong support which it enjoyed in the U.S. Treasury Department, and the Ministry of Economic Warfare in London, after consultation with the U.S. Embassy, decided to give its approval to the financial aspects of the scheme, provided certain safeguards were observed.[68] But at this point it became apparent that the reasons for British opposition were not limited to the apparent infringement of blockade restrictions. There was also a political aspect. In a letter to the Ministry of Economic Warfare on 10 December, A. Walker of the Foreign Office wrote: 'We cannot conceal from you our view that to acquiesce in this U.S. Treasury scheme . . . fills us with misgivings since it would be likely, so far as we can see, to land us in all kinds of complications.' Walker noted that the plan was singularly inexplicit as to the destination of the proposed seventy thousand emigrants from Roumania. He pointed out that Cyprus was already overcrowded and that it was most unlikely that the War Cabinet would sanction the admission of so many immigrants to Palestine.[69] Halifax was therefore informed on 11 December that the Foreign Office saw grave disadvantages in the project, which they hoped would be abandoned.[70] A letter from the Ministry of Economic Warfare to the U.S. Embassy in London explained:

The Foreign Office are concerned with the difficulties of disposing of any considerable number of Jews should they be rescued from enemy-occupied territory. . . . They foresee that it is likely to prove almost if not quite impossible to deal with anything like the number of 70,000 refugees whose rescue is envisaged by the Riegner plan. For this reason they are reluctant to agree to any approval being expressed even of the preliminary financial arrangements.[71]

[67] 'Memorandum on telegram from Bern dated October 6, 1943' from U.S. Embassy (London) Economic Warfare Division, Black List Section, 4 Nov. 1943, PRO FO 371/36747 (W 15684/15684/48).
[68] Halifax to M.E.W., 24 Nov. 1943, ibid.; Bliss (M.E.W.) to Walker (Foreign Office), 1 Dec. 1943, PRO FO 371/36747 (W 16460/15684/48).
[69] Walker to Bliss, 10 Dec. 1943, ibid.
[70] Ministry of Economic Warfare to British Embassy, Washington, 11 Dec. 1943, PRO FO 371/36747 (W 17176/15684/48).
[71] Quoted in Winant (London) to State Dept., Washington, 15 Dec. 1943, USNA 840.51 Frozen Credits 12144.

The British Government was, however, compelled to withdraw in the face of American pressure. Halifax cabled to the Foreign Office that he considered that the 'suggested line of approach' was not 'likely to be very convincing' to the American Government. He added that the State Department was letting it be known that they were willing to accede to the Jewish request, but that British opposition was blocking the project. Halifax continued:

Though I have no doubt you are tired of hearing it this is an election year, Jewish vote is very important, and Administration would certainly not wish to be identified with a British decision which all Jews here, Zionist or non-Zionist, would agree in regarding as inhumane. Consequently I have little doubt that if I act as instructed in your telegrams whole blame for refusing this Jewish request will be placed on H.M.G.[72]

Opinion in the Foreign Office remained hostile to the scheme. Ian Henderson minuted: 'The question at issue is one of balancing the advisability of helping the State Department and Treasury to meet Jewish electoral pressures and of their avoiding a crescendo of U.S. criticism about our Palestine policy, and, on the other hand, of meeting the requirements of the C.O. in relation to practical politics and Arab wishes.' A. W. G. Randall prognosticated gloomily: 'Once we open the door to adult male Jews to be taken out of enemy territory, a quite unmanageable flood may result. (Hitler may facilitate it!)'[73] The matter was taken out of the hands of the British on 20 December when the State Department decided to authorize the issue of the licence notwithstanding the British opposition. The decision was the result of a vociferous protest by Morgenthau to Secretary of State Hull that 'in simple terms, the British were apparently prepared to accept the probable death of thousands of Jews in enemy territory because of "the difficulties of disposing of any considerable number of Jews should they be rescued"'.[74] The British were consequently obliged to accept a *fait accompli*: in a letter to the American Ambassador, Eden

[72] Halifax to Foreign Office, 22 Dec. 1943, PRO FO 371/36747 (W 17686/15684/48).
[73] Henderson minute, 23 Dec. 1943; Randall minute 24 Dec. 1943, ibid.
[74] Morgenthau to Roosevelt, 16 Jan. 1944 (referring to earlier talk with Hull), in Mashberg, 'Documents', p. 176; the licence to Riegner was issued on 21 Dec. 1943, copy in WJCL.

reiterated 'that as a consequence of the financial measures proposed certain problems of transport and accommodation might arise capable of embarrassing both your Government and mine', but he added that 'having, however, made a reservation to this effect, we are prepared to agree to the financial proposals under the safeguards mentioned'.[75] Unhappily the scheme did not fulfil the hopes of its originators, mainly because the Roumanian Government, yielding to German pressure, did not sanction the departure of significant numbers of Jews. A similar arrangement for rescuing Jews from enemy territory was, however, successful in securing the exodus from France to Spain and Switzerland of over two thousand people (the magnitude of the refugee traffic across the Pyrenees occasioning protest by the British intelligence authorities).[76] And during the latter stages of the war negotiations for ransom deals involving the use of blocked funds in hard currency were instrumental in saving further considerable numbers of Jewish lives, with dollars provided by the American Jewish Joint Distribution Committee.[77]

The most notorious ransom offer made during the war, and one which received the greatest amount of attention at the highest levels of British Government, was that made by Gestapo agents in Hungary in the spring of 1944. The mass deportation of the Jews of Hungary to Auschwitz had begun in May 1944 (one trainload had already left in April) under the direction of Adolf Eichmann. On 19 May there arrived in Istanbul a representative of the Hungarian Zionist Relief and Rescue Committee, Joel Brand. He carried a message from Eichmann to the effect that the Germans would be prepared to allow all the Jews remaining in Hungary (and possibly also the remnants of the Jewish communities of neighbouring countries) to leave freely for countries other than Palestine. In return the Germans had demanded certain goods such as ten thousand lorries, two million bars of soap, eight hundred tons of coffee, two hundred tons of cocoa, and eight hundred tons of tea. The Germans had further offered a guarantee that the lorries would be used 'on the eastern front only'. Dieter

[75] Eden to Winant, 3 Jan. 1944, PRO FO 371/36747.
[76] See p. 211; World Jewish Congress, *Unity in Dispersion*, p. 192.
[77] See p. 219.

Wisliceny, the Gestapo agent who had initiated the contacts with Hungarian Jews, had presented references in the form of letters from leading Slovak Jews who, according to Wisliceny, had succeeded by means of bribes in preventing (for a time) the deportations of Jews from Slovakia in 1942. Later Brand had met Eichmann who had laid down the terms of the ransom offer which he was to convey to the Allies. Brand was accompanied on his journey (all arrangements for which were made by the Gestapo) by a known German agent, a converted Jew, 'Bandi' Grosz, *alias* Andre György. The latter claimed to have been entrusted by the S.S. with an entirely separate mission the purpose of which was to arrange a meeting on neutral ground between senior S.S. and Allied officers in order to discuss terms of a separate peace. Upon arrival in Istanbul Brand immediately contacted Zionist representatives there to whom he presented letters of introduction from leading Hungarian Jews and explained the purpose of his journey. Brand and the Jewish committee in Budapest that he represented were anxious that he should return with a message which would at least encourage Eichmann to believe that Allied acceptance of the scheme was not ruled out. The deportations might then be stopped to allow negotiations to proceed, and Eichmann might allow some Jews to leave as a token of his good faith. The Zionists, satisfied with the credentials offered by Brand, and gravely concerned by Brand's confirmation that twelve thousand Jews a day were being deported for liquidation, felt that any opportunity for saving lives, however remote, should be explored. They therefore informed the British authorities in the Middle East of Brand's arrival and of the message he carried.[78]

Meanwhile American representatives in Turkey interviewed Brand and formed certain impressions. The American Ambassador in Turkey forwarded to the State Department two reports which reached rather different conclusions on the matter. The first, prepared by the Istanbul representative of the American Jewish Joint Distribution Committee, accepted that there were several different interpretations to be placed on the motives

[78] High Commissioner to Colonial Office, 26 May 1944, PRO CAB 95/15/152; Alex Weissberg, *Advocate for the Dead: The Story of Joel Brand*, London 1958; Yehuda Bauer '"Onkel Saly"—Die Verhandlungen des Saly Mayer zur Rettung der Juden 1944/45', *Vierteljahrshefte für Zeitgeschichte* vol. 25, no. 2, Apr. 1977; Bela Vago, 'The Intelligence Aspects of the Joel Brand Mission', *Yad Vashem Studies*, vol. X, Jerusalem 1974.

which lay behind the German approach. But the report stressed that, whatever the German motives

it appears advisable to keep all avenues for negotiation open, first because of major military and political implications involved and also because of the possibility of effecting the rescue of a substantial number of Jews. Everyone with whom I have talked recognizes the impossibility of carrying out the proposals as they have been stated, but everyone believes that all should be done to continue exploration until it is definitely determined that no further good can be served by its continuance.[79]

The second American report, compiled by the American Vice Consul in Istanbul, came to a different conclusion. While agreeing that Brand's documentation as a Jewish emissary appeared to be 'fairly satisfactory' and accepting that it was 'obvious from the details of Brand's trip to Turkey that his journey was actively sponsored by the Gestapo', the report expressed doubt as to whether the proposal carried by Brand was seriously intended by the senior German officials from whom it undoubtedly originated. After analysing various possible German motives, the report concluded that the most probable explanation was that the move formed 'part of an effort to split the Allies, to divide Russia from Great Britain and the United States'. This conclusion was buttressed by the following reasoning:

If it is accepted that Germany can win a stalemate only by dividing the Allies, then it can be assumed that every effort will be made, up to the last minute, to split Russia away from the Allied camp. Such an end can be achieved best, if it can be achieved at all, only by convincing the Russians that the Allies are not playing an open and honest game. How better could this be attained than by demonstrating that the Allies were considering a proposal that made military equipment available to the Germans for use against the Russians.

Hence, it was argued, the 'peculiar emphasis' on lorries 'for use "only on the Eastern front"'. Hence 'the elaborate campaign to put in Allied hands a plan which the Germans obviously must have considered impossible of acceptance from the first'. If the Brand proposals were thus correctly interpreted, it was finally

[79] Memorandum by Reuben Resnick, 4 June 1944, enclosed in Steinhardt to State Dept., 5 June 1944, USNA 840.48 Refugees 6276.

surmised, it was for the Germans 'essential that they *not* be accepted. It is not acceptance that interests the Germans but a hearing.'[80] The implication of this second report was that 'to keep all avenues for negotiation open' as urged by the A.J.J.D.C. representative, would be the most dangerous possible reaction on the part of the Allies.

On 31 May a meeting in London of the Cabinet Committee on Refugees, attended, among others, by Eden, Stanley, and Lord Selborne (Minister for Economic Warfare) considered the matter. A. W. G. Randall of the Foreign Office Refugee Department told the meeting that the Foreign Office thought that there were substantial reasons for having nothing to do with the proposals as they stood. On the other hand, in putting this point of view to the United States Government, it would have to be borne in mind that the scheme might secure sympathy in Washington, where there was a considerable body of opinion, headed by Mr Morgenthau, which 'partly for electoral reasons' favoured 'the "rescue" of Jews'. Stanley said that he 'considered it should be made clear at the outset that since the evacuation of a million refugees from occupied territories and their maintenance in neutral or allied countries could not be undertaken without a major alteration of the course of military operations, the scheme in its present form could not be considered'. Selborne 'reminded the Committee that a similar form of blackmail had been tried in 1942. The Germans had made it known through their agents in Buenos Aires that they proposed to seize some Jews residing in Holland unless their American partners paid over large sums of money. The intermediaries and relatives of these men had been told that the firms would be put on the [British] black list if they complied, and some thirty Jews had in fact been sent to concentration camps. After some months nothing more had been heard of these threats.' The Committee minutes recorded among 'other points made' the following unattributed observation:

There seemed to be some danger that an indication that we might negotiate through a Protecting Power with the German Government might be followed up, and lead to an offer to unload an even greater number of Jews on our hands.

[80] Memorandum by L. A. Squires, U.S. Vice Consul, Istanbul, 4 June 1944, enclosed in Steinhardt to State Dept., 8 June 1944, USNA 840.48 Refugees 6312.

The committee decided to inform Washington that 'it was not possible to consider any scheme which involved an evacuation of the order of magnitude envisaged in the proposal, since the necessary operations could not be undertaken without altering the course of the war'; and 'that no dealings with the Gestapo or bargaining on the basis of the exchange of refugees against stores, particularly of war-like material could be permitted'.[81]

The definitive reaction of the British Government was set out in a telegram dispatched to Washington on 3 June 1944. This stated that the proposal seemed to be a 'sheer case of blackmail or political warfare' which was 'totally unacceptable' After stating the objections to the proposal, the message continued:

While, however, refusing to deal with this scheme and channels through which it has come, we realise importance of not opposing a mere negation to any genuine proposals involving rescue of any Jews and other victims which merit serious consideration. Whole record of United States Government and His Majesty's Government over refugees is a proof of their active sympathy with victims of Nazi terror. Accordingly if the German Government were willing to release Jews in position of extreme distress or danger, His Majesty's Government and United States Government would be willing to examine the possibilities of moving to and accommodating in Spain and Portugal such persons as could be handled without prejudice to vital military operations.

The Government, the telegram continued, had informed Weizmann of the proposal, and the Zionist leader had 'merely observed that it looked like one more German attempt to embarrass the United States and United Kingdom Governments'. Weizmann had added 'that he would like to reflect on the affair'. The British Government was prepared to allow the Zionists to convey 'the substance of our observations' to Brand:

This would show that, although we cannot enter into the monstrous bargain now proposed by the Gestapo, we are yet far from indifferent to the sufferings of the Jews and have not shut the door to any serious suggestions which may be made and which are compatible with the successful prosecution of the war.[82]

[81] Minutes of meeting on 31 May 1944, PRO CAB 95/15/32.
[82] Foreign Office to Washington, 3 June 1944, PRO PREM 4/51/10/1394.

Weizmann had been informed of all that was known in London of the matter on 2 June at a meeting at the Foreign Office with G. H. Hall. On 6 June he wrote to Eden saying that the story had given him 'a great and most painful shock'. He regarded it as his 'paramount duty to try and discover the course of action which offers the best hope of saving lives'. Weizmann asked that the Foreign Office should help to expedite the grant of a Turkish visa to Moshe Shertok so that he might travel immediately from Jerusalem to investigate the story thoroughly.[83] The next day (it was the day after D-Day) Eden saw Weizmann who said that while the Gestapo proposal seemed fantastic he thought it might reflect a weakening by the Germans and also second thoughts on the part of the Hungarian Government regarding the extermination of the Jews. Weizmann made three suggestions: first, 'that we might play for time'; secondly, that the Soviet Government should be informed; and thirdly, that if nothing became of the affair the story should be made public. Eden's reception of these ideas was encouraging and Weizmann later wrote to thank the Foreign Secretary for his attitude which 'was a great comfort to me in the distress I am feeling over the position of the Jews in Hungary'.[84]

Meanwhile in Jerusalem Shertok and Ben Gurion had discussed the German message with Sir Harold MacMichael, and had pleaded that it should receive serious consideration in view of the unprecedented catastrophe which had befallen European Jewry. The High Commissioner expressed no personal opinion but reported the conversation to the British authorities in Cairo.[85] Although officials there expressed scepticism about the genuineness of the German offer, Shertok was permitted to interview Brand in Aleppo where he was being held in custody by the British security authorities following his arrival from Turkey.[86] The interview took place on 11 June in the presence

[83] Weizmann to Eden, 6 June 1944, WA.

[84] Eden to Minister Resident, Cairo (on meeting with Weizmann), 7 June, 1944, PRO FO 921/227; Weizmann to Eden, 9 June 1944, WA.

[85] High Commissioner to Colonial Office, 26 May 1944, PRO CAB 95/15/152.

[86] J. S. Bennett minute, 30 May 1944, PRO FO 921/227; Brigadier I. N. Clayton minute, 30 May 1944, ibid.; Brigadier Maunsell (Cairo) to British Military Attaché, Ankara, 30 May 1944, ibid.; G. E. Kirk (Cairo) to 'Subsided, Aleppo', 6 and 7 June 1944, ibid.

of a British security officer. According to the officer's report, Brand inquired at the outset whether 'he might ask one vital question which was whether he would be allowed to return [to Hungary]. On being told by Shertok that this was doubtful, he crumpled up and stated that it was imperative that he return as the consequences of his failure to do so did not bear thinking about.'[87] After questioning Brand for six hours, Shertok returned to Jerusalem and had a further interview with the High Commissioner in the company of Ben Gurion. Shertok pronounced himself fully convinced of Brand's reliability, and did not discount the possibility that the offer had been made by the Germans in good faith. Reporting to the Colonial Office, the High Commissioner noted:

Shertok emphasised the urgent and vital need to probe the whole matter and explore every avenue. In particular he considered it was essential that there should be a meeting with accredited German representatives on the clear understanding that all political discussions should be precluded . . . Finally, Shertok urged most strongly that Brandt should be allowed to return. If he did not the Germans would assume that we had turned the whole scheme down and proceed to take drastic measures against the Jews in their hands.[88]

In further representations to the American and British Governments during June and July the Jewish Agency reiterated that it was vital to keep the matter open and to send Brand back to Budapest.[89]

At the end of June Shertok arrived in London and took charge of Jewish Agency discussions with the Government concerning Brand. He pleaded that 'in spite of the fantastic and inacceptable features of the proposals', the British and American Governments should dangle a 'carrot' before the Germans by offering to discuss with them the question of Jewish emigration as well as the possible payment of some *quid pro quo*. The Government was at first prepared to consider some indirect approach to the Germans. In a memorandum

[87] Assistant Defence Security Office, Northern Syria, to Lt. Col. G. E. Kirk, S.I.M.E., G.H.Q., Cairo, 12 June 1944, ibid.

[88] High Commissioner to Colonial Office, 15 June 1944, PRO FO 921/227.

[89] Shertok to Goldmann and Ben Gurion, in Foreign Office to Washington, 9 July 1944, PRO FO 371/42807/41; I. L. Henderson minute, 30 June 1944, PRO FO 371/42807/73.

to the Cabinet Committee on Refugees on 29 June Eden commented:

The plan . . . which reached us through Brandt arrived in circumstances so suspect, and was worded in such a mixture of terrorist threats and blackmail that we should have been justified in rejecting it forthwith. With our well-known solicitude for the Jews and for all who are suffering under the German terror, we have, however, carefully considered what, arising out of this affair, can be done by both Governments.[90]

The British Government therefore proposed to the State Department that Brand might be sent back with a message that the Allies were ready to consider any practicable scheme for saving Jews, that all further discussions on the subject should be conducted through the medium of the Swiss Government, and that as an initial earnest of good faith the Germans should be requested by the Swiss to release immediately a small number of Jews, particularly children.[91] Although this did not go as far as the Zionists asked, it fulfilled what was in their eyes the vital condition of keeping the matter open. But by the middle of July several further developments combined to change the Government's attitude.

An important consideration which greatly influenced the Government's thinking was the attitude of the Soviet Government. The Russians had been informed of the affair by the British Ambassador in Moscow on 14 June; the decision to notify Moscow had been taken mainly because it was reported from Washington that a journalist there had learnt of the story, and great fear was expressed lest relations with the Russians (already strained) should be adversely affected by a leak.[92] The Soviet reaction was emphatic. In a letter to the American Embassy on 18 June, Deputy Foreign Commissar Vyshinsky stated that the Soviet Government did 'not consider it expedient or permissible to carry on any conversations whatsoever with the German Government'.[93] On 30 June the British

[90] Eden to Cabinet Committee on Refugees, PRO CAB 95/15.

[91] Foreign Office to British Embassy, Washington, 1 July 1944, PRO CAB 95/15/188.

[92] Foreign Office to British Embassy, Moscow, 12 June 1944, PRO PREM 4/51/10/1393; Eden to Churchill, 20 June 1944, PRO PREM 4/51/10/1391.

[93] Quoted in Harriman to State Dept., Washington, 19 June 1944, *FRUS 1944* vol. I, p. 1074.

Ambassador in Moscow sounded a warning note in a cable to the Foreign Office. Notwithstanding Vyshinsky's letter, the cable began, discussions concerning Brand seemed to have gone much further than originally envisaged. Reminding the Foreign Office that the Russians had still not been told of one crucial fact, the German stipulation that the ten thousand lorries which were demanded would not be used on the western front, the ambassador warned that the Soviet reaction 'would probably be violent' if they now learnt that such a condition had been set and that discussions on the matter were proceeding. He therefore urged that nothing further should be done until the Russians had been fully informed and their reply received.[94] In the light of all this the Foreign Office decided that the proposed reply to the German Government 'and still more any kind of discussion of the subject would not be undertaken without the Soviet Government's prior consent'. The agreement of the United States Government to this position was secured, and it was proposed that the British and American Ambassadors in Moscow should jointly inform the Soviet Government of the suggestion that Brand be sent back to Hungary with a message 'that the Allied Governments would convey their views through the Protecting Power [Switzerland], those views to be to the effect that the Allies would be prepared to grant hospitality to certain numbers of Jews if the German Government would release them to neutral countries'.[95]

However, before the proposed joint *démarche* to the Russians could be effected, the British attitude towards the idea of 'dangling a carrot' before the Germans, even with Russian consent, grew more sceptical. The further doubts arose primarily from British intelligence service interpretations of the affair. While the discussions in London were proceeding, Brand and his travelling companion, Grosz, had been taken to Cairo for interrogation. There certain significant details had emerged. Brand stated that he had been a member of the Communist Party's youth movement for ten years prior to 1931, and also that he had participated in efforts to organize Jewish military

[94] Sir A. Clark Kerr (Moscow) to Foreign Office, 30 June 1944, PRO FO 371/42807/3.

[95] Foreign Office to Cabinet Committee on Refugees, 12 July 1944, PRO FO 371/42810/71.

resistance in Hungary during the war, an activity which he termed *haganah*.[96] Neither a communist past nor connection with any organization with the name *haganah* was likely to establish Brand's credentials in the eyes of the British security services. Nevertheless, the interrogator's conclusion, after lengthy questioning of Brand, was that he seemed 'a very naive idealist' and should be 'regarded as cleared from the security point of view'.[97] A different conclusion was reached regarding Grosz, who, under interrogation, drew a squalid self-portrait. It emerged that he had been involved in passport rackets, smuggling, and intelligence work on behalf of half a dozen countries, and had connections with shady figures in the Istanbul underworld, among them 'casino dancers' and 'impresarios' who were believed to be Nazi agents. Grosz gave a confused account of the objects of his mission, alleging that he had received separate instructions from the German and Hungarian secret services: both, it appeared, had instructed him to make soundings about a separate peace with the western allies.[98] Brand's mission was inevitably tainted by its connection with the sinister person of Grosz and his purported peace offer. The waters were further muddied in early June by reports that the Nazis were seeking contact with the allies through Jews in Lisbon. A British intelligence appreciation on 5 July was that the new reports 'lend support to Brandt's story that his discussions have been with senior Gestapo officials (e.g. in particular, Eichmann), rather than with local get-rich-quick Hungarian Gestapo men'. The appreciation continued:

There is nothing novel in this Gestapo scheme which, as so often happens in German bargaining, is two-edged, i.e. it is a dodge (a) to acquire funds and (b) if the attempt fails, to turn it into a nice piece of psychological warfare. . . A feature of present Gestapo planning is preparation for post-armistice activity in neutral countries. In order to ensure the survival of its hideouts, e.g. in the Argentine, this organisation needs respectable funds (e.g. Swiss francs or dollars). Trafficking in Jewish lives is a notorious way of acquiring these funds

---

[96] *Haganah* (defence) was the name of the main Zionist underground army in Palestine. See p. 3.

[97] Report on interrogation of Brand by W. B. Savigny, 2 July 1944, PRO FO 921/228.

[98] Report on interrogation of Grosz by N. J. Strachan, 24 June 1944, PRO FO 371/42810/79 ff.

and the present scheme bears a strong resemblance to general Gestapo marketing of this nature.[99]

In the light of the probable Russian reaction to any further discussion of the Brand proposal and of increased scepticism about the whole affair in intelligence quarters, official opinion in London now moved strongly towards the view that all German overtures should be totally rejected. On 11 July Churchill wrote to Eden:

There is no doubt that this is probably the greatest and most horrible crime ever committed in the whole history of the world, and it has been done by scientific machinery by nominally civilized men in the name of a great State and one of the leading races of Europe. It is quite clear that all concerned in this crime who may fall into our hands, including the people who only obeyed orders by carrying out the butcheries, should be put to death after their association with the murders has been proved.

I cannot therefore feel that this is the kind of ordinary case which is put through the Protecting Power as, for instance, the lack of feeding or sanitary conditions in some particular prisoners' camp. There should therefore in my opinion be no negotiations of any kind on this subject. Declarations should be made in public, so that everyone connected with it will be hunted down and put to death.

The project which has been put forward through a very doubtful channel seems itself also to be of the most nondescript character. I would not take it seriously.[100]

The Prime Minister's view was endorsed by a meeting of the Cabinet Committee on Refugees two days later. Eden, who took the chair, told the committee that the British 'object had been to spin out the affair, but he had been conscious of the danger of being dragged into negotiations'. He observed that there was evidence that the Brand proposal was a cover for a separate peace intrigue designed to embroil Britain with the U.S.S.R. This, 'together with other information he had about the present attitude of the Gestapo leaders, appeared to afford the strongest confirmation of the suspicion which the committee had held from the beginning that the proposals put forward

[99] Major C. H. Dewhurst, M.I.2(a), to I. L. Henderson, Foreign Office, 5 July 1944, enclosing memorandum entitled, 'Joel Brandt and the Gestapo Jew Offer', PRO FO 371/42807/115.

[100] Churchill to Eden, 11 July 1944, PRO FO 371/42809/115.

were a mere trap'. After further discussion the committee agreed that 'any offer of negotiation through the Protecting Power was now proved to be dangerous'. It was decided that the United States Government should be informed that

> we had had secret information of a very reliable nature that the proposals brought by Brandt were definitely intended to trap the United States and United Kingdom Governments into negotiations with the Gestapo, that this would be used as a cover for a separate peace intrigue with the object of embarrassing the two Governments with the Soviet Government; that we therefore proposed to lay aside entirely the idea of any kind of negotiation, whether direct or indirect, and that if the Germans or the Jews themselves made the facts public the United States and United Kingdom Governments should make a public statement.[101]

This decision marked the end of serious official consideration of the ransom offer relayed by Brand.

It is evident that the primary consideration which influenced British handling of the affair was apprehension of a German scheme to split the western allies from Russia. At the time when the 'second front' so long demanded by the Russians was at last being opened on the beaches of Normandy, such a manoeuvre would have been in the logic of the German position. Whether this was indeed the German intention is unclear: The German Foreign Ministry appears to have had no knowledge of the matter;[102] it seems most probable that it was an independent Gestapo enterprise rather than a concerted move by the German Government. The British intelligence interpretation of the proposal may well have been near the truth. It was no secret at the time that the U.S.S.R. was intensely suspicious of the possibility of a separate peace between Germany and the western allies. Indeed in January 1944 Churchill had found it necessary to complain to Stalin of a false report in *Pravda* alleging that secret talks had taken place in Cairo between Ribbentrop and British representatives.[103] (The Russian

[101] Minutes of meeting on 13 July 1944, PRO FO 371/42810/73.

[102] Veesenmayer (Budapest) to Ribbentrop, 22 July 1944, in Braham, *Destruction of Hungarian Jewry*, p. 630.

[103] Churchill to Stalin (received 24 Jan. 1944), in *Correspondence between the Chairman of the Council of Ministers of the U.S.S.R. and the Presidents of the U.S.A. and the Prime Ministers of Great Britain during the Great Patriotic War of 1941–1945*, 2 vols., Moscow 1957, vol. I pp. 188–90.

accusations were perhaps made in a *tu quoque* spirit: until October 1944 there were secret contacts in Stockholm between German and Russian representatives who discussed the possibility of a separate peace between Germany and Russia; these relations appear to have been initiated by the Russians.[104]) During the spring and summer of 1944 relations between Russia and the west were increasingly soured by disagreements over the Polish question. Conscious that the Germans might seize the opportunity to try to drive a wedge between Russia and her allies, the British and American Governments showed the utmost possible solicitude for the susceptibilities of the U.S.S.R. regarding German peace feelers. In these circumstances Brand's arrival on the eve of D-Day with a companion who openly stated that he had come to make peace soundings could not but arouse official scepticism as to the seriousness of the German ransom offer. However, if this was the primary consideration in official minds, it is plain that there was also a subsidiary anxiety which affected British (but rather less American) consideration of the matter: this was the 'danger', as it had been termed in the Cabinet Committee on 31 May 1944, that the proposal might after all be genuine 'and lead to an offer to unload an even greater number of Jews on our hands'. From such a prospect, with its implications for the maintenance of the White Paper policy in Palestine, the official mind shrank as if faced with a major calamity.

A few days after the Cabinet Committee's decision, the story became public property. Because of a leak to two American newspaper correspondents in London, the British Government released an account of the affair to the press and gave official 'guidance' on its treatment.[105] All British newspapers were unanimous in their condemnation of the ransom offer as blackmail and in their support of the Government's contemptuous repudiation of the proposal.[106] *The Times* called it 'monstrous', and the *Manchester Guardian* commented: 'Nothing shows more clearly the depths of satanic wickedness to which the Germans will sink or their perverted ingenuity.'[107] There

[104] H. W. Koch, 'The Spectre of a Separate Peace in the East: Russo-German 'Peace Feelers', 1942–44, *Journal of Contemporary History*, vol. X, no. 3, July 1975.

[105] Foreign Office to Washington, 19 July 1944, PRO FO 371/42810/41.

[106] Sharf, *British Press*, p. 115.

[107] *The Times* and *Manchester Guardian*, 20 July 1944.

was general press agreement that the offer was a German trick to increase dissension between the western allies and Russia. With the publication of the story and of the emphatic allied rejection of the German offer there no longer seemed any point in permitting Brand to return to Hungary. Brand remained anxious to return, but the British Ambassador in Moscow pointed out that the Russians might 'feel surprise' at Brand's being allowed to go home. Mainly for this reason it was decided to detain Brand in Cairo until the end of the war.[108] The Brand episode had a number of bizarre aspects which made it difficult to take seriously. It was, however, immediately followed by a much more straightforward test of British readiness to accept the emigration of large numbers of Jewish refugees from enemy territory.

On 18 July the Foreign Office received a message from the British Legation in Berne reporting that the Hungarian Government had told Swiss diplomats in Budapest that all Jews possessing entry permits for other countries, including Palestine, would be permitted to leave Hungary. It was further stated that the German Government would provide transit permits for such emigrants to cross occupied territories.[109] Subsequent reports from various sources, including the International Red Cross, indicated that the Hungarian Government had decided in early July to exert its authority more vigorously and to curtail the activities of Gestapo agents in Hungary engaged in the deportation of Jews to Auschwitz. Between mid-April and early July Eichmann and his collaborators had deported nearly all the Jews in provincial towns in Hungary. But on 7 July the Hungarian Regent, Admiral Horthy, had called a halt: the deportations abruptly ended, leaving the largest Jewish community, that of the capital, alive. Horthy, who had received appeals, protests, and warnings against the deportations from President Roosevelt, the International Red Cross, the Pope and the King of Sweden rejected German demands that the deportations should be resumed. In spite of a message from Hitler demanding a resumption and charging

[108] Sir A. Clark Kerr (Moscow) to Foreign Office, 11 Aug. 1944, PRO FO 371/42814/22; Foreign Office minutes, 14–18 Aug. 1944, PRO FO 371/42814/21–4; Moyne (Cairo) to Foreign Office, 12 Aug. & Foreign Office to Moyne, 21 Aug. 1944, PRO FO 371/42814/49–51.

[109] Norton (Berne) to Foreign Office, 18 July 1944, PRO FO 371/42809/151.

Horthy with 'treason', the Regent, no doubt with an eye on what now seemed a probable allied victory, asserted that 'his conscience' forbade him to acquiesce in the German demands. Eichmann was induced to leave Hungary, and the offer to allow the unconditional departure for allied territory of certain categories of Jews was reiterated.[110]

The 'Horthy offer' confronted the British Government with a much more serious challenge than the Brand proposal. In this case there could be no doubt as to the source of the offer, and as there was no demand for a *quid pro quo* objections based on arguments concerning economic warfare or negotiation with the enemy did not apply. Moreover, while Horthy's motives might be suspect, the offer was not accompanied by a peace proposal, and there was no discernible psychological warfare element in it. Consequently the British response was rather more positive than it had been in the case of the Brand proposal. But here too the recurrent British nightmare of a mass exodus of Jews from Europe towards Palestine affected policy-making. On 28 July the Colonial Office declared itself 'somewhat concerned (from the point of view of the limited room that there is in Palestine) at the recent turn of events in the Balkans. We are afraid that we may be on the verge of a flood of refugees.'[111] A memorandum by Eden circulated to the Cabinet Committee on Refugees on 3 August accepted that the Hungarian offer appeared to be genuine and that it seemed 'desirable to agree with the United States Government that it should be accepted with the least possible delay.' However, he objected to an American suggestion that the two governments should issue a declaration announcing that they would 'undertake to care for all Jews who are permitted to leave Hungary'. He pointed out that there were formidable difficulties of accommodation and transport, and that the Colonial Office were 'already much disturbed by the numbers in which Jews

[110] Eden to Churchill, 8 Aug. 1944, PRO PREM 4/52/5/Part I; A. E. Zollinger (International Red Cross) to State Dept., Washington, 24 July 1944, *FRUS 1944* vol. I, p. 1103; C. J. Burckhardt (I.R.C.) to British Consul, Geneva, 26 July 1944, PRO FO 371/42815/121; Ribbentrop to Veesenmayer, 16 July 1944, in Braham, *Destruction of Hungarian Jewry*, pp. 450–4; Veesenmayer to Foreign Ministry, Berlin, 24 Aug. 1944, ibid., p. 476.

[111] Eastwood (Colonial Office) to I. L. Henderson (Foreign Office), 28 July 1944, PRO FO 371/42811 (WR 453/3/48).

have been arriving in Palestine from Constantsa'. Eden continued:

According to a report just received from the International Red Cross the first contingent of a total number of 40,000 Jews are to start leaving Hungary for Palestine in ten days. Palestine cannot accept at the moment anything like so many immigrants. Nevertheless, British and American public opinion would probably not view with favour any qualification of an acceptance by His Majesty's Government of the 'Horthy offer'. It is therefore suggested that unless there are strong military reasons to the contrary His Majesty's Government should confine themselves to telling the United States Government that while they agree to join in the proposed declaration, British capacity to receive, as they know, has now become limited and we would thus accept an indefinite commitment, counting on them not to face us with the impossible.[112]

Eden's reservations were echoed at a meeting of the Cabinet Committee on Refugees the next day. Eden could not be present and the dominant voice in the proceedings was that of the Colonial Secretary, Oliver Stanley. Referring to the reported imminent departure of forty thousand Jews for Palestine, Stanley said that 'the sudden influx of large numbers of Jewish refugees into Palestine would immediately bring about a most critical situation.' He continued:

It was not clear that the figure of 40,000 might not turn out to be much larger and he recalled that the Brandt proposals recently considered by the Committee had spoken of 800,000 to a million Jews. He felt most strongly that it was imperative that urgent action should be taken to stop this movement pending decision of our general line of action and to prevent matters from slipping still further. At the same time it should be made clear to the International Red Cross that they had no right to attempt to send the refugees to territories for which His Majesty's Government had responsibility without permission.

After Stanley's statement the committee's discussion followed a familiar course. There was some consideration of the availability of places in refugee camps, and of the possibility of opening a new camp in Sicily. The War Office representative saw 'considerable difficulties' in the way of the latter suggestion. The

[112] Eden to Cabinet Committee on Refugees, 3 Aug. 1944, and attached telegrams, PRO CAB 95/15/198.

Home Office representative 'observed that there was now negligible accommodation in this country'. And Stanley said 'that repeated investigations had shown that there were no other possible places in the British Empire or territories over which we had control'. In a minute to Churchill, Eden summed up the 'general feeling of the meeting' as one of opposition to joining the U.S.A. in '"signing a blank cheque which we could not honour"'. Eden suggested that the matter should go to a full meeting of the War Cabinet for a decision.[113]

Taking account of the reservations which had been expressed, the Cabinet decided on 9 August that it would suggest certain amendments to the proposed Anglo-American declaration, in order to limit the potential British share of the refugee burden.[114] However, the Cabinet decision came under contradictory pressures, on the one hand from those who thought it offered too much, and on the other from those who considered it inadequate. Powerful ammunition for the former view was provided by Sir Harold MacMichael who, in an exhaustive analysis of the numerical possibilities for immigration to Palestine under the remainder of the White Paper quota, concluded that there was room for a maximum of 4,000 immigrants from Hungary.[115] In later telegrams MacMichael, with the support of the Minister Resident in Cairo, Lord Moyne, argued that no larger number of immigrants could be admitted even on a temporary basis to Palestine (nor, added Moyne, to any other part of the Middle East). Any Jewish refugees from Hungary in excess of the authorized figure should therefore, insisted MacMichael, be sent 'direct from Turkey to whatever country may be considered a practicable receptacle for them'.[116] But these restrictive arguments were countered by the United States Government which objected that the proposed British amendment to the joint declaration appeared 'to commit [the] United States Government to unlimited liability only partially supported subject to definite qualifications by His Majesty's

[113] Cabinet Committee on Refugees, minutes of meeting on 4 Aug. 1944, PRO FO 371/42814/87; Eden to Churchill, 6 Aug. 1944, PRO PREM 4/52/5/Part I/829.

[114] Cabinet minutes, 9 Aug. 1944, PRO CAB 65/43.

[115] High Commissioner to Colonial Office, 7 Aug. 1944, PRO FO 371/42813/98.

[116] High Commissioner to Colonial Office, 17 Aug. 1944, PRO FO 371/42815/84; Minister Resident, Cairo, to Foreign Office, 25 Aug., PRO FO 371/42816/40.

Government'.[117] Under strong American pressure the British eventually agreed to drop their proposed reservations. A joint declaration broadcast by the BBC at midnight on 16/17 August accepted the Hungarian offer to release Jews and stated that 'temporary havens of refuge' would be found for Jews leaving Hungary. The declaration added that the two governments 'in accepting the offer . . . do not in any way condone the action of the Hungarian Government in forcing the emigration of Jews as an alternative to persecution and death'.[118] However, the British Government, while agreeing to an apparent 'blank cheque' in this public statement, insisted privately on American acceptance of the British view that the capacity for receiving refugees in British-controlled territory was limited. The American Ambassador in London therefore delivered a formal note to Eden agreeing that it was 'understood between the United States and British Governments that the British capacity to accommodate refugees is limited, so that while the British Government has accepted in principle an indefinite commitment, the British Government rely on the United States Government to assume its fair share of the burden and not to face the British Government with a practical impossibility'.[119]

The Horthy offer too proved to be a false hope for the Hungarian Jews. The main reason was that the German Government did not, as was hoped, permit Jewish emigrants to leave. At Eichmann's suggestion German agreement was given 'in principle' to the emigration of 7,400 Jews to Sweden and Switzerland. However, no emigration was to be permitted to Palestine on the ground that this would conflict with German propaganda in the Muslim world in which the Grand Mufti of Jerusalem (at this time a privileged resident of Nazi Germany) played a leading role. Moreover, the departure of the limited number of emigrants was to be dependent on the resumption of the deportations of all remaining Hungarian Jews to Auschwitz. And even the limited emigration was to be stopped as soon as Hungarian acquiescence in the resumption of depor-

[117] British Embassy, Washington, to Foreign Office, 12 Aug. 1944, PRO FO 371/42814/45.
[118] Text in Winant (London) to State Dept., 16 Aug. 1944, *FRUS 1944* vol. I, p. 1127.
[119] Winant to Eden, 16 Aug. 1944, PRO FO 371/42815/29; War Cabinet minutes, 16 Aug. 1944, PRO CAB 65/43.

tations had been secured.[120] In mid-October the Horthy regime was deposed, and a pro-German puppet government assumed power in Budapest: Eichmann was permitted to return to Budapest and resume his activities against the remaining Jews in Budapest.[121] No Hungarian Jews therefore were enabled to emigrate as a result of the Allied acceptance of the Horthy offer.

On the other hand, the keenly expressed interest of the allied and certain neutral governments in the fate of the Hungarian Jews, if it did not secure the emigration of more than a tiny number, probably helped during the crucial summer months of 1944 to prevent the deportation to Auschwitz of the Jewish population of Budapest. As has been seen, an important part was played by the activities of neutral states (especially Sweden) whose diplomats granted protective documents to Jews. Britain also made a contribution of a similar nature by acting on a suggestion made to the Colonial Office by Moshe Shertok in July 1944. In an interview with the Permanent Under-Secretary, Sir George Gater, Shertok had drawn attention to the apparent tendency of German and Hungarian officials to accord some degree of recognition to Palestine immigration certificates: it appeared that, notwithstanding German concern for their relations with the Grand Mufti of Jerusalem, the holders of such certificates were often considered by the Germans as potential candidates for exchange, were accorded privileged treatment, and frequently managed to avoid being deported to Poland to be killed. Shertok accordingly suggested a means whereby some at least of the Jews remaining in Hungary might be protected:

He did not ask that these Jews should be granted full Palestinian naturalisation or that the law of naturalisation should be set aside. What he had in mind was some fictitious device by which they might be regarded for present purposes as Palestinian citizens, without becoming Palestinian citizens for permanency. Such a course would of course be completely unorthodox, but on the other hand the position of these Jews was a tragedy without parallel. The Agency were prepared to give a written undertaking that no claim to full Palestinian citizenship would be made on the strength of any

[120] Memorandum from Reichel to Wagner (German Foreign Ministry) on directives of the Reich Security Main Office regarding emigration of Jews to Palestine, 15 Aug. 1944, in Braham, *Destruction of Hungarian Jewry*, p. 708.

[121] See p. 321.

document now given to these Jews and that if any of them wished at some subsequent date to qualify for Palestinian citizenship they would have to qualify in accordance with the law.

In reply to Shertok, Gater said that he recognized the desperate situation. He imagined that what Shertok wanted was 'some kind of document which would appear to be a document of Palestine citizenship but which would really be a fake and could be acknowledged as such once the present emergency was passed'. Rather surprisingly Gater did not immediately rule out this proposal that the British Government should, as it were, forge its own documents. Shertok was told that the suggestion would receive 'sympathetic consideration . . . in consultation, if need be, with the High Commissioner'.[122]

Sir Harold MacMichael, however, expressed 'grave misgivings' about the idea. He argued that 'so demonstrable an act of bad faith' might prejudice the prospects for a fourth Palestinian-German exchange, and he expressed doubt as to the protection which the documents might afford to Jews in Hungary. But the main burden of MacMichael's objection was his scepticism about the good faith of the Zionists. In a message to the Colonial Office he emphasized:

You will, of course, appreciate how little permanent value could be attributed to any undertaking, formal or otherwise, which the Jewish Agency would give. They would certainly not hesitate to demand release from any such pledge whenever it suited them politically to do so; and when the time came they would seek by every means in their power to establish irrefutable evidence, which in the circumstances we should find it very hard to rebut, that persons upon whom bogus certificates had been conferred were bona fide Palestine citizens.[123]

In spite of the High Commissioner's misgivings, the Colonial Secretary agreed to issue 5,000 'bogus' Palestine immigration certificates to 'veteran Zionists' in Hungary; the documents were distributed by Swiss diplomats in Budapest. The arrangement was based on an understanding between the Colonial Office and the Jewish Agency that the certificates 'constituted no claim to admission' to Palestine.[124] Four

[122] Record of discussion at Colonial Office, 7 July 1944, PRO CO 733/455/75113/72A.
[123] High Commissioner to Colonial Office, 19 July 1944, PRO FO 371/42810/64.
[124] Stanley to Eden, 6 Dec. 1944, PRO FO 371/42825/23.

months later, at the end of November 1944, as Soviet forces moved into Hungary, the question arose (as the High Commissioner had forecast) of whether the certificates should be honoured. The Jewish Agency adhered to its undertaking to the Colonial Office, but for a while the Foreign Office, under strong American pressure to honour the documents, wavered. One Foreign Office official declared that failure to honour the certificates would be 'more in keeping with the traditions of a disreputable Balkan or South American Government, than with those of H.M.G.'[125] It was ultimately agreed that the holders of the documents would 'not be regarded as having the automatic right to be admitted to Palestine' but would have to be 're-selected' for admission within the normal quota.[126] No holders of these documents were, in fact, able to reach Palestine before the liberation of Hungary. However, the primary purpose of the strategem was partly fulfilled: as in the case of the Swedish passports, the Palestine certificates proved to have a certain protective value to their holders, by securing preferential treatment from some German and Hungarian officials.

The acquiescence of the British Government to this device was possible because, the High Commissioner's fears notwithstanding, it did not endanger the maintenance of the White Paper policy in Palestine. This, indeed, was the essential criterion by which the British Government judged all schemes for the rescue of Jews from Nazi Europe during the war. Approval could be given to the exchanges of small numbers of civilians or the plans for the movement of Jews to neutral states because these did not involve any commitment by the British Government to a significant increase in Jewish immigration to Palestine. On the other hand, the Government manifested the greatest reluctance to agree to any scheme which might lead to such a mass influx. Only strong pressure from the United States could induce the British to modify their attitude, as occurred in the case of the 'Horthy offer'. Such pressure led to much British resentment of the apparent American tendency to urge the admission of large numbers of refugees to British-controlled

[125] Hall-Patch minute, 4 Nov. 1944, PRO FO 371/42823/16; Eden to Cabinet, 30 Nov. 1944, PRO CAB 95/15/214; Colonial Office to Gort (Jerusalem), 1 Nov. 1944, PRO FO 371/42823/145.
[126] Gort to Colonial Office, 4 Dec. 1944, PRO FO 371/42823/144.

territories while the U.S.A. showed no eagerness to liberalize its own immigration restrictions. But, in the event, neither the British nor the Americans found themselves faced with mass migrations. A total of 22,971 Jews succeeded in reaching Palestine in 1943 and 1944; an unknown but almost certainly smaller number reached the U.S.A.[127] For the great majority of the surviving Jews in Europe during these years there was no realistic prospect of emigration, nor any effective shield against persecution in the countries where they lived. Any lingering expectation of help from the outside world in resistance against the process of mass murder also now proved to be a false hope.

[127] Gurevich, *Statistical Handbook of Jewish Palestine* p. 116. In 1943 4,705 Jewish immigrants to the U.S.A. were officially recorded. After 1943 there was no separate official classification of Jewish immigrants to the U.S.A.

7

Resistance

No FORM of resistance to the Nazi anti-Jewish terror could have hoped to save the lives of the majority of the victims. Neither the allied governments nor the Jews themselves had the capability to do more than attempt to save the lives of a small minority. Jews, of course, participated in the allied armies and in the resistance movements of occupied Europe in common with others, but the special nature of the Jewish predicament necessitated in many areas a response which, if it was to be effective, had to be specifically Jewish. But Jewish resistance could not hope to have any effect unaided. All resistance movements depended heavily on external assistance, but for the Jews, marked out from others by the yellow star, isolated in ghettos and camps, possessing no government-in-exile, no weapons, and few trained military personnel, and often surrounded by a hostile population, help from outside was the indispensable condition of effective resistance. Various schemes were put forward during the war for British support for Jewish resistance to the Nazi onslaught. The most formidable was the plan for a Jewish army, whose primary purpose would be the defence of Palestine (which remained under threat from Axis forces until the British victory at Alamein in November 1942). It was further proposed that Jewish volunteers from Palestine, with special knowledge of conditions behind Axis lines, should be infiltrated into Europe in order to carry out espionage and sabotage activities for the allies, and in order to bring succour to Jews in occupied areas. Suggestions were made that the resistance of the Jews and of their non-Jewish neighbours to the Nazi deportations might be stiffened by means of wireless broadcasts and the dissemination of leaflets, warning the Jews of what awaited them, appealing to non-Jews to offer refuge to the threatened victims, and threatening retribution to all who collaborated with the Nazis' system of mass murder. Pleas were made by Jewish resistance groups in Europe, most notably in the Warsaw ghetto rising in the spring of 1943, for supplies and other assistance from the allies. There were demands for retributive bombing of German cities by the allies in order to try to deter the Nazis from further atrocities. And there was strong pressure for the bombardment of the Auschwitz and Treblinka camps, or of the railway lines leading to them, in order to halt, or at least slow down, the massacres. These proposals differed greatly in their nature and in their practicability. But they shared the common end of seeking to provide some tangible resistance to the Nazi campaign of annihilation.

The most elaborate scheme for promoting a distinctive Jewish military role during the Second World War was the project for the establishment of a Jewish Army. The idea was one which had a natural attraction for the Zionists. The formation of such a force, they felt, would help to ensure recognition of the Jews as an allied nationality, and so strengthen their claim to a Jewish state in Palestine after the war. The Zionists recalled that during the First World War small Jewish units had participated within the British army in the Gallipoli landings and in Allenby's Palestine campaign. That 'Jewish Legion' had helped to secure the favourable atmosphere towards Zionism in which the Balfour Declaration had been issued in 1917. Now perhaps history might be repeated. The Zionists argued that the formation of a Jewish army would facilitate the withdrawal of the substantial British forces retained for internal security duties in Palestine. Britain would be able, by means of such an army, to draw on a large reservoir of otherwise unavailable man-power, including stateless refugees and nationals of neutral and enemy states, often with special skills or expert knowledge of value to the British war effort. The force might be able to extend some aid to their suffering co-religionists in Europe. Looking further ahead the Zionists privately calculated that such a force would provide large numbers of Jews with sophisticated military training helpful to the *Haganah* in any post-war conflict in Palestine. It was this consideration, among others, which provoked strong opposition to the project in Whitehall. That the scheme was considered at all as a serious proposition by the British Government was primarily due to the countervailing weight of the support of Winston Churchill, who strongly favoured the withdrawal of most of the British troops tied down in Palestine, and had long advocated the arming of the *Yishuv* for self-defence.

The possibility of recruiting Jewish units which would include large numbers of Jewish refugees to serve in the British army was mooted immediately upon the outbreak of the war both by the Jewish Agency and by the 'New Zionist Organisation' of Vladimir Jabotinsky (who had been the chief originator of the 'Jewish Legion' in the First World War).[1] The approaches by the latter were rejected out of hand by the British Government, but those of the Jewish Agency proved more difficult to brush aside. Weizmann discussed the idea with R. A. Butler at the Foreign Office on 11 September 1939, and was warned to expect 'great opposition in Whitehall to the formation of Jewish units as such to serve with the British forces'. Weizmann did not seem deterred, merely remarking that 'we had a similar difficulty in 1914'.[2] Weizmann had already talked about the idea with Churchill (not then in office) in late August, and at a further meeting over dinner on 19 September Churchill declared himself 'all for it', and asked for a detailed plan to be prepared.[3] Preparation of the plan was consigned by Weizmann to Orde Wingate, the strongly pro-Zionist British army officer, who had commanded the force of 'Special Night Squads', composed of Palestinian Jews, who had operated with considerable success against Arab guerrillas in Palestine during the later stages of the Arab revolt in 1938. Wingate was a hero among the *Yishuv*, and it was his lifelong ambition to lead a Jewish army to victory. He quickly prepared a 'plan for the employment of Jewish forces in the prosecution of the war'. The preamble to the scheme prudently stated that the object was to raise and equip a Jewish force without committing the Government to a change of policy in Palestine. The plan called for the force to be set up in three stages: first, a thousand junior officers were to be trained; then, a Jewish force

[1] V. Jabotinsky to N. Chamberlain, 4 Sept. 1939, PRO FO 371/23250 (E 6680/6342/31); C. G. L. Syers (for Chamberlain) to Jabotinsky, 21 Sept. 1939, ibid.

[2] Note by Butler, 11 Sept. 1939, PRO FO 371/23250 (E 6528/6343/31).

[3] Bauer, *From Diplomacy to Resistance*, p. 84; Rose ed., *Dugdale Diaries*, p. 152 (entry dated 20 Sept. 1939); Weizmann to Shertok, 24 Sept. 1939, WA.

of twenty thousand men was to be organized for internal security duties in Palestine; finally, the force would be mobilized for active combat duties elsewhere.[4]

Meanwhile Weizmann set about the task of mobilizing support for the scheme in the British political and military establishment. He had several conversations about Wingate's memorandum with Brendan Bracken, whom Churchill had designated as his liaison with the Zionists. Bracken reported to Churchill on 31 October:

The Jews are perhaps unreasonably impatient, and Dr Weizmann is pressing strongly for immediate and definite statements regarding this scheme for training officers. Although I am not one of Mr Malcolm MacDonald's 'familiars', I shall be very surprised if he does not offer strong opposition to Wingate's proposal. He is notoriously hostile to the Zionists and I understand that Weizmann and his friends believe that it is almost useless to attempt to negotiate with him.[5]

Bracken's prognostication as to the view of MacDonald proved correct: in the course of a long talk with Weizmann on 27 November the Colonial Secretary said that he 'certainly was averse' to the raising of a Jewish army.[6] MacDonald's remark reflected a general hostility in the Colonial, Foreign, and War Offices, and in the Government of Palestine, to the raising of specifically Jewish units whether for service in Palestine or elsewhere.[7] Weizmann and his associates, however, continued to lobby in favour of the project. On 30 November Weizmann discussed it with the Foreign Secretary, Halifax.[8] The Zionist leader also had two conversations at this time with the Chief of the Imperial General Staff, General Ironside. After the first of these, on 29 October, Ironside noted in his diary:

One had strongly the impression that he merely regarded the British Empire as something likely to further his ends . . . He gave one an eerie sensation . . . I had strongly a feeling of half-resentment that I

[4] Memorandum dated 13 Oct. 1939, PRO PREM 4/51/9 Part 2/1281.
[5] Bracken to Churchill, 31 Oct. 1939, PRO PREM 4/51/9 Part 2/1278.
[6] Record of conversation by MacDonald, PRO FO 371/23242 (E 8142/6/31).
[7] PRO FO 371/23240/176 ff. (E 6904/6/31), *passim*.
[8] Halifax to MacDonald, 30 Nov. 1939, PRO FO 371/23242/196 (E 8075/6/31).

was being 'used' for somebody else's benefit. I have never felt that before in my life.[9]

However, Weizmann's ability to charm the British officer class had not totally forsaken him: after a second meeting a fortnight later Ironside's reaction was more sympathetic:

I must say that I agreed with him completely. We are probably missing a chance to get the Jews on our side . . . The complication of the war has upset things so much that it is difficult for us to do anything at the moment except mark time.[10]

With the agreement 'in principle' of Ironside to the scheme, Weizmann next saw the Commander-in-Chief of British forces in the Middle East, General Wavell. But Wavell, concerned as to the potential Arab reaction, expressed no enthusiasm for the idea.[11]

In spite of Zionist efforts no progress was made at this stage. Although the Cabinet approved a limited programme of recruitment of Palestinian Jews, they were not to form separate units. Churchill argued forcefully in Cabinet that

it might have been thought a matter for satisfaction that the Jews in Palestine should possess arms, and be capable of providing for their own defence. They were the only trustworthy friends we had in that country, and they were much more under our control than the scattered Arab population. He would have thought that the sound policy for Great Britain at the beginning of the war would have been to build up, as soon as possible, a strong Jewish armed force in Palestine.[12]

But these views encountered no support from Churchill's colleagues. It was only in the changed political atmosphere following Churchill's formation of a new government in May 1940 that the proposal was reconsidered. In spite of Churchill's strong backing, the idea once again aroused formidable opposition. The new Colonial Secretary, Lord Lloyd, said that 'if we accept Jewish military assistance in any form, we cannot

[9] General Sir Edmund Ironside, *The Ironside Diaries 1937–1940*, eds. R. Macleod and D. Kelly, London 1962, pp. 135–6 (entry dated 31 Oct. 1939).

[10] Ibid., p. 137 (entry dated 14 Nov. 1939).

[11] Macleod (for Ironside) to Weizmann, 4 Dec. 1939, WA; Bauer, *From Diplomacy to Resistance*, p. 86.

[12] MacDonald to Cabinet, 20 Jan. 1940, memorandum on 'Recruitment of Palestinian Armed Forces—Release of British Garrison', PRO CAB 67/4 (W.P. (G.) (40) 16); Cabinet minutes, 12 Feb. 1940, PRO CAB 65/5/187 ff.

altogether escape future political embarrassment'.[13] The Foreign Office view remained that there was 'no reason why any special arrangement should be made for the recruitment of Jews, any more than for Scotchmen or bus-conductors or people with red hair'.[14] However, armed with the support of the Prime Minister, Weizmann saw Lloyd on 29 May, and secured his assent in principle to the formation of a Jewish force. Lloyd specified that his agreement was conditional on the incorporation of the force within the British Army and its deployment 'for general service in any theatre of war outside Palestine'. Jews were to be recruited in any country where such enlistment was permissible, and to be trained 'at the most convenient centres, though not in Palestine'. The practical details of the scheme were to be settled between the Jewish Agency and the War Office, but Lloyd warned Weizmann 'that the War Office see certain practical difficulties in any scheme to form purely Jewish units of the British Army'.[15]

Although the green light appeared to have been given to the plan, a strong rearguard action continued to be waged against it by the War Office. While Churchill's energetic support kept it alive, the scheme was whittled down in the course of the summer. The only tangible result seemed to be an announcement by Eden in the House of Commons on 6 August that two battalions (one Jewish, and one Arab) would be raised in Palestine. The Zionists protested vociferously. David Ben Gurion said that the reduction of the proposal to such a minuscule size meant 'letting down the Jews of Palestine and leaving them to be destroyed by invaders and Arabs'.[16] Weizmann wrote to Churchill:

Should it come to a temporary withdrawal from Palestine—a contingency which we hope will never arise—the Jews of Palestine would be exposed to wholesale massacre at the hands of the Arabs, encouraged and directed by the Nazis and Fascists. This possibility reinforces the demand for our elementary human right to bear arms which should not normally be denied to the loyal citizens of

[13] Quoted in A. V. Coverley-Price minute, 5 June 1940, PRO FO 371/24566 (E 2044/187/31).
[14] Ibid.
[15] Lloyd to Weizmann, 15 June 1940, PRO FO 371/24566/47.
[16] Memorandum by Ben Gurion, 7 Aug. 1940, WA.

a country at war. Palestinian Jewry can furnish a force of 50,000 men.[17]

Churchill again intervened in favour of the scheme, and on 3 September he met Weizmann and told him that he had written to the War Office about it. Weizmann said that he wanted Wingate to command the projected force. A few days later Weizmann discussed the plan with Eden and Dill (who had succeeded Ironside as C.I.G.S.) at the War Office.[18] At a further meeting on 13 September Eden produced a written draft scheme: this provided for the raising of Jewish units for service outside the Middle East; the condition was laid down that in the case of stateless or foreign Jews, each recruit must present 'a certificate from his country of origin that he would be taken back'. It was explained that this was necessary lest the British Government at the end of the war should 'have left on their hands a large body of stateless and homeless Jews and be subjected to great pressure to bring them to Palestine'. With these reservations Eden indicated that he was now prepared to approve the Jewish Army proposal. It would have to obtain Cabinet sanction, but as all ministers now agreed on it there would be no difficulty. The only criticism was likely to come from the Prime Minister who might consider the scheme too modest.[19] Although he did not like the conditions attached to the scheme by Eden, Weizmann now thought that he had finally secured Government approval for the idea. Elated by what Eden had told him, Weizmann said, 'It is almost as great a day as the Balfour Declaration!'[20]

But Weizmann's jubilation was misconceived. On 10 October Eden presented for Cabinet approval a scheme for the recruitment of 10,000 Jews 'for incorporation in special Jewish units'. It was specified that not more than 3,000 of these were to be drawn from Palestine, most of the rest to be drawn from the U.S.A., although some would be refugees from Germany. In the ensuing discussion 'the view was expressed that it was right

[17] Weizmann to Churchill, 6 Aug. 1940, WA.

[18] Churchill to Wavell, 12 Aug. 1940, Churchill, *Second World War*, vol. II, p. 377; memorandum by Weizmann, 4 Sept. 1940, WA; note on meeting of Weizmann with Eden and Dill, 10 Sept. 1940, CZA Z4/302/24.

[19] Account of meeting by Weizmann, 16 Sept. 1940, CZA Z4/302/24; account by H. L. Baggallay, 14 Sept. 1940, PRO FO 371/24567/146 (E 2609/187/31).

[20] Rose ed., *Dugdale Diaries*, p. 175 (entry dated 13 Sept. 1940).

and natural that Jews who had been maltreated by the enemy should be given an opportunity to take up arms against them'. However, fears were expressed as to the 'risk of a propaganda outcry being raised that the Jews, who were responsible for the outbreak of the war, were now seeking to drag America into the quarrel'. Lloyd said that while he had done all he could to help arrive at an agreed scheme 'in deference to the views held in the Cabinet on White Paper policy', he nevertheless

felt it his duty to warn the Cabinet of the importance of doing nothing to upset Moslem feeling. This had been continually stressed by every important British authority without exception in the areas concerned. He did not ask that the proposal under consideration should be abandoned, but that it should be deferred until the highly critical situation now present in the Middle East cleared up or developed.

In view of these hesitations, the Cabinet, while giving the scheme 'general approval in principle' decided that nothing should be done to give effect to the scheme until after the American presidential election in early November, after which the matter would be considered again.[21] The Cabinet decision was conveyed to Weizmann confidentially by Lloyd who stressed that no action should be taken and no announcement made until after the American elections.[22] Although the postponement appeared to be only for a period of three weeks, it was the first of several which were eventually to kill the scheme altogether.

By the end of the year the only tangible move towards implementation of the scheme was the appointment of a commander for the projected force. The man chosen was not the Zionists' nominee, Wingate (who, angry at being rejected, went off to fight in Ethiopia), but Brigadier L. A. Hawes, a former Indian army officer. While exchanges continued between the Jewish Agency and the Government as to the precise terms of the announcement of the formation of the force, renewed opposition to the scheme gathered force in the Foreign, Colonial, and War Offices.[23] The Permanent Under-

[21] Cabinet minutes, 10 Oct. 1940, PRO CAB 65/9.
[22] Lloyd to Weizmann, 17 Oct. 1940, PRO FO 371/27126/9 (E 60/60/31).
[23] Weizmann to Lloyd, 6 Jan. 1941, WA; Weizmann to Dill, 8 Jan. 1941, WA; Foreign Office note on Weizmann-Butler interview, 21 Jan. 1941, PRO FO 371/27126

Secretary of the Foreign Office, Sir Alexander Cadogan, wrote on 24 February:

I am afraid that, in my ignorance, I deplore the scheme. There are thousands of Britishers in this country whom we do not take into the army because we cannot yet equip them. We do *not*, therefore, want these Jews, and the whole attitude of Dr Weizmann shows that it is purely a political stunt. If such a stunt were to do our cause any good, it would be worth considering, but the value of Jewish support seems to me questionable.[24]

Eden shared this view, commenting that there was no military importance in the scheme, and that the question was 'purely political'.[25] On 26 January, General Wavell cabled to the War Office:

I am strongly opposed to raising this force at present time. It is vitally important that for the next six months at least I should be as free as possible from commitments and anxieties in Palestine.[26]

On 28 February a ministerial meeting was held to consider the future of the scheme. Present were David Margesson (who had succeeded Eden as Secretary of State for War in December 1940), Lord Moyne (appointed Colonial Secretary following the death of Lloyd in early February), and R. A. Butler, representing the Foreign Office. Moyne said that he had been studying the proposal and had reached the conclusion that it was bound to give rise to serious difficulties. These misgivings were, he said, shared by Sir Harold MacMichael. The telegram from Wavell was produced by Margesson and shown to the meeting. It was agreed that the plan must either be postponed for six months, as recommended by Wavell, or modified drastically. Immediately after the meeting Moyne wrote to Churchill informing him of these recommendations by the three departments.[27]

(E 93/60/31); Foreign Office note on Weizmann-Eden talk, 24 Jan. 1941, ibid.; Jewish Agency note on Weizmann-Eden talk, 24 Jan. 1941, WA: Baxter minutes, 14, 23, and 29 Jan. 1941, PRO FO 371/27126 (E 93/60/31); Shuckburgh (Colonial Office) to Eyres (Foreign Office), 14 Feb. 1941, PRO FO 371/27126 (E 589/60/31).

[24] Cadogan minute, 24 Feb. 1941, PRO FO 371/27126 (E 612/60/31).

[25] Marginal note by Eden, 31 Jan. 1941, PRO FO 371/27126 (E 93/60/31).

[26] Wavell to War Office, 26 Feb. 1941, PRO FO 371/27126 (E 739/60/31).

[27] Note on meeting by C. W. Baxter, 3 Mar. 1941, PRO FO 371/27126 (E 739/60/31); Moyne to Churchill, 28 Feb. 1941, ibid.

Churchill's reaction was characteristic:

General Wavell, like most British army officers, is strongly pro-Arab. At the time of the licences to the ship-wrecked illegal immigrants being permitted, he sent a telegram, not less strong than this, predicting widespread disaster in the Arab world, together with the loss of the Busra—Baghdad—Haifa route. The telegram should be looked up, and also my answer in which I overruled the General and explained to him the reasons for the Cabinet decision.[28] All went well and not a dog barked. It follows from the above that I am not in the least convinced by all this stuff. The Arabs, under the impression of recent victories, would not make any trouble now. However, in present circumstances I do not wish General Wavell to be worried now by lengthy arguments about matters of no military consequence to the immediate situation . . . Dr Weizmann should be told that the Jewish Army project must be put off for six months, but may be reconsidered again in four months. The sole reason given should be lack of equipment.[29]

Although the decision to postpone further the recruitment of the force met Moyne's recommendation, he was uneasy about the proposed reason to be given to Weizmann:

I fear . . . Weizmann will feel that lack of equipment is a very unconvincing reason for postponing an announcement . . . Weizmann will have an added grievance if he feels that we are merely making excuses. Would it not be better for me to tell him the true reason, that you have decided that the matter must be postponed in view of the development in the Middle East situation and the necessity of not risking any unrest in the Arab world at the present time.[30]

However, the Prime Minister insisted that his decision must stand: 'The equipment is the true and best reason. Otherwise you will find the argument endless.'[31]

The Zionist reaction was predictable. Weizmann pronounced the decision 'a sore blow', but refused to give up altogether.[32] On 12 March he obtained an interview with Churchill who (according to Weizmann's account) told him

[28] The reference is to the decision to permit the survivors of the *Patria* disaster to remain in Palestine: see pp. 71–2.

[29] Churchill to Moyne, 1 Mar. 1941, PRO FO 371/27126 (E 739/60/31).

[30] Moyne to Churchill, 3 Mar. 1941, ibid.

[31] Churchill minute, 4 Mar. 1941, ibid.

[32] Weizmann to Moyne, 6 Mar. 1941; Weizmann to Shertok, 7 and 12 Mar. 1941, WA.

that whenever he saw the Zionist leader he felt 'a twist in his heart'; Churchill assured him that the postponement of the Jewish army plan was only temporary and that he would continue to support it.[33] Shortly after the interview Weizmann left for the U.S.A., but he, from afar, and his colleagues in London and Jerusalem continued to press for the early implementation of the idea.[34] Their anxiety to assure the security of the *Yishuv* by means of a Jewish force was increased by widespread rumours in the spring of 1941 that Britain was seriously considering withdrawal from Palestine.[35] The rumours were denied by the Government of Palestine, although a contingency plan had in fact been prepared for the evacuation of Palestine. The plan provided for the withdrawal of all British personnel, as well as of several hundred German and Italian internees. Asylum elsewhere would also be sought for 'about one thousand Allied nationals, mainly Poles'. As for the remainder of the population, Arab and Jewish, they would be issued with instructions to 'stay put'.[36] The prospect that the Jewish population of Palestine might share the fate of the Jews of Europe heightened the apprehensions of the Zionists, and their determination to ensure that the *Yishuv* was not thus abandoned defenceless to face enemy occupation. However, at the end of the six-month waiting period, the continued opposition to a Jewish army of Margesson, Eden, and Moyne, led to a further postponement, although at Churchill's suggestion the period was shortened to only three months.[37]

Zionist patience was now exhausted. In a letter to Churchill, circulated to the Cabinet by the Prime Minister, Weizmann protested bitterly that 'during these two years our readiness to serve has earned us only rebuffs and humiliations'. He pointed out that thousands of Palestinian Jews had fought for the allied cause, 'but our people are never mentioned; our name is shunned; all contact or co-operation with us is kept dark as if it were

[33] Notes by Weizmann on meeting, WA.

[34] Weizmann to J. M. Martin, 17 Apr. 1941 WA; Isaiah Berlin to Weizmann, 22 Apr. 1941 WA.

[35] U.S. Consul, Jerusalem, to State Dept., Apr. 1941., *FRUS 1941*, vol. III, p. 602; High Commissioner, Jerusalem, to Colonial Office, 5 May 1941, PRO PREM 3/348/26.

[36] Moyne to Churchill, 16 June 1941, PRO PREM 3/348/15.

[37] Moyne to Churchill, 26 Aug. 1941; Eastwood (Colonial Office) to Harvey (Foreign Office), 28 Aug. 1941, PRO FO 371/27128 (E 5160/60/31).

compromising'. Even in Palestine, where, Weizmann stressed, defence of the country might be for the Jews 'literally a matter of life and death', Jews were recruited 'only under humiliating limitations and conditions'.[38] The letter did not, however, win Weizmann any official support. Moyne told Eden that he considered that the letter did 'not accurately state' the position. A Foreign Office official minuted that Weizmann appeared 'to be opening his mouth wider than before'. And Eden commented: 'It's no doubt my fault, but this letter makes me feel less inclined to help Dr Weizmann than I was before.'[39] On 13 October the matter was again considered by the Cabinet. The meeting was told that Weizmann had said he would prefer a definite refusal to a further postponement, and that although the Zionists were not now asking that the proposed Jewish units be stationed in Palestine 'this demand was certain to come later on'. The final decision of the Cabinet was 'against the adoption of a scheme for the recruitment of Jewish units'; some concession towards the Zionists' demands might be permitted by means of increased recruitment of Jews in Palestine; in that context, 'if practicable, it would be desirable that a few purely Jewish units should be formed, provided that this could be done without undue publicity'.[40]

The Zionists reacted with bitter indignation to what they regarded as a further betrayal by the British Government of its pledged word. Recalling that the Cabinet had decided in principle in favour of the scheme Weizmann wrote to Moyne that the Cabinet had now broken its 'promise'.[41] On 17 October Moyne defended the Government's decision in the presence of a deputation of pro-Zionist M.P.s. Moyne denied that the Jews were being 'snubbed or ignored'. He said there had never been any attempt by the authorities to deny 'full credit to the Jews for their services . . . There was nothing to prevent the Jews from getting all the publicity they wanted for themselves'. He added:

It was on military grounds and on account of the supply and shipping

[38] Weizmann's letter circulated to Cabinet, 14 Sept. 1941, PRO CAB 67/9 (W.P. (G.) (41) 95.)

[39] Moyne to Eden, 16 Sept. 1941, PRO FO 371/27128 (E 5160/60/31); H. M. Eyres minute, 18 Sept. 1941, PRO FO 371/27128 (E 5746/60/31); Eden minute, 16 Sept. 1941, PRO FO 371/27128 (E 5160/60/31).

[40] Cabinet conclusions, 13 Oct. 1941, PRO FO 371/27128/91.

[41] Weizmann to Moyne, 28 Oct. 1941, WA.

situation that the project had been abandoned. The formation proposed was not what the War Office required, and it was evident that, if there were difficulties when supplies were comparatively plentiful, they would be much greater now when this country was giving away almost more than we could afford to our Russian allies. Someone must go short.[42]

Clearly embarrassed by the reaction of Weizmann and of his supporters, Moyne undertook to consider a more modest suggestion for the formation of a Palestinian Jewish air squadron based in Britain. In a letter to Sir Archibald Sinclair, the Secretary of State for Air, on 24 October, Moyne inquired whether the suggestion was feasible. Sinclair, a friend of Weizmann, had long been a noted supporter of the Zionists. In his reply to Moyne he pointed out practical difficulties in the idea, and continued:

I should like the Government to change its policy towards the Jewish people. I should like them to welcome on a big scale the help which they are prepared to offer us, and to form a Jewish Army under the Jewish flag. That would hearten 16,000,000 Jews of World Jewry, rally the influential Jews in the United States, and stiffen the resistance to oppression of the unhappy Jews in Europe. If such a policy were to be embarked upon, I certainly think that in spite of the practical difficulties we in the Air Ministry and the Royal Air Force ought to play our part. I cannot, however, see much attraction in the proposal that we should fling to the Jews a Royal Air Force Squadron as a sop to keep them quiet.[43]

The Zionists, in spite of the apparently final nature of this rebuff, did not relent in their pressure on the Government on the Jewish Army issue.[44] The matter came to a head again in June 1942 when, after the fall of Tobruk, it appeared that a British withdrawal from Palestine might be imminent. Weizmann again appealed to Churchill to allow the *Yishuv* the 'elementary human right' of self-defence against a threat to their 'actual physical existence'.[45] The demand was supplemented

[42] Note of interview of Moyne with Captain V. A. Cazalet M.P., J. C. Wedgwood M.P., and Sir P. Harris M.P., 17 Oct. 1941, PRO AIR 19/177/12A.

[43] Moyne to Sinclair, 24 Oct. 1941, PRO AIR 19/177/13A; Sinclair to Moyne, 28 Oct. 1941, PRO AIR 19/177/16A.

[44] See e.g. Weizmann to Moyne 1 and 10 Dec. 1941, WA; Weizmann to Churchill, 9 Feb. 1942, ibid; Weizmann to Cranborne, 6 Mar. 1942, ibid.

[45] Weizmann to Churchill, 25 June 1942, WA.

vociferously by a clamorous agitation organized in the United States by the Revisionist Zionists whose 'Committee for a Jewish Army of Stateless and Palestinian Jews' took out full-page advertisements in major American newspapers, held mass demonstrations, and mobilized Congressional support. On 5 July Churchill yet again intervened in support of Weizmann's proposal. In a note to the Colonial Secretary, Cranborne, he wrote:

Pray let me have some proposals about this. The strength of opinion in the United States is very great, and we shall suffer in many ways there by indulging the British military authorities' and the Colonial Office officials' bias in favour of the Arabs and against the Jews. Now that these people are in direct danger, we should certainly give them a chance to defend themselves. Colonel Orde Wingate should not be put on one side, but be given a fair chance and proper authority. It may be necessary to make an example of some of these anti-Semite officers and others in high places. If three or four of them were recalled and dismissed, and the reason given, it would have a very salutary effect.[46]

On 7 July Weizmann secured another influential backer for the project. In a meeting with Roosevelt at the White House, the President told him: I always wanted to make a statement about the Jewish Army, which I think is a good thing.' Roosevelt added that he considered Wingate 'a wonderful fellow'.[47] The Jewish Army plan now had the support of the two most powerful men in the Anglo-American alliance. But again success was to elude the Zionists. The British authorities in the Middle East put up renewed opposition to the scheme. In consequence the Cabinet decided in August 1942 that, rather than accede to the Zionist demand for a Jewish division, a Palestinian Regiment would be formed, consisting of separate Jewish and Arab battalions, with at least 10,000 new recruits. There would also be some expansion of the Palestinian police and internal security forces.[48] Although the decision represented some concession to the Zionists' demands, it was received both in Britain and the U.S.A. as a rejection of the Jewish Army proposal. The *Daily*

[46] Churchill to Cranborne, 5 July 1942, PRO PREM 4/51/9/Part 2/938.

[47] Note by Weizmann on meeting, WA.

[48] Joint memorandum of Secretary of State for War and Secretary of State for Colonies to Cabinet, 1 Aug. 1942, PRO CAB 66/27/60; Cabinet Conclusions, 5 Aug. 1942, PRO CAB 65/27.

Telegraph commented that it was a 'wise decision to form a Palestine regiment representing the population of that country as a whole and not merely one section of it'. The *Chicago Daily News* headlined its report: 'British Reject Jews' Demand for Own Army'.[49] The Zionists welcomed the news as 'a step forward', but complained that it did not go nearly far enough.[50] As for Wingate, he was stated by the War Office to be 'not available' because of his involvement in long-range guerrilla warfare in Burma; Dill added privately that Wingate was unsuitable as 'his nerves were very distraught'.[51]

The Zionists continued with unflagging tenacity for the next two years their efforts to persuade the British Government to fulfil the original design. However, it was only in mid-1944, when the danger to the British position in the Middle East (and to the Jews of Palestine) had receded, that the force, in a truncated form, finally received the Government's authorization. In March 1944 Weizmann had sent to the War Office an appeal for the formation of 'a Jewish Fighting Force within the British Army to take part in the liberation of Europe'. Arguing that the 'irritating effect of the Jewish Force on Arab countries' could not possibly be invoked as an objection to such a force participating in the invasion of Europe, Weizmann stressed that

collective participation in the battle of Europe is a definite Jewish concern. Europe is now the graveyard of millions of massacred Jews. The remnants live in the shadow of death. The world outside has failed to save them. The least we can ask is that a force of free, fighting Jews be enabled to uphold the honour of their people, avenge its martyrs, and help to liberate the survivors.[52]

The opposition in Whitehall to a Jewish force had hardly diminished, and was given authoritative expression in a Cabinet memorandum by the War Secretary, Grigg.[53] At War Office insistence the size of the scheme was reduced from the proposed division to a brigade group. Once again it was only

[49] *Daily Telegraph*, 7 Aug. 1942; *Chicago Daily News*, 7 Aug. 1942.

[50] *New York Herald Tribune*, 11 Aug. 1942; *New York Times*, 10 Aug. 1942.

[51] C.I.G.S. (Brooke) to Dill (in Washington) 5 July 1942, PRO PREM 4/51/9/Part 2/939; Dill to C.I.G.S., 3 July 1942, PRO PREM 4/51/9/Part 2/942.

[52] Weizmann to Grigg, 28 Mar. 1944, WA.

[53] Grigg to Cabinet, 26 June 1944, PRO FO 371/40144 (E 3531/628/31); Foreign Office minutes, ibid.

repeated, energetic interventions by Churchill which prevented the proposal being obstructed. On 10 July Churchill
wrote to the Cabinet Secretary:

In your report you say it was decided that a Brigade Group would be
carefully examined. I certainly understood and hold very strongly
that a Brigade Group should be made. When the War Office say they
will carefully examine a thing, they mean they will do it in. The
matter must be set down for an early meeting of the War Cabinet only
this week, and the Secretary of State for War should be informed of
my objections.[54]

At Churchill's instruction a plan was finally presented by the
War Office, although Grigg continued to voice doubts as to the
military and political wisdom of the project.[55] These objections
were swept aside by the Prime Minister. In a minute to Grigg
he wrote:

I like the idea of the Jews trying to get at the murderers of their
fellow-countrymen in Central Europe, and I think it would give a
great deal of satisfaction in the United States ... Remember the
object of this is to give pleasure and an expression to rightful sentiment.[56]

In a message to Roosevelt, asking for his support for the
scheme, Churchill again emphasized his personal backing for
the idea:

This will give great satisfaction to the Jews when it is published, and
surely they of all other races have the right to strike at the Germans as
a recognisable body. They wish to have their own flag, which is the
Star of David on a white background with two light blue bars. I
cannot see why this should not be done. Indeed I think that the flying
of this flag at the head of a combat unit would be a message to go all
over the world. If the usual silly objections are raised I can overcome
them, but before going ahead I should like to know whether you have
any views upon it.[57]

The President's reply was favourable, and in the course of
August and September details of the scheme were finally

[54] Churchill to Bridges, 10 July 1944, PRO PREM 4/51/9/Part 2/843.

[55] Churchill to Grigg, 12 July 1944; Grigg to Churchill, 21 July 1944; Grigg to
Churchill, 6 Aug. 1944, PRO PREM 4/51/9/Part 2/810–840.

[56] Churchill to Grigg, 26 July 1944, PRO PREM 4/51/9/Part 2/824.

[57] Churchill to Roosevelt, 23 Aug. 1944, in Loewenheim, ed., *Roosevelt–Churchill
Correspondence*, p. 566.

approved.[58] On one point Churchill found it impossible to overcome official objections: he informed Weizmann that while the Brigade would be permitted to fly its flag in Italy, 'administrative difficulties' precluded the flag being flown in Egypt.[59] The Zionists were also disappointed in another respect: Wingate, whom they had hoped to see as commander of the force, had been killed in an air crash in Burma the previous spring. An English Jew, Brigadier E. F. Benjamin, was appointed commander instead. After the years of obstruction by the British authorities in the Middle East and by Whitehall departments, the creation of the Brigade represented a signal diplomatic triumph for the Zionists, and a considerable personal achievement by Weizmann (who had been much criticized by Ben Gurion and by the Revisionist Zionists for not pressing the scheme with sufficient vigour). American Zionists received the news with jubilation, and the British Embassy in Washington noted with relief that it was likely to lead to the diminution or disappearance of American Zionist attacks on the British Government.[60] But in Palestine there was some dark speculation among Zionist leaders that the scheme had now been approved only in order to remove Jewish troops from Palestine.[61] The general reaction in Britain to the announcement of the Brigade's formation was one of welcome.[62] But the long struggle for a Jewish army contained warning elements for the Zionists. Churchill's role in securing approval for the idea had been paramount: without his relentless prodding of the Colonial and War Offices the plan would have died an early bureaucratic death. The episode showed how dangerously dependent the Zionists were on the favour of the Prime Minister. When, as a result of the assassination of Lord Moyne in November 1944, even Churchill's support was placed in doubt, the real friendlessness of the Zionists in the British establishment was revealed.

The Jewish army had been seen by its advocates as having

[58] Roosevelt to Churchill, 28 Aug. 1944, ibid., p. 469; Cabinet minutes, 9 Aug. 1944, PRO CAB 65/43.   [59] Churchill to Weizmann, 28 Oct. 1944, WA.

[60] Memorandum on American reaction to the formation of the Jewish Brigade, forwarded to the Foreign Office by Lord Halifax, 20 Oct. 1944, PRO FO 371/40132 (E 6804/67/31).

[61] Bauer, *From Diplomacy to Resistance*, p. 349.

[62] *The Times* and *Manchester Guardian*, 20 Sept. 1944.

two immediate military roles: first, the defence of Palestine; secondly, participation in the war against the Nazi domination of Europe. In the event it was prevented from playing more than a minor role in either. Formed in Italy in October 1944, the Jewish Brigade went into action against the Germans in March 1945. The suggestion made at the beginning of the war thus finally bore fruit as the war neared its end. The formation of the brigade, although it gave heart to the small numbers of Jews who survived in previously occupied areas of Europe at the end of the war, could do nothing to counter the Nazi massacres of the Jews of Europe. As a conventional military formation it was impossible for it to take any action behind enemy lines. After the war members of the brigade played an active part in the organization of illegal immigration of Jewish survivors from Europe to Palestine. But by the time the brigade was formed the majority of the Jews of Nazi Europe had already been murdered. However, while the Jewish Brigade scheme was being considered in Whitehall in the spring and summer of 1944, another plan proposed by the Jewish Agency, which had as its aim the rendering of direct help to the Jews of Europe, was secretly being effected in co-operation with the British authorities. This was a scheme for the dispatch of trained Palestinian Jewish saboteurs by parachute behind enemy lines to make contact with surviving Jewish communities and, where possible, to try to stimulate resistance to the Nazis. Jews from Palestine had been trained by the British early in the war for such action behind enemy lines, and there had been secret collaboration between British security organs and the *Haganah* in several such missions. In 1940 Jewish agents had participated in secret activities in Roumania on behalf of the British Government—culminating in the embarrassing incident of the *Darien*.[63] Later in the war Jewish agents from Palestine operated in various parts of the Middle East and in the Balkans. Notwithstanding the Anglo-Zionist clashes over the White Paper and illegal immigration, these secret contacts provided a basis for undercover co-operation on which the Jewish Agency sought to build in early 1944 when it presented the British authorities with a plan for the fostering of Jewish resistance to the Nazis in south-east Europe.

[63] See p. 78.

The Zionist proposal was set out in two memoranda addressed not to the Government of Palestine but to the British political and military headquarters in the Middle East in Cairo. The first memorandum was drafted by Reuven Zaslani, who had been involved in earlier secret Anglo-Zionist contacts, and who was a popular figure among British officials. Zaslani's paper, entitled 'Proposals to Organise Jewish Communities in the Balkans for Resistance against Massacre by the Germans', stated that five million Jews had already been put to death by the Nazis. Zaslani argued that resistance, while it might not save many Jewish lives, might at least make the price of mass murder, in time, in men, and in equipment, much higher for the enemy:

The theory that quiescence and passivity would mitigate the terror has been entirely exploded. That annihilation wherever it could be applied has been complete, irrespective of whether there was resistance or not. Had resistance been offered, it could in no way have increased the disaster which has already reached a maximum degree. In those few cases where resistance has been offered, losses were inflicted on the enemy, and had this resistance been better organised and on a larger scale, it might even have saved certain Jewish communities, as well as causing considerable difficulty to the enemy.

Zaslani pointed out that matters were now coming to a head in south-eastern Europe: in that area Jewish populations which had so far survived might soon face direct German occupation and deportation to Poland where they would be killed. He therefore proposed

that steps should be taken to organise the Jewish population of the Balkans and prepare them for resistance without delay. The Jews in the Balkans alone, without moral encouragement and expert direction from outside, will not be able to achieve the necessary organisation, and it is suggested that a number of picked men from Palestine with previous knowledge and experience of conditions in the Balkan countries should be introduced there for the purpose of setting up that organisation. These men should be in communication [with] and under the direction of British Headquarters and their work to be co-ordinated with the general strategy of the war.[64]

A further memorandum, addressed by Shertok to the British

[64] R. Zaslani to Brigadier I. Clayton, 25 Jan. 1944, PRO FO 921/152.

Minister Resident in the Middle East, gave further details of the proposed scheme. Shertok urged that four countries should be included in the plan: Bulgaria, Roumania, Hungary, and Slovakia. Two men should be sent immediately into each country, one to act as chief organizer, the other to be his assistant and wireless operator. These would establish contact with Jewish youth organizations and organize small cells of potential resisters. Meanwhile cadres of instructors should be selected for each country, and at a given signal these would be sent to train the recruits. Later 'larger groups, say at least fifty for each country' would be sent 'to bring in equipment and to provide a stiffening as well as a commanding personnel for the guerillas'. Shertok added that all these men would be selected from Palestinians already serving in the army as well as from the civilian population. 'A lead from Palestine', he argued, was essential to the success of the plan:

That lead will not play its full part if it takes the form merely of a signal sent from outside . . . The Palestinian Jewish community . . . represents an accumulator of fighting energy which has only to a very limited extent been utilised in the present war. Nowhere outside Nazi-dominated Europe have young Jews smarted more bitterly under the humiliation of their brethren being slaughtered like sheep than they have done in Palestine. Nowhere has their desire for revenge been more intense. The formation of the Jewish guerrillas and their command in battle must, therefore, it is submitted, be entrusted to Palestinians. The whole organisation in both the preparatory and the operational stages would be under British military control.[65]

The scheme received a mixed response from the British authorities. Sir William Croft, Chief Civil Assistant to the Minister of State, minuted on Zaslani's memorandum: 'I am afraid the demands upon facilities for sorties are so heavy that the idea of enabling the Jews to protect themselves and save themselves from extermination will not cut much ice. The proposal will have to stand on its merits from the operational point of view.'[66] The project was submitted for consideration to the military authorities, but 'Mr Shertok's disingenuous offer' met with an unfavourable response:

[65] Shertok to Minister Resident, Cairo, 7 Feb. 1944, ibid.
[66] Minute dated 27 Jan. 1944, ibid.

The military policy of GHQ ME is to organise and support resistance groups in which all parties, colours and creeds can join. We are already giving the maximum support to resistance groups in various parts of the Balkans. Our resources are limited and we could not in present circumstances undertake the organisation and support of special resistance groups restricted to a particular type of personnel, even if this were desirable. This view point fits in no doubt with the political unsuitability of Mr Shertok's proposals.[67]

A negative reaction to the scheme was also expressed by the High Commissioner in Jerusalem, Sir Harold MacMichael, to whom it had been referred for advice. MacMichael's response reflected his concern as to the possible post-war consequences of any Jewish military participation in the war:

I cannot regard Palestinian inspiration and leadership as essential to such operations. Desperation, as it has done elsewhere, is likely to provide the necessary determination and drive. From our point of view any avoidable extension of further opportunities to Palestine Jews for training in and organisation of guerilla warfare is most strongly to be deprecated from the aspect of the future internal security of this country. The training previously given them for post-occupational purposes at the time when this part of the world was threatened by the enemy is likely to prove embarrassing enough as it is.[68]

However, the Jewish Agency's proposal encountered some support among British officials in Cairo. J. S. Bennett considered it 'a reasonable proposal which deserves serious study', and added:

The German occupation of Hungary makes it particularly topical. The point is, briefly, will it be of any assistance to the war effort if the Jewish communities in the Balkans go down fighting—killing some Germans in the process—rather than submitting to liquidation without a struggle? If so, are we prepared to give any facilities to enable this to come about? If the answer to both questions is 'no', then we must say so to the Jewish Agency; but we shall need to be in a position to give a reasoned answer on military grounds.[69]

The plan had another powerful advocate in Brigadier I. N. Clayton, who wrote a forceful minute in its defence following a

[67] H. G. Curran to Sir W. Croft, 28 Feb. 1944, ibid.
[68] MacMichael to Croft, 8 Mar. 1944, ibid.
[69] J. S. Bennett minute, 24 Mar. 1944, ibid.

conversation about it with Zaslani in early April. Zaslani had pointed out that the 'very set of circumstances which were envisaged in his note and Mr Shertok's have now come about. Hungary and Rumania have been occupied by the Germans who have already put out on the radio that they propose eliminating a million Jews in Hungary'. Any action would therefore have to be taken immediately if it were to be effective. Clayton minuted that he agreed with Bennett's view, and did 'not see any real force in Jerusalem's objections':

It is not proposed to give these Jews training in guerilla organisation (in any case they know a lot about it already), but to train them as parachutists and possibly in W/T [wireless-telegraphy]. This appears to present no great danger as the Jews are not likely to be able to make parachute descents in Palestine. To quote Zaslani again, we ought to be glad to get two or three score of tough Jews out of Palestine.[70]

However, these arguments did not convince the military authorities who insisted that their objections stood and that there was 'no necessity to justify in detail the rejection of Mr Shertok's proposals'.[71] The matter was referred to the Minister Resident, who approved the sending of a negative answer. On 1 May, therefore, Shertok was informed that 'any attempt to organise groups separate and distinct from the present unified and centrally controlled organisation could only result in a dispersion of effort and would defeat its purpose'. Both the Commander-in-Chief and the Minister Resident shared 'an earnest desire to help the persecuted Jews and to make use of their capacity for resistance' but Shertok's scheme was not judged likely to achieve this object nor to be 'to the advantage of our common war effort'.[72]

As in the case of the Jewish army the Zionists refused to accept a negative answer as final. Having failed to secure the approval for the plan of the authorities in Cairo, they pursued what was for them the common tactic of transferring their pressure to a different department. In July Zaslani visited Italy and succeeded in convincing the Minister Resident in Bari, Harold Macmillan, of the value of his scheme at least so far as it applied to Hungary. The British security authorities were per-

[70] Clayton minute, 6 Apr. 1944, ibid.
[71] H. G. Curran minute, 14 Apr. 1944, ibid.
[72] Croft to Shertok, 1 May 1944, ibid.

suaded that it was 'an attractive offer', and an intelligence appreciation stated:

There is no doubt that if successful contacts can be made inside Hungary, it will be of great value to us. At the moment, Intelligence about Hungary is almost entirely lacking and no activities are being carried out against the enemy. Should the enemy withdraw to the Danube-Sava line, it will be of great assistance to have contacts inside the country not only for intelligence purposes but also to stir up resistance against the enemy. Although there may be objections on political and religious grounds to our using the Jewish Agency for our own purposes, there may be no objections to the selection of a few of these men, preferably from those who are already serving in North Africa and Italy.[73]

Macmillan supported the recommendation of the security organs that, in the first instance, ten Hungarian-Jewish volunteers, who had already received intelligence training, should be sent to Hungary. Support was also given to the scheme by the Prime Minister's personal intelligence adviser, Major Desmond Morton.[74] Lord Moyne now reconsidered his view and gave the proposal guarded approval. He noted that, even from the Palestine viewpoint, the idea contained certain potential advantages for British policy:

The scheme would remove from Palestine a number of active and resourceful Jews, and their training need not take place in Palestine. The chances of many of them returning in the future to give trouble in Palestine seem slight ... Authorities in Bari appear to welcome scheme and this is known to Jewish Agency. To turn it down now on purely Palestine political and security grounds would lay us open to considerable criticism both from Jews and from humanitarian opinion, and I recommend despite Palestine's objections that the scheme be given consideration.[75]

In a later message to the Foreign Office, however, Moyne emphasised that he still agreed with the High Commissioner that 'the employment of any organised group with close affiliation to the Jewish Agency would be undesirable and potentially

[73] 'Use of Palestinian Jews for SOE Work in Hungary', Note by G – 3, 24 July 1944, ibid.

[74] Minister Resident, Bari, to Minister Resident, Cairo, 21 July 1944, ibid.; Minister Resident, Caserta, to Minister Resident, Cairo, 1 Aug. 1944, ibid.; Shertok to J. M. Martin, 31 July 1944, PRO PREM 4/52/5/Part I.

[75] Moyne to Foreign Office, 25 July 1944, ibid.

dangerous'. He urged that the plan be limited to the recruitment of a 'few individual Jews from Palestine and elsewhere'.[76] Notwithstanding Moyne's reservations, the Chiefs of Staff authorized the recruitment of ten Hungarian-speaking Jews, as recommended by Macmillan. But it was stressed that 'they must be used as individuals under S[pecial] O[perations] E[xecutive] Command, and not in groups under Palestinian Jewish direction'. No authorization was given for the recruitment of the larger numbers envisaged by the Jewish Agency plan.[77]

Limited approval was thus given to the proposal in August 1944 (seven months after it had originally been put to the British authorities). Meanwhile, a handful of Jewish agents had already been infiltrated into Europe by the British in the spring of 1944. In March 1944 four Palestinian Jewish parachutists were dropped into Yugoslavia. Among them was a Hungarian-born woman, Hannah Szenes aged twenty-three. Szenes crossed the border into Hungary in June 1944, but was captured almost immediately by the Hungarian police. Other agents who followed Szenes into Hungary were also captured. When a report on their seizure arrived in Berlin it was sent direct to Hitler who inscribed on the document the words 'to be shot'.[78] Szenes was executed in Budapest on 7 November. A similar fate awaited most of the other parachutists who were dropped into Europe. Some of those dropped into Bulgaria, Roumania, and Slovakia were, however, able to accomplish something. Others, such as Enzo Sereni, dropped in error directly on to the German lines in northern Italy, were immediately captured and killed. The far-reaching aims of the Zionists for stimulating active resistance by European Jews were not fulfilled, although some of the parachutists were able to contact Jewish communities and to organize some partisan activity and illegal immigration to Palestine from Roumania and Bulgaria. But the number of agents dispatched was too minute to have any real military effect; the extension of the scheme to larger numbers of agents was never authorized by the British

[76] Moyne to Foreign Office, 2 Aug. 1944, ibid.

[77] Foreign Office to Moyne, 16 Aug. 1944, ibid.

[78] Veesenmayer (Budapest) to Ritter (Berlin), transmitting SS report, 8 July 1944, in Braham, *Destruction of Hungarian Jewry*, p. 619; Altenburg (Berlin) to Veesenmayer, 12 July 1944, quoting Hitler's order, ibid., p. 445.

authorities. The parachutists episode marked the only occasion during the war when the British Government approved the rendering of direct assistance to Jewish resistance against the Nazis in Europe. As a symbolic legend it was to make an important contribution to the historical myth of Zionism, but as an effective contribution to the salvation of the Jews of Europe it was a tragic failure.[79]

During the last three years of the war a more indirect, but apparently more practicable form of aid to Jewish resistance in Europe was urged on the British Government by Jewish organizations and others: it was suggested that propaganda warfare, by means of broadcasts and leaflets, might have some effect in warning Jews about Nazi atrocities, and thereby stimulating resistance or flight. It was also argued that such propaganda might induce the non-Jewish populations to offer shelter to Jews, and that threats of retribution against war criminals might have some effect on the persecutors. But, although the British Government took some limited steps to accede to such requests, official opinion remained generally sceptical as to the effectiveness or desirability of such action. There were a number of reasons for this. In the first place, the general policy pursued by the BBC and the Political Warfare Executive (which directed propaganda to enemy territory) was one of sobriety and restraint, particularly in transmissions to Germany, 'Exaggeration, excitement, threats and extravagance in all forms were avoided', stated an official spokesman.[80] The British propaganda organs were 'rather averse to "Greuel-propaganda"' (as one Foreign Office official, borrowing from the vocabulary of Dr Goebbels, put it in 1940).[81] This position was modified after the United Nations Declaration of December 1942, but the reluctance to indulge in atrocity propaganda continued until the end of the war. For example, in July 1943, when the Foreign Office was engaged in discussions regarding a further Allied declaration on German atrocities in Poland, officials agreed that evidence of the use of gas chambers for mass murder was untrustworthy and inconclusive. The

[79] *Hannah Senesh: Her Life and Diary*, London 1971; Bauer, *From Diplomacy to Resistance*, pp. 274–82.

[80] Asa Briggs, *The History of Broadcasting in the United Kingdom vol. III The War of Words*, London 1970, p. 429.

[81] Minute by F. K. Roberts, 12 Feb. 1940, PRO FO 371/24422/131 (C 1977/1977/18).

Chairman of the Joint Intelligence Committee, V. Cavendish-Bentinck, commented: 'The Poles, and to a far greater extent the Jews, tend to exaggerate German atrocities in order to stoke us up.'[82] In consequence, it was agreed, at the British Government's suggestion, to delete the reference to gas chambers from the declaration, which was signed by Stalin, Roosevelt, and Churchill, and issued on 1 November 1943.[83]

Such hesitations were not merely the product of squeamishness or incredulity. There was also serious doubt about the effects of such propaganda. The general feeling in the Foreign Office was that broadcast threats were unlikely to deter the Germans.[84] Indeed, it was felt that BBC news reports on the deportations of Jews 'would not materially aid the refugees' and that 'the effect might be to increase measures of persecution'.[85] In March 1944 when the United States Government proposed yet another declaration, the British response was far from enthusiastic:

Our own view is that [the] hope that [the] Allied declaration of December 1942 would have [a] restraining influence on Germans has not been realised. Subsequent German persecution of Jews was intensified, and we have been inclined to think that by seeing us attach such intense public importance to the Jewish question, [the] Germans may have felt that they could hit Allied nations by tormenting or killing large numbers of Allied Jewish nationals. Whether this reading of German psychology is correct or not, we think repeated warnings tend to debase the currency and that fanaticism in the Nazi ranks will need breaking down a good deal by other means before repeated solemn declarations can have much deterrent effect.[86]

Under pressure from Jewish bodies, and from the Americans, the Government gave publicity to several further official denunciations of German war crimes, but Eden repeatedly

[82] Minutes by V. Cavendish-Bentinck and R. Allen, July 1943, PRO FO 371/34551 (C 9705/34/G).

[83] Foreign Office to British Embassy, Washington, 27 Aug. 1943, PRO FO 898/225/367; Secretary of State (Washington) to U.S. Ambassador in U.S.S.R., 30 Aug. 1943, *FRUS 1943* vol. I, p. 416.

[84] See e.g. D. S. Laskey minute, 26 Oct. 1943, PRO FO 371/37286 (R 10575/4200/22).

[85] D. Hall (Foreign Office) to A. L. Easterman (World Jewish Congress), 18 Jan. 1944, WJCL.

[86] Foreign Office to British Embassy, Washington, 11 Mar. 1944, PRO FO 371/42728 (W 3420/16/48).

expressed the fear that (as he put it in a letter to Lord Melchett in March 1944) such pronouncements 'instead of scaring the Germans and making them refrain from further bestialities . . . may simply "harden their hearts"'.[87] Churchill, however, appears to have been a little less pessimistic. In October 1943 he wrote that a declaration would 'strike a chill to the evil heart'. When a further declaration was proposed in October 1944, he wrote in a minute to Eden: 'Surely publicity given about this beforehand might have a chance of saving the multitudes concerned.'[88]

The reluctance to single out Jews which had marked Foreign Office thinking about the December 1942 declaration, affected propaganda policy throughout the war. The '"air for the Jew String"', as one Foreign Office humorist described it, was not regarded as a particularly efficacious propaganda theme.[89] A report to Lord Beaverbrook in 1940 warned that BBC broadcasts to Germany were 'unconsciously aiding Goebbels' propaganda' because 'most of the announcers appear to be German Jews,' thereby providing 'proof that Britain is "run" by Jews'.[90] A Ministry of Information memorandum in 1941 recorded general agreement on the need 'to eliminate as much as possible the Hungarian Jewish intellectual voice and content from our Hungarian broadcasts'.[91] A Special Operations Executive report to the Political Warfare Executive in January 1943 stated that the reaction to the broadcasts following the United Nations Declaration did not appear to have been uniformly favourable:

In conversation with two young Frenchmen who have just arrived in this country after doing good work for us in France, I learn that the continued reference in BBC broadcasts to the persecution of the Jews tends to be resented by the French, who themselves have so many relatives imprisoned in German prison camps or concentration camps.[92]

[87] Eden to Melchett, 11 Mar. 1944, WJCL.

[88] Churchill to Eden, 25 Oct. 1943, PRO PREM 4/100/9; Churchill to Eden, 1 Oct. 1944, PRO FO 371/39454 (C 13824/131/55).

[89] A. Walker minute, 4 Apr. 1944, PRO FO 371/42724/3.

[90] Extract from report to Lord Beaverbrook, 18 Jan. 1940, PRO FO 371/24387 (C 1424/6/18).

[91] M.O.I. memorandum on meeting on 29 May 1941, PRO FO 371/26624/33.

[92] Storrs (S.O.E.) to Gielgud (P.W.E.), 2 Jan. 1943, PRO FO 898/26.

Another obstacle to such propaganda which occasionally arose derived from difficulties with Britain's allies, or anticipated complications for British foreign policy. For example, in 1943 the Government rejected a suggestion by the World Jewish Congress that the Latvian Minister in London should broadcast to the Latvian people warning them not to collaborate with the Nazis in the persecution of the Jews. The Foreign Office felt it inadvisable to lend support to any such scheme without the approval of the U.S.S.R. (which had annexed Latvia in 1940).[93] The Russians (who frequently refused to co-operate with Britain and the U.S.A. in matters relating to war crimes) were not prepared to comply with a request in 1944 that Moscow Radio join the B.B.C. and American radio stations in broadcasting a reaffirmation of allied warnings of retribution for war crimes.[94] Foreign policy considerations of a different kind led the Foreign Office to reject a suggestion in the summer of 1944 that Lord Rothermere should make a broadcast to Hungary in the hope of alleviating the persecutions of the Hungarian Jews at that time. Rothermere's father had once been offered the Hungarian throne, and his name was therefore thought to count for something in the country.[95] But the Political Warfare Executive registered strong objections to the proposed broadcast, because the first Lord Rothermere had been strongly identified with Hungarian revisionist claims to the territory of her neighbours after the Treaty of Trianon in 1920, and it was feared that a broadcast by his son 'under official auspices could hardly fail to suggest both to the Hungarians and to the peoples who would be adversely affected by a revision of frontiers to Hungarian advantage that H.M.G. regard revision with favour'.[96]

A final, but probably fundamental, reason for British reluc-

[93] A. L. Easterman (W.J.C.) to Foreign Office, 11 Jan. 1943, PRO FO 371/34361 (C 524/18/62); minutes by D. Allen, 14 Jan., and G. M. Wilson, 15 Jan. 1943, ibid; F. K. Roberts (Foreign Office) to Easterman, 22 Jan. 1943, WJCL.

[94] State Dept., Washington, to A. Harriman (Moscow), 17 Apr. 1944, *FRUS 1944* vol. I, p. 1033 (and note on p. 1037); State Dept. to Harriman, 10 June 1944, ibid., p. 1064.

[95] The 'offer' was not an official one, and Rothermere probably exaggerates its significance in his own account (Viscount Rothermere, *My Campaign for Hungary*, London 1939, chap. 8: 'Myself and the King Question'); but there is no doubt of the popularity in Hungary of both first and second viscounts.

[96] Minute by P. W. S. Y. Scarlett (P.W.E.) 12 July 1944, PRO FO 371/42810/5.

tance to acquiesce in requests for a massive propaganda campaign on behalf of the Jews of Europe was that, in the total context of allied psychological warfare, the fate of the Jews was regarded as having a low priority. In this as in other spheres, everything had to give way before the central objective of victory. Richard Law, for example, explained to David Robertson M.P. in March 1943 that 'as a matter of policy we cannot afford to give this question such prominence that it would overshadow or exclude other themes which it is important for our propaganda to put across at the present stage of the war'.[97] When Sir Clifford Heathcote-Smith, in 1944, suggested a whirlwind propaganda campaign to save Jewish lives in the final stages of the war,[98] Sir Robert Bruce Lockhart, Director of the Political Warfare Executive, commented:

P.W.E. has always recognized the importance of doing everything possible through the media at its disposal to protect from maltreatment the many thousands of refugees and internees in German hands, and in the course of its activities over a period of several years has covered a fairly exhaustive range of propaganda themes bearing directly or indirectly on this topic, including, of course, the widest possible distribution of all official warnings regarding the punishment of those found guilty of crimes and atrocities against these unfortunate people . . . Experience has shown that certain types of declarations are not only without beneficial effect, but sometimes result in increased maltreatment . . . As regards his project for a whirlwind campaign of leaflets and radio concentrated on this particular object, it should be realised that paper, planes, and broadcasting hours are limited, and that our other commitments are heavy.[99]

This was the view that generally prevailed. The result was that deputations who went to the Foreign Office to plead for such action usually left unsatisfied. Harold Nicolson, who participated in one such deputation to the Foreign Secretary in January 1944, described in his diary how he had left Eden 'thinking how reasonable, how agreeable, and how helpful he has been, and then [one] discovers that in fact he has promised nothing at all'.[100]

[97] Law to Robertson, 22 Mar. 1943, PRO FO 371/34365 (C 2957/31/62).
[98] See p. 219.
[99] Minute dated 1 Dec. 1944, PRO FO 371/42897/25 (WR 1732/1554/48).
[100] Harold Nicolson, *Diaries and Letters 1939–1945*, ed. Nigel Nicolson, London 1967, p. 344.

In spite of these difficulties, some propaganda was directed to occupied Europe with the object of assisting the Jews. In the summer of 1942 General Sikorski broadcast to Poland condemning the massacres of Polish Jews. Szmul Zygielbojm, representative of the Jewish Socialist Bund on the Polish National Council, made a broadcast in Yiddish (the first in the history of the BBC). Cardinal Hinsley, Archbishop of Westminster, broadcast a speech directed specifically at Catholics about the persecution of Jews. The Dutch Prime Minister, Professor Gerbrandy, broadcast a denunciation of the deportations of Dutch Jews. A broadcast to Belgium on 29 December 1942 (following the Allied declaration of 17 December) appealed to the general population to offer shelter to Belgian Jews.[101] The Czechoslovak Foreign Minister, Jan Masaryk, made an impassioned speech on the Czechoslovak programme of the BBC in which he urged his countrymen to 'do everything in their power to make easier the life of their Jewish fellow-citizens'. Masaryk declared:

It seems that millions of Jews will be slaughtered. You know that I have always condemned anti-Semitism. But today any sign of anti-Semitism, when this small, minute, freezing, dying, ill-treated minority is handed over to the mercies of the German anti-Christs, in these times even a sign of anti-Semitism is a proof of shameful and disgusting cowardice . . . I hate cruel cowardice, and I am horrified if I think that the people which gave birth to my father helps these bestialities, even if in an insignificant fashion.[102]

In October 1943 the BBC broadcast sixteen times a warning to Germany and occupied Europe in eleven languages, informing Jews that compulsory registration as Jews was generally the first step to deportation, urging non-Jewish populations to shelter Jewish refugees, and declaring that the German people should 'realise [that] these atrocities committed in their name merely increase [the] horror and hatred which Germany brings upon herself by tolerating such barbarism'.[103] Several broad-

[101] *The Times*, 10 June 1942; *Jewish Chronicle*, 10 July 1942; Netherlands Foreign Office to World Jewish Congress, London, 27 Jan. 1943, enclosing text of Gerbrandy broadcast on 24 July 1942, WJCL; *Bulletin documentaire* no. 101, of the Office Belge d'Information et de Documentation, 15 Jan. 1943, WJCL.

[102] Transcript of Masaryk broadcast, 9 Dec. 1942, WJCL.

[103] Quoted in A. L. Kubowitzki (World Jewish Congress, New York) to Greek

casts to Hungary in the spring and summer of 1944 sought to mitigate the lot of Hungarian Jews threatened with deportation, by warning the Hungarian Government 'that they and those who carry out their orders will be treated as war criminals if they indulge in political persecution or in atrocities on the German model'. The Hungarian people were called upon to emulate the example set by the Danes, who had offered succour to their Jewish fellow-citizens and enabled them to escape from the country. The Archbishop of Canterbury delivered an address to Hungarian Christians begging them to do their utmost 'even taking great personal risks in order to save some [Jews] if you can'.[104]

A further propaganda weapon which was considered by the British authorities was the publication of lists of known war criminals who would be threatened with retribution after the war. The idea was considered to have certain disadvantages: it might simply encourage those not on the lists to believe themselves immune, while doing little to deter those named (since the latter might reason that they had nothing more to lose). The security authorities encountered difficulties in drawing up lists of war criminals. As one of those responsible pointed out:

Atrocities are usually not committed with press reporters in attendance, and, even if on rare occasions somebody has seen something happening and lives to tell the tale, he has not been given the names of individual torturers . . . Result: if black lists are kept at all—they must be kept on the basis of a different conception! As we know who is being used for committing atrocities in general, e.g. certain groups of officials and certain SS units etc., we might (and have done so in propaganda) speak of a collective responsibility of all people coming under these known headings. In practice one might say: 'Every SS-man is guilty—unless *he* gives proof that he is not.'[105]

Eden at first opposed the preparation of lists of criminals, declaring himself 'far from happy about all this War Criminals business' and 'most anxious not to get into the position of

Consul General, New York, 10 Nov. 1943, WJCNY, Drawer 177A, File 'W.J.C. British Section, Misc. Corresp. 1944 I – X'.
[104] P.W.E. Special Directive on the German Occupation of Hungary, 24 Mar. 1944, PRO FO 898/218; transcripts of broadcasts to Hungary by G[eorge] B[uday], 14 and 15 May 1944, PRO FO 898/58; sim., 9 and 23 July 1944, PRO FO 898/59; text of Archbishop of Canterbury's appeal, 8 July 1944, WJCL.
[105] G. S. W[agner] to A. D. Wilson, 26 Sept. 1942, PRO FO 898/25.

breathing fire and slaughter against War Criminals and promising condign punishment, and a year or two hence have to find
pretexts for doing nothing'.[106] In spite of these doubts some
names were used in propaganda to Europe. For instance, a
P.W.E. propaganda leaflet, directed at German troops, and
entitled *Soldaten-Nachrichten*, carried a heading 'Das sind
Kriegsverbrecher' ('These are war criminals') over a list of
Germans 'who are responsible for atrocities in Poland and who
will be punished'.[107] In October 1944 the BBC broadcast to
Germany a list of names of those known to be responsible for
the murders of prisoners at Auschwitz; another broadcast in
Polish also included the list (which had been supplied by the
Polish underground forces to the Polish Government-in-Exile
in London).[108]

The total quantity of British wartime propaganda to Europe
concerning the Jewish question was small: with the exception of
the month immediately following the United Nations Declaration of December 1942, there was never anything in the nature
of a concerted campaign on the subject. The effect of the limited
number of broadcasts and leaflets which were disseminated is
very difficult to judge. It is possible that the vigorous broadcast
appeals (coupled with diplomatic protests) in 1944 concerning
the deportation of the Jews of Hungary may have helped to save
some lives there.[109] Elsewhere the propaganda may have stiffened the resolve of those among the occupied populations who
offered shelter to Jews. It does not appear that the determination of the perpetrators of war crimes was seriously affected by
threats of retribution—except perhaps in the final stages of the
European war when some leading Nazis, including Himmler,
were anxious to ingratiate themselves with the victors.[110] Probably the only real value of such propaganda was in its effect on
the Nazis' victims, in offering them the knowledge that their
sufferings were known to those outside and that their fate was a
matter of concern to others. If it could not give them any
realistic basis for hope, it could at least relieve their loneliness.

[106] Eden minute, 9 Oct. 1943, PRO PREM 4/100/9; see also diary of Oliver Harvey,
BL 56398 (entry dated 7 Oct. 1941).
[107] Leaflet dated, 26 Nov. 1943, PRO FO 898/122.
[108] PRO FO 371/39454 (C 14352/131/55 & C 14402/131/55) *passim*.
[109] See p. 262.
[110] See p. 341.

Emmanuel Ringelblum, the chronicler of the Warsaw Ghetto, recorded the reaction of the Jews of Warsaw to BBC broadcasts in the summer of 1942 on the mass murder of the Jews in Poland:

Friday, June 26, has been a great day . . . This morning the English radio broadcast about the fate of Polish Jewry. They told about everything we know so well: about Slonim and Vilna, Lemberg and Chelmno, and so forth. For long months we had been suffering because the world was deaf and dumb to our unparallelled tragedy . . . But now it seems that all our interventions have finally achieved their purpose . . . Today there was a broadcast summarising the situation: 700,000 the number of Jews killed in Poland, was mentioned. At the same time, the broadcast vowed revenge, a final accounting for all these deeds of violence.

In a later note Ringelblum added:

The last few days, the Jewish populace has been agitated by the broadcast from London. The news that the world has finally been deeply stirred by the account of the massacres taking place in Poland has shaken us all to the very depths. For long, long months, we tormented ourselves in the midst of our suffering with the questions: Does the world know about our suffering? And if it knows, why is it silent? . . . And then the speeches delivered by the Archbishop of Canterbury, by the Rev. Dr Hertz [Chief Rabbi of Britain], and by the deputy Zygielbojm—all this news excited Jewish public opinion in Warsaw. There was joy, mingled with fear . . .[111]

But the relief of solidarity was soon transformed into bitter disillusion and accusations of betrayal, when it became plain to the survivors in the Warsaw ghetto in the winter of 1942–3 that the encouragement held out by such broadcasts was as insubstantial as the ether through which they were transmitted. When the remnants of the ghetto rose in revolt in April 1943 their deperate pleas to the Polish underground movement and to the allies for arms and supplies went largely unheeded. On 26 April 1943, eight days after the outbreak of the revolt (while the Bermuda Conference was still deliberating), the commander of the Jewish Fighting Organisation in Warsaw, Mordechai Anielewicz, wrote: 'Our last days draw near, but so long as we hold a weapon in hand we will fight and resist . . . Send aid to those to be delivered at the last moment from enemy hands so

[111] Sloan ed., *Ringelblum Journal*, pp. 295–7.

that they may keep up the struggle.'[112] Anielewicz and most of his supporters were killed on 8 May, but sporadic resistance continued for some time. Two of the last messages from Warsaw Jews were sent by representatives of the Jewish National Council and of the Bund to the two Jewish deputies to the Polish National Council in London, Zygielbojm and Schwarzbart, on 28 April and 21 May. The first stated:

The ghetto is ablaze; clouds of smoke envelop the city . . . The tragic epilogue [is] now being played out. Let the heroic struggle, without precedent in history, of the doomed sons of the ghetto at last arouse the world to deeds equal to the gravity of the hour.[113]

The second message stated: 'The world of freedom and justice is silent and does nothing.'[114] By this time nearly all the Jews in the ghetto had been killed or deported. However, as late as November 1943 a message from members of the Bund in Warsaw was smuggled out to the Bund Central Committee in New York. It reported that the last remnants of Polish Jewry were being wiped out. Declaring that 'responsibility to posterity for murder of the innocent also falls upon the democracies', the message ended with the words: 'Why don't you maintain contact with us?'[115]

On 12 May 1943 the Bundist deputy to the Polish National Council, Szmul Zygielbojm, committed suicide in London. In a note written shortly before his death, Zygielbojm (whose wife and children had been shot near Warsaw the previous autumn) expressed bitter resentment of what he saw as the indifference of the allied governments to the Jewish tragedy in Poland:

The responsibility for this crime—the assassination of the Jewish population in Poland—rests above all on the murderers themselves, but falls indirectly upon the whole human race, on the Allies and their governments, who so far have taken no firm steps to put a stop to these crimes . . . My companions of the Warsaw Ghetto fell in a last heroic battle with their weapons in their hands. I did not have the honour to die with them, but I belong to them and to their common grave. Let

[112] Letter dated 26 Apr. quoted in Ber Mark, *Uprising in the Warsaw Ghetto*, New York 1975, pp. 53–4.
[113] Text of message (in translation) in Mark, *Uprising*, pp. 154–5, and in PRO FO 371/34550 (C 5913/34/55).
[114] Text in Mark, *Uprising*, pp. 160–1.
[115] Text ibid., p. 185.

my death be an energetic cry of protest against the indifference of the world which witnesses the extermination of the Jewish people without taking any steps to prevent it.[116]

But although Zygielbojm's death was widely reported in the press, the motive behind it received little notice.[117] The ghetto rising was sympathetically reported in both the British and American press, and the BBC in its 'London Calling Europe' transmission on 25 May broadcast an account of the last days of the struggle which, said the broadcast, would 'go down to history as one of the most tragic and yet one of the most heroic chapters of the war'.[118] But, in the spring of 1943, there was little beyond words of comfort that the Allies could offer Jewish resistance in eastern Europe. Communications with Poland from the west were extremely limited until the start of regular supply flights to Polish underground forces from the airfield at Brindisi in the spring of 1944. Nor did the Polish underground forces outside the ghetto (strongly impregnated with anti-Semitic feeling) offer much help from the resources at their disposal. In the spring of 1943 the Polish Home Army had 600 heavy machine-guns at their disposal; none were supplied to the Jewish Fighting Organisation in the ghetto. Of the Home Army's 1,000 light machine-guns, one was supplied to the Jews; of 25,000 rifles, the Jews were given ten; of 6,000 pistols, the Jews received ninety; out of 30,000 hand grenades the Ghetto was assigned five hundred.[119] As for the Soviet Union it offered only moral support to the Jewish resistance. As a result, the Warsaw Ghetto revolt and later attempts at Jewish resistance elsewhere in eastern Europe were lonely and hopeless gestures of moral defiance.

A further suggestion for Allied aid to the Jews which was pressed on the British by the Polish Government was that for

[116] Quoted in Alex Grobman, 'The Warsaw Ghetto Uprising in the American Jewish Press', *The Wiener Library Bulletin*, 1976, vol. XXIX, new series nos. 37/38, pp. 53–61.

[117] See Sharf, *The British Press*, pp. 113–14.

[118] Grobman, 'Warsaw Ghetto'; Sharf, *The British Press*, pp. 111–14; *Jewish Chronicle*, 28 May 1943.

[119] These figures are all drawn from Polish Home Army sources and may over-state the amount of aid given to the resistance in the ghetto: see S. Krakowski, 'The Slaughter of Polish Jewry—A Polish "Reassessment"', *The Wiener Library Bulletin*, 1972/3, vol. XXVI, nos. 3/4, new series nos. 28/9, pp. 13–30; and note by J. Kermish and S. Krakowski, in Emmanuel Ringelblum, *Polish-Jewish Relations During the Second World War*, Jerusalem 1974, pp. 172–3.

retributive bombing of Germany. In a memorandum to Churchill in June 1942, General Sikorski demanded that in addition to the confiscation of German property and 'drastic measures' against German citizens in allied countries, the allies should undertake the 'bombing on a large scale of non-military objectives in Germany . . . in retaliation for German savagery'. Such action, Sikorski maintained, 'would undoubtedly restrain the Germans from pursuing their present policy of terrorism'.[120] Although the bombardment of German cities by R.A.F. Bomber Command was being conducted on a vast scale in the summer of 1942, the idea of announcing that such air raids were reprisals for German atrocities was rejected by the British Government.[121] This decision was taken in spite of a memorandum, prepared on Churchill's instructions by the Commander-in-Chief of Bomber Command, Air Marshal Harris, which concluded that 'Operation "Retribution"' (the complete elimination of a small town from the air) was practicable.[122]

The possibility of reprisal bombing was seriously considered again by the British Government in January 1943, when, in the aftermath of the United Nations declaration of 17 December 1942, the Polish Government renewed its demand for such action. The idea was considered by the Foreign Office and by the Air Ministry, but both rejected it. In a note to Churchill, Eden pointed out some of the difficulties involved:

If we link a legitimate measure of war with German bestiality,
(1) There would always be the danger that the reaction of the Germans would merely be to massacre a whole lot more Poles or Jews; and
(2)—a less cogent reason perhaps—the Germans might thereafter claim that if they refrained from murdering Poles and Jews, we were morally bound to give up bombing cities.
There is the further point that, whatever the German people might think about their Government's atrocity policy, they know very well that in no circumstances would we be likely to give up bombing them.[123]

[120] Sikorski to Churchill, 22 June 1942, PRO PREM 4/100/13.
[121] See F. K. Roberts minute, 6 Aug. 1942, PRO FO 371/30917/60 (C 7794/61/18).
[122] Harris to Churchill, 15 June 1942, PRO AIR 14/3507.
[123] Eden to Churchill, 2 Jan. 1943, PRO PREM 3/351/4.

The Chief of Air Staff, Air Chief Marshal Portal, noted other difficulties:

At the Staff Conference on Thursday, at which General Sikorski's telegram was considered, you [Churchill] suggested that if Berlin was raided in the near future leaflets should be dropped during the raid telling the Germans that our attacks were reprisals for the persecution of the Poles and the Jews. At the time I was attracted by the idea, but on further consideration I think I ought to ask you to consider the objections to it which seem to me to be rather formidable.

First, by labelling as a "reprisal" any raid even on Berlin (particularly as there is no special feature or weapon that we can introduce into it) we would automatically abandon our previous position, which is that our attacks on cities are attacks on military objectives (including industry) and therefore "lawful" and justifiable.

Alternatively, if we claimed that the raid had been an especially violent or effective one, should we not have the dilemma (a) 'Why not always do the same?' or (b) 'You are competing in brutality with the Germans'?

Then again, we should almost certainly be overwhelmed with requests from all the other Allies that we should also redress their grievances in the same way. This would result in nothing but a series of 'token' reprisals which would not only be completely ineffective as deterrents but would also destroy the last shreds of the cloak of legality which at present covers our operations.

Finally, we should make it much easier for the Germans to institute reprisals against our captured air crews.[124]

Churchill minuted at the foot of this document: 'I agree.' Although the Prime Minister toyed with the idea of retaliation bombing as a counter to the German 'V-weapon' in July 1944, the Air Staff again advised against it.[125] Thus, although at least half a million German civilians were killed by bombardment from the air in the course of the war, Operation 'Retribution' was never carried out.

Meanwhile, a proposal was put to the British Government for a different form of bombing which, it was argued, might have a direct effect on the Nazi process of mass murder: this was the suggestion that camps such as Auschwitz and Treblinka, in which mass murder of Jews and others was being committed,

124 Portal to Churchill, 6 Jan. 1943, ibid.
125 Note by Air Staff (sent to Churchill), 5 July 1944, PRO PREM 3/12.

should be bombed from the air. A telegram on 24 August 1943 from the Polish Government in London to the leaders of the Polish Home Army underground in Poland stated:

The British Staff expresses readiness to bomb Auschwitz, in particular factories of synthetic rubber and gasoline, and other factories of this kind in Silesia. For our part we would like to combine it with a mass liberation of inmates from Auschwitz. Your extensive cooperation is necessary to liberate them immediately after the raid and in granting them help. Apart from that you must help us in arranging the targets in order of their importance and in guiding the airoplanes to their targets to avoid Polish casualties. Let us know what you think about it and what you expect from us in this respect, and also whether you can prepare the inmates for this beforehand. The operation is scheduled for the period of the longest nights.[126]

Notwithstanding the first sentence of the cable, there is no evidence that the British Air Staff seriously considered such a scheme at this stage. The plan was, in any case, fraught with difficulties. Although the Polish underground movement was in contact with an underground organization within the Auschwitz camp,[127] there is no record of any reply to this cable from Poland. The distance of the camps from air bases in Britain was such that heavy bombers would have had difficulty reaching targets with an adequate bomb load. Nor could there be a sufficient probability of locating the targets accurately.

These difficulties which confronted the proposal in mid-1943 had, however, greatly diminished by the summer of 1944. By this time the capture of airfields at Foggia and Brindisi in southern Italy had rendered bombing of targets in eastern Europe less difficult. Technical advances in precision bombing had progressed considerably by 1944 so that the likelihood of the bombers successfully pinpointing a target was much greater than in 1941 when it had been estimated by Air Marshal Viscount Trenchard (who, in the debates over air strategy between the wars, had been a prominent advocate of the efficacy of the bomber) that 'taking all in all the percentage of bombs which hit military targets at which they are aimed is

[126] Polish Underground Movement (1939–45) Study Trust 4514/43.
[127] Józef Garliński, *Fighting Auschwitz: The Resistance Movement in the Concentration Camp*, London 1975.

not more than one per cent'.[128] However, in spite of the territorial and technical advances which had been made by 1944, some difficulties remained. The distance from Foggia to Auschwitz (in Upper Silesia) by air was about six hundred miles—close to the limit of range for effective bombing. The range of bombers operating from Italy might have been extended by landing on Russian-held territory after dropping the bombs, thereby avoiding the need to conserve fuel for the return flight from target to base. The Russians were highly reluctant to permit such landings. On 21 June 1944 some American bombers landed in Russia after completing bombing missions, but, as Liddell Hart puts it, 'after their cool reception there the experiment was discontinued.'[129] The head of the British air mission in Moscow in February 1944 spoke of an 'entire lack of understanding between allied air forces', and friction increased during the summer and autumn of 1944.[130] The controversy assumed a dangerous political aspect in August and September 1944, when Stalin refused to allow British and American planes to land on Russian soil during the revolt of the Polish Home Army in Warsaw.[131] It was against this background that the British Government, in the summer of 1944, considered a renewed request for the bombing of Auschwitz.

The request was made on behalf of the Jewish Agency by Weizmann and Shertok at a meeting at the Foreign Office with G. H. Hall (Parliamentary Under-Secretary for Foreign Affairs) on 30 June.[132] The suggestion had been made to Shertok by Jewish Agency officials to Budapest, Geneva, and Jerusalem.[133] At a further meeting at the Foreign Office on 6 July, Weizmann and Shertok presented to Eden a number of proposals for action to try to save the lives of Hungarian Jews, among them the suggestion 'that the railway-line leading from

---

[128] Memorandum by Trenchard, 19 May 1941, in Sir Charles Webster and Noble Frankland, *The Strategic Air Offensive Against Germany vol. IV Annexes and Appendices*, London 1961, pp. 194–7.

[129] B. H. Liddell Hart, *History of the Second World War*, London 1973, p. 637.

[130] Air Commodore D. N. Roberts (Moscow) to Secretary of State for Air (London), 5 Feb. 1944; Lieutenant-General M. B. Burrows (Moscow) to British Ambassador (Moscow), 28 Apr. and 21 Sept. 1944, PRO FO 800/302.

[131] See Churchill, *Second World War*, vol. VI, chap. 9.

[132] Record of meeting, PRO FO 371/42807/73.

[133] Ibid.; Lichtheim (Geneva) to Jewish Agency, London, 26 June 1944, CZA L22/77; Grünbaum (Jerusalem) to Schwarzbart (London), 19 June 1944, YV M2/488.

Budapest to Birkenau [an annex of the Auschwitz camp where the gas chambers and crematoria were situated] and the death-camps at Birkenau and other places should be bombed'.[134] A memorandum from Shertok to the Foreign Office a few days later outlined the reasoning behind the Zionist request. Shertok admitted that the proposed bombing was unlikely to save many lives:

The bombing of the death camps is . . . hardly likely to achieve the salvation of the victims to any appreciable extent. Its physical effects can only be the destruction of plant and personnel, and possibly the hastening of the end of those already doomed. The resulting dislocation of the German machinery for systematic wholesale murder may possibly cause delay in the execution of those still in Hungary (over 300,000 in and around Budapest). This in itself is valuable as far as it goes. But it may not go very far, as other means of extermination can be quickly improvised.

But, while conceding that the direct effect of bombing might not be great, Shertok argued that 'the main purpose of the bombing should be its many-sided and far-reaching moral effect':

It would mean, in the first instance, that the Allies waged direct war on the extermination of the victims of Nazi oppression—today Jews, tomorrow Poles, Czechs, or whatever race may become the victim of mass murder during the German retreat and collapse. Secondly, it would mean the lie to the oft-repeated assertions of Nazi spokesmen that the Allies are not really so displeased with the work of the Nazis in ridding Europe of the Jews. Thirdly, it would go far towards dissipating the incredulity which still persists in Allied quarters with regard to the report of mass extermination perpetrated by the Nazis. Fourthly, it would give weight to the threats of reprisals against the murderers, by showing that the Allies are taking the extermination of Jews so seriously as to warrant the allocation of aircraft resources for this particular operation, and thus have a deterrent effect. Lastly, it would convince the German circles still hopeful of Allied mercy of the genuineness of Allied defamation of the murder of Jews, and possibly result in some internal pressure against a continuation of the massacres. The first report that the R.A.F. or the American Air Force had bombed the death camps in Upper Silesia is bound to have a demonstrative value in all these directions.[135]

[134] Aide-mémoire left with Eden by Weizmann and Shertok on 6 July 1944, WA.
[135] Memorandum dated 11 July 1944, in Barlas, *Hatzalah Bimei Shoah*, pp. 293–5.

Eden's initial reaction to the proposal, at the meeting with Zionist leaders on 6 July, was to say that the possibility of bombing had already been considered and rejected. But he added that, in view of the appalling slaughter which was reported to be taking place at Auschwitz, the matter would be re-examined. In a note to the Prime Minister on the same day Eden informed Churchill of Weizmann's request and suggested that the matter might be put before the Cabinet.[136] Churchill replied: 'Is there any reason to raise these matters at the Cabinet? You and I are in entire agreement. Get anything out of the Air Force you can and invoke me if necessary.'[137] On 7 July Eden therefore wrote to the Secretary of State for Air, Sir Archibald Sinclair, outlining Weizmann's proposal:

Dr Weizmann admitted that there seemed to be little enough that we could do to stop these horrors, but he suggested that something might be done to stop the operation of the death camps by
(1) bombing the railway lines leading to Birkenau (and to any other similar camps if we get to hear of them); and
(2) bombing the camps themselves with the object of destroying the plant used for gassing and burning.

After informing Sinclair of the undertaking that had been given that the matter would be re-examined, Eden's letter concluded:

Could you let me know how the Air Ministry view the feasibility of these proposals? I very much hope that it will be possible to do something. I have the authority of the Prime Minister to say that he agrees.[138]

But although the proposal had secured the rapid and clear-cut support of the Prime Minister and the Foreign Secretary it was never implemented. Sinclair's reply to Eden on 15 July stated:

I entirely agree that it is our duty to consider every possible plan that might help, and I have, therefore, examined:

    (a) interrupting the railways
    (b) destroying the plant
    (c) other interference with the camps.

I am informed that (a) is out of our power. It is only by an enormous

[136] Eden to Churchill (draft), 6 July 1944, PRO FO 371/42809/132.
[137] Churchill to Eden, 7 July 1944, PRO FO 371/42809/135.
[138] Eden to Sinclair, 7 July 1944, PRO FO 371/42809/142.

concentration of bomber forces that we have been able to interrupt communications in Normandy; the distance of Silesia from our bases entirely rules out our doing anything of the kind.

Bombing the plant is out of the bounds of possibility for Bomber Command, because the distance is too great for the attack to be carried out at night. It might be carried out by the Americans by daylight but it would be a costly and hazardous operation. It might be ineffective, and, even if the plant was destroyed, I am not clear that it would really help the victims.

There is just one possibility, and that is bombing the camps, and possibly dropping weapons at the same time, in the hope that some of the victims may be able to escape. We did something of the kind in France, when we made a breach in the walls of a prison camp and we think that 150 men who had been condemned to death managed to escape. The difficulties of doing this in Silesia are, of course, enormously greater and even if the camp was successfully raided, the chances of escape would be small indeed.

Nevertheless, I am proposing to have the proposition put to the Americans, with all the facts, to see if they are prepared to try it. I am very doubtful indeed whether, when they have examined it, the Americans will think it possible, and I do not wish to raise any hopes. For this reason, and because it would not be fair to suggest that we favoured it and the Americans were unwilling to help, I feel that you would not wish to mention the possibility to Weizmann at this stage. I will let you know the result when the Americans have considered it.[139]

The Foreign Secretary was highly dissatisfied with this reply. Next to Sinclair's expression of doubt that the bombing would help the victims Eden minuted: 'He wasn't asked his opinion of this; he was asked to act.' And on the letter as a whole, Eden (who did not share Sinclair's reputation for sympathy with Zionism) commented acidly: 'A characteristically unhelpful letter. Dept. will have to consider what is to be done about this. I think that we should pass the buck to this ardent Zionist in due course, i.e. tell Weizmann that we have approached Sir A. Sinclair & suggest that he may like to see him.'[140]

The United States Government had, in fact, already considered and rejected the idea. The Assistant Secretary of the War Department, John J. McCloy, had stated on 4 July:

[139] Sinclair to Eden, 15 July 1944, PRO FO 371/42809/147.
[140] Minutes by Eden, 16 July 1944, ibid.

The War Department is of the opinion that the suggested air operation is impracticable. It could be executed only by the diversion of considerable air support essential to the success of our forces now engaged in decisive operations and would in any case be of such very doubtful efficacy that it would not amount to a practical project.[141]

Further pressure by Jewish organizations in favour of the project did not alter the War Department's view. In a statement on 14 August McCloy repeated his view that the idea was impracticable, adding: 'There has been considerable opinion to the effect that such an effort, even if practicable, might provoke even more vindictive action by the Germans.'[142]

Meanwhile, in London, in contrast to the speed with which the original idea had been considered and approved by the Prime Minister and the Foreign Secretary, officials at the Foreign Office and the Air Ministry did not pursue the matter with any sense of urgency. On 18 July A. W. G. Randall, head of the Foreign Office Refugee Department, suggested that it would not be necessary to inform Weizmann immediately about the difficulties raised by Sinclair. Randall added: 'I don't see how the F.O. could pursue the matter in the face of the technical objections. In the meantime Jewish circles here (Mr Shertok) tell me there has been a slackening of the deportations. I am trying to verify this and get some explanation of the fact—if correct.'[143] On 3 August the Chairman of the Joint Intelligence Committee, Cavendish-Bentinck, noted:

The Air Staff are anxious to obtain more precise details regarding the locality of this 'death camp' at Birkenau. It may be within ten miles or more of that place. Unless the Air Staff can be given an exact pinpoint of this camp the airmen will experience difficulty in finding it.[144]

Inquiries were made through the Polish Government in the hope of securing detailed plans of the camp. But the Foreign Office and the Air Ministry were clearly very sceptical as to the

[141] McCloy (War Dept.) to J. W. Pehle (War Refugee Board) 4 July 1944, in Barlas, *Hatzalah Bimei Shoah*, p. 293.

[142] McCloy to A. L. Kubowitzki (World Jewish Congress), 14 Aug. 1944, in *Unity in Dispersion: A History of the World Jewish Congress*, New York 1948, p. 167. For an analysis of the United States Government's attitude to the proposal for the bombing of Auschwitz, see David S. Wyman, 'Why Auschwitz Was Never Bombed', *Commentary*, vol. 65 no. 5, May 1978, pp. 37–46.

[143] Minute dated 18 July 1944, PRO FO 371/42809/146.

[144] V. Cavendish-Bentinck minute, 3 Aug. 1944, PRO FO 371/42809/127.

practicability or value of the entire scheme. The Foreign Office believed that 'the whole position' had changed as a result of the reported halt to the deportations from Hungary. The Air Staff said 'that for operational reasons they [were] far from anxious to pursue the project . . . and [had] only been going into the matter because of the Secretary of State's letter to Sir A. Sinclair'.[145] Doubt was expressed as to whether mass murder was still being committed at Auschwitz.[146] However the Air Staff continued (without enthusiasm) to investigate the proposal, and a Foreign Office official pointed out the idea could not simply be dropped: 'We cannot . . . let this die without the S[ecretary] of S[tate]'s approval, as it arose out of a minute from him to the P.M., which the P.M. approved.'[147]

On 13 August Air Ministry impatience with the Foreign Office's apparently indecisive and dilatory attitude was revealed in a letter from Air Commodore G. W. P. ('Tubby') Grant to Cavendish-Bentinck:

I am perturbed at having heard nothing more from the Foreign Office about the problem of Birkenau since Allen telephoned me on the 5th of this month.[148]

You will appreciate that as the Secretary of State for Air has instructed the Air Staff to take action on Mr Eden's request, it is a matter of the greatest urgency for me to obtain photographic cover of the camps and installations in the Birkenau area. The information at present in our possession is insufficient for a reconnaissance aircraft to have a reasonable chance of obtaining the cover required, and only the Foreign Office can obtain the information which I need.

In view of the urgency of the problem which Mr Eden has raised I shall be grateful if I can have a reply, whether it be positive or negative, to my request with the utmost expedition.

In his conversation Mr Allen hinted that the Foreign Office were tending to reconsider the importance they had placed upon the liberation of the captives at Birkenau. This, however, does not help me. If, in fact, further information about the Germans' intentions in that particular camp has caused the Secretary of State for Foreign Affairs to revise his opinion, it will be necessary for him to inform the Secretary of State for Air who will, no doubt, then modify or rescind

[145] Minute by D. Allen, 5 Aug. 1944, PRO FO 371/42809/127–8.
[146] Minute by D. Allen, 10 Aug. 1944, PRO FO 371/42809/129.
[147] G. E. Millard minute, 10 Aug. 1944, ibid.
[148] The reference is to R. H. S. Allen.

Resistance 315

the instructions which he has issued to the Air Staff. Only if and until such official action is taken can the priority of cover of Birkenau, which is now of the very highest, be lowered.[149]

On receipt of this letter the Foreign Office 'passed the buck' to the Jewish Agency by suggesting that in view of the reported halt to the deportations from Hungary, the Zionists might wish to withdraw their request for the bombing. The Zionist reply was immediate:

The reasons which were advanced for the bombing of the death-camps are still valid. There are still many Jews in the hands of the Germans who can be sent to those camps to their doom. There is another reason why the destruction of the camps is urgent: in the situation in which the Germans find themselves today, it will be more difficult for them to construct new camps, and this might be the means of saving Jewish lives.[150]

Upon being told by the Foreign Office that the project could not go ahead unless more detailed topographic information were made available, the Jewish Agency quickly secured plans and descriptions of the Auschwitz and Treblinka camps from the Polish Ministry of the Interior, and forwarded these documents to the Foreign Office.[151]

At this point the Foreign Office officials dealing with the matter decided to block further action. Notwithstanding the minutes by the Prime Minister and the Foreign Secretary, and in spite of the Air Ministry's request for topographic data, nothing further was done. Instead of being forwarded to the Air Ministry, the plans and descriptions supplied by the Jewish Agency were consigned to the Foreign Office files. Meanwhile the officials considered how best to dispose of the matter. On 18 August I. L. Henderson minuted:

Mr Grant of the Air Ministry says that this idea would cost British lives and aircraft to no purpose. I think it is fantastic, and should be dropped. But if the Air Ministry have strong objections they should say so and we can return a negative reply to the Jewish Agency.[152]

[149] Grant to Cavendish-Bentinck, 13 Aug. 1944, PRO FO 371/42814/190.
[150] I. J. Linton to I. L. Henderson, 16 Aug. 1944, CZA Z4/15202.
[151] Linton to G. E. Millard (Foreign Office), enclosing plans and descriptions, 18 Aug. 1944, PRO FO 371/42806/31; these documents were submitted following a telephone conversation between Linton and Millard on the afternoon of 18 Aug.
[152] Minute dated 18 Aug. 1944, PRO FO 371/42814/188.

R. H. S. Allen disagreed:

We cannot now shift the responsibility to the Air Ministry, by asking
them to say that for technical reasons they are opposed to the whole
venture. If the political situation has changed and we no longer wish
on political grounds to proceed with this project, it is up to us to tell
the Air Ministry so in a form that will have the effect of revoking the
Secretary of State's previous communication to Sir A. Sinclair. From
the Air Ministry point of view this matter is urgent, since the reconnaissance has been given the highest priority and they can do nothing
about it until either (a) we put them in touch with the source of the
topographical information or (b) we tell them that the whole scheme
is now dead.[153]

Henderson, however, saw no reason for pursuing course (a):

I cannot understand why, in view of the *very* negative import of Sir A.
Sinclair's letter . . . instructions should have been issued in the Air
Ministry to go ahead with this scheme. However, the only way out of
the impasse would appear to be a draft for the signature of the
Secretary of State saying that in view of the technical difficulties of
carrying out our request we do not intend to pursue it.[154]

A minute was therefore prepared for the Secretary of State
outlining the history of the scheme, and stressing the reports
that the deportations of Jews from Hungary had halted. The
minute suggested that 'in the circumstances, i.e. the apparent
cessation of the deportations, but most of all the great technical
difficulties involved, it may be considered advisable to inform
the Secretary of State for Air that we do not wish to pursue the
idea'. The minute prepared for Eden made no reference to the
Air Ministry's request for topographic data, nor to the fact that
the data had been received and withheld by the Foreign
Office.[155]

The result was a striking testimony to the ability of the
British civil service to overturn ministerial decisions: although
it had secured the explicit backing of the Prime Minister and
the Foreign Secretary, the scheme was rejected. Churchill was
abroad at the end of August and does not appear to have been
told of the decision. Eden was preoccupied with the severe
crisis in relations with the U.S.S.R. as a result of the Warsaw

[153] Minute dated 21 Aug. 1944, ibid.
[154] Minute dated 22 Aug. 1944, ibid.
[155] Note for Secretary of State by A. Walker, 25 Aug. 1944, PRO FO 371/42814/196.

rising and the Soviet refusal to grant landing rights to British or American supply planes. The task of dealing with the Jewish Agency bombing proposal was left to the Minister of State, Richard Law. Letters announcing that the scheme had been rejected were signed by Law and dispatched to Weizmann and Sir Archibald Sinclair. A subtle difference in formulation marked the two communications. The letter to Weizmann stated that 'in view of the very great technical difficulties involved' the Government had decided it had 'no option but to refrain from pursuing the proposal in present circumstances'.[156] No reference was made to any other reason for the decision. But the letter to Sinclair placed the technical objection in a secondary position:

For the last month our reports have tended to show that Jews are no longer being deported from Hungary. In view of this fact and also because we understand from the Air Ministry that there are serious technical difficulties in the way of carrying out the suggestion, we do not propose to pursue it.[157]

That the Foreign Office's handling of the matter had not been entirely straightforward did not pass unnoticed. A few weeks later, the newly-appointed head of the Refugee Department, Paul Mason, happened to come across the plans of Auschwitz and Treblinka in the departmental files. He recorded his surprise that they had never been forwarded to the Air Ministry, and minuted:

The Minister of State on Sept. 1 (on behalf of S[ecretary] of S[tate]) agreed in writing to the S[ecretary] of S[tate] for Air that in view of the difficulties of the operation of bombing the camps as represented by the Air Min[istry] (they said they had no detailed inf[ormatio]n of the topography) the idea of bombing them might be dropped. We are therefore technically guilty of allowing the Air Min[istr]y to get away with it without having given them (tho' we had it) the inf[ormatio]n they asked for as a prerequisite.

But, although the Jewish Agency were still pressing for the scheme to go forward, Mason felt the matter should be left where it stood, 'though', he added, 'I feel a little uneasy about

[156] Law to Weizmann 1 Sept. 1944, WA.
[157] Law to Sinclair, 1 Sept. 1944, PRO FO 371/42809/149.

it'.[158] Further requests from Jewish organizations for the bombing of Auschwitz were ruled out by the Foreign Office on the ground that the Hungarian deportations were now known to have ceased. Official minutes suggested that 'possibly the Soviets might consider doing this'.[159] A representative of the Board of Deputies of British Jews returned to the matter on 12 October, and at an interview at the Foreign Office asked whether the Government had considered bombing the camp in association with the Red Air Force. In reply, Mason 'invited his attention to the risk of Germany claiming that *we* had done our best, by bombing the camps, to exterminate the inmates ourselves'.[160] In fact, no suggestion was ever made by the British Government to the U.S.S.R. that the camp be bombed by the Red Air Force.[161] It is, however, very unlikely that, given the highly strained relations between the U.S.S.R. and the western allies on matters relating to aviation and to war crimes, anything would have been achieved by such an approach.

Auschwitz was not bombed partly because of the technical difficulties involved in such an operation, and partly because the Foreign Office believed that the deportations and killings had stopped. How valid were these reasons? It is clear from the chain of official communications that the technical objection, although a genuine and serious one, was not alleviated by the decision of the Foreign Office officials to withhold the topographical data insistently requested by the Air Ministry. The data could not have eliminated all the technical problems even if they had been taken into account by the Air Ministry, but they might have eased the difficulty. That pinpoint bombing of a target such as Auschwitz from air bases in Italy was possible was demonstrated on 13 September 1944 when the U.S. 15th Air Force bombed the I.G. Farben industrial complex adjacent to Auschwitz. The raid was conceived solely as an attack on a war production target, and was not connected with the pro-

[158] Minute by Mason, 18 Sept. 1944, PRO FO 371/42806/30.

[159] Minute by Lady Cheetham, 25 Sept. 1944, PRO FO 371/42818/29; see also minute by P. Mason, 21 Sept. 1944, PRO FO 371/42806/28.

[160] Minute by Mason, 12 Oct. 1944, PRO FO 371/39454 (C 14201/131/55); note by A. G. Brotman, 12 Oct. 1944, BD C 11/7/1/6.

[161] The suggestion to the contrary in Morse, *While Six Million Died*, pp. 360–1, is based on a confusion of the proposal for the bombing of Auschwitz with a separate proposal for a declaration by the Soviet Government warning of retribution for war crimes.

posed bombing of the camp. Nevertheless, some bombs landed in the camp itself: according to one account, fifteen SS-men, forty prisoners, and thirty civilian workers were killed.[162] As to the second objection which influenced the Foreign Office, the halt to the deportations from Hungary, this too was based on incomplete information (although in this instance the fault did not lie with the Foreign Office). While it was true that the deportations of Jews from Hungary to Auschwitz had stopped in July 1944, Jews continued to be deported there from other areas until the autumn. The last remaining Jewish ghetto in Poland, that of Lodz, was not liquidated until early September, when its 60,000 inhabitants had been transported to Auschwitz (and other destinations) where they were killed. The scale of the slaughter during this final period was immense. During one twenty-four hour period in August more than 24,000 bodies were cremated in the Auschwitz crematoria and in open trenches nearby.[163] The gas chambers continued to operate until the end of October. Murder of camp inmates continued until the eve of the liberation of Auschwitz by Russian forces on 27 January 1945. The Foreign Office view that the end of the Hungarian deportations to Auschwitz in July 1944 had disposed of any necessity for an attack on the camp was therefore based on a misconception.

Both of the main objections to the plan which influenced the decision of the British Government were therefore open to question. The bombardment of the camp might not have saved many lives, as had indeed been conceded by Weizmann and Shertok at the outset. It is, however, known that the Germans considered the possibility of an air raid on Auschwitz as a serious hazard. The Germans had learnt of the proposed bombardment by intercepting a telegram from the British Legation in Berne to the Foreign Office; the cable contained a message from the Jewish Agency representative in Geneva urging that the camp should be bombed. The intercepted message was forwarded to the chief of the Reich Security Police, Kaltenbrunner, and the proposed bombing of Auschwitz and of the railway lines to the camp from Hungary was drawn to the

[162] See Garliński, *Fighting Auschwitz* p. 242; and Webster and Frankland, *Strategic Air Offensive*, vol. III, map opposite p. 46.
[163] Garliński, *Fighting Auschwitz*, p. 199.

attention of Ribbentrop and of the Hungarian Government.[164] The danger of an air attack on Auschwitz later led to a cessation of the burning of bodies in open trenches at night, a decision taken as a consequence of protests by anti-aircraft units at the camp.[165] The potential results of an attempt to bomb the camp are, in terms of the direct effects, impossible to assess. But, as Weizmann and Shertok had also pointed out, quite apart from the immediate effects, the mere fact that such a raid had been attempted would have been of considerable moral significance in providing an unequivocal demonstration that the Allies were not indifferent to the fate of the Jews of Europe, that they were prepared to allocate resources to an effort to save Jewish lives, and that they were prepared to risk the lives of some of their own airmen in that cause. In the absence of such an attempt, there endured a lasting suspicion of the motives underlying the decision not to attack Auschwitz, and a long series of bitter Jewish recriminations against the British and American Governments.[166]

Resistance to the Nazi mass murder of the Jews of Europe could hope to be effective only with outside support. The common purpose of the project for a Jewish army, of the scheme for the bombing of Auschwitz, of the pleas for underground help to Jewish resistance in Europe, for propaganda broadcasts and leaflets, for assistance to the fighters in the Warsaw Ghetto, and for warnings, threats, and reprisals, was to provide that external buttress without which no resistance movement could expect to operate. Such resistance, it was argued, would contribute to the general war effort and to the eventual defeat of Nazism. But the saving of Jewish lives was not regarded as a primary British war aim which would make a direct contribution to an Allied victory. Resistance to the Nazi genocide was not, therefore, considered as a high priority, but, at most, as a secondary aim to be realized only if it would in no way impair the resources required for the central objective of British victory over Germany. By that test there was, in the official British view, little that could be done to diminish the savagery of the Nazi anti-Semitic terror.

[164] Wagner to Kaltenbrunner, 5 July 1944, in Braham, *Destruction of Hungarian Jewry*, p. 734; Hilberg, *Destruction*, p. 549.   [165] Garliński, *Fighting Auschwitz*, p. 199.
[166] See e.g. Gideon Hausner, *Justice in Jerusalem*, London 1967, p. 243; George Steiner, *Language and Silence*, London 1967, p. 183.

8

Unconditional Surrender

By the autumn of 1944, as the German armies were driven into retreat on all fronts, and as the area under German domination shrank, an allied victory began to seem no longer a distant dream but an imminent reality. However, the nightmare did not yet give way to dawn for the surviving remnants of the Jews in Nazi Europe. The gas chambers of Auschwitz were dismantled in November 1944, but in the increasing chaos of the collapsing Nazi state the systematic process of mass murder gave way to a more disorganized but hardly less brutal regime of inhumanity and terror. Surviving inmates of Auschwitz and of other camps on the periphery of the Reich were transferred to camps such as Dachau, Buchenwald, and Bergen-Belsen, situated in the heart of Germany not yet under immediate threat from the allied armies. In October 1944 Eichmann began organizing the forced march from Budapest of thousands of Jews who had survived the deportations of the previous spring; they were to be used as slave labour for the German war effort. In this final stage of the holocaust multitudes died of hunger, disease, and exposure, as well as in massacres by Germans and collaborators of other nationalities. However, the increasing probability of defeat led some elements among Germany's junior allies as well as some Nazi officials to calculate that, notwithstanding the failure of the Brand mission, it might be possible to use Jews as bargaining counters in peace negotiations or in order to secure funds to facilitate escape. The allies remained committed to the war aim of 'unconditional surrender' enunciated at the Casablanca Conference in January 1943. Nevertheless, towards the end of the war, differences emerged in the attitudes of the three major allies towards the question of German war crimes. On the allied side too the prospect of victory concentrated the attention of governments on the formulation of policies to deal with the problems of victory. In the U.S.A. this led to a modification of policy on the refugee question, in Britain to renewed consideration of the vexed problem of the future of Palestine. On both issues the British and American Governments now found themselves drifting dangerously apart.

A notable change in the public stance of the U.S.A. on the refugee problem occurred on 22 January 1944 when President Roosevelt issued an executive order establishing a War Refugee Board charged with 'taking all measures within its power to rescue the victims of enemy oppression who are in imminent danger of death, and otherwise to afford such victims all possible relief and assistance consistent with the successful prosecution of the war'.[1] The W.R.B., which consisted of the Secretaries of State, Treasury, and War, was formed as a result of an initiative by the Treasury Secretary, Henry Morgenthau, who, on 16 January, had sent to Roosevelt a strong-worded 'personal report', denouncing vehemently the 'utter failure of certain officials in the State Department . . . to take effective action to prevent the extermination of the Jews in German-controlled Europe'. Morgenthau named as the chief culprit Assistant Secretary of State Breckenridge Long, who was in charge of refugee policy at the State Department. Morgenthau's memorandum went into considerable detail, alleging that the State Department had suppressed deliberately the facts of German atrocities against the Jews, and had procrastinated in dealing with schemes for the relief and rescue of Jews from Nazi Europe. He accused the State Department of being 'indifferent, callous, and perhaps even hostile' in their attitude towards the problem.[2] The Board was allocated a million dollars from the President's emergency funds, and later received further public funds as well as donations from the American Jewish Joint Distribution Committee. Organized after the style of a 'New Deal' agency, the W.R.B. swiftly went into action in an energetic and well-publicized manner. In an effort to cut red tape, agents were sent to neutral countries with instructions to take whatever measures might be necessary to save Jewish lives.

[1] State Dept. to U.S. Embassies in London, Lisbon, Madrid, Berne, and Ankara, 25 Jan. 1944, in Mashberg, 'Documents', pp. 180–2.
[2] Morgenthau to Roosevelt, 16 Jan. 1944, ibid., pp. 174–9.

The creation of the W.R.B. was greeted with a certain amount of cynicism in London, where it was recalled that 1944 was an election year. In a caustic note to the Cabinet Committee on Refugees, Eden suggested that, in addition to the announced humanitarian aims, the W.R.B. was formed with the further intention of

(1) placating the large Jewish vote, and
(2) spiking the guns of Congress whose Foreign Affairs Committee had recently applied much pressure to the State Department over this refugee question, and was agitating for a 'committee of rescue'.

Recalling that there had recently been increasing pressure by the U.S.A. on Britain regarding the admission of Jewish refugees to Palestine, Eden continued:

Although these possibilities contrast strongly with the United States Government's reticence over admissions to their own territory, which have recently been the subject of sarcastic comment in the American Jewish papers, I think we should welcome the President's move.[3]

A strikingly similar response was recorded (privately) by Assistant Secretary Long, who confided to his diary:

We have not heard from England, but I expect they will not look with favor on it. However, I think it a good move—for local political reasons—for there are 4 million Jews in New York and its environs who feel themselves related to the refugees and because of the persecutions of the Jews, and who have been demanding special attention and treatment. This will encourage them to think the persecuted may be saved, and possibly satisfy them—politically—but in my opinion the Board will not save any persecuted people I could not save under my recent and long-suffering administration.[4]

Long's gloomy prognostications, at least as regards the British reaction to the activities of the War Refugee Board, proved to be accurate.

Anglo-American friction arose almost immediately over the question of the dispatch of funds for relief of Jews in occupied Europe. There had already been disputes between the British and Americans over the allocation of funds to the World Jewish Congress for attempts to smuggle Jews to safety.[5] The British

[3] Eden to Cabinet Committee on Refugees, 7 Feb. 1944, PRO CAB 95/15/131.
[4] Long, *Diary*, pp. 336–7 (entry dated 24 Jan. 1944).
[5] See p. 247.

Government, concerned that the blockade of Nazi Europe should be strictly maintained, had consistently rejected most applications for permission to send relief supplies to Jews in Europe. The first notable relaxation of the rules permitted by the Ministry of Economic Warfare was in late 1942 when the Board of Deputies of British Jews (with funds granted by the Jewish Colonisation Association and the Central British Fund) was allowed to send relief supplies to Polish Jewry to the value of £3,000 per month. The results, however, were very disappointing. A first batch of 12,559 packages, all containing figs, were dispatched to addresses in Poland through the office of the American Jewish Joint Distribution Committee in Lisbon. Only 925 of the parcels were confirmed as having reached the addresses, 849 of these confirmations being signed by representatives of the *Judenrat* (Jewish Council) set up by the occupying authorities in many localities in Poland. More than four thousand of the remainder were confiscated by the German authorities. Following the first consignment in the spring of 1943, two further consignments of 7,226 packages were dispatched, mostly to addresses from which confirmation of receipt had been received in the earlier batch. The packages contained sardines, almonds, and fruit juice.[6] The scheme was discontinued after packages worth a total of £9,000 had been sent to Poland, without in most cases reaching the addresses. However, a similar scheme for the transfer of £3,000 per month to Lisbon for the dispatch of food parcels for Jewish prisoners in the Theresienstadt concentration camp was authorized in 1943. According to an International Red Cross report some ninety per cent of these packages reached their destinations.[7] Nevertheless, the Ministry of Economic Warfare remained consistently reluctant to sanction large-scale relief plans which went beyond the relatively modest sums involved in these limited parcel schemes.

The United States Government approached the question in a very different spirit. In the first two years of the European war, when the U.S.A. was neutral, the British Government had

[6] H. Katzki (A.J.J.D.C., Lisbon) to A. G. Brotman (Board of Deputies, London), 2 July 1943, BD C11/12/92/2.

[7] E. Frischer (Czechoslovak State Council, London) to Prof. S. Brodetsky (Board of Deputies), 6 May 1943, BD C11/12/92/5.

resisted pressure from the U.S.A. to permit relief supplies to be sent through the British blockade to enemy-occupied territory. But, in spite of British opposition, American Jewish organizations, particularly the Joint Distribution Committee, had succeeded in pumping millions of dollars into Axis Europe for food and medical supplies to Jewish populations. Even after Pearl Harbor the J.D.C. had continued to send large amounts of aid to enemy territory: according to one estimate over a million dollars was sent by the J.D.C. to Poland after the German declaration of war on the U.S.A.[8] In 1943 the J.D.C. had an operating budget of over ten million dollars.[9] The United States Treasury tended to adopt a rather more relaxed attitude than the British to the danger of giving indirect assistance to the enemy war effort by permitting infringements of the blockade. The matter came to a head in the spring of 1944 when the War Refugee Board approved a proposal by the J.D.C. to give $100,000 to the International Red Cross for the purchase of food and other supplies in Hungary and Roumania. The remittance was stated to be the first of several such transfers and led to a direct confrontation with the British Government.

In a note circulated to the Cabinet Committee on Refugees in March 1944, Eden warned of 'the possibility of serious differences of opinion between His Majesty's Government and the United States Government over details of refugee policy'. Eden commented on the W.R.B.'s authorization of remittances to Hungary and Roumania:

If we object, we run the risk of being held up by the War Refugee Board, which is engaged on a publicity campaign, as obstacles to a humanitarian measure which would probably save many Jewish lives. If we merely acquiesce, we allow the United States Government to get the credit for a piece of rescue work which critics will say should have been attempted long ago, while if we, too, agree to remit money to the International Red Cross, we may be committed to a relaxation of our financial blockade which may prove of real advantage to the enemy.

'In considering these three disagreeable possibilities', Eden continued, it would be necessary to bear in mind that the W.R.B., 'whatever the transient electoral motives behind its

[8] Herbert Agar, *The Saving Remnant*, London 1960, pp. 14–15.
[9] Tartakower and Grossmann, *The Jewish Refugee*, p. 451.

creation', had been officially welcomed by the British Government which had given assurances of co-operation.

None the less, this departure is so serious that I suggest that we ask His Majesty's Ambassador to enquire whether, in granting this first licence, the United States have duly considered the effect which such a breach of the blockade will, if repeated, produce on the conduct of the war, or, if they have considered the point, what safeguards they have devised to prevent benefit to the enemy out of proportion to the advantage gained. In putting these questions we should emphasize that we wish to help the refugee cause as much as the United States Government and desire to cooperate with them fully. But we cannot overlook the fact that providing the enemy with foreign currency may increase his powers of resistance, and so ultimately cause more suffering than will be relieved.[10]

The underlying issues were discussed during a visit to London in April 1944 by the U.S. Under-Secretary of State, Edward Stettinius, whose report on his visit contained the following account of conversations on the subject with Churchill and Eden:

The Prime Minister stated that he objected strongly to any relief shipments of food to the occupied countries of Europe because of the danger of security leaks concerning the coming operations. He said that he is interested in the providing of relief, but that he feels we must take no chances whatsoever of jeopardizing the success of our military operations.

Mr Eden stated that it was hopeless to raise the food relief question again with the War Cabinet. He said that they had taken a firm position that the best thing for the people in the occupied areas is to turn those areas into liberated areas as soon as possible and that any food relief plans must be turned down for operational and security reasons. The whole question is tied up, of course, with Britain's historical dependence on blockade as a principal weapon of war.

The Under-Secretary told Mr Eden that it is very important from the American political point of view to open negotiations promptly with Germany, through Switzerland or Sweden, on the subject of food relief.

Mr Eden felt that his Government would never agree to such action.[11]

[10] Eden to Cabinet Committee on Refugees, 10 Mar. 1944, PRO CAB 95/15/138.
[11] Report by Stettinius, 22 May 1944, on visit to London, 7–29 Apr. 1944, *FRUS 1944* vol. III, p. 7.

Before the disagreement over relief had been resolved, further actions by the W.R.B. compounded the dim view taken by the British of American refugee policy. In the spring of 1944 the Roumanian Government, sensing imminent defeat, began to moderate its anti-Semitic policy. Jewish survivors from the 'Transnistrian' region of the occupied U.S.S.R., now reconquered by the Red Army, were permitted to return to Roumania. In April American representatives in Turkey secured British, Turkish, Russian, and Roumanian acquiescence in a scheme for the evacuation of at least 1,500 Jewish refugees from the Roumanian port of Constanza. They were to be transported to Palestine aboard the s.s. *Tari* which had been chartered for the purpose by the Americans. In Constanza there were reported to be 'indescribable' scenes as large masses of Jews fought 'pitched battles' with 'Christian Jews', and with White Russians and others who hoped for a berth on the *Tari* to escape not the Germans but the advancing Russians.[12] On 3 April, the American Ambassador in Ankara, Laurence Steinhardt, wrote to the Jewish Agency representative in Istanbul that he expected the *Tari* to 'be prepared to sail within three or four days'.[13] However, before the *Tari* could sail (under the Turkish flag) a safe-conduct was required for the ship from the Germans. This was not forthcoming in spite of representations made by the International Red Cross, by the Apostolic Delegate in Istanbul, Mgr. Roncalli (later Pope John XXIII), and by the German Ambassador to Turkey, von Papen.

The failure to secure a German safe-conduct was attributed by the British to two injudicious actions by the Americans. First, the American Ambassador, determined to hasten the realization of the scheme, persuaded the Turkish Government to make an official request to the Germans for a safe-conduct. The Red Cross representative in Turkey was subsequently informed that the Germans had turned down the request because, emanating from the Turkish Government at a time when German-Turkish relations were deteriorating, the proposal had a political flavour; if the request had been made solely by the Red Cross, it was alleged, it might have been acceptable. The Red Cross representative was said to be 'wild

[12] British Embassy, Ankara, to Foreign Office, 25 May 1944, PRO FO 371/42726/41.
[13] Steinhardt to Barlas, 3 Apr. 1944, in Barlas, *Hatzalah Bimei Shoah*, pp. 358-9.

at what the Americans had done', accusing them 'of having sabotaged the whole scheme by their stupidity'.[14] Meanwhile the prospects of securing a safe-conduct had been further reduced as a result of publicity given to the plan by the War Refugee Board's representative in Turkey, Ira A. Hirschmann. A former department store executive at Bloomingdale Bros. in New York, Hirschmann was described by the British Embassy in Ankara as 'a go-getter, somewhat tenacious of his own ideas and impatient of official methods'; he was said to be looking at the Jewish refugee problem 'mainly from the point of view of [the] coming Presidential election in [the] U.S.'[15] At a press conference in New York on 18 April Hirschmann claimed that 'thousands' of Jews had been saved by the W.R.B., and announced that the *Tari* would sail from Constanza to Haifa as soon as a German safe-conduct had been secured.[16] Both the British Government and the Jewish Agency condemned the publicity given to the scheme by the W.R.B. as the main reason for its failure since the Germans were reported to have given as the reason for their refusal of a safe-conduct their desire not to offend the Arabs by appearing to promote Jewish emigration to Palestine.[17] British confidence in the sincerity of American zeal to rescue Jewish refugees was not enhanced by statements made by Ambassador Steinhardt to Knox Helm of the British Embassy in Ankara. According to Helm, Steinhardt had told him that 'the essential thing . . . was that the United States Government should be able to announce that they had arranged for this ship to carry Jews to safety'. When Helm mentioned that a group of three hundred Jews had arrived in Istanbul that weekend, Steinhardt was said to have replied that 'he knew, but the arrivals of these hundreds of Jews were no use as propaganda for the President'.[18]

British suspicion of American motives in the refugee issue were further aggravated in mid-1944 by a decision of President

[14] British Embassy, Ankara, to Foreign Office, 25 May 1944, PRO FO 371/42726/41.

[15] British Embassy, Ankara, to Minister Resident, Cairo, 20 June 1944, PRO FO 921/227.

[16] *New York Times*, 19 Apr. 1944; Jewish Telegraphic Agency report, 19 Apr. 1944, in PRO FO 371/42725/92.

[17] Eden to Cabinet Committee on Refugees, 29 June 1944, PRO CAB 95/15/181 ff.; Moshe Shertok to I. J. Linton, 26 May 1944, WJCL.

[18] Minute by Helm, 23 May 1944, quoted in British Embassy, Ankara, to Foreign Office, 25 May 1944, PRO FO 371/42726/41.

Roosevelt. On 12 June 1944 the President delivered a special message to Congress on refugee policy. The message began by praising the work of the War Refugee Board, which, said Roosevelt, 'operating quietly, as is appropriate', had saved many innocent lives. The message then announced that, in order to help relieve refugee congestion in southern Italy, it had been decided to bring to the U.S.A. about a thousand refugees, 'predominantly women and children', who were to be placed 'in a vacated Army camp on the Atlantic coast'. The refugees were to be held 'under appropriate security restrictions', and were to be maintained under the supervision of the War Relocation Authority, the agency responsible for organizing the internment of Japanese-Americans. At the end of the war the refugees were to be sent back to their homelands.[19] The decision, devised in such a way as to circumvent American immigration laws, over which Congress maintained a jealous, defensive scrutiny, had been taken against the advice of the Secretary of War, and it aroused some congressional opposition.[20] The refugees were brought to the U.S.A. shortly afterwards, and taken to Fort Ontario, near Oswego on the shore of Lake Ontario in upper New York State. The wide publicity given to the announcement irritated the Foreign Office, where some anger was aroused by a further comment by the President that he was 'canvassing the possibility' of refugees being received in Cyprus. It was pointed out that Cyprus had already taken in 5,000 Greek refugees, plus an additional 1,083 Greeks from the Dodecanese, as well as 'a considerable number of Jewish refugees from the Balkans'. Lady Cheetham of the Foreign Office Refugee Department minuted: 'Thus this little island has taken in over 6,100 refugees. Compared to the U.S.A.['s] paltry 1,000 this is a stupendous effort. Cyprus should "canvas" the U.S.A.' The head of the Refugee Department, A. W. G. Randall, agreed: 'This U.S. publicity is sometimes hard to bear.'[21]

But much more serious than such British resentment of the ballyhoo surrounding the activities of the War Refugee Board was growing evidence in the course of 1944 of a divergence

[19] Text of message in U.S. Embassy, London, to Foreign Office, 17 June 1944, PRO FO 371/42726/131.

[20] Feingold, *Politics of Rescue*, pp. 260–4.

[21] Minutes by Lady Cheetham and A. W. G. Randall, 21 July 1944, PRO FO 371/42809/170 (WR 297/3/48).

between British and American attitudes to the Palestine problem. In January the British Ambassador in Washington, Lord Halifax, warned the Foreign Office that 'Zionist pressure' in the United States was rising. Stressing the importance of the Jewish vote in the Congressional and Presidential elections due to take place in November, Halifax noted that several prominent members of the administration and of Congress had recently signed pro-Zionist statements. The Ambassador continued:

The small band of Americans with knowledge of the Middle East, in the Near East Division of the State Department and elsewhere, have small chance of prevailing against this formidable array. One of them recently told a member of my staff that he feared that unless a decision on Palestine policy was soon taken which would provide a line to hold on to, the pressure on the Administration to intervene with His Majesty's Government in favour of the Zionists would soon prove irresistible.[22]

A further cable from Washington in January noted that 'the campaign against the White Paper' was 'rising to a climax'.[23] In March Roosevelt met Rabbis Stephen Wise and Abba Hillel Silver, Co-Chairmen of the American Zionist Emergency Council, and authorized them to announce publicly that the American Government had never given its approval to the White Paper, and that 'when future decisions are reached full justice will be done to those seeking a Jewish National Home'.[24] In the course of the election campaign later in the year Roosevelt was more specific, pledging his aid for 'the establishment of Palestine as a free and democratic Jewish Commonwealth'.[25] Nor did Roosevelt's apparent pro-Zionist enthusiasm disappear upon re-election: on 10 November he told Under-Secretary of State Stettinius privately that he thought 'Palestine should be for the Jews, and no Arabs should be in it'.[26]

[22] Halifax to Foreign Office, 8 Jan. 1944, PRO PREM 4/52/5/Part 2/1030.

[23] Halifax to Foreign Office, 10 Jan. 1944, PRO FO 371/38537 (A 221/20/45).

[24] M. Wright (British Embassy, Washington) to N. Butler (Foreign Office), 21 Mar. 1944, enclosing account of Wise-Silver-Roosevelt interview, PRO FO 371/40135/23 ff. (E 1994/95/31).

[25] *New York Times*, 16 Oct. 1944.

[26] T. M. Campbell & G. C. Herring, eds., *The Diaries of Edward R. Stettinius Jr.*, New York 1975, p. 170 (entry dated 10 Nov. 1944).

British reaction to the growing political strength of Zionism in the U.S.A. was mixed: on the one hand there was resentment at what was felt to be uninformed and electorally motivated criticism of the White Paper policy; but at the same time there was an increasing realization in British official circles that co-ordination of British and American policies over Palestine after the war would be essential in view of the strategic and economic interests of both powers in the area, especially given signs of heightened Soviet diplomatic activity in the Middle East. The first line of thought led Foreign Office officials to express concern at the 'public auction for Jewish votes'. One official ruminated darkly: 'It is at bottom (and elections apart) the old Anglo-Saxon penchant for distant underdogs. This time it is we who are "on the receiving end" as regards Palestine, India, etc. If we didn't care what effect it had on America we could quickly whack up an analogous agitation for the Negroes in America.'[27] The desire to co-ordinate policies had led in 1943 to a proposal, favoured by the U.S. State Department and by the Foreign Office, for a joint Anglo-American statement, designed to damp down Zionist agitation in the U.S.A. The draft text stated that it was 'undesirable that special viewpoints should be pressed while the war is in progress to such an extent as to create undue anxiety among other friendly governments and peoples'. Noting recent 'public discussions and activities of a political nature relating to Palestine (a thinly veiled reference to vociferous Zionist demands for the establishment of a Jewish 'Commonwealth' in Palestine), the draft recommended that 'these speculations should cease and that all efforts should be concentrated on the war'.[28] However, the statement was never issued, because, at the last moment, the U.S. Secretary of War, Henry Stimson, withdrew his earlier approval—a change of opinion which was generally attributed to Zionist influence in Washington.[29] Halifax regarded the American *volte-face* as 'a

[27] Minute by R. M. A. Hankey, 16 Oct. 1944, PRO FO 371/40132 (E 6298/67/31); Foreign Office minute (signature unclear), 10 Feb. 1944, PRO FO 371/38538 (A 548/20/45).

[28] PRO PREM 4/51/6/307.

[29] Memorandum by W. Murray (Near East Division of State Dept.) to Secretary of State, 16 Aug. 1943, *FRUS: Conferences at Washington and Quebec 1943*, pp. 673 ff.; Isaiah Berlin, *Zionist Politics in Wartime Washington: A Fragment of Personal Reminiscence* (Yaacov Herzog Memorial Lecture), Jerusalem 1972, p. 31.

rather sinister indication of the power of Jewish pressure groups in this country'.[30] British official anxiety about the trend of American opinion on Palestine increased in the course of 1944.

Meanwhile British thinking on the post-war solution of the problem was also changing. In July 1943 the Cabinet had decided to set up a committee to report on future policy in Palestine. The chairman of the committee was the Labour Home Secretary, Herbert Morrison, and other members included Sir Archibald Sinclair and Leopold Amery, both noted pro-Zionists, the latter appointed at Churchill's insistence.[31] The committee's terms of reference included an instruction that they 'should start by examining the Peel Commission's Report, and considering whether that scheme, or some variant of it, can now be adopted'.[32] By November 1943 the committee had reached agreement on a partition plan which divided Palestine into a Jewish state, a British mandatory area, and an Arab state to be joined in a large Arab federation of Greater Syria. The scheme had secured the approval of ministers unsympathetic to Zionism, such as Oliver Stanley and Lord Moyne, although not of the Foreign Office representative on the committee, Richard Law. Sinclair and Amery were disappointed with the small size of the proposed Jewish state, but Amery wrote to Churchill that they were prepared to accept it 'as an irreducible minimum'. Amery added:

The one thing that can make a judgement of Solomon possible is the swift and clean cut. What we cannot afford to do is to saw away slowly at a squealing infant in the presence of two hysterical mothers and amid the ululations of a chorus of equally hysterical relatives in the Arab and Jewish world.[33]

Amery's injunction was not heeded. Although the Cabinet approved the partition plan in principle in January 1944, strong opposition by the Foreign Secretary (who was supported by the Chiefs of Staff and by some British representatives in the Middle East, most notably Lord Killearn, British Ambassador

[30] Halifax to Foreign Office, 9 Aug. 1943, PRO PREM 4/51/6/293.
[31] Churchill to Eden, 11 July 1943, PRO PREM 4/52/1/202.
[32] Note by Cabinet Secretary, 14 July 1943, PRO PREM 4/52/1/200.
[33] Amery to Churchill, 22 Jan. 1944, PRO PREM 4/52/1/177.

in Cairo) delayed any further consideration of the proposal at Cabinet level until the autumn of 1944.

Meanwhile in Palestine there began in early 1944 a resurgence of terrorist activity by Jewish groups who launched bomb attacks on government immigration and tax offices, and on police stations, killing a number of British policemen. The main organization responsible was the *Irgun Tsevai Leumi*, revived under the leadership of Menahem Begin; but the *Irgun* was outflanked by a more militant offshoot, the Fighters for the Freedom of Israel, known to the *Yishuv* by its Hebrew acronym, *Lehi* and to the British as the 'Stern Gang' (after the name of its founder). The anti-British violence aroused concern among the mainstream Zionists and in the Government. Weizmann strongly condemned the dissidents, particularly after an attempt on the life of the High Commissioner, Sir Harold MacMichael, in August 1944.[34] MacMichael himself warned of the 'growth in the numbers of Jewish young men and women who are becoming infected with the gangster virus' which he attributed to 'persistent insidious propaganda' against the Government, and to the 'reiterated innuendo that countless Jewish lives were sacrificed in the abbatoirs of Europe to the deliberate obstructionism of the "Struma Government"'. He did not exempt the orthodox Zionists from his strictures, drawing attention to their 'aggressive nationalism', to their youth movements which, he reported, were 'unpleasantly reminiscent of Hitler Youth', and to 'the totalitarian organization and regimentation of the *Yishuv* by the [Jewish] Agency'.[35] In October 1944 the Jewish Agency was invited by the Colonial Secretary to co-operate in the suppression of the terrorists.[36] While not prepared to collaborate directly with the Palestine Police, the Agency decided to conduct a campaign of its own against the separatists, and a special unit of the *Haganah* was detailed to 'arrest' members of the *Irgun* and *Lehi*, several of whom were confined and interrogated by the *Haganah*. The Government too adopted a tougher policy in October 1944, with the arrest and deportation from Palestine to East Africa of

[34] See letter to editor of *The Times*, 18 Feb. 1944, from Weizmann; and statement by Weizmann reported in *The Times*, 11 Aug. 1944.

[35] High Commissioner to Colonial Office, 2 Oct. 1944, PRO FO 921/153.

[36] Cabinet minutes, 9 Oct. 1944, PRO PREM 4/52/5/Part I.

251 suspected members of the *Irgun*. However, neither the *Haganah* nor the Government proved capable of eradicating the terrorist groups.

Government consideration of future policy in Palestine was now once again approaching a point of decision. The principle of partition had by now gained an important new adherent in Sir Harold MacMichael who, in a lengthy dispatch on 17 July, had declared that the crucial issue was control of immigration. Were it practicable to stop mass immigration 'almost any political structure' could be made to work in Palestine. But the High Commissioner had lost faith in the British Government's capacity to prevent large-scale Jewish immigration at the end of the war. 'Since I became persuaded that His Majesty's Government would not, and probably could not, strictly and effectively control immigration, I have come, if for no other reason, to regard partition as faute de mieux inevitable.'[37] On 15 September Eden circulated to the Cabinet a cogently argued memorandum, entitled 'The Case Against Partition', in which he strongly opposed the recommendations of the Cabinet Committee. Eden described the view of Amery and others that partition would at least afford some 'finality' as 'pure illusion'. He warned that partition would 'remove all restrictions on Jewish immigration' and that the Zionists would 'not be deterred by the small size of the Jewish State from filling it up with immigrants beyond its capacity'. The Zionists would continue to hope for a larger state covering the whole of Palestine and Transjordan, the Arabs would 'be kept in a state of continual tension', and there would be endless disorders and bloodshed. The crux of Eden's argument was his appreciation of the dependence of British interests in the Middle East on good relations with the Arabs:

Obviously, if British interests in the Middle East are so important that we cannot afford to alienate the Arabs, it is essential to find some policy in which the Arabs can be expected to acquiesce even if it means the strict control of Jewish immigration into Palestine.

The Committee on Palestine should first, I think, make up its mind on the question whether or not the Middle East is vital to British interests. If not, then we can perhaps afford to gamble on a partition

[37] High Commissioner to Secretary of State for the Colonies, 17 July 1944, PROCO 733/461 Part I (75872/44).

policy. But if, as I believe, Middle Eastern oil and Middle Eastern communications are indeed vital to us, then it is essential to follow a different policy which will not alienate the Arab peoples.[38]

The Cabinet Committee, however, while making minor revisions in its recommendations, adhered to the principle of partition. In view of the difference of opinion, Churchill pressed for an early discussion of the committee's report by the Cabinet.[39]

The Zionist attitude to the renewed partition scheme was, as with the Peel Commission plan in 1937, ambivalent. The prospect that a sovereign Jewish state, however small, would be able to provide a sanctuary to any Jewish refugees fleeing persecution continued to attract many moderate Zionists to the idea of partition. But the public stance of the movement had by now hardened: the position now taken by most Zionist leaders, including Weizmann, was that enunciated at a Zionist Conference at the Biltmore Hotel, New York, in May 1942. The 'Biltmore programme' declared:

that the new world order that will follow victory cannot be established on foundations of peace, justice, and equality, unless the problem of Jewish homelessness is finally solved.

The Conference urges that the gates of Palestine be opened; that the Jewish Agency be vested with control of immigration into Palestine and with the necessary authority for upbuilding the country, including the development of its unoccupied and uncultivated lands; and that Palestine be established as a Jewish Commonwealth integrated in the structure of the new democratic world.[40]

In discussions with British ministers and officials, Weizmann, who had been apprised of the partition plan notwithstanding a Cabinet decision that it be kept secret, generally adhered to the Zionist demand for a Jewish state in the whole of Palestine. Nevertheless, the Colonial Secretary, Oliver Stanley, considered that Weizmann's opposition to partition was merely 'good tactics'.[41] Some substance was lent to this view by remarks made by Weizmann in October 1944 in a conversation with the Prime Minister's principal Private Secretary, J. M.

[38] Memorandum by Eden, 15 Sept. 1944, PRO CAB 95/14.
[39] See minute by C. W. Baxter, 4 Nov. 1944, PRO FO 371/45376/42.
[40] Text in Laqueur, *Israel-Arab Reader*, pp. 77–9.
[41] Stanley to Eden, 12 May 1944, PRO FO 371/40135/177.

Martin (who in 1936–7 had served as Secretary to the Peel Commission). Martin's account of the discussion stated:

I mentioned that I had seen propaganda against partition in the Zionist press, which published quotations from the Prime Minister's speech at the time of the Peel Report arguing against partition. Dr Weizmann's immediate comment was that what they feared was a variety of partition which would leave the Jews an impossibly small State and take from them some of the areas which they had already developed. He made it clear that he did not regard it as impossible to devise some form of partition which would be acceptable and frankly gave his reason as being that it was possible to take two bites at the cherry. So long as sufficient elbow room was given at the start, he did not see why all the burden should fall on the present generation and why one could not look to the possibility of future expansion by some means or other.[42]

On 4 November 1944 Weizmann secured an interview with Churchill, who told him that no pronouncement would be made on policy in Palestine until the end of the war with Germany. Questioned as to rumours about the Cabinet Committee's partition scheme, Churchill admitted that it existed, and said that, although he had not studied the proposals in detail, he was in favour of partition. While refusing to discuss details on a map, the Prime Minister added that in his own opinion the Negev desert in the south of Palestine should form part of the Jewish state. Weizmann did not argue for or against partition, saying that his only requirement was that the area allotted to the Jews should provide room for a large number of Jews, perhaps a million, who might be displaced after the war. While stressing the opposition to Zionism, particularly in his own party, Churchill assured Weizmann that such opposition only hardened his heart. Weizmann was much encouraged by the interview and declared that he put his faith in the Prime Minister and President Roosevelt.[43] Churchill did not mention to Weizmann that a Cabinet discussion of the partition plan was imminent. In the event, however, Cabinet consideration of

[42] Note by Martin, 4 Oct. 1944, PRO PREM 4/52/3/419.

[43] Accounts of interview in J. M. Martin to Sir G. Gater, 4 Nov. 1944, PRO PREM 4/52/3/410; and Weizmann to Rabbi Abba Hillel Silver, 7 Nov. 1944, WA. There are some discrepancies between these two versions of the conversation. According to Weizmann, the figure of 1½ million immigrants was mentioned. As for partition, Weizmann wrote to Silver: 'I gave the Prime Minister our reasons against partition.'

future policy in Palestine was indefinitely postponed, for on 6 November news arrived from Cairo of the assassination there of the Minister Resident in the Middle East, Lord Moyne.

The murder of Moyne by two *Lehi* gunmen came as a profound shock to the British and to the Zionists, and was to mark a fateful stage in the deterioration of Anglo-Zionist relations. Oliver Stanley broke the news to Weizmann, who said he was leaving immediately for Palestine, where he would tell the Jewish Agency Executive that 'there must now be war to the knife against these extremists. There must no longer be any reservation or hanging back, but complete cooperation with the Government in crushing them'.[44] In a talk with J. M. Martin two days later, Weizmann said that the news of the murder had shocked him as much as that of the loss of his son (reported missing in action with the R.A.F. in 1942), and he declared that he would make it his first duty upon arrival in Palestine to deal with 'this cancer'.[45] In fact, even before Weizmann's arrival, the Agency decided to co-operate fully with the Government of Palestine in rooting out the terrorists. Ben Gurion declared: 'To England terrorism like the murder of Lord Moyne is like a fly stinging a lion, but to Jewry it is a dagger plunged at the heart.'[46] Collaboration with the authorities was rendered easier by the arrival on 1 November of Lord Gort who succeeded Sir Harold MacMichael as High Commissioner. Although the private views of Gort on the politics of Palestine resembled those of MacMichael, he was to prove a much more popular figure among the *Yishuv* than the generally execrated Mac-Michael.

The most serious effects of the assassination, however, were upon British opinion, and above all on that of the Prime Minister, who had been a friend of Moyne, and who felt his loss as rather more than a 'sting'. The murder marked something of a watershed in Churchill's attitude to Zionism. Hitherto he had been forthright and unwavering in his advocacy of a Jewish state in Palestine after the war, and in his condemnation of the White Paper policy. After the killing of Moyne Churchill told the House of Commons: 'If our dreams for Zionism are to end

[44] Stanley to Churchill, 6 Nov. 1944, PRO PREM 4/51/11/1466.
[45] Martin to Churchill, 8 Nov. 1944, PRO PREM 4/51/11/1518.
[46] *The Times*, 23 Nov. 1944.

in the smoke of assassins' pistols and our labours for its future to produce only a new set of gangsters worthy of Nazi Germany, many like myself will have to reconsider the position we have maintained so consistently and so long in the past.'[47] Horror and indignation were widely felt in Britain, and in the immediate aftermath of the murder few were disposed to share the view of the *Manchester Guardian*, which pressed the 'case for a little more sympathy' for the Zionists.[48] The sternest reaction came, not unnaturally, from the British military and civil authorities in the Middle East. The Middle East Defence Committee, supported by Lord Killearn, urged that 'something drastic or dramatic' should be done by the British, on the model of the firm action taken in response to the murder in 1924 of Sir Lee Stack, Sirdar of the Egyptian Army and Governor-General of the Sudan.[49] On that occasion, the British High Commissioner in Egypt, Viscount Allenby, had delivered a humiliating ultimatum to the Egyptian Government, declaring that the murder held up Egypt 'to the contempt of civilised peoples', ordering payment by the Egyptian to the British Government of a fine of £500,000, and insisting on 'ample apology'.[50] In the present case it was urged that there should be a complete disarmament of the irregular Jewish forces (that is, the *Haganah* as well as the terrorist groups), and suspension of all further Jewish immigration to Palestine. Neither of these courses was in fact adopted. The first was rejected because the Government was informed that disarmament of the *Haganah*, now a well-organized force with more than 36,000 members, would require two British infantry divisions, two air squadrons, and a 'show of force' by a battleship at Haifa and a cruiser at Jaffa; these forces were not available for use in Palestine at the end of 1944.[51] Nor was immigration completely halted, for Churchill concluded that suspension of immigration might merely play into the hands of the terrorists.[52]

[47] HC vol. 404, col. 2242 (17 Nov. 1944).   [48] *Manchester Guardian*, 18 Nov. 1944.
[49] Minister Resident's Office, Cairo, to Foreign Office, 18 Nov. 1944, PRO FO 371/42823/23.
[50] Text of Allenby's ultimatum, 22 Nov. 1924, in Viscount Wavell, *Allenby in Egypt*, London 1943, p. 113.
[51] Commander-in-Chief, Middle East (General Paget) to Chiefs of Staff, 27 Nov. 1944, PRO FO 371/40138/42.
[52] Churchill to Colonial Secretary, 17 Nov. 1944, in Winston S. Churchill, *The Second World War*, vol. VI, London 1954, p. 612.

According to the terms of the White Paper, Jewish immigration to Palestine was due to come to a full stop on 31 March 1944, save in the unlikely event of Arab acquiescence in its continuation. However, in July 1943 the Cabinet decided, on the initiative of the then Colonial Secretary, Lord Cranborne, that as more than 30,000 out of the 75,000 immigrants envisaged by the White Paper had not yet reached Palestine, immigration would be permitted to continue beyond the original terminal date until the total of 75,000 had been attained.[53] The decision was announced to the House of Commons in November 1943 by Cranborne's successor, Oliver Stanley. It marked a departure from the strict letter of the White Paper, albeit one which had little immediate effect because it was made at a time when immigration was in any case at a very low ebb owing to the difficulties of escape from Nazi Europe. The concession was made in spite of the view of Sir Harold Mac-Michael that any Jewish immigration after 31 March 1944 would be 'a grave political mistake'.[54] So long as departure from Europe remained virtually impossible save for isolated individuals or small groups, the Government was able to maintain its policy intact, and the guarantee given to the Jewish Agency in July 1943 (and later relayed to the Turkish Government) that all Jewish refugees reaching Turkey would, after a security screening, be permitted to proceed to Palestine was honoured. But in the autumn of 1944 Russian victories in south-east Europe, culminating in the Roumanian withdrawal from the war in August and the Russian arrival at Budapest in December, suddenly rendered refugee movement out of the area possible again, and confronted the British Government with the unpalatable prospect that the quota of 75,000 might be filled before the end of the war. The Government shrank from the dilemma which would in that circumstance face it of deciding either to halt immigration altogether, thereby further alienating the Zionists, or permitting it to continue, thus

[53] Cabinet Conclusions, 2 July 1943, Confidential Annex, PRO CAB 65/39/3 ff.; Michael J. Cohen, 'The British White Paper on Palestine, May 1939: Part II The Testing of a Policy 1942–5', *Historical Journal*, vol. 19, no. 3, pp. 727–758.

[54] High Commissioner to Colonial Office, 1 Mar. 1944, quoted in J. S. Conway, 'Between Apprehension and Indifference: Allied Attitudes to the Destruction of Hungarian Jewry', *The Wiener Library Bulletin*, 1973/4, vol. XXVII, new series nos. 30/31, pp. 37–48.

alienating the Arabs. The former alternative might require large British forces to repress Jewish opposition. The latter would introduce a dangerous disturbing element into Anglo-Arab relations at a time (September–October 1944) when the founding conference of the Arab League was meeting in Cairo under the benevolent eye of the British.

Until the end of the war, therefore, all British efforts were bent towards reducing to a minimum Jewish immigration to Palestine in order to avoid such a difficult decision. In October 1944 the Colonial Office informed the Jewish Agency that

In view of the changed situation in the Balkans the undertaking conveyed to the Jewish Agency in . . . July 1943, that in future all Jews, whether adults or children, who may succeed in escaping to Turkey, will be eligible for onward transport to Palestine, is now withdrawn.

In its place the Colonial Office agreed to allow a total of 10,300 Jews to enter Palestine at a rate of not more than 1,500 per month.[55] This would prevent any breach of the 75,000 limit for at least a further seven months, that is until April 1945. The withdrawal of the guarantee to the Jewish Agency did not, however, halt the flow of Jewish refugees, especially from Roumania, which by November 1944 threatened to become a flood. The Government at first refrained from withdrawing the guarantee given to the Turkish Government that all Jews reaching Turkey would be given refuge somewhere by the British Government. In practice, however, no alternative destination to Palestine was available for most Jewish arrivals in Turkey. News that masses of Jews were now seeking to emigrate to Palestine gravely disturbed the British authorities. A report on 27 November from the British mission in Bucharest stated that 150,000 Jews in Roumania were destitute and that 'several tens of thousands' had already registered for emigration.[56] Alarmed by such reports, official thinking now tended to return to the moulds set during the illegal immigration wave of 1939–41. For example, R. M. A. Hankey of the Foreign Office Eastern Department minuted:

---

[55] Colonial Office to Jewish Agency, 5 Oct. 1944, PRO FO 371/42819/62–3 (WR 1403/3/48).

[56] Le Rougetel (Bucharest) to Foreign Office, 27 Nov. 1943, PRO FO 371/42823/44.

We must really be most careful to avoid a recurrence of illegal immigration from the Balkans if we possibly can. It is an absolute hydra. We should also send Jews back to Roumania if unauthorised parties start moving—unless we have somewhere outside Palestine as a destination. This may sound drastic, but we have our backs to the wall in Palestine and the Chiefs of Staff cannot provide forces to keep things in real order, unless they reduce the pressure on Germany; so it is the business of the civil departments now to prevent any aggravation of the situation there.[57]

In an effort to impede Jewish emigration, the Turkish Government was informed in December 1944 that the British guarantee to find some destination for Jewish refugees arriving in Turkey had been withdrawn.[58] This did not, however, prevent Jewish efforts to get out of Europe. By January 1945 it was reported from Bucharest that over 100,000 were now registered with the Jewish Agency for emigration to Palestine. The Foreign Office Refugee Department drew comfort from the fact that 'fortunately, the Soviet authorities on the Roumanian Control Commission take the line that they will not give Jews exit permits until they know that our people have given them visas for Palestine'.[59] Nevertheless, in the final weeks of the war, the *Mossad*, the Jewish Agency's underground organization of illegal immigration, re-established its network of agents in various parts of Europe, including Roumania. A renewed and even more bitter struggle over the White Paper now loomed.

With the end of the war in sight, some German officials, fearful of the fate which awaited them after defeat, sought to use surviving groups of Jews under their control as bargaining counters, in order to gain financial or political credit which might be drawn upon after the war. In Switzerland in December 1944 a representative of the American Jewish Joint Distribution Committee succeeded, after lengthy and dextrous negotiations with senior German officials (during which the bait of large financial rewards was dangled before the Germans), in extricating 1,684 Jewish prisoners from the Bergen-Belsen concentration camp, who were put across the Swiss frontier by the Germans. Further such discussions led to the

[57] Minute dated 29 Nov. 1944, PRO FO 371/42823/40–1 (WR 1835/3/48).
[58] Foreign Office to Angora, 18 Dec. 1944, PRO FO 371/42824/125 (WR 2082/3/48).
[59] P. Mason minute, 23 Jan. 1945, PRO FO 371/51111/35 (WR 195/4/48).

arrival in Switzerland in February 1945 of 1,210 prisoners from the Theresienstadt camp. Larger numbers of Jews were probably saved from death by virtue of these tortuous bargaining sessions, although they remained in German custody. An important part in these proceedings was played by the representative in Switzerland of the United States War Refugee Board.[60] Separate discussions on the Italian-Swiss border between German generals and American intelligence agents concerning a local surrender, led to a German offer to release several hundred Jews interned at Bolzano.[61] Meanwhile in Sweden discussions began in February with representatives of Heinrich Himmler for the unconditional release of Jews from Nazi concentration camps. In April thousands of Jews were released on orders from Himmler, and allowed to proceed to neutral territory. In these final months of the war, the International Red Cross, acting with more assurance than hitherto, was permitted some access to concentration camps, and was able to give succour to some prisoners. Hitler appears to have opposed these moves, which seem to have derived from a delusion on the part of Himmler that he might by such means earn credit which would save him from punishment for war crimes. This, at any rate, was the interpretation of the British Government, which refused to lend countenance to such negotiations.[62] Churchill's opinion, recorded in a minute to Eden, was adamant: 'No truck to Himmler.'[63]

At the close of the war in Europe British policy on the Jewish question had, in several important respects, turned almost full circle since 1939. Once again, after lengthy consideration of the possible partition of Palestine and of the creation of a Jewish state, the White Paper policy held the field. In 1945, as in 1939, considerable British efforts were being made to impede the flow of Jewish immigration to Palestine, with diplomatic representations being made by British representatives in south European capitals, and expedients such as deportation of illegal immigrants being mooted. At the end of the war the British Government appeared hardly more enthusiastic than at the

---

[60] See Bauer, 'Onkel Saly'.
[61] Allen Dulles, *The Secret Surrender*, London 1967, pp. 99 ff.
[62] PRO FO 371/51194 *passim*.
[63] Churchill minute, 5 Apr. 1944, PRO PREM 4/52/5/Part I/786.

beginning about efforts by the German authorities to promote the departure of large groups of Jews from the Reich. In other ways, too, official attitudes seemed to have returned to the moulds of the late 1930s. There was general agreement that the Jewish problem in post-war Europe must be solved in the countries where Jews lived, and not by emigration. British disapproval was expressed of the tendency of U.N.R.R.A. officials (mainly Americans) to recognize Jews as a distinct category among refugees. The Home Office in February 1945 advocated the compulsory renationalization as German or Austrian citizens of Jewish refugees from those countries who had lost their nationality as a result of discrimanatory Nazi decrees.[64] When a complaint was received that Jewish refugees in liberated Belgium in October 1944 were being imprisoned by the local authorities on the ground that they were 'enemy aliens', one Foreign Office official commented: 'I trust we shall not rush in with representations to the Belgian Government. Apart from the fact that Belgian feeling towards Germans and Austrians, whether anti-Nazi or not, is very bitter, there is an important security aspect.' Another official concurred, remarking that he would 'have more sympathy with the Jews' if they regarded the war as a 'general' rather than as a 'private' conflict.[65]

It was only with the liberation of the concentration camps in western Germany by British and American troops in the final weeks of the war that there was a dawning realization in Britain of the magnitude of the catastrophe that had befallen European Jewry. The United Nations declaration of December 1942 had provided ample grounds for such an appreciation, but, as has been seen, there endured until almost the end of the war a tendency in official circles to dismiss Jewish reports of the scale of atrocities as exaggerated. The advance of Russian forces through Poland in 1944, and the capture of Auschwitz by the Red Army in January 1945 (with under three thousand inmates left alive), had provided further evidence. But the British public consciousness was fully awakened only when British soldiers, officials, and correspondents sent home first-hand

[64] Home Office to Foreign Office, 27 Feb. 1945, PRO FO 371/51085/21.
[65] Minutes by C. W. Harrison & R. M. A. Hankey, 17 Oct. 1944, PRO FO 371/42892/2 (WR 1362/1362/48).

accounts of what they had seen in the liberated camps. On 21 April 1945 a British Parliamentary Delegation visited the concentration camp at Buchenwald, which had been liberated by American forces ten days earlier. The delegation's report, published as a White Paper, gave a harrowing description of conditions in the camp, which, they concluded, marked 'the lowest point of degradation to which humanity has yet descended'.[66] Richard Crossman, at that time Assistant Chief of the Psychological Warfare Division of S.H.A.E.F.,[67] described the effect on him of the first direct reports from Buchenwald: 'Though we had heard and reported many stories of Nazi massacres of Jews and Slavs, we had never believed in the possibility of "genocide" . . . Now we were to realize that our propaganda had fallen far behind the truth.'[68] 'Unconditional surrender' had now been achieved. But for the majority of European Jewry it had come too late. The sombre fear recorded in the Warsaw Ghetto in 1941 had proved to be grimly prophetic:

There are pessimists who are afraid the English will finally arrive, declaring, "We have conquered!"—to our graves.[69]

[66] *Buchenwald Camp: The Report of a Parliamentary Delegation*, Cmd. 6626, London, Apr. 1945.

[67] Supreme Headquarters Allied Expeditionary Force.

[68] Richard Crossman, *Palestine Mission: A Personal Record*, London 1946, p. 18.

[69] Sloan ed., *Ringelblum Journal*, p. 125.

Conclusion

THERE IS little to celebrate in this account of British policy towards the Jews of Europe between 1939 and 1945. A few flashes of humanity by individuals lighten the general darkness. Churchill's attitude towards the Jews was one of sympathy and compassion. But the effectiveness of his interventions in favour of the Jews was repeatedly blunted by the actions of his subordinates. The generous impulses of a small number of officials and politicians stand out from the documents mainly by virtue of their isolation amidst an ocean of bureaucratic indifference and lack of concern. The overall record leaves a profoundly saddening impression.

During the first two years of the war, when the German authorities bent their efforts to securing the exodus of Jews from the Reich and from Nazi-occupied territory, it was the British Government which took the lead in barring the escape routes from Europe against Jewish refugees. On the second day of the war an overcrowded hulk, carrying terrified refugees, including women and children, in flight from the terror of Britain's enemies, was fired on by British forces when those on board sought haven on British-held territory (in a country which Britain, under the different exigencies of a previous war, had thought fit to declare their 'national home'). In January 1940 the Colonial Office considered it necessary, in order to preserve British security in the Middle East, to seek to prevent an American charity sending food to dying families who had been marooned for months on the frozen Danube. The Government of Palestine, in December 1940, after the *Patria* explosion, was so anxious to get rid of the surviving passengers from the *Atlantic*, that it was not prepared to delay their deportation for a matter of days in order to isolate typhoid carriers: the result was an epidemic and many deaths. A few days later, when the

Salvador sank in the Sea of Marmara with the loss of two hundred lives, the head of the Foreign Office Refugee Department wrote that he considered the event an 'opportune disaster'.[1] When the Jews complained, a standard response was that given by Sir Harold MacMichael to Moshe Shertok on the occasion of the *Atlantic* deportations: 'One might think that the British Government were going to do something inhuman.'[2]

Some apologists for British policy seek to impugn the Zionists on the ground that they allegedly concentrated exclusively on immigration to Palestine, and were not prepared to countenance the diversion of refugees elsewhere. John Marlowe writes:

If the Zionists and their supporters had concentrated on the humanitarian, instead of on the political and propagandist aspect, and if they had in consequence asked H.M.G. to treat these wretched people as refugees and not as prospective Palestine immigrants, there is no doubt that H.M.G. (which had a far better pre-war record than the U.S. Government over the relief of Jewish refugees) would have done everything possible to assist them.[3]

Christopher Sykes writes:

The Jewish Agency were determined . . . not to budge an inch from their essential principle: the flow of refugees was to come into Palestine and was to be diverted nowhere else: better that they should die than be so used as to enfeeble Zionist resolve.[4]

Against the happy retrospective generosity of Mr Marlowe we may set such incidents as the voyage of the *Alsina*, or the reaction of the British Government to suggestions that Jews from Luxemburg or Vichy France might be admitted to Britain. The not inconsiderable expanse of the British Empire was found, as one official put it, to have an 'absorptive capacity [of] nil' when it came to the admission of Jewish refugees.[5] The Labour Home Secretary considered the danger of anti-Semitism in Britain during the war so menacing as to preclude the admission of any significant numbers of Jewish refugees to

[1] See p. 77.
[2] See p. 68.
[3] John Marlowe, *The Seat of Pilate: An Account of the Palestine Mandate*, London 1959, p. 171.
[4] Christopher Sykes, *Cross Roads to Israel*, London 1965, pp. 271–2.
[5] See p. 47.

the United Kingdom. At the end of the war he urged that refugees from Germany should be compulsorily renationalized as Germans, and he is represented in Cabinet minutes as arguing for their return to Germany on the basis that anti-Semitism was a lesser threat there than in Britain.[6] Yet, these facts notwithstanding, a peculiar inversion of logic leads historians such as Mr Marlowe and Mr Sykes to condemn not the British Government but the Zionists for the failure to find Jewish refugees safe havens in places other than Palestine. It is perhaps necessary to state the obvious fact that it was not in the power of the Zionist Organization to decree that Jews be admitted to British colonies or to the United Kingdom; that power resided in the British Government; we have seen how it was exercised. As for the further allegation by Mr Sykes that the Zionists preferred that Jewish refugees perish rather than permit them to be diverted to destinations other than Palestine, this may be described as a lie within a lie. For not only was there in reality nowhere else that refugees might have gone in substantial numbers, but, as has been shown, the Zionists were in fact prepared to countenance, and indeed to co-operate in, such a diversion of Jewish refugees to safe destinations. The Zionist Organization's reiterated offers in this sense were rejected by the British Government out of an anxiety lest the Zionists might somehow gain political credit by such an arrangement.[7] Yet we find the charge levelled not at the British Government but at the Zionists that they concentrated on the 'political and propagandist aspect' at the expense of humanitarian considerations.

If comment is to be made on the 'propagandist aspect' it is worth remarking the frequent disparity between the public professions of the British Government as to its concern for the fate of Jewish refugees and the reality of British policy. In public on 17 December 1942 Eden, in a memorable scene in the House of Commons, read out the Allied declaration condemning the Nazi persecutions of the Jews. In private on 31 December 1942 Eden presided over a meeting of the Cabinet Committee on the Reception and Accommodation of Jewish Refugees at which it was agreed that Britain could not admit

[6] See p.131.
[7] See pp. 65 and 73.

more than 1,000 to 2,000 further refugees. It was later agreed
that no substantial numbers could be admitted to the Dominions or the colonies.[8] In response to public concern it was
decided to convene an Anglo-American conference in Bermuda
to consider the refugee problem. The conference, meeting (privately) in April 1943, was based on an implicit understanding
that the United States delegates would not raise the thorny
issue of immigration to Palestine, while their British colleagues
would avoid the contentious subject of American immigration
laws. After 'ten days of agreeable discussion' the British delegates reported to London that 'so far as immediate relief to
refugees is concerned, the conference was able to achieve very
little'.[9] It is hardly surprising that it was considered imprudent
to publish the final report of the conference. The meagre results
of the Bermuda deliberations did not deter Eden from pronouncing the conference a 'marked success'.[10] Nor did he
shrink from informing the House of Commons on 19 May 1943
that 'if there were the slightest prospect' of refugees reaching
Palestine in excess of the thirty thousand vacancies still remaining under the White Paper quota he would be 'willing and
eager' to discuss the admission of these larger numbers.[11] The
true value of these protestations may be assessed by weighing
them against the (non-public) statement handed to the American Ambassador in London in December 1943, when there
appeared a possibility of securing the departure of seventy
thousand Jews from Roumania. The Ambassador was
informed that 'the Foreign Office are concerned with the difficulties of disposing of any considerable number of Jews should
they be rescued from enemy-occupied territory'.[12] When the
fate of Hungarian Jewry hung in the balance in mid-1944 the
attitude of most ministers and officials was similar. In the final
year of the war, when escape from Europe again became a
practicable proposition for a few of the Jewish survivors, the
British Government resumed its practice of earlier years in
seeking to prevent the departure of Jews from Europe. Because
of the stringency of the Government's attitude even the limit of

[8] See p. 183.
[9] See p. 201.
[10] See p. 205.
[11] See p. 204.
[12] See p. 247.

seventy-five thousand immigrants to Palestine permitted under the White Paper had not been attained by the end of the war.

Nor did other aspects of British policy towards Jewish refugees during the war bring greater credit on the Government. The 'fifth column' panic of 1940 led to the needless internment of thirty thousand 'enemy aliens', the overwhelming majority of whom were refugees friendly to the allied cause. Among the many bizarre products of this policy was the diversion of valuable shipping space for the deportation of eight thousand aliens (including many Jewish refugees) to Canada and Australia, a proceeding accompanied by much ill-treatment of the deportees. Among all the resistance movements of occupied Europe that of the Jews stood almost alone in the near-total absence of aid, whether in weapons, outside advisers, or propaganda, from the Allies. The persistent efforts of the Zionists to secure the establishment of a Jewish fighting force within the British Army (on the lines of the 'Jewish Legion' in the First World War) were rejected by the British Government until 1944 ostensibly on grounds of lack of equipment, in fact because such a force was regarded as a potential political liability. Pleas to the Government to relax the economic blockade of Axis Europe to permit some food and medical relief to be sent to the ghettos and concentration camps met with little substantial success. The proposal for the bombardment of Auschwitz by the Allies, although favoured by Churchill and Eden, was obstructed by officials in the Foreign Office and the Air Ministry.

What is the explanation for this unimpressive record?

Ignorance of the persecution of Jews in Europe cannot be seen as a major element. It is true that until the end of 1942 many British officials refused to believe most of the reports of atrocities which were presented to them. They recalled the atrocity propaganda of the First World War and what were regarded as the exaggerated accounts of pogroms in Eastern Europe in the period 1918–21, and they suspected that Nazi barbarities were being magnified in the telling. Even after the Allied declaration of 17 December 1942 some officials persisted in their criticism of Jewish reports of mass murders as exaggerations. Yet it cannot be argued that the Foreign Office had no inkling of what the results of its actions might be when its representatives in several continents played a foremost part in sealing the escape routes of Jewish refugees fleeing for their lives. The written record of Foreign Office consideration of the problem presented by the *Struma*, for example, makes it clear that some at least of the officials who dealt with the matter were aware of the probable consequences of sending the boat back into the Black Sea. Nevertheless, strong pressure was exerted by Britain on the Turkish Government to pursue that very course. It was perhaps less a matter of ignorance than of blindness to the reality of the Jewish catastrophe in Europe. Churchill, with his broader imagination, was almost alone in his grasp of the magnitude of the disaster. He wrote: 'This is probably the greatest and most horrible crime ever committed in the whole history of the world, and it has been done by scientific machinery by nominally civilised men in the name of a great State and one of the leading races of Europe.'[13] The narrower horizons of the official mind rarely stretched to encompass the vastness of the horror which had overtaken the Jews of Europe.

It was not, however, unthinking obedience to orders, sometimes held to explain the murderous actions of German soldiers and bureaucrats in this period, that animated British officials in many of the incidents discussed in this book. For, as we have seen, it was frequently the officials themselves, particularly in the Colonial Office and the Government of Palestine, who pressed for the adoption of radical methods, such as the suggestion for firing on unarmed refugee vessels to keep them away from the shores of Palestine.[14] Indeed, in some instances officials ignored orders which were not to their liking, or by inaction permitted them to wither away. Delay, one of the chief weapons in the bureaucrat's armoury, repeatedly prevented the implementation of schemes for aid to the Jews of Europe. The process by which officials of the Foreign Office and Air Ministry rendered null a clear instruction from the Prime Minister and the Foreign Secretary to arrange for the bombing of Auschwitz is one such instance—a notable illustration of the capacity of Whitehall to thwart the will even of the most powerful Prime Minister in British history. Part of the explana-

---

[13] See p. 259.
[14] See pp. 79–80.

tion for the common official attitude towards the Jewish problem may lie in the weight of precedent, in particular in the continuation of attitudes towards Jewish refugees formed before the outbreak of the war, when the British Government had been devoting strenuous efforts to combat illegal Jewish immigration to Palestine. The blunting of ordinary human feelings when institutionalized in the straitjacket of bureaucratic procedure may also form a partial explanation. And simple irritation with the persistence, ubiquity, and (it was felt) selfishness of Jewish complaints, demands, and pleas, led to such comments as that of J. S. Bennett of the Colonial Office that 'The Jews have done nothing but add to our difficulties by propaganda and deeds since the war began';[15] the remark of Sir John Shuckburgh that 'I am convinced that in their hearts they hate us and have always hated us; they hate all Gentiles';[16] and the view expressed in September 1944 by A. R. Dew, head of the Southern Department of the Foreign Office (commenting on submissions made by the Board of Deputies of British Jews urging measures to help Jews in Hungary and Roumania): 'In my opinion a disproportionate amount of the time of this office is wasted in dealing with these wailing Jews.'[17]

Certainly there was a tinge of anti-Semitism in the words of some British officials and politicians, as such minutes demonstrate. But anti-Semitism does not by itself explain British conduct. There is no doubt that anti-Semitism was in the air in Britain during the war, partly as a result of general xenophobia and war hysteria, partly arising from resentment of immigrants and complaints of black market activity and war profiteering. Officials and politicians were not immune from infection by the public mood. There was a definite Government tendency, exemplified most notably by Herbert Morrison in his attitude to wartime refugee immigration, to bend with the wind of hostility to refugees, rather than give a lead or build upon the more generous elements in public opinion. However, even in the cases of those such as Eden, who thought it opportune in 1941 to 'murmur' to his private secretary that he 'prefer[red]

[15] See p. 50.
[16] Ibid.
[17] Minute dated 1 Sept. 1944, PRO FO 371/42817/16 (WR 993/3/48).

Arabs to Jews',[18] conscious anti-Semitism should not be regarded as an adequate explanation of official behaviour.

It was rather that within the context of the total war effort aid to the Jews of Europe was seen as a low priority which must give way to what were believed to be inexorable strategic realities. The immigration provisions of the 1939 White Paper were regarded by British officials and by most leading politicians (but not Churchill) as an essential bulwark of the shaky British position in the Middle East. Total economic warfare against the Axis, it was argued, precluded the dispatch of large-scale relief to Jews in occupied Europe. The war aim of 'unconditional surrender' was invoked to justify the refusal to countenance negotiation, bargains, or deals with the enemy for the release of Jews. The support of the Jews for the Allied cause could be taken for granted and therefore required no additional stimulation from the British Government. As one Foreign Office official minuted in 1941: 'When it comes to the point, the Jews will never hamper us to put the Germans on the throne.'[19] The Jewish Agency's protestations of loyalty to the struggle against Nazism therefore cut little ice in official circles. 'World Jewry', that supposedly powerful international force which had so impressed the British Government at the time of the Balfour Declaration in 1917, now stood nakedly exposed in its true defencelessness; it was no longer a factor of much apparent international consequence. Halifax (at the time Foreign Secretary) expressed the view in a letter to Weizmann in December 1939:

Let me assure you that I am the last to underrate the value of Jewish sympathy and cooperation with the Allied war effort. But, highly as His Majesty's Government appreciated Jewish offers of assistance on the outbreak of war, it must not be overlooked that those offers were made unconditionally and were welcomed on that footing. So far as this country is concerned, we are putting our whole energy into a life-and-death struggle with Nazi Germany, the persecutor of Jewry in Central Europe, and by ridding Europe of the present German régime we hope to render a supreme service to the Jewish people.[20]

[18] See p. 34.
[19] See p. 37.
[20] Viscount Halifax to Dr Weizmann, 19 Dec. 1939, PRO FO 371/24563/273 (E97/31/31).

At the heart of the matter was a political element which helps to explain the low priority accorded to aid for the Jews of Europe. The retreat from the Balfour Declaration policy was also a retreat from the perception of the Jews as a nation. The Jews lacked the essential attribute of state sovereignty, and (by contrast with the position during the First World War) it was a cardinal principle of British policy that the Jews should not gain state sovereignty. Moreover, during the struggle against Nazism, liberal principle might appear to demand that the Jews be seen not as a distinct entity but merely as part of the nations among whom they lived. The British Government therefore tended to regard the notion that the Jews were an allied people as (to quote an official minute) 'a major fallacy'.[21] The Jews of Europe were, of course, in many cases citizens of allied countries, such as Poland or Czechoslovakia, but this benefited them little, for they were persecuted not as Poles or Czechs but as Jews. The British Government would not, however, allow that they had thereby any special claim to help. Indeed, in certain instances the contrary was the case. For example, in July 1940, when arrangements were being made to evacuate Polish soldiers from south-east Europe to Palestine, the High Commissioner cabled to the Colonial Office to 'suggest that only non-Jews be regarded as acceptable'. He added that he had 'reason to believe that [the] Polish authorities would be willing to arrange that only non-Jews should come to Palestine'.[22]

This political element lay at the basis of much official thinking, and is vital to an explanation of one of the most depressing features of British policy towards the Jews: the unavoidable conclusion that, when set in the context of total war and of British policy towards Allied nations in general, the Jews received peculiarly ungenerous treatment. Far from shedding a more favourable light on Britain's Jewish policy, an examination of it within the broader context merely highlights its deficiencies. There is, for example, a painful contrast between the niggardly quantities of food relief which the Ministry of Economic Warfare permitted to be sent to Jews in central and

[21] Marginal comment by J. S. Bennett on cable from Colonial Secretary to High Commissioner for Palestine, 4 Dec. 1942, PRO FO 921/10.
[22] High Commissioner to Colonial Office, 10 July 1940, PRO CO 733/431 (76039).

eastern Europe, and the wholesale operation by which the Allies supplied the entire food needs of the population of Axis-occupied Greece between 1942 and the end of the war. As against a total of 4,500 tons of foodstuffs which the International Red Cross was permitted to send to inmates of concentration camps between autumn 1943 and 1945,[23] $40,000,000 worth of foodstuffs (comprising up to 35,000 tons per month) were permitted to go through the blockade to Greece. The huge disparity between those figures calls for explanation. According to the official British history of the economic blockade, 'it was accepted from the start that Greece, in view of her valiant resistance to the Axis, and her normal dependence on imported food, was a special case, and the Foreign Office took the lead in pressing the view that something effective, whether consistent with the blockade or not, must be done . . . As the Allied Governments were unable to enter on a battle of wills with the Germans over the dying bodies of their former allies they accepted the principle of relief on terms which led naturally to increasing shipments.'[24] Whatever the merits of the Greek case, there is a striking incongruity between the solicitude shown towards the Greeks on the question of relief, and the *non possumus* attitude characteristic of British handling of proposals for the relief of Jews in occupied Europe. There is a similar dissonance between the welcome accorded to tens of thousands of Yugoslav and Greek refugees from Nazism in the Middle East after 1941 and the more chilly reception accorded to Jews. Even more remarkable is the contrast between the official preparations which were undertaken in early 1940 for the reception of up to 300,000 Dutch and Belgian refugees in Britain, and the consistent refusal of the Home Secretary to consider the admission to the United Kingdom of more than one or two thousand Jewish refugees. But then, as a Foreign Office minute pointed out, the Jews of Luxemburg were 'simply racial refugees'.[25] That was not, in itself, a sufficient qualification for entry to Britain; indeed, it appears from the record, rather the contrary. Most poignant is the disparity

---

[23] *Report of the International Committee of the Red Cross on its Activities during the Second World War*, 3 vols., Geneva 1948, vol. III, p. 80.
[24] W. N. Medlicott, *The Economic Blockade*, vol. II, London 1959, pp. 263 and 272.
[25] See p. 109.

between the extraordinary efforts devoted by the Western powers to the provision of assistance to the Warsaw rising (of the Polish Home Army) in August–September 1944, and the unanswered cries of the Jewish rebels on the Warsaw Ghetto in April–May 1943. The Jews suffered more than any other group in Europe; their commitment to the Allied cause was firmer than that of any other nationality. Yet the Jews, it is plain, were not regarded as a 'special case', except perhaps in a negative sense.

An explanation only in terms of priorities, balances of interest, strategic calculation, and rational decision-making remains inadequate if we are fully to understand what lay behind British official attitudes towards the Jews. Part of the explanation may also be found in the collective paranoia to which modern nations involved in total war are prone. The exaggerated fears which led to the mass internment of 'friendly enemy aliens' in Britain in the summer of 1940, accompanied by such comic-opera episodes as the police raid on Hampstead Public Library, or the arrests of elderly gentlemen who had lived in Britain continuously since infancy, are hard to explain in other terms. Similarly the repeated insistence of the Government of Palestine and the Colonial Office on the supposed danger that Nazi agents might be smuggled into Palestine among Jewish immigrants, and the determination of the authorities on that account to exclude all immigrants emanating from enemy or enemy-occupied territories (that is, all refugees), derived from demonstrably baseless anxieties. For these authorities, when challenged by the Foreign Office and invited to produce the evidence on which they based their fears, found themselves compelled to admit that not a single such agent had ever been unearthed.[26] This confession annoyed the Foreign Office which had used the 'agents' threat as a propaganda argument in the USA in justification of British immigration policy in Palestine. The admission that no evidence existed was made in January 1941, and the documentation now available does not suggest that there was any significant change in the position later in the war. Yet at the time of the *Struma* affair in December 1941, Lord Moyne returned to the alleged threat as the main prop of his argument in favour of sending the ship

[26] See p. 49.

back into the Black Sea.[27] The notion was to crop up in similar discussions throughout the war, drawing the apt comment from a Foreign Office official that it had 'fatal attraction . . . like the candle-flame for the moth—though they get burnt every time they come near it'.[28]

A final element in an explanation of British behaviour may lie in an imaginative failure to grasp the full meaning of the consequences of decisions, when those consequences were distant, unseen, and bore no direct personal relation to the actor. Dr Anthony Storr notes that the majority of men, given a can of petrol and told to pour it over a child of three and ignite it, will tend to disobey the order. Yet put the same decent men in aircraft a few hundred feet above a town, and they will often be ready without compunction to inflict death or appalling pain on masses of men, women, and children. Distance has a disinhibiting effect. Moreover, as Dr Storr further points out, distance need not be physical; it may simply be psychological.[29] The average British official lived in a different mental world from that of the Jewish refugee. The Pall Mall club and the Palestine internment camp were not merely different places: they were different psychological universes, conditioning attitudes and reflexes which rarely found points of contact. The effects of such distancing and of the fissure between the official and refugee mentalities were perceptively analysed by Richard Crossman in a diary entry written after a visit to the Dachau concentration camp immediately after V-E day:

The abyss which separates the outside world from the concentration camp influences both sides equally. Even the most sensitive and intelligent people whom we met in Dachau seemed to accept it as the only reality, and to think of the outside world as a mirage. Similarly the incoming troops, after the first uprush of indignation, seemed to slump back into accepting Dachau, not as 32,000 fellow human beings like themselves, but as a strange monstrosity to be treated on its own standards. How else can one explain that ten days after the liberation no one thinks it strange that there are no trucks to carry the dying to hospital and no proper diet in the hospital? If a town of 32,000 people had been struck by a cyclone, an immense rescue apparatus would be organised. But these 32,000 outcasts are so

[27] See p. 145.
[28] See p. 51.
[29] Anthony Storr, *Human Aggression*, London 1970, p. 152.

remote from civilisation as we know it that we are content to leave them as they are, improving slightly their living standards.[30]

It may be objected that if Britain's record on the Jewish question during the war was unimpressive, that of other countries was often far worse. There is some truth in this. But it was not by the standards of others that a lone and justifiably proud Britain chose to fight without allies in this her 'finest hour'. The Jews, in their most desperate and dependent hour, looked in particular to Britain for some gesture of concern as token of her adhesion to the values for which she waged war. The response has been described in this book. The men chiefly responsible for sending the *Struma* to her doom, for refusing to admit significant numbers of Jewish refugees to Britain, Palestine, or the Empire, for blocking the bombardment of Auschwitz, and for the other decisions which have been discussed, were the sort who would probably have played the part of the Good Samaritan if their neighbour had fallen among thieves. But the agony of European Jewry was enacted in a separate moral arena, a grim twilight world where their conventional ethical code did not apply. And so they 'came and looked, and passed by on the other side.'

[30] Crossman, *Palestine Mission*, p. 21.

Who was who

Below are brief notes on British politicians and officials of particular relevance to this book. Information given is in general restricted to the period 1939 to 1945. Names are listed according to the form used in the text; where the form subsequently changed, the later form is also noted.

WILLIAM DENIS ALLEN (b. 1910): Second Sec., Br. Embassy in China, 1939–41; Chargé d'Affaires, Chungking 1942; transferred to Foreign Office Central Dept. 1942; K.C.M.G. 1958.

RICHARD HUGH SEDLEY ALLEN (b. 1903): First Sec., Br. Embassy in Santiago, 1939–42; transferred to Bogotá 1942; subsequently transferred to Foreign Office; promoted to Counsellor 1946.

LEOPOLD CHARLES MAURICE AMERY (1873–1955): Con. M.P. for Birmingham, Sparkbrook, 1918–1945; Sec. of State of India 1940–1945.

SIR JOHN ANDERSON, 1st Viscount Waverley from 1952 (1882–1958): Ind. Nat. M.P. for Scottish Universities 1938–50; Lord Privy Seal 1938–9; Home Sec. and Min. of Home Security 1939–40; Lord President of the Council 1940–3; Chancellor of the Exchequer 1943–5.

CLEMENT RICHARD ATTLEE, 1st Earl Attlee from 1955 (1883–1967): Lab. M.P. for Limehouse 1922–50; Leader of the Opposition 1935–40; Lord Privy Seal 1940–2; Sec. of State for Dominions 1942–3; Lord President of the Council 1943–5; Deputy Prime Minister 1942–5; Prime Minister 1945–51.

CHARLES WILLIAM BAXTER (1895–1969): Seconded from Foreign Office to Min. of Economic Warfare 1939–40; resumed duties at Foreign Office as head of Eastern Dept., and promoted to Counsellor 1940.

JOHN SLOMAN BENNETT (b. 1914): Entered Colonial Service 1936; seconded to Office of Minister of State in Middle East, 1941–5.

EDMUND BLAIKIE BOYD (1894–1946): Entered Colonial Office 1919;

Private Sec. to successive Colonial Secs. 1930–7; member of Palestine Currency Board 1941–5.

BRENDAN RENDALL BRACKEN, 1st Viscount Bracken from 1952 (1901–58): Con. M.P. for Paddington N., 1929–45; Min. of Information 1941–5; First Lord of the Admiralty 1945.

RICHARD AUSTEN BUTLER, Lord Butler of Saffron Walden from 1965 (b. 1902): Con. M.P. for Saffron Walden 1929–65; Under-Sec. of State for Foreign Affairs 1938–41; Min. of Education 1941–5.

SIR ALEXANDER GEORGE MONTAGU CADOGAN (1884–1968): Permanent Under-Sec., Foreign Office 1938–46.

VICTOR FREDERICK WILLIAM CAVENDISH-BENTINCK (b. 1897): Acting Counsellor (Counsellor from 1942), Foreign Office, and head of Services Liaison Dept. from 1940; Chairman of Joint Intelligence Committee from 1940; Asst. Under-Sec. of State, Foreign Office 1944.

ARTHUR NEVILLE CHAMBERLAIN (1869–1940): Con. M.P. for Birmingham, Edgbaston, 1929–40; Prime Minister 1937–40; Lord President of the Council 1940.

WINSTON LEONARD SPENCER CHURCHILL (1874–1965): Con. M.P. for Epping 1924–45; First Lord of the Admiralty 1939–40; Prime Minister and Minister of Defence 1940–45; K.G. 1953.

VISCOUNT CRANBORNE, ROBERT ARTHUR JAMES GASCOYNE-CECIL, Marquess of Salisbury from 1947 (1893–1972): Paymaster-General 1940; Sec. of State for Dominions 1940–2 and 1943–5; Sec. of State for Colonies 1942; Lord Privy Seal 1942-3.

RICHARD HOWARD STAFFORD CROSSMAN (1907–74): Dep. Director of Psychological Warfare, A.F.H.Q., Algiers 1943; Asst. Chief of Psychological Warfare Division of S.H.A.E.F. 1944–5; Member of Anglo-American Committee of Inquiry on Palestine 1945–6; Asst. Editor of *The New Statesman and Nation* 1938–55.

HAROLD FREDERICK DOWNIE (1889–1966): Head of Middle East Dept. of Colonial Office to 1941; appointed one of Crown Agents for Colonies 1942; K.B.E. 1951.

ROBERT ANTHONY EDEN, K.G. 1954, Earl of Avon from 1957 (1897–1977): Con. M.P. for Warwick and Leamington 1923–57; Sec. of State for Foreign Affairs 1935–8 and 1940–5; for Dominions 1939–40; for War May–Dec. 1940.

SIR HERBERT WILLIAM EMERSON (1881–1962): League of Nations High Commissioner for Refugees 1936–46; Director of Inter-Governmental Committee for Refugees 1939–47.

HARRY MAURICE EYRES (1898–1962): Consul in Foreign Office Eastern Dept., 1938–44.

SIR GEORGE HENRY GATER (1886–1963): Permanent Under-Sec., Colonial Office 1939–47.

LORD GORT, FIELD-MARSHALL JOHN STANDISH SURTEES PRENDER-GAST VEREKER (1886–1946): Chief of Imperial General Staff 1937–9; Commander-in-Chief of British Field Force 1939–40; Inspector-General to Forces for Training 1940–41; Governor of Gibraltar 1941–2; of Malta 1942–4; High Commissioner for Palestine and Transjordan 1944–5.

SIR PERCY JAMES GRIGG (1890–1964): Nat. M.P. for Cardiff East 1942–5; Permanent Under-Sec., War Office, 1939–42; Sec. of State for War 1942–5.

LORD HALIFAX, EDWARD FREDERICK LINDLEY WOOD, Earl of Halifax from 1944 (1881–1959): Sec. of State for Foreign Affairs 1938–40; Br. Ambassador to U.S.A. 1941–6.

GEORGE HENRY HALL, 1st Viscount Hall from 1946 (1881–1965): Lab. M.P. for Aberdare 1922–46; Parliamentary Under-Sec., Colonial Office 1940–42; Financial Sec., Admiralty 1942–3; Parliamentary Under-Sec., Foreign Office 1943–5.

ROBERT MAURICE ALERS HANKEY, 2nd Baron Hankey from 1963 (b. 1905): First Sec. Br. Embassy, Bucharest 1939; transferred to Cairo 1941; to Tehran 1942; later transferred to Foreign Office.

OLIVER CHARLES HARVEY, 1st Baron Harvey of Tasburgh from 1954 (1893–1968): Private Sec. to Sec. of State for Foreign Affairs 1936–9 and 1941–3; Asst. Under-Sec., Foreign Office 1943–6.

SIR CLIFFORD HEATHCOTE-SMITH (1883–1963): Br. Consul-General in Alexandria 1924–43; Representative in Italy of Inter-Governmental Committee for Refugees 1944–5.

IAN LESLIE HENDERSON (1901–71): Chargé d'Affaires in San Salvador 1940; transferred to Foreign Office 1942; K.B.E. 1958.

SIR SAMUEL HOARE, 1st Viscount Templewood from 1944 (1880–1959): Con. M.P. for Chelsea 1910–44; Lord Privy Seal 1939–40; Sec. of State for Air 1940; Br. Amb. to Spain 1940–4.

DAVID VICTOR KELLY (1891–1959): Counsellor in Foreign Office 1938–9; Br. Minister in Berne 1940–1; Ambassador to Argentina 1942; K.C.M.G. 1942.

SIR HUGHE MONTGOMERY KNATCHBULL-HUGESSEN (1886–1971): Br. Ambassador to Turkey 1939–44; to Belgium 1944–7.

RICHARD THOMAS EDWIN LATHAM (d. 1943): Temporary clerk in Foreign Office General Dept., Refugee Section, 1939–41; Fellow of All Souls College, Oxford; Barrister of Lincoln's Inn; author of *The Law and the Commonwealth*, Oxford 1949.

RICHARD KIDSTON LAW, 1st Baron Coleraine of Haltemprice from 1954 (b. 1901): Unionist M.P. for S.W. Hull 1931–45; Financial Sec., War Office 1940–41; Parliamentary Under-Sec., Foreign Office, 1941–3; Min. of State, Foreign Office 1943–5; Min. of Education 1945.

REGINALD WILDIG ALLEN LEEPER (1888–1968): Counsellor at Foreign Office from 1933; Asst. Under-Sec., Foreign Office 1940; Ambassador to Greece 1943–6.

LORD LLOYD, SIR GEORGE AMBROSE LLOYD (1879–1941): Sec. of State for Colonies and Leader of House of Lords 1940–1.

STEPHEN ELLIOT VYVYAN LUKE (b. 1905): Sec. Palestine Partition Commission 1938; Principal in Colonial Office 1937–42; Asst. Sec. 1942–7; K.C.M.G. 1953.

MALCOLM JOHN MACDONALD (b. 1901): Nat. Lab. M.P. for Ross and Cromarty 1936–45; Sec. of State for Colonies 1938–40; Min. of Health 1940–1; High Commissioner in Canada 1941–6.

SIR HAROLD MACMICHAEL (1882–1969): High Commissioner for Palestine & Transjordan 1938–44.

MAURICE HAROLD MACMILLAN (b. 1894): Unionist M.P. for Stockton-on-Tees 1931–45; Parliamentary Sec., Ministry of Supply 1940–42; Parliamentary Under-Sec., Colonial Office 1942; Minister Resident A.F.H.Q. Algiers (later Caserta, Italy) 1942–5; Sec. of State for Air 1945.

JOHN MILLER MARTIN (b. 1904): Sec. of Palestine Royal Commission 1936; Private Sec. to Prime Minister 1940–5 (Principal Private Sec. from 1941); Asst. Under-Sec., Colonial Office 1945–56; K.St. J. 1966.

PAUL MASON (1904–78): First Sec. Br. Embassy, Lisbon 1941; head of Foreign Office Refugee Dept. 1944–5; Acting Counsellor 1945; K.C.M.G. 1954.

HERBERT STANLEY MORRISON, Lord Morrison of Lambeth from 1959 (1888–1965): Leader of London County Council 1934–40; Sec. to London Labour Party 1915–47; Lab. M.P. for S. Hackney 1935–45; Min. of Supply 1940; Home Sec. and Min. of Home Security 1940–5; Member of War Cabinet 1942–5.

LORD MOYNE, WALTER EDWARD GUINNESS (1880–1944): Joint Parliamentary Under-Sec., Ministry of Agriculture 1940–41; Sec. of State for Colonies and Leader of House of Lords 1941–2; Dep. Min. of State, Middle East 1942–3; Min. Resident, Cairo, 1944; assassinated Nov. 1944.

OSBERT PEAKE, 1st Viscount Ingleby from 1955 (1897–1966): Con. M.P. for Leeds N., 1929–55; Parliamentary Under-Sec., Home Office 1939–44; Financial Sec. to Treasury 1944–5.

ALEC WALTER GEORGE RANDALL (1892–1977): Counsellor in Foreign Office 1938–45; head of Refugee Dept. 1942; K.C.M.G. 1949.

FRANK KENYON ROBERTS (b. 1907): Acting First Secretary in Central Dept. of Foreign Office 1940–3; head of Central Dept. 1943; Chargé d'Affaires to Czechoslovak Govt. 1943.

FRANK SAVERY (1883–1965): Consul-Gen. in Warsaw 1939; Counsellor, Br. Embassy to Polish Govt. 1939–45.

SIR JOHN EVELYN SHUCKBURGH (1877–1953): Dep. Under-Sec. of State, Colonial Office, 1931–42; retired 1942.

SIR ARCHIBALD SINCLAIR, 1st Viscount Thurso from 1952 (1890–1970): Sec. of State for Air 1940–5; Leader of Parliamentary Liberal Party 1935–45.

THOMAS MAITLAND SNOW (b. 1890): Br. Minister to Cuba 1935–7; to Finland 1937–40; transferred to Foreign Office 1940; Br. Minister to Colombia 1941–4.

OLIVER FREDERICK STANLEY (1896–1950): Con. M.P. for Westmorland 1924–45; President of Board of Trade 1937–40; Sec. of State for War 1940; for Colonies 1942–5.

EDWARD ALAN WALKER (b. 1894): First Sec., Br. Embassy, Angora, 1939–41; transferred to Foreign Office Refugee Dept. 1941.

JOHN GUTHRIE WARD (b. 1909): Second Sec. in Foreign Office 1936; First Sec. 1941; Counsellor 1946; K.C.M.G. 1956.

FIELD-MARSHAL SIR ARCHIBALD PERCIVAL WAVELL, 1st Earl Wavell from 1947 (1883–1950): Commander-in-Chief, Middle East 1939–41; in India 1941–3; Supreme Commander, S.W. Pacific 1942; Viceroy and Governor-General of India 1943–7.

Sources

(A) UNPUBLISHED SOURCES

British Library, London (BL)
Diaries and Papers of Oliver Harvey (Lord Harvey of Tasburgh),
  Add. Mss. 56397–56402
Cambridge University Library
Papers of 1st Viscount Templewood (Sir Samuel Hoare)
Central Zionist Archives, Jerusalem (CZA)
L22 Jewish Agency Geneva Office
S25 Jewish Agency Political Department, Jerusalem
Z4   Zionist Organisation, London Office
Israel State Archives, Jerusalem (ISA)
Record Group 2 Chief Secretary's Office
Middle East Centre, St Antony's College, Oxford
Papers of Sir Harold MacMichael
Papers of Sir Edward (Louis) Spears
Polish Underground Movement (1939–1945) Study Trust, London
Papers of the Polish underground movement
Public Record Office, Kew (PRO)

AIR 14	CAB 66	CAB 98	FO 800	PREM 4
AIR 19	CAB 67	CO 733	FO 898	
CAB 21	CAB 68	FO 195	FO 916	
CAB 23	CAB 78	FO 369	FO 921	
CAB 65	CAB 95	FO 371	PREM 3	

Rhodes House, Oxford
Sidney and Flora Moody Papers
United States National Archives, Washington D.C. (USNA)
740.00116   European War 1939
840.48   Refugees
Weizmann Archives, Rehovot (WA)
Papers of Chaim Weizmann (classified in date order)
Woburn House, London
Papers of the Board of Deputies of British Jews (BD)
World Jewish Congress Archives, London (WJCL)
Papers classified in date order
World Jewish Congress Archives, New York (WJCNY)
Drawer 177A

Drawer 266
Yad Vashem Archives, Jerusalem
Papers of Dr. I. Schwarzbart M–2
Unpublished Doctoral Thesis
Sheffer, Gabriel, *Policy Making and British Policies Towards Palestine, 1929–1939*, Oxford 1971.

(B) PUBLISHED SOURCES

PUBLISHED OFFICIAL DOCUMENTS

Germany
Documents on German Foreign Policy 1918–1945 Series D (1937–1945), Vols. VIII–XIII, London 1954–64.
Great Britain
Palestine Royal Commission: Memoranda Prepared by the Government of Palestine, Colonial No. 133, London 1937
Palestine Royal Commission Report, Cmd. 5479, London, 1937
Palestine Royal Commission: Minutes of Evidence Heard at Public Sessions, Colonial No. 134, London 1937
Report of the British Guiana Refugee Commission to the Advisory Committee on Political Refugees appointed by the President of the United States of America, Cmd. 6014, London 1939
Palestine: A Statement of Policy, Cmd. 6019, London, 1939
Appendices to the Report of the British Guiana Refugee Commission to the Advisory Committee on Political Refugees appointed by the President of the United States of America, Cmd. 6029, London, 1939
Papers Concerning the Treatment of German Nationals in Germany 1938–1939, Cmd. 6120, London 1939.
German and Austrian Civilian Internees, Cmd. 6217, London 1940.
Summary of the Arandora Star Inquiry conducted by the Rt. Hon. Lord Snell C.B.E., LL.D. Cmd. 6238, London 1940.
Buchenwald Camp: The Report of a Parliamentary Delegation, Cmd. 6626, London, 1945.
Report of the Anglo-American Committee of Enquiry Regarding the Problems of European Jewry and Palestine, Cmd. 6808, London 1946.
Mauritius
Interim Report on the Detainment Camp 26th December 1940 to 30th September 1941, Port Louis 1941.
Interim Report on the Detainment Camp 1st October 1941 to 30th September 1942, Port Louis 1942.
Interim Report on the Detainment Camp 1st October 1943 to 30th September 1944, Port Louis 1945.
Palestine
A Survey of Palestine, 3 vols. Jerusalem 1946.

Poland
Documents on Polish-Soviet Relations 1939–1945, 2 vols., London 1961.
U.S.A.
Foreign Relations of the United States, volumes covering years 1939–1945, Washington, D.C. 1955–70.
U.S.S.R.
Correspondence between the Chairman of the Council of Ministers of the U.S.S.R. and the Presidents of the U.S.A. and the Prime Ministers of Great Britain during the Great Patriotic War of 1941–1945, 2 vols. Moscow 1957.
Vatican
Actes et Documents du Saint Siège Relatifs à la Seconde Guerre Mondiale, vols. 6–9, Vatican 1972–5.

NEWSPAPERS
Jewish Chronicle
The Times
Cuttings from the British and foreign press in Chatham House Press Cuttings Library, London.

BOOKS, PAMPHLETS, AND ARTICLES
ABRAHAMS, A. *Background of Unrest: Palestine Journey 1944*, London 1945.
ADAM, COLIN FORBES, *Life of Lord Lloyd*, London 1948.
ADAM, UWE DIETRICH, *Judenpolitik im Dritten Reich*, Düsseldorf, 1972.
ADDISON, PAUL, *The Road to 1945: British Politics and the Second World War*, London, 1975.
AGAR, HERBERT, *The Saving Remnant*, London 1960.
AINSZTEIN, REUBEN, *Jewish Resistance in Nazi-Occupied Eastern Europe*, London 1974.
ALAMI, MUSA, 'The Lesson of Palestine', *Middle East Journal*, Vol. 3, No. 4, October 1949.
ALIAV, RUTH and MANN, PEGGY, *The Last Escape*, London 1974.
AMERY, L. S., *My Political Life vol. III The Unforgiving Years 1929–1940*, London 1955.
ANGELL, NORMAN and BUXTON, DOROTHY FRANCES, *You and the Refugee*, London 1939.
ANTONIUS, GEORGE, 'The Machinery of Government in Palestine', *American Academy of Political and Social Science Annals*, vol. 164, 1932.
——*The Arab Awakening*, London 1938.
ARAD, YITZHAK, 'Concentration of Refugees in Vilna on the Eve of the Holocaust', *Yad Vashem Studies*, IX, Jerusalem 1973, pp. 201–14.
ARENDT, HANNAH, *Eichmann in Jerusalem: A Report on the Banality of Evil*, London, 1963.

'Argus', 'Friendly Enemy Aliens', *Contemporary Review*, Jan. 1941, pp. 53–60.

Association of Latvian and Estonian Jews in Israel, *The Jews in Latvia*, Tel Aviv 1971.

AVITAL, ZVI, 'The Polish Government in Exile and the Jewish Question', *The Wiener Library Bulletin*, vol. XXVIII, 1975, New Series Nos. 33–4, pp. 43–51.

AVNI, HAIM, 'Spanish Nationals in Greece and their Fate during the Holocaust', *Yad Vashem Studies*, VIII, Jerusalem 1970, pp. 31–68.

——*Sefarad Ve-hayehudim Bimei Ha-shoah Ve-ha-emansipatsiah*, Tel Aviv 1975.

AVON, EARL OF (SIR ANTHONY EDEN), *The Eden Memoirs: The Reckoning*, London 1965.

AVRIEL, EHUD, *Open the Gates!*, London 1975.

BARBOUR, N. *Nisi Dominus: A Survey of the Palestine Controversy*, London 1946.

BARKER, ELISABETH, *British Policy in South-East Europe in the Second World War*, London 1976.

BARLAS, HAIM, *Hatzalah Bimei Shoah*, Tel Aviv, 1975.

BAUER, YEHUDA, *Flight and Rescue: Brichah*, New York, 1970.

—— *From Diplomacy to Resistance: A History of Jewish Palestine 1939–1945*, New York, 1973.

—— 'Rescue Operations Through Vilna', *Yad Vashem Studies*, IX, Jerusalem 1973, pp. 215–23.

—— 'Contemporary History: Some Methodological Problems', *History*, October 1976.

—— '"Onkel Saly" – Die Verhandlungen des Saly Mayer zur Rettung der Juden 1944/45', *Vierteljahrshefte für Zeitgeschichte*, vol. 25, no. 2, April 1977.

BEGIN, MENACHEM, *The Revolt*, 5th English edn., with additional chapter, Jerusalem 1972.

BELL, J. BOWYER, *Terror out of Zion: Irgun Zvai Leumi, Lehi, and the Palestine Underground, 1929–1949*, New York 1977.

BEN ELISSAR, ELIAHU, *Le facteur juif dans la politique étrangère du IIIe Reich (1933–1939)*, Paris, 1969.

BEN GURION, DAVID, *Ben Gurion Looks Back*, ed. M. Pearlman, London 1965.

BEN SHALOM, RAFI, *Neevaknu Lema'an He-hayim*, Tel Aviv 1977.

BENTWICH, NORMAN, 'England and the Aliens', *Political Quarterly*, vol. XII, no. 1, January–March 1941, pp. 81–93.

—— *They Found Refuge*, London 1956.

—— *My Seventy-Seven Years*, London 1962.

BENTWICH, NORMAN and HELEN, *Mandate Memories*, London 1965.

BÉRECZKY, ALBERT, *Hungarian Protestantism and the Persecution of Jews*, Budapest, n.d.

BERGER, GEORGE M. 'Australia and the Refugees', *The Australian Quarterly*, December 1941.

BERLIN, SIR ISAIAH, *Zionist Politics in Wartime Washington: A Fragment of Personal Reminiscence*, Jerusalem 1972.

BONNÉ, A. *The Economic Development of the Middle East*, London 1943.

BOWLE, JOHN, *Viscount Samuel: A Biography*, London 1957.

BRACHER, KARL DIETRICH, *The German Dictatorship*, London 1973.

BRAHAM, RANDOLPH, *The Destruction of Hungarian Jewry*, 2 vols, New York 1963.

—— 'The Role of the Jewish Council in Hungary: A Tentative Assessment', *Yad Vashem Studies*, X, Jerusalem 1974.

BRAMSTED, ERNEST K., *Goebbels and National Socialist Propaganda 1925–1945*, London 1965.

BRENNER, Y. S., 'The "Stern Gang" 1940–48', *Middle Eastern Studies*, vol. 2, No. 1, October 1965.

BRIGGS, ASA, *The History of Broadcasting in the United Kingdom, vol. III: The War of Words*, London 1970.

BRODETSKY, SELIG, *Memoirs: From Ghetto to Israel*, London 1960.

BROWN, FRANCIS J., 'Refugees', special number of *American Academy of Political and Social Science Annals*, vol. 203, May 1939.

BULLOCK, ALAN, *Hitler: A Study in Tyranny*, revised ed. London 1962.

BURNS, JAMES MACGREGOR, *Roosevelt: The Soldier of Freedom 1940–1945*, New York 1970.

BUXTON, DOROTHY F., *The Economics of the Refugee Problem*, London, n.d. (1939?)

CADOGAN, SIR ALEXANDER, *The Diaries of Sir Alexander Cadogan O.M., 1938–1945*, ed. David Dilks, London 1971.

CALDER, ANGUS, *The People's War: Britain 1939–45*, London 1969.

CANAAN, T., *Conflict in the Land of Peace*, Jerusalem 1936.

—— *The Palestine Arab Cause*, Jerusalem 1936.

CARLYLE, MARGARET, *Documents on International Affairs 1939–1946 vol. II Hitler's Europe*, London 1954.

CASEY, LORD, *Personal Experience 1939–1946*, New York 1962.

Central British Fund for Jewish Relief and Rehabilitation, *Report for 1933–1943*, London 1944.

CHANDOS, VISCOUNT [OLIVER LYTTELTON], *The Memoirs of Lord Chandos*, London 1962.

CHANNON, SIR HENRY, *Chips: The Diaries of Sir Henry Channon*, ed. Robert Rhodes James, London 1970.

CHARY, FREDERICK B., *The Bulgarian Jews and the Final Solution 1940–1944*, Pittsburgh 1972.

CHURCHILL, WINSTON S., *The Second World War*, 6 vols. London 1948–54.

CIANO, COUNT GALEAZZO, *Ciano's Diaries 1939–1943*, ed. Malcolm Muggeridge, London 1947.

COHEN, GAVRIEL, *The British Cabinet and the Question of Palestine April – July 1943*, Tel Aviv 1976.

—— *Churchill and Palestine 1939–1942*, Jerusalem 1976.

COHEN, HAYYIM, J., 'The Anti-Jewish *Farhud* in Baghdad, 1941', *Middle Eastern Studies*, vol. 3, no. 1, October 1966.

COHEN, MICHAEL J., 'British Strategy and the Palestine Question 1936–9', *Journal of Contemporary History*, vol. 7, nos. 3–4, July – October 1972.

—— 'Direction of Policy in Palestine 1936–48', *Middle Eastern Studies*, October 1975.

—— 'The British White Paper on Palestine, May 1939: Part II The Testing of a Policy, 1942–1945', *Historical Journal*, 19, 3 (1976) pp. 727–58.

—— *Palestine: Retreat from the Mandate: The Making of British Policy 1936–1945*, London 1978.

COHN, N., *Warrant for Genocide*, London 1967.

COLVILLE, J. R., *Man of Valour: The Life of Field-Marshal the Viscount Gort V.C.*, London 1972.

CONWAY, J. S., 'Between Apprehension and Indifference: Allied Attitudes to the Destruction of Hungarian Jewry', *The Wiener Library Bulletin*, 1973/4, vol. XXVII, new series nos. 30/31, pp. 37–48.

CROSSMAN, R. H. S., *Palestine Mission*, London 1946.

DALLIN, ALEXANDER, *German Rule in Russia 1941–1945*, London 1957.

DALTON, HUGH, *The Fateful Years: Memoirs 1931–1945*, London 1957.

DAWIDOWICZ, LUCY S., *The War Against the Jews 1933–1945*, London 1975.

DINUR, BEN–ZION, ed. *Sefer Toldot Ha-haganah*, 3 vols. bound as 8, Tel Aviv 1954–72.

DJILAS, MILOVAN, *Conversations with Stalin*, London 1963.

DONOGHUE, BERNARD, and JONES, G. W., *Herbert Morrison: Portrait of a Politician*, London 1973.

DRIBERG, TOM, *Ruling Passions*, London 1977.

DUFF, D. V., *Palestine Unveiled*, London 1938.

DUGDALE, BLANCHE, *Baffy: The Diaries of Blanche Dugdale 1936–1947*, ed. N. A. Rose, London 1973.

DULLES, ALLEN, *The Secret Surrender*, London 1967.

ECK, NATHAN, 'The Rescue of Jews with the Aid of Passports and Citizenship Papers of Latin American States', *Yad Vashem Studies*, I, Jerusalem 1957.

EHRENBURG, ILYA, *Memoirs 1921–1941*, New York 1966.

EMERSON, SIR HERBERT, 'Postwar Problems of Refugees', *Foreign Affairs*, vol. 21, no. 2, January 1943, pp. 211–20.

ESCO FOUNDATION FOR PALESTINE, *Palestine: A study of Jewish, Arab, and British Policies*, 2 vols., New Haven 1947.

EUROPEAN RESISTANCE MOVEMENTS, INTERNATIONAL CONFERENCE ON, *European Resistance Movements 1939–1945 (First International Conference on the History of the Resistance Movements held at Liège – Bruxelles – Breendonk 14–17 September 1958)*, Oxford 1960.

—— *European Resistance Movements 1939–45 (Proceedings of the Second International Conference on the History of the Resistance Movements held at Milan 26 February–9 March 1961)*, Oxford 1964.

FARAGO, L., *Palestine on the Eve*, London 1936.

FEINGOLD, HENRY L., *The Politics of Rescue: The Roosevelt Administration and the Holocaust 1938–1945*, New Brunswick, N.J., 1970.

FEIWEL, T. R., *No Ease in Zion*, London 1938.

FENYO, MARIO D., *Hitler, Horthy, and Hungary: German-Hungarian Relations 1941–1944*, New Haven, Conn. 1972.

FOOT, M. R. D., *Resistance: An Analysis of European Resistance to Nazism 1940–1945*, London 1976.

FOX, JOHN P., Great Britain and the German Jews 1933', *The Wiener Library Bulletin*, 1972, vol. XXVI, nos. 1 and 2, New Series nos. 26 and 27, pp. 40–6.

—— 'The Jewish Factor in British War Crimes Policy in 1942', *English Historical Review*, vol. XCII, no. 362, January 1977.

FRIEDLÄNDER, SAUL, *Pius XII and the Third Reich: A Documentation*, New York 1966.

—— *Counterfeit Nazi: The Ambiguity of Good*, London 1969.

—— 'L'extermination des Juifs d'Europe. Pour une étude historique globale', *Revue des études juives*, CXXXV, 1 – 3, jan. – sept. 1976.

FRIEDMAN, SAUL S., *No Haven for the Oppressed: United States Policy Toward Jewish Refugees, 1938–1945*, Detroit 1973.

FURLONGE, GEOFFREY, *Palestine is My Country: The Story of Musa Alami*, London 1969.

GARLIŃSKI, JÓZEF, *Poland, S.O.E., and the Allies*, London 1969.

—— *Fighting Auschwitz*, London 1976.

GERSHON, KAREN, ed., *We Came as Children: A Collective Autobiography*, London 1966.

GILBERT, MARTIN, *Winston S. Churchill*, vols. IV and V, London 1975 & 1976.

—— *Britain, Palestine, and the Jews 1891–1939*, Sacks Lecture, Oxford 1977.

—— *Exile and Return: The Emergence of Jewish Statehood*, London 1978.

GLICKSMAN, WILLIAM, 'Emanuel Ringelblum: Chronicler of the Holocaust', *Jewish Quarterly*, vol. 25, no.3, 93, Autumn 1977.

GOEBBELS, JOSEPH, *The Goebbels Diaries*, ed. Louis P. Lochner, London 1948.

GOLDING, LOUIS, *The Jewish Problem*, London 1938.

GOLDMANN, NAHUM, *Memories*, London 1970.

GOLDSMITH, MARGARET, 'The Refugee Transit Camp at Richborough', *The Nineteenth Century and After*, Sept. 1939, pp. 315–21.

GOLLANCZ, VICTOR, *'Let my People Go'*, London n.d. [1942].

GOODMAN, PAUL, ed. *The Jewish National Home 1917–1942*, London 1943.

GROBMAN, ALEX, 'The Warsaw Ghetto Uprising in the American Jewish Press', *The Wiener Library Bulletin*, 1976, vol. XXIX, new series nos. 37/38, pp. 53–61.

GUTTERRIDGE, RICHARD, *Open Thy Mouth for the Dumb!: The German Evangelical Church and the Jews 1879–1950*, Oxford 1976.

HACOHEN, DAVID, *'Et Le-saper*, Tel Aviv 1974.

HALPERN, BEN, *The Idea of the Jewish State*, London 1970.

HALSTEAD, CHARLES R. 'Historians in Politics: Carlton J. H. Hayes as American Ambassador to Spain 1942–45', *Journal of Contemporary History*, vol. X, no. 3, July 1975.

HARVEY, OLIVER, *The Diplomatic Diaries of Oliver Harvey 1937–1940*, ed. J. Harvey, London 1970.

HATTIS, SUSAN LEE, *The Binational Idea in Palestine During Mandatory Times* Haifa, 1970.

HAUSNER, GIDEON, *Justice in Jerusalem*, London 1967.

HAWES, STEPHEN AND WHITE, RALPH, eds., *Resistance in Europe: 1939–1945*, London 1976.

HAYES, CARLTON J. H., *Wartime Mission in Spain 1942–1945*, New York 1945.

HILBERG, RAUL, *The Destruction of the European Jews*, Chicago 1961.

—— ed., *Documents of Destruction: Germany and Jewry 1933–1945*, London, 1972.

HIMADEH, S. B., ed., *Economic Organization of Palestine*, Beirut 1938.

HIRSZOWICZ, LUKASZ, *The Third Reich and the Arab East*, London 1966.

—— ed., 'The Soviet Union and the Jews during World War II: British Foreign Office Documents', *Soviet Jewish Affairs*, vol. 3, no. 1, 1973.

—— ed., 'The Soviet Union and Jews during World War II: British Foreign Office Documents' *Soviet Jewish Affairs*, vol. 3, no. 2, 1973.

—— ed., 'The Soviet Union and the Jews during World War II: Documents from the Zionist Archives, Jerusalem, and British Colonial Office Documents', *Soviet Jewish Affairs*, vol. 4, no. 1, 1974.

HOLMES, COLIN, ed., 'East End Anti-Semitism 1936', *Bulletin of Society for the Study of Labour History*, no. 32, Spring 1976, pp. 26–33.

HOROWITZ, DAN, AND LISSAK, MOSHE, 'Authority Without Sovereignty', *Government and Opposition*, Winter 1973.

HORTHY, ADMIRAL MIKLÓS, *The Confidential Papers of Admiral Horthy*, ed. Miklós Szinai and Lászlo Szucs, Budapest 1965.

HOURANI, A. H., *Syria and Lebanon: A Political Essay*, London 1946.

—— *Great Britain and the Arab World*, London 1946.

—— *Is Zionism the Solution of the Jewish Problem?* London 1946.

HOWARD, MICHAEL, *The Continental Commitment*, London 1972.

—— 'Ethics and Power in International Politics', *International Affairs*, vol. 53, no. 3, July 1977.

HUGHES, EMRYS, *Sidney Silverman: Rebel in Parliament*, London 1969.

HULL, CORDELL, *The Memoirs of Cordell Hull*, 2 vols., London 1948.

HUREWITZ, J. C., *The Struggle for Palestine*, New York 1950.

HYAMSON, A. M., *Palestine: A Policy*, London 1942.

—— *Palestine under the Mandate 1920–1948*, London 1950.

INTERNATIONAL COMMITTEE OF THE RED CROSS, *Report of the International Committee of the Red Cross on its Activities during the Second World War (September 1 1939 – June 30 1947)*, 3 vols. Geneva 1948.

IRANEK-OSMECKI, KAZIMIERZ, and LICHTEN, JOSEPH, and RACZYNSKI, EDWARD, 'The Polish Government in Exile and the Jewish Tragedy during World War Two', *The Wiener Library Bulletin*, 1976, vol. XXIX, new series nos. 37/38, pp. 62–7.

IRONSIDE, GENERAL SIR EDMUND, *The Ironside Diaries 1937–1940*, ed. R. Macleod and D. Kelly, London 1962.

ISMAY, LORD, *Memoirs*, London 1960.

JAMES, ROBERT RHODES, *Victor Cazalet: A Portrait*, London 1976.

JEDRZEJEWICZ, WACLAW, ed., *Poland in the British Parliament 1939–1945*, 3 vols, New York, 1946–62.

JEWISH AGENCY FOR PALESTINE, *Documents and Correspondence Relating to Palestine August 1939 –March 1940*, London 1940.

—— *Political Report of the London Office of the Executive of the Jewish Agency submitted to the Twenty-Second Zionist Congress at Basle, December 1946*, London 1946.

DE JONG, LOUIS, *The German Fifth Column in the Second World War*, London 1956.

—— 'The Netherlands and Auschwitz', *Yad Vashem Studies*, VII, Jerusalem 1968, pp. 39–55.

JOSEPH, BERNARD, *British Rule in Palestine*, Washington 1948.

'JUDEX', *Anderson's Prisoners*, London 1940.

KÁLLAY, NICHOLAS, *Hungarian Premier*, London 1954.

KARSKI, JAN, *Story of a Secret State*, London 1945.

KENNAN, GEORGE, *Russia and the West*, Boston 1960.

KENT, GEORGE O., 'Pius XII and Germany: Some Aspects of German-Vatican Relations 1933–1943', *American Historical Review*, vol. LXX no. 1, October 1964, pp. 59–78.

KERMISH, JOSEPH, 'Emmanuel Ringelblum's Notes Hitherto Unpublished', *Yad Vashem Studies*, VII, Jerusalem 1968, pp. 173–83.

KILMUIR, EARL OF, *Political Adventure: The Memoirs of the Earl of Kilmuir*, London 1964.

KIMCHE, JON and DAVID, *The Secret Roads*, London 1955.

KIRK, GEORGE, *Survey of International Affairs 1939–1946: The Middle East in the War*, London 1952.

KLARSFELD, SERGE, *Le Mémorial de la déportation des Juifs de France*, Paris 1977.

KLEIN, BERNARD, 'The *Judenrat*', *Jewish Social Studies*, vol. 22, no. 1, 1960.

KNATCHBULL-HUGESSEN, SIR HUGHE, *Diplomat in Peace and War*, London 1949.

KOCH, H. W., 'The Spectre of a Separate Peace in the East: Russo-German "Peace Feelers", 1942–44', *Journal of Contemporary History*, vol. X, no. 3, July 1975.

KOCHAN, LIONEL, ed., *The Jews in Soviet Russia since 1917*, London 1970.

KOESSLER, MAXIMILIAN, 'Enemy Alien Internment: With Special Reference to Great Britain and France', *Political Science Quarterly*, vol. 57 no. 1, March 1942, pp. 98–127.

KOESTLER, ARTHUR, *Promise and Fulfilment: Palestine 1917–1949*, London 1949.

KORBONSKI, STEFAN, *Fighting Warsaw: The Story of the Polish Underground State 1939–1945*, London 1956; Minerva paper edn. 1968.

KOT, STANISLAW, *Conversations with the Kremlin and Dispatches from Russia*, London 1963.

KRAKOWSKI, SAMUEL, 'The Slaughter of Polish Jewry – A Polish "Reassessment"', *The Wiener Library Bulletin*, 1972/3, vol. XXVI nos. 3/4 new series nos. 28/9 pp. 13–20.

KRANZLER, DAVID, 'The Jewish Refugee Community of Shanghai, 1938–1945', *The Wiener Library Bulletin*, 1972/3, vol. XXVI, nos. 3/4, new series, 28/9, pp. 28–37.

KRAUSNICK, HELMUT, and BROSZAT, MARTIN, *Anatomy of the SS State*, London 1970.

KUBOVY [KUBOWITZKI], ARYEH [LEON] L. 'The Silence of Pope Pius XII and the Beginnings of the "Jewish Document"', *Yad Vashem Studies*, VI, Jerusalem, 1967.

LAFITTE, F., *The Internment of Aliens*, London 1940.

LAQUEUR, WALTER, *A History of Zionism*, London 1972.

LEDERER, ZDENEK, *Ghetto Theresienstadt*, London 1953.

LEVAI, JENÖ, *Hungarian Jewry and the Papacy*, London 1968.

LEWY, GÜNTER, *The Catholic Church and Nazi Germany*, London 1964.

LIDDELL HART, B. H., *History of the Second World War*, London 1970.

LIPSTADT, DEBORAH E., 'The Media and the Holocaust: A Case Study', *Association for Jewish Studies Newsletter*, no. 20, June 1977, p, 20.

LITANI, DORA, 'The Destruction of the Jews of Odessa in the Light of Rumanian Documents', *Yad Vashem Studies*, VI, Jerusalem 1967.

LOEWALD, K. G., 'A *Dunera* Internee at Hay, 1940–41', *Historical Studies*, vol. 17, no. 69, October 1977.

LONG, BRECKENRIDGE, *The War Diary of Breckenridge Long: Selections from the Years 1939–1944* (ed. Fred L. Israel), Lincoln, Nebraska 1966.

LUCAS, NOAH, *The Modern History of Israel*, London 1974.

MacDONALD, MALCOLM, *Titans and Others*, London 1972.

McDONNELL, SIR M., 'The Fruits of Fear in Palestine', *The Patriot*, 1 June 1939.

MACMILLAN, HAROLD, *The Blast of War 1939–1945*, London 1967.

MAIN, E., *Palestine at the Crossroads*, London 1937.

MANUEL, F. E., *The Realities of American-Palestine Relations*, Washington 1949.

MARITAIN, JACQUES, *Antisemitism*, London 1939.

MARK, BER, ed., *The Report of Jürgen Stroop Concerning the Uprising in the Ghetto of Warsaw and the Liquidation of the Jewish Residential Area*, Warsaw 1958.

—— *Uprising in the Warsaw Ghetto*, New York 1975.

MARLOWE, JOHN, *The Seat of Pilate*, London 1959.

MASHBERG, MICHAEL, 'Documents Concerning the American State Department and Stateless European Jews, 1942–1944', *Jewish Social Studies*, vol. XXXIX, nos. 1–2, Winter–Spring 1977.

MASTERMAN, J. C., *The Double-Cross System in the War of 1939 to 1945*, London 1972.

MEDLICOTT, W. N., *The Economic Blockade*, 2 vols., London 1952 & 1959.

MEINERTZHAGEN, RICHARD, *Middle East Diary 1917–1956*, London 1959.

MELKA, R., 'Nazi Germany and the Palestine Question', *Middle Eastern Studies*, vol. 5, no. 3, October 1969.

MERIDOR, YA'ACOV, *Long is the Road to Freedom*, Johannesburg 1955.

MICHEL, HENRI, *The Shadow War: Resistance in Europe 1939–1945*, London 1972.

MICHMAN, JOSEPH, 'The Controversial Stand of the *Joodse Raad* in the Netherlands', *Yad Vashem Studies*, X, Jerusalem 1974.

MILLER, MARSHALL LEE, *Bulgaria During the Second World War*, Stanford, California, 1975.

MONROE, ELIZABETH, *Britain's Moment in the Middle East*, London 1963.

—— 'British Interests in the Middle East', *Middle East Journal*, vol. 2, no. 2, April 1948.

MORRISON, HERBERT (LORD MORRISON OF LAMBETH), *Herbert Morrison: An Autobiography*, London 1960.

MORSE, ARTHUR D., *While Six Million Died*, London 1968.

MOSLEY, SIR OSWALD, *My Life*, London 1970.

MUGGERIDGE, MALCOLM, *The Thirties*, London 1940, rev. edn. 1967.

MUNRO, DANA G., and others, *Refugee Settlement in the Dominican Republic*, Washington 1942.

MURPHY, ROBERT, *Diplomat Among Warriors*, New York 1964.

NAMIER, L. B., *Conflicts: Studies in Contemporary History*, London 1942.

—— *Avenues in History*, New York 1952.

NATHAN, R., GASS, O., and CREAMER, D., *Palestine: Problem and Promise*, Washington 1946.

NICOLSON, HAROLD, *Diaries and Letters 1939–1945*, ed. Nigel Nicolson, London 1967.

NOAKES, JEREMY, and PRIDHAM, GEOFFREY, *Documents on Nazism 1919–1945*, London 1974.

OREN, NISSAN, 'The Bulgarian Exception: A Reassessment of the Salvation of the Jewish Community', *Yad Vashem Studies*, vol. VIII, Jerusalem 1968, pp. 83–106.

ORWELL, GEORGE, *The Collected Essays, Journalism and Letters of George Orwell*, eds. Sonia Orwell and Ian Angus, vols. II & III (1940–1945), New York 1968.

PAPEN, FRANZ VON, *Memoirs*, London 1952.

PARKES, JAMES, *Whose Land?* London 1970.

PAXTON, ROBERT O., *Vichy France: Old Guard and New Order, 1940–1944*, New York 1972.

PINCHUK, BEN-CION, 'Soviet Media on the Fate of Jews in Nazi-Occupied Territory (1939–1941)', *Yad Vashem Studies*, XI, Jerusalem 1976.

POLIAKOW, LEON, and SABILLE, JACQUES, *Jews Under the Italian Occupation*, (Paris 1955).

POLK, W. R., STAMLER, D. M., and ASFOUR, E., *Backdrop to Tragedy: The Struggle for Palestine*, Boston 1957.

PORATH, Y., *The Palestinian Arab National Movement vol. 2 From Riots to Rebellion 1929–1939*, London 1977.

PRESSER, J., *Ashes in the Wind: The Destruction of Dutch Jewry*, London 1968.

PRICE, A. GRENFELL, 'Refugee Settlement in the Tropics', *Foreign Affairs*, vol. 18, no. 4, July 1940, pp. 659–70.

PROUDFOOT, MALCOLM J., *European Refugees: 1939–1952*, London 1957.

RACZYNSKI, COUNT EDWARD, *In Allied London*, London 1962.

REDLICH, SHIMON, 'The Jews in the Soviet Annexed Territories 1939–1941', *Soviet Jewish Affairs*, vol. I, no. 1, pp. 81–90, June 1971.

—— 'Jews in General Anders' Army in the Soviet Union 1941–2', *Soviet Jewish Affairs*, vol. I, no. 2, pp. 90–8, Nov. 1971.

REITLINGER, GERALD, *The Final Solution*, 2nd revised edn. London 1968.

RENDEL, SIR GEORGE, *The Sword and the Olive*, London 1957.

RHODES, ANTHONY, *The Vatican in the Age of The Dictators 1922–1945*, London 1973.

RICHMOND, ERNEST T., 'Dictatorship in the Holy Land', *The Nineteenth Century And After*, February 1938.

RINGELBLUM, EMMANUEL, *Notes from the Warsaw Ghetto: The Journal of Emmanuel Ringelblum*, ed. and trans. Jacob Sloan, New York 1974.

—— *Polish-Jewish Relations During the Second World War*, eds. Joseph Kermish & Shmuel Krakowski, Jerusalem 1974.

ROBINSON, JACOB, *And the Crooked Shall be Made Straight: The Eichmann Trial, the Jewish Catastrophe, and Hannah Arendt's Narrative*, New York 1965.

ROHWER, JÜRGEN, *Die Versenkung der jüdischen Flüchtlingstransporter Struma und Mefkure im Schwarzen Meer, Februar 1942, August 1944*, Frankurt/Main 1965.

ROOSEVELT, F. D. and CHURCHILL, W. S., *Roosevelt and Churchill: Their Secret Wartime Correspondence* (eds. Francis L. Loewenheim, Harold D. Langley, and Manfred Jonas), London 1975.

ROSE, N. A., *The Gentile Zionists*, London 1973.

ROSKILL, STEPHEN, *Hankey: Man of Secrets vol. III 1931–1963*, London 1974.

ROTHKIRCHEN, LIVIA, 'The "Final Solution" in its Last Stages', *Yad Vashem Studies*, VIII, Jerusalem 1970, pp. 7–29.

—— (ed.) 'Rescue Efforts with the Assistance of International Organisations: Documents from the Archives of Dr. A. Silberschein', *Yad Vashem Studies*, VIII, Jerusalem 1970, pp. 69–79.

ROTHKIRCHEN, LIVIA, 'The Czechoslovak Government-in-Exile: Jewish and Palestinian Aspects in the Light of the Documents', *Yad Vashem Studies*, IX, Jerusalem 1973, pp. 157–99.

ROYAL INSTITUTE OF INTERNATIONAL AFFAIRS, *Political and Strategic Interests of the United Kingdom: An Outline*, London 1939.

RUPPIN, ARTHUR, *Memoirs, Diaries, Letters*, London 1971.

SAMUEL, EDWIN (2nd VISCOUNT SAMUEL), *A Lifetime in Jerusalem*, London 1970.

SAMUEL, HERBERT (1st VISCOUNT SAMUEL), *Memoirs*, London 1945.

SCHLEUNES, KARL A., *The Twisted Road to Auschwitz: Nazi Policy Toward German Jews 1933–1939*, London 1972.

SCHMIDT, H. D., 'The Nazi Party in Palestine and the Levant 1932–9', *International Affairs* XXVIII, 4, Oct. 1952, pp. 460–9.

SENESH [SZENES], HANNAH, *Hannah Senesh: Her Life and Diary*, London 1971.

SERENI E. and ASHERY R. E., *Jews and Arabs in Palestine*, New York 1936.

SHARETT, MOSHE, *Yoman Medini: 1939*, Tel Aviv 1974.

SHARF, ANDREW, *The British Press and Jews Under Nazi Rule*, London 1964.

SHERMAN, A. J., *Island Refuge: Britain and Refugees from the Third Riech 1933–1939*, London 1973.

SHIMONI, Y., '*Arvei Eretz Yisrael*, Tel Aviv 1947.

SIDEBOTHAM, H., *Great Britain and Palestine*, London 1937.

SIMSON, H. J., *British Rule and Rebellion*, London 1937.

SKIDELSKY, ROBERT, *Oswald Mosley*, New York 1975.

SMITH, R. HARRIS, *O.S.S.: The Secret History of America's First Central Intelligence Agency*, Berkeley 1972.

SPIER, EUGEN, *The Protecting Power*, London 1951.

STEIN, JOSHUA B., 'Great Britain and the Evian Conference of 1938', *The Wiener Library Bulletin*, 1976, vol. XXIX, new series nos. 37/38.

STEIN, LEONARD, *The Balfour Declaration*, London 1961.

—— *Weizmann and England*, London 1964.

STETTINIUS, EDWARD R., *The Diaries of Edward R. Stettinius* (eds. Thomas M. Campbell and George C. Herring), New York 1975.

STEVENS, AUSTIN, *The Dispossessed*, London 1975.

STOCKS, MARY D., *Eleanor Rathbone: A Biography*, London 1950.

SUHL, YURI, ed., *They Fought Back*, New York 1975.

SYKES, CHRISTOPHER, *Cross-Roads to Israel*, London 1965.

—— *Troubled Loyalty: A Biography of Adam von Trott zu Solz*, London 1968.

SZAJKOWSKI, ZOSA, *Jews and the French Foreign Legion*, New York 1975.

TARTAKOWER, ARYEH, and GROSSMANN, KURT R., *The Jewish Refugee*, New York 1944.

—— 'Adam Czerniakow – the Man and his Supreme Sacrifice', *Yad Vashem Studies*, VI, Jerusalem 1967.

TAYLOR, A. J. P., *English History 1914–1945*, London 1965.

TEICH, MEIR, 'The Jewish Self-Administration in Ghetto Shargorod (Transnistria)', *Yad Vashem Studies*, II, Jerusalem 1958.

TEMPLEWOOD, FIRST VISCOUNT (SIR SAMUEL HOARE), *Ambassador on Special Mission*, London 1946.

TOYNBEE, ARNOLD and VERONICA M. eds., *Survey of International Affairs 1939–1946 vol. 7 The War and the Neutrals*, London 1956.

TREVOR, DAPHNE, *Under the White Paper*, Jerusalem 1948.

TRUNK, ISAIAH, *Judenrat: The Jewish Councils in Eastern Europe Under Nazi Control*, New York 1972.

VAGO, BELA, 'Political and Diplomatic Activities for the Rescue of the Jews of Northern Transylvania, June 1944–February 1945', *Yad Vashem Studies*, VI, Jerusalem 1967.

—— 'Budapest Jewry in the Summer of 1944: Otto Komoly's Diaries', *Yad Vashem Studies*, VIII, Jerusalem 1970, pp. 81–105.

—— 'The Intelligence Aspects of the Joel Brand Mission', *Yad Vashem Studies*, X, Jerusalem 1974.

VALE, GEORGE F., *Bethnal Green's Ordeal 1939–1945*, London 1945.

WEBSTER, SIR CHARLES, and FRANKLAND, NOBLE, *The Strategic Air Offensive against Germany: Vol. III Victory*, London 1961; *Vol. IV Annexes and Appendices*, London 1961.

WEDGWOOD, JOSIAH C., *Memoirs of a Fighting Life*, London 1941.

WEISGAL M. and CARMICHAEL J, eds., *Chaim Weizmann*, London 1962.

WEISSBERG, ALEX, *Advocate for the Dead: The Story of Joel Brand*, London 1958.

WEIZMANN, CHAIM, *Trial and Error*, London 1949.

WHEELER-BENNETT, JOHN W., *John Anderson, Viscount Waverley*, London 1962.

WILSON, EVAN M., 'The Palestine Papers 1943–1947', *Journal of Palestine Studies*, vol. II, no. 4, Summer 1973.

WINTERBOTHAM, F. W., *The Ultra Secret*, London 1974.

WISCHNITZER, MARK, *To Dwell in Safety*, Philadelphia 1948.

—— *Visas to Freedom: The History of Hias*, Cleveland 1956.

WISE, STEPHEN, *Challenging Years*, London 1951.

WISKEMANN, ELIZABETH, *The Europe I Saw*, London 1968.

WOODBRIDGE, GEORGE, *U.N.R.R.A.: The History of the United Nations Relief and Rehabilitation Administration*, 3 vols. New York 1950.

WOODWARD, SIR LLEWELLYN, *British Foreign Policy in the Second World War*, 5 vols. London 1970–6.

WORLD JEWISH CONGRESS, *Reports*, London 1942–5.

—— *Unity in Dispersion: A History of the World Jewish Congress*, New York 1948.

WRIGHT, GORDON, *The Ordeal of Total War 1939–1945*, New York 1968.

WYMAN, DAVID S., *Paper Walls: America and the Refugee Crisis 1938–1941*, Amherst, Mass. 1968.

—— 'Why Auschwitz was never Bombed', *Commentary*, vol. 65, no. 5, May 1978, pp. 37–46.

YAD VASHEM, *Rescue Attempts During the Holocaust*, (Proceedings of the Second Yad Vashem International Historical Conference), Jerusalem 1977.

YAHIL, LENI, 'Scandinavian Countries to the Rescue of Concentration Camp Prisoners', *Yad Vashem Studies*, VI, 1967.

—— 'Select British Documents on the Illegal Immigration to Palestine (1939–1940)', *Yad Vashem Studies*, X, Jerusalem 1974.

YISRAELI, DAVID, 'The Third Reich and Palestine', *Middle Eastern Studies*, vol. 7, no. 3, October 1971, pp. 343–53.

YOUNG, ROLAND, *Congressional Politics in the Second World War*, New York 1956.

ZAHN, GORDON C., *German Catholics and Hitler's Wars*, New York 1962.

ZWEIG, ARNOLD, *Insulted and Exiled: The Truth about the German Jews*, London 1937.

ZWERGBAUM, AARON, 'Exile in Mauritius', *Yad Vashem Studies*, IV, Jerusalem 1960.

Index